Beautiful Testing

Edited by Tim Riley and Adam Goucher

O'REILLY®

Beijing · Cambridge · Farnham · Köln · Sebastopol · Tokyo

Beautiful Testing
Edited by Tim Riley and Adam Goucher

Published by O'Reilly Media, Inc., 1005 Gravenstein Highway North, Sebastopol, CA 95472.

O'Reilly books may be purchased for educational, business, or sales promotional use. Online editions are also available for most titles (*http://my.safaribooksonline.com*). For more information, contact our corporate/institutional sales department: 800-998-9938 or *corporate@oreilly.com*.

Editor: Mary E. Treseler

Production Editor: Sarah Schneider

Copyeditor: Genevieve d'Entremont

Proofreader: Sarah Schneider

Indexer: John Bickelhaupt

Cover Designer: Mark Paglietti

Interior Designer: David Futato

Illustrator: Robert Romano

October 2009:   First Edition.

ISBN: 978-0-596-15981-8

[LSI]   [2013-09-20]

1379530843

All royalties from this book will be donated to the
UN Foundation's Nothing But Nets campaign to
save lives by preventing malaria, a disease that
kills millions of children in Africa each year.

CONTENTS

Preface

I DON'T THINK BEAUTIFUL TESTING COULD HAVE BEEN PROPOSED, much less published, when I started my career a decade ago. Testing departments were unglamorous places, only slightly higher on the corporate hierarchy than front-line support, and filled with unhappy drones doing rote executions of canned tests.

There were glimmers of beauty out there, though.

Once you start seeing the glimmers, you can't help but seek out more of them. Follow the trail long enough and you will find yourself doing testing that is:

- Fun
- Challenging
- Engaging
- Experiential
- Thoughtful
- Valuable

Or, put another way, beautiful.

Testing as a recognized practice has, I think, become a lot more beautiful as well. This is partly due to the influence of ideas such as test-driven development (TDD), agile, and craftsmanship, but also the types of applications being developed now. As the products we develop and the ways in which we develop them become more social and less robotic, there is a realization that testing them doesn't have to be robotic, or ugly.

Of course, beauty is in the eye of the beholder. So how did we choose content for *Beautiful Testing* if everyone has a different idea of beauty?

Early on we decided that we didn't want to create just another book of dry case studies. We wanted the chapters to provide a peek into the contributors' views of beauty and testing. *Beautiful Testing* is a collection of chapter-length essays by over 20 people: some testers, some developers, some who do both. Each contributor understands and approaches the idea of beautiful testing differently, as their ideas are evolving based on the inputs of their previous and current environments.

Each contributor also waived any royalties for their work. Instead, all profits from *Beautiful Testing* will be donated to the UN Foundation's Nothing But Nets campaign. For every $10 in donations, a mosquito net is purchased to protect people in Africa against the scourge of malaria. Helping to prevent the almost one million deaths attributed to the disease, the large majority of whom are children under 5, is in itself a Beautiful Act. Tim and I are both very grateful for the time and effort everyone put into their chapters in order to make this happen.

How This Book Is Organized

While waiting for chapters to trickle in, we were afraid we would end up with different versions of "this is how you test" or "keep the bar green." Much to our relief, we ended up with a diverse mixture. Manifestos, detailed case studies, touching experience reports, and war stories from the trenches—*Beautiful Testing* has a bit of each.

The chapters themselves almost seemed to organize themselves naturally into sections.

Part I, Beautiful Testers

Testing is an inherently human activity; someone needs to think of the test cases to be automated, and even those tests can't think, feel, or get frustrated. *Beautiful Testing* therefore starts with the human aspects of testing, whether it is the testers themselves or the interactions of testers with the wider world.

Chapter 1, *Was It Good for You?*
    Linda Wilkinson brings her unique perspective on the tester's psyche.

Chapter 2, *Beautiful Testing Satisfies Stakeholders*
    Rex Black has been satisfying stakeholders for 25 years. He explains how that is beautiful.

Chapter 3, *Building Open Source QA Communities*
    Open source projects live and die by their supporting communities. Clint Talbert and Martin Schröder share their experiences building a beautiful community of testers.

Chapter 4, *Collaboration Is the Cornerstone of Beautiful Performance Testing*
Think performance testing is all about measuring speed? Scott Barber explains why, above everything else, beautiful performance testing needs to be collaborative.

Part II, Beautiful Process

We then progress to the largest section, which is about the testing process. Chapters here give a peek at what the test group is doing and, more importantly, why.

Chapter 5, *Just Peachy: Making Office Software More Reliable with Fuzz Testing*
To Kamran Khan, beauty in office suites is in hiding the complexity. Fuzzing is a test technique that follows that same pattern.

Chapter 6, *Bug Management and Test Case Effectiveness*
Brian Nitz and Emily Chen believe that how you track your test cases and bugs can be beautiful. They use their experience with OpenSolaris to illustrate this.

Chapter 7, *Beautiful XMPP Testing*
Remko Tronçon is deeply involved in the XMPP community. In this chapter, he explains how the XMPP protocols are tested and describes their evolution from ugly to beautiful.

Chapter 8, *Beautiful Large-Scale Test Automation*
Working at Microsoft, Alan Page knows a thing or two about large-scale test automation. He shares some of his secrets to making it beautiful.

Chapter 9, *Beautiful Is Better Than Ugly*
Beauty has always been central to the development of Python. Neal Noritz, Michelle Levesque, and Jeffrey Yasskin point out that one aspect of beauty for a programming language is stability, and that achieving it requires some beautiful testing.

Chapter 10, *Testing a Random Number Generator*
John D. Cook is a mathematician and applies a classic definition of beauty, one based on complexity and unity, to testing random number generators.

Chapter 11, *Change-Centric Testing*
Testing code that has not changed is neither efficient nor beautiful, says Murali Nandigama; however, change-centric testing is.

Chapter 12, *Software in Use*
Karen N. Johnson shares how she tested a piece of medical software that has had a direct impact on her nonwork life.

Chapter 13, *Software Development Is a Creative Process*
Chris McMahon was a professional musician before coming to testing. It is not surprising, then, that he thinks beautiful testing has more to do with jazz bands than manufacturing organizations.

Chapter 14, *Test-Driven Development: Driving New Standards of Beauty*
Jennitta Andrea shows how TDD can act as a catalyst for beauty in software projects.

Chapter 15, *Beautiful Testing As the Cornerstone of Business Success*

Lisa Crispin discusses how a team's commitment to testing is beautiful, and how that can be a key driver of business success.

Chapter 16, *Peeling the Glass Onion at Socialtext*

Matthew Heusser has worked at a number of different companies in his career, but in this chapter we see why he thinks his current employer's process is not just good, but beautiful.

Chapter 17, *Beautiful Testing Is Efficient Testing*

Beautiful testing has minimal retesting effort, says Adam Goucher. He shares three techniques for how to reduce it.

Part III, Beautiful Tools

Beautiful Testing concludes with a final section on the tools that help testers do their jobs more effectively.

Chapter 18, *Seeding Bugs to Find Bugs: Beautiful Mutation Testing*

Trust is a facet of beauty. The implication is that if you can't trust your test suite, then your testing can't be beautiful. Andreas Zeller and David Schuler explain how you can seed artificial bugs into your product to gain trust in your testing.

Chapter 19, *Reference Testing As Beautiful Testing*

Clint Talbert shows how Mozilla is rethinking its automated regression suite as a tool for anticipatory and forward-looking testing rather than just regression.

Chapter 20, *Clam Anti-Virus: Testing Open Source with Open Tools*

Tomasz Kojm discusses how the ClamAV team chooses and uses different testing tools, and how the embodiment of the KISS principle is beautiful when it comes to testing.

Chapter 21, *Web Application Testing with Windmill*

Adam Christian gives readers an introduction to the Windmill project and explains how even though individual aspects of web automation are not beautiful, their combination is.

Chapter 22, *Testing One Million Web Pages*

Tim Riley sees beauty in the evolution and growth of a test tool that started as something simple and is now anything but.

Chapter 23, *Testing Network Services in Multimachine Scenarios*

When trying for 100% test automation, the involvement of multiple machines for a single scenario can add complexity and non-beauty. Isaac Clerencia showcases ANSTE and explains how it can increase beauty in this type of testing.

Beautiful Testers following a Beautiful Process, assisted by Beautiful Tools, makes for Beautiful Testing. Or at least we think so. We hope you do as well.

Using Code Examples

This book is here to help you get your job done. In general, you may use the code in this book in your programs and documentation. You do not need to contact us for permission unless you're reproducing a significant portion of the code. For example, writing a program that uses several chunks of code from this book does not require permission. Selling or distributing a CD-ROM of examples from O'Reilly books does require permission. Answering a question by citing this book and quoting example code does not require permission. Incorporating a significant amount of example code from this book into your product's documentation does require permission.

We appreciate, but do not require, attribution. An attribution usually includes the title, author, publisher, and ISBN. For example: "*Beautiful Testing*, edited by Tim Riley and Adam Goucher. Copyright 2010 O'Reilly Media, Inc., 978-0-596-15981-8."

If you feel your use of code examples falls outside fair use or the permission given above, feel free to contact us at *permissions@oreilly.com*.

Safari® Books Online

 Safari Books Online is an on-demand digital library that lets you easily search over 7,500 technology and creative reference books and videos to find the answers you need quickly.

With a subscription, you can read any page and watch any video from our library online. Read books on your cell phone and mobile devices. Access new titles before they are available for print, and get exclusive access to manuscripts in development and post feedback for the authors. Copy and paste code samples, organize your favorites, download chapters, bookmark key sections, create notes, print out pages, and benefit from tons of other time-saving features.

O'Reilly Media has uploaded this book to the Safari Books Online service. To have full digital access to this book and others on similar topics from O'Reilly and other publishers, sign up for free at *http://my.safaribooksonline.com*.

How to Contact Us

Please address comments and questions concerning this book to the publisher:

> O'Reilly Media, Inc.
> 1005 Gravenstein Highway North
> Sebastopol, CA 95472
> 800-998-9938 (in the United States or Canada)
> 707-829-0515 (international or local)
> 707-829-0104 (fax)

We have a web page for this book, where we list errata, examples, and any additional information. You can access this page at:

http://oreilly.com/catalog/9780596159818

To comment or ask technical questions about this book, send email to:

bookquestions@oreilly.com

For more information about our books, conferences, Resource Centers, and the O'Reilly Network, see our website at:

http://oreilly.com

Acknowledgments

We would like to thank the following people for helping make *Beautiful Testing* happen:

- Dr. Greg Wilson. If he had not written *Beautiful Code*, we would never have had the idea nor a publisher for *Beautiful Testing*.

- All the contributors who spent many hours writing, rewriting, and sometimes rewriting again their chapters, knowing that they will get nothing in return but the satisfaction of helping prevent the spread of malaria.

- Our technical reviewers: Kent Beck, Michael Feathers, Paul Carvalho, and Gary Pollice. Giving useful feedback is sometimes as hard as receiving it, but what we got from them certainly made this book more beautiful.

- And, of course, our wives and children, who put up with us doing "book stuff" over the last year.

—Adam Goucher

## PART I

Beautiful Testers

Let's just say I was testing the bounds of reality. I was curious to see what would happen. That's all it was: curiosity.

—Jim Morrison

## CHAPTER ONE

Was It Good for You?

Linda Wilkinson

DO YOU HEAR THAT GROUP OF PEOPLE SNICKERING IN THE CORNER? They just found out that the third-party consulting firm you hired tested their code in production and sent 14,000 form letters out to your customers with a return address of "Bertha Big Butt." While the CEO and executive management team are sweating bullets and preparing mitigation strategies, your testing team is trying (without success) to stifle their guffaws.

Testers think differently than the rest of the IT team.

It's not that they don't appreciate the seriousness of the situation. They do.

It's just that it's...well...it's FUNNY.

If you're going to manage or work with testers, it stands to reason you have to *understand* testers. They march to the beat of a different drummer when compared to the rest of the IT staff.

Have you, or has anyone you know, ever associated with someone who works in a hospital emergency or operating room? You'll see a similar phenomenon there. In order to cope with what is often difficult, stressful, and depressing work, the medical staff have a tendency to develop what would appear to be a somewhat macabre and bizarre sense of humor. And you *want* that kind of behavior. It's infinitely better for your future health and well-being that your surgeon not be weeping copiously, hands shaking, into your internal organs....

Testers are trained to find and report problems. They view their contribution as helping the company, the development organization, and the customer or end user by exposing risks. They do that by finding and reporting software anomalies, often contributing information about the consequences of those errors.

Are testers policemen? Not usually. They can't "arrest" anyone for breaking a law, even if the world of software development could figure out what those laws should be, and most do not have the authority to keep something from moving to production, regardless of the generic goodness (or badness) of the software.

Their roles are more that of advisors. In fact, it is difficult and somewhat unfair for an organization to place testers in "gatekeeper" positions. A "gatekeeper" is someone who has to bless the software as Good before it can be moved to production. Most testers have difficulty balancing risk against need, marketing requirements, and cost. When you think about it, assessing and accepting risk is really a project and/or executive management task.

Testers know that no matter how many errors they've found and have been fixed, there are more lurking somewhere in the code. They are often reluctant to "bless" anything as Good. This means your project might be held up for a very long time while your "gatekeepers" make damn sure everything is as error-free as possible—which is often far beyond the point where it is economically intelligent to continue to find and fix errors.

What's more, you can actually end up training your testers *away* from finding and reporting errors. Instead, they spend their time attempting to assess *how important* each error is, when balanced against all of the considerations that feed into go/no go decisions. They might even lose their unique perspective and sense of mission—not bothering to write up what they discover, judging it to be "unimportant" in the scheme of things as they understand it. The problem is that their perspective is inevitably limited. Testers are not end users. They are not marketing experts. They are not project managers, vendors, accountants, or executive managers. They have valuable information to give you in regard to your project risks, and they should be used and respected in the advisory capacity that allows them to do what they do best: test your products and drive out error. Testers are excellent contributors to any team that might have go/no-go decision-making authority, but there are problems inherent in expecting them to function as the entire team.

Because of their mission, the types of software errors, issues, and problems that keep project managers awake at night, sweating and shaking uncontrollably, are the very things that make the life of a tester interesting.

Software testers know they're the "dark side of the force." They often joke about it ("Come to the Dark Side—We Have Cookies"). They view themselves as rebels, as the Bad Guys in the Black Hats, as Indiana Jones, Captain Jack Sparrow, and Sherlock Holmes all rolled into one. You never knew testing groups view themselves as the original Bad Asses, did you? Well, they're about to kick down your pretty house of cards. And they're going to enjoy it. Good testers almost always have an "attitude" of sorts. It can make them kind of irritating at times. After all, *they* never would have tested in production. *They* would have tried scenario X before shipping. *They* told you something was wrong and you didn't listen, did you? Sometimes it's enough to make you want to hit them with a stick. Especially when they're right....

And they *like* finding bugs. Many of the really ugly bugs are especially funny to a tester. Smart testers find out early that nontesters aren't going to understand them or their humor. They also (sadly) come to realize their role might not be especially appreciated, understood, or rewarded. So they learn not to share their unique perspective of the software world with the rest of the organization.

There is nothing in the IT world that equates to working as a tester. How many jobs in the business venue pay you to tell the truth? Testers are not paid to tell you everything is peachy when it is clear that the only "peach" involved is somewhat rotten. You can expect that kind of misplaced optimism or doubletalk from other members of your project or IT teams. Testers, however, are paid to tell you the truth as they know it. Sometimes that means telling you that your baby is ugly and why.

It's helpful when you manage or work with testers to understand how they think, which means you need to understand what motivates and excites them about their work.

So what *is* a tester, exactly? If you were to pick just a few key qualities, one of the first would be that a tester is *curious*. They want to know how things work. They are *experimental*. They want to see what happens when they try different scenarios or experiments against what has been presented to them. A good tester is also relatively *fearless*. They aren't afraid they'll break something. They aren't afraid to tell you the truth about what they've found, regardless of your position. And they aren't afraid to stand their ground and fight to get it fixed if they believe it negatively impacts the potential success of the product. A tester is *intelligent, analytical,* and *learns fast*. They are, in fact, always learning. Their jobs require it. Technology changes on a constant basis, and every project they receive is different in some way from the last. Sometimes they have great specifications. Sometimes not. Sometimes they have no written documentation at all. They need the ability to ask the right questions, investigate the right issues, put together the pieces of the puzzle, and draw the right conclusions. Testers are also generally *apolitical*. If you find a tester who is particularly good at politics, chances are pretty good they aren't especially great at their jobs. It is very difficult to play political games successfully when your job involves discovering and reporting issues. Testers are often accused of being blunt, rude, not team players, and the like. That's rarely true. Chances are good that anyone making such accusations does not understand or appreciate the role of the tester on a project team. Their jobs do not allow them to sweep any information that is "inconvenient" under the carpet.

Those are the good qualities of testers. There are other qualities that are less desirable, but still part and parcel of the overall persona of most testers, particularly those with a lot of experience. A tester tends to be *distrustful*. This is a learned behavior. They've been told over and over again that X doesn't need to be tested or Y code "hasn't been touched." That information has been wrong more times than they can count. So you can tell a tester the grass is green and they're still going to go check for themselves. A tester is *critical*, and it bleeds into other areas of their lives. They've been trained to find and report problems. That means if you send them an email with a misspelling, the entire team is going to helpfully point that out, or any other mistakes you (or anyone else) makes. Testers *question everything*, and that includes authority. It's generally a bad idea to try to lie to or finesse a test team with whatever politically correct propaganda that would be successful with some other group of people. You'll get far better results telling them the bitter truth. It's the only way to earn their respect and trust.

You may know testing staff who really don't have any of the qualities previously mentioned. Not everyone who works in a testing organization is a tester. Not everyone with the *title* of tester is a tester. Some are comfortable, happy, and adept at running existing tests. They aren't gifted at analysis, curious, or experimental. They may not be particularly fearless, getting easily intimidated by stronger personalities, people in positions of authority, or the thought of having to tackle something new. They may not report bugs, as they are afraid of the repercussions; their primary concern is to not rock the boat. Some may be so "into" politics and their own personal agendas and success that they lose the very qualities that set them apart and made them valuable to the test team. Overall, depending on the size of your team, all types of personnel can contribute and help project efforts be successful, but it pays to recognize and nurture the "real" testing talent on your team.

An executor of someone else's test ideas may or may not be a tester. A tester, when given a bank of existing tests to run, is probably going to be pretty bored. It's likely they'll run them as quickly as possible, just to get them off their plate. This means they may not pay close attention to those tests, missing things a dedicated and thorough executor would find as a matter of course. On the plus side, however, a "real" tester is going to take ownership of those tests. They'll think about the ideas in those tests, ask questions, add to them, change them, and explore some things the original analyst never considered. If the original analyst was talented, it's likely they won't find much to update or add, which will add to the boredom factor for them. You'll find that, over time, any truly creative, engaged, intelligent tester gets their spirits, initiative, and creativity crushed when the bulk of their jobs consist of anything that is merely rote, and that certainly includes executing large banks of existing manual test cases. It is inevitably best for the morale of your testers to either farm that stuff out to people who find comfort in routine, automate it, ship it offshore, or get it off their plates. They want to be working on something new. They want to be finding and reporting bugs. They want to be adding value that no one else can add.

It's the tedium involved that makes many testers vocally denigrate running existing regression test banks. You'll find that most understand the necessity and even agree with it, but it's like doing a puzzle someone else has already solved. It takes away the joy of exploration and the pleasure of the hunt. Most testers are aware that regression tests find a fraction of the error resident in an area of code; they'd really much rather be finding the bulk of the errors, which are lurking in the new stuff. It's all about the hunt and the joy of discovery.

So what about that attitude thing? Isn't it all about working together as a team? Yes. And testers *want* to be on your team. They want to help; they want to contribute. They want to be appreciated very badly. Their focus, however, makes it hard for *other* project team members to accept and appreciate their contributions. Even their humor can make it difficult to get them integrated into a team. What's worse, if you work for the type of organization that is not focused on quality and does not recognize or fix anything your testers have worked so hard to find, a test team is going to view that as a lack of respect for them or their work. And if you don't give your testers the respect they deserve, you'll demoralize them pretty quickly, and you will be unable to retain anyone with a skill set that is marketable in your region.

Overall, the testing field as a whole is all very civilized and evolved now, and testers have become better at "playing with others." Your most experienced testing staff will sympathetically pat you on the back and tell you that everyone knows there's more to it than just finding errors. They will nod understandingly and totally support your decisions not to fix errors A, B, and C. No one will fling himself to the floor and throw a tantrum. In fact, testers with some years of experience will tell you whatever you'd like to hear, which they've learned through experience at your particular company will get them (and thus your organization) the highest quality results. But what needs to be remembered is that it's likely they're willing to sacrifice errors A, B, and C in order to get you to fix D and E, which are more serious. Most testing staff secretly want you to fix everything they find. Testers have a definite and distinct bias toward getting stuff fixed. They care that things are wrong, and they want them to be better. When you think about it, do you really want your testing staff to be any other way?

Overall, an experienced test team can present bugs in such attractive wrapping paper (words) and ribbons (understanding of your problems and issues) that it will take you some time to realize the present you've just been given is really just an exceptionally large bag of poop. They're actually just re-gifting; it's the large bag of poop you gave them to start with, but somehow you didn't realize it smelled quite that bad when you turned it over to them. And what they say to you in polite and politically correct language and what they talk about back at the ranch with the other cowboys—well out of earshot—are two different things. They've learned through painful experience that the "dudes" they work with in other areas aren't really going to appreciate the humor or enjoyment involved in systematically finding every cow patty in the field and presenting them to the project team in a nice colorful box with a big red bow....

Finding software glitches—bugs—is much like a treasure hunt. Bugs are often hidden, and it takes a combination of logic, technique, and intuition (or luck) to find them. It's no coincidence that many testers are inordinately fond of puzzles. Testers like to hunt for and find stuff. The hunt is exciting, and finding an error (or an answer) is the ultimate motivation. When a tester finds a bug, they're earning their pay. From their perspective, that's one more problem that won't be found by the end user, one more opportunity for development to make the product better, and one less element of risk for their company. Finding a bug is a Eureka Moment. What a development or management resource regards with unmitigated dislike, disgust, or dismay is actually a Thing of Beauty to a tester. It's buried treasure. It's a gold doubloon.

Different testers prepare for a bug hunt in different ways. Their preparations will depend on your environment and your development methodologies. Some will be personal preference. They may write test cases in advance. They may work from a list of notes. But regardless of methodology, some activities are normally common across all methodologies.

They're going to read everything available on what they need to test. And they're going to ask questions—many, many questions. They'll ask questions until they're satisfied they understand the application as well as possible, and then they'll decide how best to do their testing and devise a plan. The plan might be formal or it might just be in their heads, but most testers know what they want to examine before they begin testing, and they have some idea as to how the system should look and behave as they begin to experiment.

This is where technique, training, and experience kick in. A trained, experienced tester tends to find more error than their untrained, inexperienced counterparts. This has nothing to with intelligence and everything to do with mentoring and learning. Nor does it mean neophytes never find anything of value. They do. But an experienced tester knows where to look. They know what is likely to break, and they've learned what types of techniques have been successful in helping them find bugs under similar circumstances. It doesn't really matter whether a tester has been "classically" trained (boundary analysis, etc.) or trained in agile technique (heuristics, tours, etc.) or both. Once a tester has learned to read between the lines, look beyond the obvious, ask the right questions, and expand their horizons, you have a real testing powerhouse on your hands. And it's a testing powerhouse that will continue to learn and add new "tools" to their testing toolbox throughout their career.

Smart project teams take advantage of all that knowledge and intuition. The reason experienced project managers customarily get testers involved early in the project is not because they're lonely and want some company in their meetings. No, they want those testing gurus asking their questions early in the process, when it's faster, easier, and cheaper to fix discrepancies. They want the development staff to pay attention to what the testers are going to be looking at so they can develop better code. Testers used in this capacity often help the team find design flaws well before they ever get a chance to manifest themselves as bugs further down the line.

There have been arguments about the roles of a tester for literally decades now. Some feel their role is to "assure quality," which would be fine if anyone could decide what "quality" actually means. Some feel it is to help development staff build better code by training *them* to look for bugs and to start building code that doesn't contain them. Some testing experts focus on why and how bugs are found: the strategy, technique, and nomenclature involved in finding bugs in various environments. All of that is interesting, and all of it benefits the field in some way.

But, in essence, the purpose of testing is to find bugs.

Testers "assure quality" by presenting bugs/issues/discrepancies to project teams and management to help them make better decisions. They help developers become better at their jobs by showing them the types of errors found in their code so they can fix those errors, learn from their mistakes, and stop making the same mistakes in future work. Testers learn new strategies and techniques to help them find more (or more important) bugs. They categorize what they do into new strategies, such as tours, to help train others to find bugs. And if no (or few) errors are found during the testing period, well, that is important information as well.

Any tester will tell you, however, that there are bugs and then there are BUGS. Generally speaking, it's not the number of bugs that are found that makes things interesting. For example, a tester can find thousands of cosmetic errors in a large web application. What is a cosmetic error? A misspelling. A message to the user that is grammatically incorrect. The wrong color on an icon. Something put in the wrong place on the screen.

Testers don't like these kinds of errors any more than anyone else does, especially when they find 10 quadzillion (QC technical term for "a lot") of them. It takes longer to write up the defect for one of these errors than to locate them, and they are inevitably low-priority errors. On the positive side, usually they are also easy to fix and they do get fixed quickly.

You might wonder why anyone would bother with cosmetic errors anyway, but someone who has worked in the IT field for a while would tell you that the end users of a given application might care deeply about issues that you find trivial. Part of it might be something called the "irritation factor." Sure, that misspelling in the field title or an informational message might not bother anyone much at the moment, and everyone on the project team will agree the level of severity is roughly the same as that of dirt. But to the end user staring at it two thousand times a day, the "irritation factor" is very high. Often a project team has difficulty understanding how minor issues, functionally speaking, can be major issues to an end user. Consider navigation problems—simple tabbing on a screen. If negotiating through a given job function now takes 25% longer than it used to or three extra keystrokes are required, you are potentially impacting the bottom line of your end users. Their jobs, bonuses, or the output of their workgroup might be part of their evaluation process. If your changes lower their output, they would rightfully consider such issues urgent.

So testers report everything they find. Those with experience report severity from their perspective, but generally do not attempt to dictate business priority. Often their understanding of business priority, like the development team's understanding of business priority, is somewhat incomplete and not based on personal experience with the job function. On occasion, disciplining oneself to not "speak for the users" can involve swallowing one's own tongue. It is very common for business users to be willing to "live with" code that contains grievous errors, but insist that something that appears inconsequential or trivial get fixed or added at the last minute. What can you say? It's their dime. The only advice you can give a tester under such circumstances is Let It Go.

If end users are willing to work around serious issues, that's their decision. It generally does not go over well to dictate to people what they do or do not want. The job of the tester is to seek, find, and report, not to pass judgment in some sort of godlike capacity. Testers should feel free to offer their professional opinions; in fact, everyone on the team should feel free to offer professional opinions. Ultimately, however, the people that need to weigh in on impact to the business users are, well, the business users themselves. A difference of opinion in regard to production-readiness needs to be escalated and passed up the chain to executive management. Part of management's job is to assess risk and make hard decisions for the company. That said, the bias of the tester should be (and usually is) toward getting errors fixed.

One of the saddest situations in the field is one where the tester does *not* report all of the errors he finds. The reasons can be myriad, but the most common is the feeling on the part of the tester that there is no point in reporting certain types or categories of errors because they'll never be fixed anyway. This is "learned" behavior, and you'll normally find testers with this type of attitude to be disillusioned, jaded, cynical, and uninterested in their work. Their interest and desire to report bugs has been beaten out of them over time because of their working environment. Another reason may be that they've been convinced that, politically and practically, it's not "smart" to report everything they find. They should report only what the company cares about. Well, if the company isn't getting a complete picture, how do they know whether they care or not?

Everyone is aware that many errors cannot—or from a financial perspective, should not—be fixed prior to production. Part of the "art and craft" of successful project management is making the right decisions as to what to defer and what to fix. For example, say the project team decides to fix 14 errors and defer 32. But the tester opted not to report 324, because development "never fixes" field errors. This means the project manager and upper management staff are making decisions based on faulty, incomplete information. In this case, the UI is probably not yet ready for Prime Time.

In addition, reporting every error, even in a company with a history of not addressing certain errors, can eventually turn around corporate policies (or "that's the way we've always done things"). If a tester reports 40 errors, none of which get addressed, the application goes to production, and the users report those same errors with urgent priorities and demands that they get fixed as soon as possible, then development and project managers will start to pay more attention to those types of bugs in the future.

Overall, however, reporting cosmetic errors is time-consuming and isn't overly exciting for most testers. They do it because they are obligated to do so in order to provide a complete and accurate picture of the state of the application and because those errors might matter a lot to an end user.

So what kinds of bugs *do* make the life of a tester worth living?

The nasty ones. The complicated, multifaceted errors that seriously impact the ability of the end users to do their work. Those that are subtle and have serious impact on some process down the line. And those that cause an application to tank. ("Tank" is another "scientific" QC testing term for going belly-up like a dead fish.)

To understand the nature of an "ugly" error, some understanding of the development process is necessary.

A standard GUI, UI, or screen error is typically the result of an oversight. Either someone left something out because it wasn't specified, they misunderstood what the user wanted, they misinterpreted a requirement, or they simply misspelled a word. These errors are usually easy to find, easy to recreate, and easy to fix.

Beyond that, however, things get more complex and therefore more interesting. A developer is often working in somewhat of a vacuum on her own piece of code. That piece may be invoked by multiple other pieces of code and feed data into still other modules/applications or some sort of database. Consider that at the time developers write their code, all of the other pieces of code they need to interact with are *also* under development. This means that developers, in order to test their code, are likely to "dummy up" (simulate) the input they're supposed to receive and feed the data to yet another set of dummy entities, examining the end results as best they can at the time.

The problem is that the actual data received might be different from what was anticipated. Consider how many changes are made during the life of a project. It may turn out the data output by any one piece of code is no longer in a format that can be used by the next entity down the line. So even an excellent developer who does good unit testing is likely to run into issues at those points where his code intersects with someone else's code.

It's at these points—where code and applications interface with one another—that testers often find the majority of their most significant errors. There are a few lessons that can be learned from this.

The first is that testers inevitably benefit from understanding the virtual design of a system. It tells them where to focus their effort and highlights where errors are most likely to "hide."

The second is that testers understand that testing isn't "done" until they've followed a given piece of the puzzle all the way through the entire maze.

What is meant by that?

Say I develop a piece of code that collects information from a business user, massages it, and sends it to a database. So I, as the developer, test exactly that and verify my data is properly stored in each appropriate database field.

Much to my surprise, the tester finds 37 bugs in my code.

What the heck happened???

Well, it's likely that I only used "good" data for my own tests, lacking both the time and the desire to break my own stuff. I might not have fully understood what the end user was going to do with the data, I might have massaged it incorrectly, and it may have populated the database with data that could not be retrieved and formatted properly by other programs. Those programs that interface with mine might not have been expecting the data in quite the format I provided (or anticipated a given field might be empty), and therefore errors manifested down the line. When my "massaged" data is actually retrieved by the business user, it might not be displayed in the way they require, necessitating changes in my code, the database, and the retrieval code.

The tester, unlike the developer, tests all the way through, from A to Z. This doesn't mean they can't assist with more limited testing and help out with more of a unit type of testing. It means they recognize the testing isn't "done" until a given piece of information is taken through the entire process, from beginning to end.

Good testers are also creative and imaginative. Testing is usually a destructive process, which is why a great deal of care needs to be taken if decisions are made to run a test in production. A good tester is not necessarily trying to prove software works correctly; they're trying to prove it doesn't. That difference in attitude is one of the primary reasons testers find so many bugs. They *want* to find bugs. They analyze all of the information available and sit down and *think* about how they can break the application. There is no one else on the team with that kind of mission. Developers customarily aren't even given enough time to reliably create their own code, let alone try to find sufficient time to think about ways to break it. End users typically just execute what they normally do in the course of their jobs and might actually be panicked and upset if something "breaks." Testers, on the other hand, are going to fearlessly wade in there and kick the tires as hard as they can, and they're going to be happy if one of them blows up in their face. They'll be even happier if one of the doors falls off instead, or if their kicking makes the engine fall out.

This is just a validation of what your mother always told you. If you only look for the bad in people, that's all you'll find. Testers are systematically looking for the bad in a system. Along the way, they'll end up verifying what is working correctly as well. But their focus is on driving out what is wrong, not what is right. If your only goal with testing is to prove the system does what it is supposed to do under perfect conditions, your developers will tell you it does exactly that, and you can save yourself a pile of money.

Ah. You don't believe them? Neither does your testing team.

So how *do* you work with these quirky people? How do you motivate and integrate them into your team? How do you encourage them to do what they do best: find and report error?

First of all, recognize and appreciate their contributions to your company and project teams. Involve them in project efforts early, like every other pivotal member of the team. Listen to what they have to say and pay attention to what they find during their testing. Fix some of that stuff and give them a pat on the back when they're working late due to buggy code or late deliveries. Try to express a "woo-hoo!" when a particularly heinous error is uncovered; it will show them you "get it" and understand their work and how they think. When you give kudos to the team at the end of a project, include their names as well and thank them for their efforts. If they've done a particularly fine job, send them an email; copy their bosses and yours. Testers are like any other staff members: they'll knock themselves out for people who they know will recognize and thank them when they go that extra mile.

Recognize that choosing testing as a career requires some level of bravery and commitment. Many testers spend a significant portion of those careers striving for recognition, respect, and success. You can't go to school at this time and learn what you need to learn to become a successful tester. You need to learn at the School of Hard Knocks. To add insult to injury, many other IT professionals think "anyone can test." They do not recognize any difference between an end user, developer, BA, or person off the street performing testing, even when their own numbers clearly show their testing staff finds 1,000% more error than any of those other groups. That's not a coincidence. Do you pull in people from the street to do your programming? This is exactly the same thing. Testing involves more than just a warm body or mere intelligence; it also involves technique. You'll find that if you treat testing staff with the same type of respect you would give to your development staff, DBAs, etc., you will encourage and build the type of testing organization that will attract and retain top personnel.

If you're in a position to do so, reward your test team with an even hand. Testers who are paid and rewarded significantly less than your development team will move to greener pastures when the opportunity arises. Those who remain will be cynical and uninspired. Hard as it might be to believe, it is more difficult to find good testers than it is good developers. Most talented IT professionals want to be Luke Skywalker, not Darth Vader. You also need some talent on "the dark side of the force," so you need to encourage strong testing resources to stick around.

If you understand the issues testers go through to learn and grow professionally and their hunger for recognition, respect, and success, you will invest in (or encourage your company to invest in) training for your testing personnel. Software testing is a specialized field, and at the time of this writing, good courseware at standard learning institutions is limited, to say the least. Bring in some talented teachers and experts to offer their ideas and expand your team's capabilities. Send them to conferences. Encourage a learning atmosphere. Allow them to try new techniques on small projects.

If you show your test team you value them—through training, recognition, and a policy of equal reward—you will end up with a team that will walk on hot coals for you, and they'll recommend your company to their equally talented cohorts in the field. You'll attract and retain The Best of the Best, and that does not necessarily equate to the highest paychecks in the field.

So the next time your testers put in 500 hours of overtime due to late code deliveries and buggy code, and drive out 1,200 errors, 40% of which are showstoppers, tell me…

Was it good for you?

Well, it was good for them. And, ultimately, good for your customers, your company, and your bottom line.

## CHAPTER TWO

Beautiful Testing Satisfies Stakeholders

Rex Black

WHEN WE DESCRIBE SOMETHING AS BEAUTIFUL, WE MEAN that it has qualities that give great pleasure or satisfaction. In this chapter, I write primarily about the latter, not the former. Yes, testing should provide pleasure. However, testing that pleases the tester may prove a superficial form of beauty, because it does not satisfy the stakeholders.

We are all familiar with superficial forms of beauty that fade. In the entertainment world, we find some actors and actresses beautiful for a time, but in the long run many of them fade. However, some actors and actresses remain beautiful to watch throughout their careers. This is not due solely to physical beauty, but rather because we find beauty in their ability to satisfy us as viewers of their performances. Their performances tell us something that is deeply true, that is moving, and that inspires us to change the way we see the world we live in.

Similarly, in testing, although some approaches to testing might strike us as beautiful at first, in the long run those approaches to testing that satisfy our needs are those that are truly beautiful. Beautiful testing tells us something that is true. Beautiful testing moves us. Beautiful testing inspires a change in our beliefs about and actions toward the projects we work on— and the organizations we work within.

In this chapter, I address the beauty of testing that does not fade. What is it about testing, done really well, that provides long-term satisfaction to the stakeholders? Who are the stakeholders and what do they want from testing? What are the external and internal forms of beauty in testing that truly satisfy? How can testers and test managers build testing organizations that provide this satisfaction over the long term? How can we, as test professionals, create elegance, effectiveness, efficiency, and even delight for ourselves and our stakeholders in our work?

For Whom Do We Test?

Let's start by identifying these people whom we want to satisfy. I'll use the broad term *test stakeholders* for these people. This term goes beyond test participants, though it includes them. And it goes beyond project participants, though it includes them. It even goes beyond the members of the organization for which we are testing, though it includes them, too. Everyone with a stake—an interest—in the testing we do and the quality of the final deliverable is ultimately a test stakeholder.

We can divide the list of test stakeholders into external and internal stakeholders. We can choose any number of boundaries between internal and external, but let's take an obvious one: the internal stakeholders are those doing, leading, or managing the test work, and the external stakeholders are all other applicable stakeholders.

So, who are these stakeholders? The answer varies from one project, product, and organization to the next. However, here are some typical answers, starting from the most immediately obvious stakeholders (the ones we work with daily) to the ones perhaps less obvious but no less important (the ones who ultimately are satisfied that testing accomplished what it must):

Fellow testers
> The people doing the testing work.

Test leads and managers
> The people who plan, direct, measure, and manage the testing work and its results.

Developers, development leads, and development managers
> The people who implement the system. They receive our test results, and often must respond to our findings when they indicate a need for changes and improvements.

Database and system architects
> The people who design the products. They also receive our test results and often must respond to our findings when they indicate a need for changes and improvements.

Marketing and business analysts
> The people who determine the features—and their quality attributes—that must be present in the system as designed and implemented.

Project managers
> The people responsible for bringing the project to a satisfactory conclusion. They must achieve a proper balance between quality, schedule, feature, and budget priorities.

Technical support and help desk staff
> The people who must support the users, customers, and sponsors who eventually receive, pay for, and benefit from the features and quality of the final deliverable.

Sales managers, engineers, and staff

The people who find the customers, determine how to employ our systems to satisfy their needs, and manage the profitable delivery of our systems.

Executives, officers, ministers, and/or directors

The people who run the organization, either on a daily basis or as an oversight body. These roles—and the needs of those in these roles—tend to vary depending on whether we consider a public organization (e.g., a government agency), a nonprofit organization (e.g., a charity), a publicly held organization (e.g., a listed corporation), or a privately held organization (e.g., a partnership or sole proprietorship).

Company shareholders

For publicly or privately held companies, the people who own the company.

Elected officials and voters

For public agencies, the people who pass laws and make decisions that affect the organization, and those who elected them.

Regulators and law enforcement

The people who ensure compliance by the organization, its people, and its systems with applicable laws and regulations.

Users

The people who use the system directly or who receive its results, reports, data, etc. For companies that use systems internally, such as utilities or insurance companies, their customers are indirect users of their systems.

Vendors

The people who might provide components incorporated into our systems or who might be users of our systems.

Customers and sponsors

The people who pay for the development, acquisition, purchase, and/or installation.

Public and society

The people who live in the communities where the system exists or is used.

This list is not exhaustive and does not apply to all projects.

I should mention another important point. Every stakeholder in the preceding list—and perhaps others on your project—has an interest in your testing. Most of these stakeholders typically want to see your testing and the project succeed. However, not all necessarily have such a motivation.

Some stakeholders are neutral. For example, regulators and law enforcement typically care more about ensuring that you, the project team, and the organization follow the rules. If failure to follow the rules results in negative consequences, their attitude is likely to be, in the words of the 1970s TV serial, "If you can't do the time, don't do the crime." In some cases, failure to adhere to the rules might well constitute a crime, so know your obligations. Running afoul of regulators or law enforcement is not a beautiful experience.

And, although blessedly infrequent, some stakeholders are inimical. In my rare encounters with such stakeholders, I have called them *anti-stakeholders*. For example, some projects to replace legacy systems require the involvement of the very people who continue to support and maintain these legacy systems. These people might feel that the legacy system works just fine, thanks very much. Since the organizational dictate requires that they participate in the project, they do, but passive aggression is the order of the day. These anti-stakeholders hope that the project as a whole fails, and have no problem with your test work contributing to that failure. Contributing to project failure is not a beautiful experience.

Take the first step toward beautiful testing and determine who your test stakeholders are. If you do not know who the stakeholders are, you might achieve beautiful testing according to some, but others will not find it beautiful. In our consulting work, RBCS assessors see many examples of neglected stakeholders who are unhappy with the test team's work. Our clients who have thought carefully about testing stakeholders stand a much better chance of testing beautifully. Clients who neglect neutral stakeholders and anti-stakeholders can have a very ugly experience indeed.

What Satisfies?

Each stakeholder has a set of objectives and expectations related to testing. They want these carried out effectively, efficiently, and elegantly. What does that mean?

Effectiveness means satisfying these objectives and expectations. Unfortunately, the objectives and expectations are not always clearly defined or articulated. So, to achieve effectiveness, testers must work with the stakeholder groups to determine their objectives and expectations. We often see a wide range of objectives and expectations held by stakeholders for testers. Sometimes stakeholders have unrealistic objectives and expectations. You must know what people expect from you, and resolve any unrealistic expectations, to achieve beautiful testing.

Efficiency means satisfying objectives and expectations in a way that maximizes the value received for the resources invested. Different stakeholders have different views on invested resources, which might not include money. For example, a business executive will often consider a corporate jet an efficient way to travel because it maximizes her productive time and convenience. A vacationing family will often choose out-of-the-way airports and circuitous routings because it maximizes the money available to spend on the vacation itself. You must find a way to maximize value—as defined by your stakeholders—within your resource constraints to achieve beautiful testing.

Elegance means achieving effectiveness and efficiency in a graceful, well-executed fashion. You and your work should impress the stakeholders as fitting well with the overall project. You should never appear surprised—or worse yet, dumbfounded—by circumstances that stakeholders consider foreseeable. Elegant testers exhibit what Ernest Hemingway called "grace under pressure," and there's certainly plenty of pressure involved in testing. You and your work should resonate as professional, experienced, and competent. To achieve beautiful testing, you cannot simply create a superficial appearance of elegance—that is a con man's job. Rather, you prove yourself elegant over time in results, behavior, and demeanor.

As I mentioned, the perspectives on effectiveness, efficiency, and elegance can vary considerably according to the stakeholder. They can also vary considerably by group and by organization. To illustrate that, consider the following examples for two of the stakeholder groups I mentioned earlier.

For some clients, we have found that testers tend to gauge their effectiveness in terms of finding bugs. The more severe the bug, the happier the tester, even if these severe bugs are highly unlikely in real-world usage and not related to important usage scenarios. The more bugs the testers find, the more efficient the testers consider themselves. Such testers consider it elegant to construct a particular devilish—sometimes even tortured—test case that causes a crash, abnormal application termination, computer lock-up, data loss, or similarly spectacularly severe system crash. Test leads and managers, if they encourage such a bug-focused culture, tend to make this perspective even more prevalent. At the extreme end of the scale, some test managers even pay bonuses or measure testers on their yearly performance evaluations based on the number of severe bugs found.

Development managers and projects managers generally do not appreciate such a one-dimensional outlook. They do not consider bug-obsessed testing beautiful at all, but rather antagonistic, disruptive, and obstructive. Effectiveness means that testers focus their efforts on important areas and typical workflows, and find whatever bugs exist there. Efficiency means covering critical and typical scenarios and finding important bugs early in the project. Elegance means clear reporting of results based on functional areas and key quality risks, not on obscure corner cases.

Conflict results from these divergent perspectives. This conflict generally reaches its most intense stage during test execution. During test execution, testing is on the critical path for release. During this stage, each bug found and each test case failed represents a possible delay to the project. Tempers can become short and patience limited. So, conflict can reduce team cohesion and efficiency. The product often goes into production late, or with more bugs than necessary, or both. Further, a residue of bitterness and resentment begins to build between the test team and others on the project. Often, organizations choose to dissolve or reorganize such test teams after a while.

This situation is not very beautiful, is it? What if we could establish a consensus with our fellow stakeholders about what constituted effective, efficient, and elegant testing before we reached such a sorry, often irretrievable, state? Assuming we can achieve the objectives we set to a level of capability that is possible, then we could achieve widespread satisfaction with our testing work. Ah, satisfied stakeholders: now that is beautiful!

Take the second step toward beautiful testing and determine what objectives and expectations your test stakeholders have. If you do not know your stakeholders' objectives and expectations, only by luck will you achieve beautiful testing, and usually only for a few of the stakeholders. When my associates and I assess test teams, we see many examples of unfulfilled objectives and expectations, leading to a lower-than-necessary degree of satisfaction in the test team's work. Our clients who have identified stakeholder objectives and expectations often test beautifully.

What Beauty Is External?

Consider a world-class distance athlete, such as an Olympic marathon runner or an Ironman triathlete. Such athletes have a rugged external beauty, a form-fits-function appearance. They are lean. They have extremely well-toned and well-defined—but usually not bulky—muscles. During their competitions, they show a determined face, and they bear the pain of the long event with grace. We can measure their effectiveness, efficiency, and elegance by their final times, their race standings, and their sportsmanlike behavior—win or lose.

A good test team also displays an external beauty, similar to a long-distance athlete. After all, testing is much more like a marathon than like a sprint!

Suppose that, by working with your testing stakeholders, you identify a number of objectives for testing. One includes a typical objective, that of finding bugs, especially important bugs. How might you determine your externally visible effectiveness and efficiency for this objective? Consider the following questions:

- What percentage of the bugs delivered to us do we find?
- Do we find a higher percentage of the important bugs?
- What is our cost per bug found and fixed during testing compared to the cost of a failure in production?

For each of these questions, devise a metric. Start with the percentage of bugs that you find. You can measure this with the defect detection percentage (DDP), shown in Equation 2-1. If your testing is the last quality assurance activity prior to user acceptance test and then deployment, you can simplify the metric as shown in Equation 2-2. Typically, there is a characteristic period of time in which most of the bugs that will be found in production have been found, so you can calculate the defect detection percentage after that period of time has passed since deployment.

EQUATION 2-1. Defect detection percentage (DDP)

$$DDP = \frac{bugs\ detected}{bugs\ present}$$

$$DDP = \frac{test\ bugs}{test\ bugs + production\ bugs}$$

Based on our assessments and feedback from clients around the world, an independent test team's defect detection percentage for a system test or system integration test averages around 85%. However, significant variation exists on this metric. For systems developed for internal use, you should target a higher number, closer to 95%, since the users are typically less varied and the set of use cases and supported environments smaller. For systems developed for a mass market, wide variations in users, their skill levels, their usage of the system, and the environments in which they will use it make achieving a high defect detection percentage much harder. That said, for mission-critical or safety-critical systems, you will need to achieve a very high defect detection percentage.

With a measure of our bug-finding effectiveness in hand, devise a metric to check your focus. Does your test team find a higher percentage of the important bugs? You can check this by using the defect detection percentage metric again. First, calculate the defect detection percentage for all bugs. Then, calculate the defect detection percentage for the critical bugs only, however you define "critical bugs" in your organization. The relationship shown in Equation 2-3 should hold.

EQUATION 2-3. Bug-finding focus

$$DDP\ (all\ bugs) < DDP\ (critical\ bugs)$$

Generally, our clients that practice successful risk-based testing can achieve a satisfactory defect detection percentage for critical bugs, and their defect detection percentages adhere to Equation 2-3. If you need to adopt risk-based testing in your organization, you can see my book *Pragmatic Software Testing* (Wiley) or some of my articles on risk-based testing in the RBCS Library (*http://www.rbcs-us.com*). In any case, you should try to achieve a defect detection percentage for critical bugs that consistently comes close to 100%. You should carefully analyze any critical bugs that do escape to production, to see how you can improve your testing and catch such bugs in the future.

Finally, not only should we find a sizeable percentage of the bugs, and not only should we find more of the critical bugs than of the less critical bugs, but we should also find bugs more cheaply than the alternative: customers and users finding bugs in production. The recognized technique for measuring the cost of failures is called "cost of quality." You can find a complete description of this technique in my book *Critical Testing Processes* (Addison-Wesley), or in my article "Testing ROI: What IT Managers Should Know," which you can find at the RBCS Library.

Using cost of quality, you can identify three main costs associated with testing and quality:

Cost of detection

The testing costs that we would incur even if we found no bugs. For example, performing a quality risk analysis, setting up the test environment, and creating test data are activities that incur costs of detection.

Cost of internal failure

The testing and development costs that we incur purely because we find bugs. For example, filing bug reports, fixing bugs, confirmation testing bug fixes, and regression testing changed builds are activities that incur costs of internal failure.

Cost of external failure

The support, testing, development, and other costs that we incur because we don't deliver 100% bug-free, perfect products. For example, much of the costs for technical support or help desk organizations and sustaining engineering teams are costs of external failure.

So, we can identify the average costs of a bug in testing and in production, as shown in Equations 2-4 and 2-5. Typically, the average cost of a test bug is well below the average cost of a production bug, often by a factor of 2, 5, 10, or more. Equation 2-6 shows a calculation of the return on the testing investment basted on these figures. The logic behind Equation 2-6 is that each bug found by testing gives the organization the opportunity to save money, specifically the difference between the cost of a test bug and the cost of a production bug. The cost of the investment in testing is the cost of detection (since the cost of internal failure is not an investment).

EQUATION 2-4. Average cost of a test bug (ACTB)

$$ACTB = \frac{cost\ of\ detection\ +\ cost\ of\ internal\ failure}{test\ bugs}$$

EQUATION 2-5. Average cost of a production bug (ACPB)

$$ACPB = \frac{cost\ of\ external\ failure}{production\ bugs}$$

EQUATION 2-6. Calculating the testing return on investment (Test ROI)

$$Test\ ROI = \frac{(ACPB - ACTB) \times test\ bugs}{cost\ of\ detection}$$

In RBCS assessments and projects, my associates and I have found return on the testing investment to range from a respectable low around 25% all the way up to more than 3,500%. Generally, as the cost of external failure goes up relative to the cost of internal failure, the return on the testing investment also goes up. In other words, the more expensive it is for your organization to deal with bugs in production, the more it should invest in testing.

In terms of setting a target metric for your return on investment, be careful. Sometimes optimizing the return on the testing investment (your bug-finding efficiency) can reduce your defect detection percentage, your bug-finding focus, or both (your bug-finding effectiveness). During assessments, if the test team has a positive return on the testing investment, we recommend only those efficiency changes unlikely to reduce effectiveness. I'll discuss an example of such an improvement in the next section.

Now you can take the third step toward beautiful testing: establish metrics for effectiveness and efficiency and goals for those metrics. In this section, I used Victor Basili's *goal-question-metric* approach to do so. You've already understood the objectives and expectations of your stakeholders, so those are the goals. Now, what questions would you need to answer to know whether your testing achieved those goals? Finally, what metrics could demonstrate the extent to which you achieved those goals? Now you have a way of measuring your testing in terms of what satisfies your stakeholders. How beautiful is that?

You're not quite done yet, though. You still have to consider the elegance element of beauty. Establish an ethic of elegance, in terms of graceful work, a service-oriented outlook toward your stakeholders, and a focus on what really matters to the organization. Years ago, someone coined the term *egoless programming*. Similarly, beautiful testing is *egoless testing*.

In our assessments, RBCS consultants have seen shining examples of test teams that know their stakeholders, know the objectives and expectations those stakeholders have, and know how to achieve and measure success for those objectives and expectations. These clients almost always test beautifully.

What Beauty Is Internal?

There is one more element to beautiful testing we need to consider: internal beauty. Let's return to the metaphor of a test team as an Olympic marathon runner or an Ironman triathlete. Underneath the surface, their internal organs all serve the purpose of athletic performance. Muscles are trained for hour after hour of endurance. The digestive system enables the conversion of carbohydrates to fuel and protein to muscle, and distributes water into the body to maintain healthy hydration. So, we can measure effectiveness, efficiency, and elegance by calories burned, body fat percentages, and long-term health.

A good test team also displays a similar internal beauty. Since testing is like a marathon, we need a test team that can go the distance on project after project, often under trying circumstances.

Suppose you have determined that your team spends a sizeable percentage of its time doing regression testing manually. Even if the defect detection metric indicates that you don't miss many bugs, manual regression testing is tedious, expensive, error-prone, slow, and morale-sapping. So you could decide to use automation to reduce the manual effort while continuing to maintain a low level of regression risk in delivered products. How might you determine your externally visible effectiveness and efficiency for this objective? Consider the following questions:

- What percentage of regression tests have we automated?
- What percentage of regression-related quality risks do we cover?
- How much more quickly can we run our automated regression tests?

For each of these questions, devise a metric. Start with the percentage of regression tests automated, as shown in Equation 2-7. This metric typically cannot—and should not—reach 100%, since some tests require human judgment or interaction during test execution. Many of our clients do achieve regression test automation as high as 90%. You'll need to do some careful analysis to determine your target.

EQUATION 2-7. Regression test automation percentage (RTA)

$$RTA = \frac{automated\ regression\ tests}{manual\ regression\ tests + automated\ regression\ tests}$$

Test automation should preserve or lower the level of regression risk. So, you should measure the percentage of regression-related quality risks covered, as shown in Equation 2-8. To calculate this, you need the ability to establish the relationship between your tests—both automated and manual—and the underlying regression risks. (If you're not familiar with this idea of traceability between the tests and the test basis—i.e., what the tests are based on—you can find a description of it in my book *Managing the Testing Process*, published by Microsoft.) Many test management tools include the ability to establish test traceability and to measure coverage. As you proceed to automate more and more tests, the regression risk coverage metric should at least stay constant or, better yet, increase.

EQUATION 2-8. Regression risk coverage (RRC)

$$RRC = \frac{regression\ risks\ covered}{regression\ risks\ identified}$$

Automated regression tests should make regression test execution quicker, too. You should measure the acceleration of regression test execution, as shown in Equation 2-9. Note that the duration figures for both manual and automated regression testing should include the time required to run all the regression tests, even if you don't typically run all the regression tests due to time constraints. You want to measure the time savings realized to achieve the same level of regression risk. If some portion of your regression tests remain manual, you should include the time required to run them in the *automated regression test duration* figure, to keep this metric accurate.

EQUATION 2-9. Acceleration of regression testing (ART)

$$ART = \frac{manual\ regression\ test\ duration - automated\ regression\ test\ duration}{manual\ regression\ test\ duration}$$

For example, suppose it takes 20 days to run all the regression tests manually. You can now run them overnight with analysis of the results complete on the second day. You have achieved 90% regression test acceleration. That's quite a gain in efficiency.

Notice that this acceleration not only makes testing more efficient, it allows us to tolerate a higher rate of change without any increase in regression risk. This benefit is critical for teams implementing agile methodologies. Without good regression test automation, agile methodologies tend to result in a significant increase in regression risk, and ultimately in regression bugs found in production.

In addition, if we automate carefully, the costs of detection and internal failure mentioned in the previous section should go down. Thus, you can use regression test automation to improve your efficiency without reducing effectiveness. Isn't that beautiful?

You can take the fourth step toward beautiful testing. You can set objectives and expectations for your testing from an internal point of view. You can establish metrics for effectiveness and efficiency in meeting these objectives, and establish goals for those metrics. Now you have a way of measuring your testing in terms of what allows you to do your job better, quicker, cheaper, and smarter. How beautiful is that?

Don't stop there, though. Again, consider the elegance element of beauty, and add to it the element of delight. You and your fellow testers should adopt leading-edge techniques that make your test team an example of testing best practices. Beautiful testing means working in a test team that practices—and advances—the state of the art in testing. Beautiful testing raises the standard for all testers. Beautiful testers share what they have learned about testing in articles, books, and training courses, to the delight and enlightenment of their colleagues in the testing community.

In assessments, we sometimes see test teams that know their stakeholders, know the objectives and expectations of those stakeholders, have objectives and expectations to improve their internal processes, and know how to achieve and measure success for all those objectives and expectations. They inculcate an ethic of smart work, elegant work, and delightful work into their testing. They advance the field of testing and generously share those advances with others. These clients test beautifully, every day.

Conclusions

Testing has many stakeholders. Beautiful testing satisfies those stakeholders. The tester knows the stakeholders and their objectives and expectations for testing. The tester works with the stakeholders to ensure realistic objectives and expectations, and defines metrics to measure effectiveness and efficiency. He takes special care with neutral stakeholders and anti-stakeholders.

The tester knows how internal test processes support effectiveness and efficiency, too, and takes steps to improve those over time. Through a concerted focus on delivering ever-improving test services, and continuously improving his testing practices, he works effectively, efficiently, and elegantly. Not only is he delighted in his own work, but the other stakeholders are delighted, too. Such testers do beautiful work.

In this chapter, I've given you some ideas on objectives and metrics for those objectives that will help you make your testing more beautiful. You'll need to take those ideas further, as these objectives and metrics are just a starting point. I recommend a thorough assessment to kick off your journey toward beautiful testing, considering these four steps:

1. Know your stakeholders.
2. Know their objectives and expectations for testing.
3. Establish metrics and targets for stakeholder objectives and expectations (external beauty).
4. Establish metrics and targets for testing objectives and expectations (internal beauty).

Once you have a framework in place for achieving beautiful testing, start working toward that. Although it won't happen overnight, you'll be pleasantly surprised at how quickly these four steps can improve your testing.

## CHAPTER THREE

Building Open Source QA Communities

Martin Schröder
Clint Talbert

AN OPEN SOURCE PROJECT LIVES AND DIES BY ITS VOLUNTEER BASE. The tinier the project, the more true that is. As we grow to use more social networks online, we have the chance to make every project, even those that were traditionally closed source, into a participatory project. We worked on the Mozilla Calendar Project, which is a project to create a calendar application based on the Mozilla Platform. We produced two products: Sunbird, a standalone calendar application, and Lightning, an add-on for the popular Thunderbird email client.

In the early days of the project, there were four volunteer developers, and two others who were paid to spend significant amounts of their time on the project. The only quality assurance (QA) that existed was one person who alternately tested new features and triaged the incoming bugs. As the code base matured, it became very apparent that we had gone as far as we could without anything but the barest minimum of QA. We decided to organize a QA Team for the Calendar Project. It took almost six months to create a viable group that was doing regular QA. It was a beautiful process, both in its most difficult periods and in its most successful.

Communication

Communication on the project was crucial. We used IRC (Internet relay chat) as our primary means of communication. In IRC, you log onto a forum and all users that are logged in there can see the conversations in real time. It is important to have a mechanism for your community to interact with you, but it is equally important for the community to interact with each other.

If people feel that they are part of something bigger, they will identify with that larger group and become committed volunteers from that point forward.

For our other means of communication, since we worked on QA, our bug tracking system almost functioned as a social networking site. We used Bugzilla (*http://www.bugzilla.org/*), and very often there would be entire threads of conversation occurring around various bugs in each bug's comment stream.

In general, communication over the Internet, especially IRC, is limited in certain aspects that have to be overcome. Like any electronic medium, emotion is difficult to gauge and disagreements can easily cause conflagrations. Be mindful that you never know what your volunteer's first language actually is (unless you ask), so give them the benefit of the doubt and endeavor to clear up any misunderstandings. One thing we learned early on was that idiomatic phrases do not translate well, so you have to be wary of using them and vigilant in explaining their meaning.

Should you ever have a chance to meet with volunteers in person, or organize a meeting among the volunteers, even if you can't be there, you should do it. All our technology still cannot take the place of face-to-face interaction, so if you can find a way to bring your community together, it will galvanize their commitment to the project.

Volunteers

The tiny group of people working on the Mozilla Calendar Project in the beginning were either computer scientists or had been around software development long enough to know the jargon. We did not anticipate that our users and volunteers would be much different from us. The first time we got asked the question "What is QA?", we realized exactly how wrong we were about our ideas of the typical volunteer. Arcane jargon did not inspire people. We had some people who did QA as their daily job volunteering their time, but they wanted something different than "QA." Replacing the idea of "QA" with "testing" didn't work either. We began asking the volunteers who showed up in the channel what had brought them to the project and what they wanted to gain from it. The two primary reasons for being involved were "giving back to open source" and "being a part of the project." We worked hard to create and maintain an open, welcoming group identity, which eventually became an inseparable part of the Calendar Project's DNA.

"Volunteering" (from Latin *voluntarius*, "of one's free will") is a concept that implies working for a project without being motivated by financial or material gain. From this definition, the following questions arise: why are people interested, what are they interested in, and what could be achieved? The community includes individuals with a variety of prior knowledge regarding testing software and quality assurance. It ranges from the novice user with basic general knowledge to the day-to-day user of a software product to programmers with established skills.

The range of possible tasks that can and have to be solved is likewise diverse. In the Calendar Project, we started with the creation of test cases, followed by testing sessions. Each person's prior knowledge determines what activities are feasible for the emerging QA community. Although most users are oblivious to what software quality assurance entails, we found that the learning curve for a regular user to become a QA volunteer is not as steep as we had believed. A typical user, with some mentoring, would become a decent tester after about three to four weeks of consistent, part-time involvement.

The motivations that drive people to engage in the project differ widely among the volunteers. There are students spending spare time on testing because they want to gain skills in open source software development. Others are regular users who want to bring the project forward because they want to see improvement or want to "give back" something for using a free product they like. Many of the volunteers were newer users, which had the added benefit that they allowed us to see the product through fresh eyes on a regular basis. It is important to find out what the volunteers expect from their participation. These expectations must be identified to understand the community and to find ways to engage them further on the project.

The community of volunteers is a dynamic group, and you cannot expect everyone to spend the same amount of time on and show the same dedication toward the project. It's important to determine how much time a given volunteer will dedicate to the project so that you can ask them to perform tasks best suited to the amount of time they have available. A phenomenon we observed many times was "the vanishing and reappearing member." It is not uncommon that regular contributors disappear suddenly and then return some months later and continue with the same passion as before. When we encounter these cases, we always welcome them back, and let them know we're happy to see them again.

You can visualize the volunteer process as a series of steps, which we identified and experienced ourselves. Most of the interested people start by lurking and listening in the communication channel to begin learning the communication style. After getting familiar and confident enough, they begin to interact with other volunteers. Following a period of participation in regular testing activities, they sometimes ask for or even identify projects they would like to assume responsibility for. But, don't wait for them to ask. As we'll talk about later, it's important to give them small responsibilities as soon as you can. Increasing responsibilities deepen identification with the project and help encourage volunteers to become permanent members of the community.

Coordination

At first, as we gained success at creating a group, we tried calling what we were doing "leading." While ostensibly true, it never seemed to really tell the truth of what we were doing on a regular basis. Eventually, we began to call it "coordinating," and that stuck. The Calendar QA Team is a self-selected group of individuals; they have never needed a leader in the traditional sense. They had decided to come to this project, they decided to get involved, and their loyalty was to the project, not some person who had been self-anointed through word or deed as a leader. So, once we began to think of ourselves as coordinators, the entire project began to run more smoothly. Having a volunteer community force is much like having a river at your disposal. You cannot demand that it flows in a certain direction, but if you dig a canal for it to run in, then you can entice it to follow you.

So, coordinating a project like this means there are a few principles to keep in mind:

- You are not special.
- You are always recruiting.
- You are always engaging.

You Are Not Special

Often, when someone becomes a leader, there is a seductive quality to it. It is almost like we are children once more on the playground, directing all the other kids around us. You cannot do this in an online community. You must always be the first among equals. Everyone in the group must see you as part of that larger group, not separate from it; otherwise, they will not have any desire to be in your group. It essentially comes down to the fact that no one likes the idea of being bossed around by someone who claims to "know better" but does not back up words with action.

You have to do everything that you ask the volunteers to do. You are never too busy to do the same work that they do. Perhaps you will do less of that work because you are mentoring a new person, but you must always be doing some of that work. Often when a project is successful, the leaders tend to focus on new tasks, and move away from the core work that their volunteers are doing. This always results in a drop-off of participation as the volunteers see the leader's new focus as a "more important" area, and so logically whatever they are doing is "less important." It is good for you as the organizer of your community to explore new avenues and areas and increase the depth of your testing, but when you do so, you should actively encourage your volunteers to leap into that new area as well. By bringing them with you into the new area, they are discovering it with you.

We made this mistake with writing out manual test cases. We had some stellar volunteers who were cranking out test case after test case. Eventually we stopped writing test cases, our thoughts being that the volunteers would simply continue doing so, even without our aid, and we would redirect that time and focus toward our test day events. For a little while, this strategy worked. If we had returned and started writing test cases again, we might have been able to salvage the situation. Instead, we became even more tied up in ad-hoc testing and test day preparations. As a result, before we realized what was happening, we lost our test case writers. They stopped working on them because they perceived test case writing as being less important since we were no longer focused on it.

Avoid the tendency to explore an area first and report back. This also creates a false dichotomy between you as someone "in the know" and the rest of the group as those who are "not in the know." It is much better to bring people into a new area early and let them see you stumble. You do not have to be perfect; in fact, it is better if you aren't. Let them see you learn the new areas alongside them. It takes courage to do this, because no one likes to be seen as inadequate. But, in the eyes of the volunteer, it shows that you are all equal, and that you are all doing what you can for the project. It will help further their attachment to the project and the effort at hand.

Likewise, you do not have a monopoly on good ideas. You might be leading an effort, but that does not mean that your word is golden. Allow the rest of the community to drive. Allow them to debate and change the way you do things. If it does not work, channel them back to methods that do work, but do not fear change. Do not fear failure. It is only through failure that you can grow. On the Calendar Project, we had a set of manual tests that people could run. We worried that people would grow bored of running the manual test cases, so we attempted to encourage people to do ad-hoc testing. However, without intensive training and knowledge of how software is put together, it is very hard to do relevant ad-hoc testing. Every attempt at this failed, not through any fault of the community, but because we simply could not provide a deep enough channel for them to be successful in this effort. We eventually gave up on the idea of community-driven ad-hoc testing, and instead focused our efforts on writing better manual test cases.

You Are Always Recruiting

This is very self-explanatory. Everything you do on your project must be with an aim to build your volunteer base. This means not only being welcoming when you are in a public space, but it also means getting to know people personally. It means unceasingly hunting for ways to lower the barrier to entry on your project. So for every event we did, we always ensured that we gave people a simple, easy-to-understand way to contribute. We always gave plenty of detailed instructions. We always looked at how to make things easier and easier. Our home channel on IRC was more like a giant group of people sitting in a living room around a burning fire than a workplace. While we were all there for the work, it was very important to allow people to connect with each other, and these chats also gave us a chance to connect with them. These random, nontechnical discussions allowed people who had merely been lurking in the background to feel confident in speaking out. You have to balance that with real work in order to accomplish your goals, but always try to find ways to draw people out and engage them. You never know what will pull people out of their shells and get them involved. Make everything you do as welcoming as possible.

You Are Always Engaging

There is a meritocracy around open source projects. The more you do, the more privileges you have and the more you can do. Rewarding participation is exactly the right behavior. However, it is important to allow people to get engaged early on. This is not like a martial art where the newcomers are expected to kneel on rice for the first three months of their training. When an individual appeared in channel asking for access to write manual test cases, we originally balked. There was a bug in our test case manager that meant everyone who could write a test case could also administer the entire system (including delete it). He came back to our events and kept asking for access. We did not have much to go on, but he seemed persistent and determined, so we gave him the keys to the kingdom, and cautioned him about the problems. He wrote most of the test cases that currently exist for the Calendar Project.

You do need to be careful. But you cannot be so careful that you do not engage your volunteers. You must find simple ways to give them power early on so that they feel they are contributing and making a difference. Many times, simply calling out a good behavior publicly is enough encouragement that it causes more engagement. We held test days every week. Each week we would blog about the test day, and we would blog about the results of the test day, and thank each person who attended by name in the post. When we stopped blogging the results of the test days, we lost many of our repeat volunteers. We had stopped engaging them. They probably felt (and rightly so) that we were taking them for granted. You must always be on the lookout for ways to engage a volunteer.

There is a simple mechanism for moving a volunteer through the process of becoming engaged in your project: motivation, cooperation, responsiveness, and success. The optimal result of engaging an interested volunteer is to get sustaining support from him. To reach this state, the volunteer's motivation must be maintained, so it is important to understand how it is influenced by other elements. Remember that a single volunteer can never be as effective as a team, and you should do everything you can to foster cooperation among all members of your QA community. Friendly competition is fine, but the product suffers if people do not help each other. Members acting as veteran volunteers or coordinators are expected to maintain the highest possible degree of responsiveness to questions and requests from the other volunteers. Whenever a volunteer stalls in a dead end and does not know how to proceed, she needs someone to react to her call for help. Otherwise, she might start to turn away from the project. Also, never underestimate the momentum that success brings to a volunteer. It is vital to tell volunteers how much impact their actions have had on the project. This in turns feeds back into motivation, creating a virtuous circle.

Events

The cornerstones of coordination are the events you do with the volunteers. Creating events to coordinate QA activities is the best way to engage volunteers and generate excitement about the project. There are many parallels to creating an online event and an event in "real life," but there are also some unique challenges to creating and publicizing events on the Net. Just like any event, you have to pick a location and time. The location is usually simple; you just use whatever media you normally use to communicate with your volunteers. In our case, IRC was a natural choice. We made it clear that people were not required to join IRC to participate, but we also marshaled our resources and did not attempt to man several different communication channels on our event days. This helped increase the activity, responsiveness, and focus in the IRC channel and made for a more engaging, exciting event.

Although location is simple, time is anything but. Our volunteers were spread throughout the world, primarily in North America, Europe, Asia, and Australia. No one time would work for all of these locations, but there are multiple ways to resolve this challenge as your volunteer group develops. If you have the depth of volunteers in each location, you can charge them with taking a "shift" on your event, and allow them the freedom to lead that shift and work with new volunteers in their time zone. This is the best way to address the problem, but of course it assumes you have a volunteer base.

In the beginning, we simply held 12-hour events that covered a decent swath of convenient times for locations with the highest number of contributors. This originally meant running events from noon to midnight UTC time. Another option we attempted was multiday events, but they were failures. It seemed that people had an easier time understanding hour offsets than day offsets, and the entire concept of a multiday event seemed too unspecific. One way to combat this might be to combine the two ideas and have specific hours on two adjoining days, but that was not something we ever tried. The best advice with time planning is to start small and grow the timing of your events as you grow the volunteer base to staff the extra shifts.

Publicity

Promoting the event is the next step. You can think of your potential volunteer base as fans in a stadium. Some of them are already playing on the field; others are sitting on the bench. Still others are in the front rows, and even more are far above you in the nosebleed seats. Ideally, your publicity should reach all of them, and entice each one to come down to the field. Realistically, you can only move the people who are sitting on those lowest levels of the stadium, but once those people get involved, the resulting activity will bring more curious people closer to the field and within reach of your next event.

On the Calendar Project, we made use of the larger Mozilla Community forums to announce our events to a larger audience of people. We would regularly announce through our blog (*http://weblogs.mozillazine.org/calendar/*), which is syndicated to Planet Mozilla (*http://planet .mozilla.org/*). We posted to mailing lists, Mozilla project newsgroups, and Mozilla forums. For your project, you'll have to answer the question: "What are your users watching?" That is the place where you want to promote the most. For example, if your users are on Facebook, create a group there and use that. We attempted this, but we did not know enough Calendar users on Facebook for the group to be successful.

Another idea is to take some of your events and submit them to press outlets using standard press releases. Traditional technology press outlets will rarely run a story for a small QA event unless you have something truly unique. However, if you are lucky enough to snag traditional press coverage for your event, you will reach people who have never heard of your project. So, it is worth the time and energy to throw press releases toward the traditional outlets from time to time. On a stroke of incredible luck, we stumbled into traditional press coverage for one of our early Calendar events, and it was that coverage, more than any other action we took, that galvanized and engaged the Calendar QA team. We had over 50 volunteers show up that day, and about 15 of them remained on the project for a time afterward. Some of them are still involved to this day.

What We Actually Did

We held several types of QA events, each with a different QA theme. We hoped to entice volunteers with different skills and interests by offering the different events. The first and most successful event we tried was the test day. A test day is exactly what it sounds like: a block of time set aside when you invite your volunteers to come test some feature of your application. The best test days are those that were the most specific. When we could point to a complete set of tests, with complete documentation and instructions on how to run those tests, people were more engaged than they were when we attempted to do ad-hoc testing. In our test days, we encouraged our more veteran volunteers to work on the more difficult test cases, such as time zone support. We directed the newer volunteers toward the better-documented manual test cases. In both cases, encouraging users to participate in test days had a direct impact on the quality of the project, because it exposed the applications to many different running environments and a wide variety of operating system and hardware configurations.

Our test days became so crucial to the project that we created templates and how-to documents so that even volunteers could run the test days. This was important once we began to do different time-zone shifts for the test days. However, you have to be careful that your how-to and communication documents do not sound recycled. This was a problem we have encountered more recently on the Calendar Project and have lost quite a few volunteers because of it. The documents must still sound fresh and exciting, even if it is the thousandth time you have written them.

Bug days are entire events devoted to bug triage. In the Mozilla Bug system, we get a fair number of new bugs each day, and we have several old bugs that were reported and have sat orphaned for some time. On bug days we endeavor to lead people through the process of bug triage to deal with these outdated bugs, to see if they are still valid and to try to reproduce and clean up the newer bug reports into something actionable by a developer. It is important to set specific goals when working on a large project such as this in order to keep volunteers from feeling overwhelmed. For example, on the Calendar Project alone, we had a thousand new and old bugs needing triage when we began. It was important to focus the volunteers on only a subset of them.

You also need to evaluate the constraints of your bug system from an outside user's perspective. One of the critical things we wanted the volunteers to help us with was declaring a bug as "verified." This indicated that QA had reviewed the changes the developer made and found that the bug was indeed fixed properly. However, in Mozilla's Bugzilla installation, you need special privileges to set the "verified" flag. We tried to be as liberal as possible with granting those privileges to our users, and we also invented workarounds for under-privileged users so that they could still contribute. But that was always a weak piece of our bug days, and we have never had the amount of help verifying bugs that we wanted.

Our least-used event was Test Case Writing Days. The first time we did this unusual event, we got that unexpected press coverage mentioned earlier. On a test case writing day, we invited the community to write both manual and automated test cases for us. The success or failure of an event like this is directly related to the templates you provide for writing a test case. We found many people were daunted by the prospect of writing these, but when we explained it as "writing down what someone should do, then writing what the application should do in response to those actions," people immediately understood the concept. We did not use this event very often, simply because it was so difficult to do with success.

Goal Setting and Rewards

For all your events, you should have a well-defined goal in mind: the number of test cases run, the number of bugs triaged, the number of test cases written. We experimented with giving out gift certificates for top performers at our events, which was somewhat successful. When you are a small volunteer project, it is hard to provide any sort of real incentive, and the people are there because they want to help out, not because they expect material gain from helping out. So, although the rewards were a fun way to spur on some inter-team competition during the events, they did not serve to motivate people as much as we expected. However, we found that public recognition of their efforts during the events was a giant motivational tool.

After each test day, we would write a blog post describing the event, naming all the people who participated and thanking them. We would also identify the people who found bugs and name the bugs they found. This simple blog post energized the community, and the day we stopped writing our "results" blog posts was the day that our returning volunteer count began to taper. It really boils down to recognizing the effort and the expenditure of each volunteer's spare time. Doing the "results" post was a way to show how grateful we were for that time, and when we stopped, they stopped showing up.

Conclusions

Creating community involvement around a QA project is one of the best things you can do for your product. It puts the product before interested users early on in the process, and allows them to use and experiment with in-development features. It also enables you to broaden your testing to a wide variety of end user configurations, hardware, and operating systems. But the number one reason that building community around a QA project is beautiful is because it brings together an interested crew of energized, active volunteers, creating a tribe of people who will follow your product. That tribe will do far more evangelism and word-of-mouth promotion than any glossy advertisement could hope to accomplish. Connecting people all over the world, from all walks of life, and bringing them to focus on a shared goal is a truly beautiful, rewarding endeavor.

## CHAPTER FOUR

Collaboration Is the Cornerstone of Beautiful Performance Testing

Scott Barber

PERFORMANCE TESTING IS ALL TOO FREQUENTLY THE MOST FRUSTRATING, complicated, understaffed, time-crunched, misunderstood, combative, and thankless aspect of a software development project, but it doesn't have to be. I have experienced beautiful performance testing firsthand on several occasions. In fact, it seems like most career performance testers have at least one story about beautiful performance testing.

So, what are the attributes of beautiful performance testing? I think that beautiful performance testing is:

- Desired
- Deliberate
- Useful
- Technical
- Social
- Respectful
- Humble
- Efficient
- (Appropriately) challenging

- Value-driven
- Value-focused

But above all, I think that for performance testing to be beautiful, it must be *collaborative*.

In the stories that follow, I share with you the critical incidents that shaped my view of performance testing beauty. Coincidentally, this chapter is also the story of how one software development company's approach to performance testing became increasingly beautiful over the course of several development projects. While you read them, pay particular attention to two things. First, notice that none of these stories starts out, shall we say, beautifully. Second, notice that in each story collaboration was the key to progress, success, and/or conflict resolution.

Setting the Stage

All of the events that follow occurred over a 14-month period during the Dot-Com Era at a boutique custom software development company where I was the performance testing technical lead and practice manager. The events span several development projects, but the core project team was substantially the same throughout—and when I say project team, I am referring to not just those who wrote the code, but also to the executives, account managers, project management, business analysts, testers, system administrators, and technical support staff.

Although I have done my best to recount these events accurately and objectively, what follows is exclusively my perspective of the events that occurred. The events did occur in the sequence in which they appear in this chapter, and I have not taken any intentional liberties with them, other than to remove or replace offensive epithets with less offensive ones. In addition, I'd be remiss if I didn't mention that much of the identifying information related to individuals, clients, and contracts has been changed to protect the innocent, the guilty, the shy, and those I've lost touch with and couldn't get permission to use their real names.

100%?!? Fail

I'd just been informed that I was to start working on a new project to build a computer-based learning delivery and student progress tracking system (I'll call it eVersity) for a Fortune 50 company on the following Monday. The project was officially entering the development phase, which meant that the client had accepted our proof of concept and it was time to bring the rest of the team onto the project. I was at my desk finishing some documentation for my previous project when Harold, the test manager for the new project, walked up and, without preamble, handed me a single sheet of paper while asking, "Can you test this?"

Though I found the question insulting, I looked at the paper. I got as far as:

"System Performance Requirements:

- 100% of the web pages shall display in 5 seconds or less 100% of the time.
- The application shall…"

before writing "FAIL" on a sticky note, slapping the note on the paper, and handing it back to Harold over my shoulder and going back to work. Harold, making no attempt to conceal his anger at my note, asked, "What's *that* supposed to mean?" Spinning my chair around to face him, I replied, "I can test it if you want, but c'mon, it's the Internet! You never get 100% of anything!" Harold walked off in a huff.

Early the next week, Harold returned with another sheet of paper. Handing it to me, he simply asked "Better?" This time I managed to read all of the bullets.

"System Performance Requirements:

- 95% of the web pages shall display in 5 seconds or less 95% of the time.
- The application shall support 1,000 concurrent users.
- Courses shall download completely and correctly on the first try 98% of the time.
- Courses shall download in 60 seconds or less 95% of the time."

"Better? Yes. But not particularly useful, and entirely untestable. What is this for, anyway?" I responded. Clearly frustrated, but calm, Harold told me that he'd been asked to establish the performance requirements that were going to appear in our contract to the client. Now understanding the intent, I suggested that Harold schedule a conference room for a few hours for us to discuss his task further. He agreed.

As it turned out, it took more than one meeting for Harold to explain to me the client's expectations, the story behind his task, and for me to explain to Harold why we didn't want to be contractually obligated to performance metrics that were inherently ambiguous, what those ambiguities were, and what we could realistically measure that would be valuable. Finally, Harold and I took what were now several sheets of paper with the following bullets to Sandra, our project manager, to review:

"System Performance Testing Requirements:

- Performance testing will be conducted under a variety of loads and usage models, to be determined when system features and workflows are established.
- For internal builds, all performance measurements greater than the following will be reported to the lead developer:
    — Web pages that load in over 5 seconds, at any user volume, more than 5% of the time.
    — Web pages that load in over 8 seconds, at any user volume, more than 1% of the time.
    — Courses that do not download completely or correctly more than 2% of the time.

- Courses that take over 60 seconds to download, at any user volume, more than 5% of the time.

- The current maximum load the system can maintain for 1 hr with 95% of all web pages loading in 5 seconds or less and 95% of all the courses downloading completely and correctly in 60 seconds or less.

- External builds will be accompanied by a performance testing report including:

    - Web pages that load in over 5 seconds, at any user volume, more than 5% of the time.

    - Web pages that load in over 8 seconds, at any user volume, more than 1% of the time.

    - Courses that do not download completely or correctly more than 2% of the time.

    - Courses that take over 60 seconds to download, at any user volume, more than 5% of the time.

    - The current maximum load the system can maintain for 1 hr with 95% of all web pages loading in 5 seconds or less and 95% of the courses downloading completely and correctly in 60 seconds or less.

- At the discretion of the project manager, other performance tests will be conducted that are deemed valuable to the project based on requests or recommendations by [client name deleted], the development team, or the performance test lead."

Much to our chagrin, Sandra replied that Harold and I should work together more often, and added our bullets verbatim into the client contract.

I fully admit that there was nothing beautiful about the *process* that led to Harold and I collaborating to turn the original System Performance Requirements into the ultimate System Performance Testing Requirements, but the *result* was. To be honest, when I found out that Harold had written the original requirements doc that I had "failed" in dramatic fashion, I fully expected to be removed from the project. But regardless of whether Harold tried to have me removed from the project, even he would have acknowledged that there was a certain beauty in the outcome that neither of us would have come up with on our own. Specifically:

- The shift from committing to achieving certain levels of performance to committing to report under what conditions the performance goals were *not* being achieved

- Calling out that it may be some time before enough information would be available to fully define the details of individual performance tests

- Leaving the door open for performance testing that supported the development process, but that didn't directly assess compliance with performance goals

Unfortunately, this was not to be the last un-beautiful interaction between Harold and me.

OK, but What's a Performance Test Case?

A few weeks later, Harold called to tell me he needed me to get all of the "performance test cases" into the eVersity test management system by the end of the following week. I said, "OK, but what's a performance test case?" As you might imagine, that wasn't the response he was expecting. The rest of the conversation was short but heated, and concluded with me agreeing to "do the best I could" by the end of that week so that he would have time to review my work.

As soon as I hung up the phone, I fired up the test management system to see if there were any other test cases for what we called nonfunctional requirements (aka quality factors, or parafunctional requirements), such as security or usability. Finding none, I started looking to the functional test cases for inspiration. What I found was exactly what I had feared: a one-to-one mapping between requirements and test cases, and almost all of the requirements were of the form "The system shall X," and almost all of the test cases were of the form "Verify that the system [does] X."

I stared at the screen long enough for my session to time out twice, trying to decide whether to call Harold back in protest or try to shoehorn *something* into that ridiculous model (for the record, I find that model every bit as ridiculous today as I did then). Ultimately, I decided to do what I was asked, for the simple reason that I didn't think I'd win the protest. The client had mandated this test management system, had paid a lot of money for the licenses, and had sent their staff to training on the system so they could oversee the project remotely. I simply couldn't imagine getting approval to move performance test tracking outside the system, so I created a new requirement type called "Performance" and entered the following items:

- Each web page shall load in 5 seconds or less, at least 95% of the time.
- Each course shall download correctly and completely in 60 seconds or less, at least 98% of the time.
- The system shall support 1,000 hourly users according to a usage model TBD while achieving speed requirements.

I then created the three parallel test cases for those items and crossed my fingers.

To say that Harold was not impressed when he reviewed my work at the end of the week would be a gross understatement. He must have come straight downstairs to the performance and security test lab where I spent most of my time the instant he saw my entry. As he stormed through the door, he demanded, "How can I justify billing four months of your time for three tests?"

Although I had been expecting him to protest, that was not the protest I'd anticipated. Looking at him quizzically, I responded by saying, "You can't. Where did you get the idea that I'd only be conducting three tests?" I'll let you imagine the yelling that went on for the next 15 minutes until I gave up protesting the inadequacy of the test management system, especially for performance testing, and asked Harold what it was that he had in mind. He answered that he wanted to see all of the tests I was going to conduct entered into the system.

I was literally laughing at loud as I opened the project repository from my previous, much smaller, project and invited him to come over and help me add up how many performance tests I'd conducted. The number turned out to be either 967 or 4,719, depending on whether you counted different user data as a different test. Considering that the five-person functional test team had created slightly fewer than 600 test cases for this project, as opposed to approximately 150 on the project I was referencing, even Harold acknowledged that his idea was flawed.

We stared at one another for what felt like a very long time before Harold dialed the phone.

"Sandra, do you have some time to join Scott and me in the lab? Thanks. Can you bring the client contracts and deliverable definitions? Great. Maybe Leah is available to join us as well? See you in a few."

For many hours, through a few arguments, around a little cursing, and over several pizzas, Harold, Sandra, Leah (a stellar test manager in her own right who was filling the testing technical lead role on this project), Chris (a developer specializing in security with whom I shared the lab and who had made the mistake of wandering in while we were meeting), and I became increasingly frustrated with the task at hand. At the onset, even I didn't realize how challenging it was going to be to figure out how and what to capture about performance testing in our tracking system.

We quickly agreed that what we wanted to include in the tracking system were performance tests representing valuable checkpoints, noteworthy performance achievements, or potential decision points. As soon as we decided that, I went to the whiteboard and started listing the tests we might include, thinking we could tune up this list and be done. I couldn't have been more wrong.

I hadn't even finished my list when the complications began. It turns out that what I was listing didn't comply with either the terms of the contract or with the deliverables definitions that the client had finally approved after much debate and many revisions. I don't remember all of the details and no longer have access to those documents, but I do remember how we finally balanced the commitments that had been made to the client, the capabilities of the mandated tracking system, and high-value performance testing.

We started with the first item on my list. Sandra evaluated the item against the contract. Harold evaluated it against the deliverables definitions. Leah assessed it in terms of its usefulness in making quality-related decisions. Chris assessed its informational value for the development team. Only after coming up with a list that was acceptable from each perspective did we worry about how to make it fit into the tracking system.

As it turned out, the performance requirements remained unchanged in the system. The performance test cases, however, were renamed "Performance Testing Checkpoints" and included the following (abbreviated here):

- Collect baseline system performance metrics and verify that each functional task included in the system usage model achieves performance requirements under a user load of 1 for each performance testing build in which the functional task has been implemented.
  - — [Functional tasks listed, one per line]
- Collect system performance metrics and verify that each functional task included in the system usage model achieves performance requirements under a user load of 10 for each performance testing build in which the functional task has been implemented.
  - — [Functional tasks listed, one per line]
- Collect system performance metrics and verify that the system usage model achieves performance requirements under the following loads to the degree that the usage model has been implemented in each performance testing build.
  - — [Increasing loads from 100 users to 3,000 users, listed one per line]
- Collect system performance metrics and verify that the system usage model achieves performance requirements for the duration of a 9-hour, 1,000-user stress test on performance testing builds that the lead developer, performance tester, and project manager deem appropriate.

The beauty here was that what we created was clear, easy to build a strategy around, and mapped directly to information that the client eventually requested in the final report. An added bonus was that from that point forward in the project, whenever someone challenged our approach to performance testing, one or more of the folks who were involved in the creation of the checkpoints always came to my defense—frequently before I even found out about the challenge!

An interesting addendum to this story is that later that week, it became a company policy that I was to be consulted on any contracts or deliverable definitions that included performance testing before they were sent to the client for approval. I'm also fairly certain that this was the catalyst to Performance Testing becoming a practice area, separate from Functional Testing, and also what precipitated performance test leads reporting directly to the project manager instead of to the test manager on subsequent projects.

You Can't Performance Test Everything

One of the joys of being the performance testing technical lead for a company that has several development projects going on at once is that I was almost always involved in more than one project at a time. I mention this because the following story comes from a different project, but did occur chronologically between the previous story and the next one.

This project was to build a web-based financial planning application. Although common today, at the time this was quite innovative. The performance testing of the system was high priority for two reasons:

- We'd been hired for this project only after the client had fired the previous software development company because of the horrible performance of the system it had built.

- The client had already purchased a Super Bowl commercial time slot and started shooting the commercial to advertise the application.

Understandably, Ted, the client, had instructed me that he wanted "every possible navigation path and every possible combination of input data" included in our performance tests. I'd tried several methods to communicate that this was simply not an achievable task before *that* year's Super Bowl, but to no avail. Ted was becoming increasingly angry at what he saw as me refusing to do what he was paying for. After six weeks of trying to solve (or at least simplify) and document a massively complex combinatorics problem, I was becoming increasingly frustrated that I'd been unable to help the developers track down the performance issues that led Ted to hire us in the first place.

One afternoon, after Ted had rejected yet another proposed system usage model, I asked him to join me in the performance test lab to build a model together. I was surprised when he said he'd be right down.

I started the conversation by trying to explain to Ted that including links to websites maintained by other companies as part of our performance tests without their permission was not only of minimal value, but was tantamount to conducting denial-of-service attacks on those websites. Ted wasn't having any of it. At that moment, I realized I was standing, we were both yelling at one another, and my fists were clenched in frustration.

In an attempt to calm down, I walked to the whiteboard and started drawing a sort of sideways flowchart representing the most likely user activities on the website. To my surprise, Ted also picked up a marker and began enhancing the diagram. Before long, we were having a calm and professional discussion about what users were likely to do on the site during their first visit. Somewhere along the way, Chris had joined the conversation and was explaining to us how many of the activities we had modeled were redundant and thus interchangeable based on the underlying architecture of the system.

In less than an hour, we had created a system usage model that we all agreed represented the items most likely to be popular during the Super Bowl marketing campaign as well as the areas of the application that the developers had identified as having the highest risk of performing poorly. We'd also decided that until we were confident in the performance of those aspects of the system, testing and tuning other parts of the application was not a good use of our time.

Within a week of that meeting, we had an early version of the test we'd modeled up and running, and the developers and I were actively identifying and improving performance issues with the system.

Once again, the story had started anything but beautifully. This time the beauty began to blossom when Ted and I started working together to build a model at the whiteboard rather than me emailing models for him to approve. The beauty came into full bloom when Chris brought a developer's perspective to the conversation. Collaborating in real time enabled us to not only better understand one another's concerns, but also to discuss the ROI of various aspects of the usage model comparatively as opposed to individually, which is what we'd been doing for weeks.

This story also has an interesting addendum. As it happened, the whiteboard sketch that Ted, Chris, and I created that day was the inspiration behind the User Community Modeling Language (UCML™) that has subsequently been adopted as the method of choice for modeling and documenting system usage for a large number of performance testers worldwide. For more about UCML, visit *http://www.perftestplus.com/articles/ucml.pdf*.

The Memory Leak That Wasn't

It was almost two months after the "OK, but what's a performance test?" episode before we were ready to start ramping up load with a reasonably complete system usage model on the eVersity project. The single-user and 10-user tests on this particular build had achieved better than required performance, so I prepared and ran a 100-user test. Since it was the first run of multiple usage scenarios at the same time, I made a point to observe the test and check the few server statistics that I had access to while the test was running.

The test ran for about an hour, and everything seemed fine until I looked at the scatter chart, which showed that all the pages that accessed the application server started slowing down about 10 minutes into the test and kept getting slower until the test ended. I surfed the site manually and it was fine. I checked the logfiles from the load generation tool to verify that I wasn't seeing the effect of some kind of scripting error. Confident that it wasn't something on my end, I ran the test again, only this time I used the site manually while the test was running. After about 15 minutes, I noticed those pages getting slow. I picked up the phone and called Sam, the architect for the project, to tell him that he had a memory leak on the application server.

Sam asked if I was running the test right then. I told him I was. I heard him clicking on his keyboard. He asked if the test was still running. I told him it was. He said, "Nope, no memory leak. It's your tool," and hung up.

I was furious. For the next two days I ran and re-ran the test. I scoured logfiles. I created tables and graphs. I brought them to project meetings. I entered defect reports. I sent Sandra the URL to the performance test environment and asked her to use the application while I ran tests. Everyone seemed to agree that it was acting like a memory leak. By the end of day two, even Sam agreed that it looked like a memory leak, but followed that up by saying, "…but it isn't."

Late on the third day after I'd first reported the issue, Sam called me and asked me to try the test again and hung up. I launched the test. About 20 minutes later, Sam called back to ask how the test looked. It looked great. I asked how he fixed it. He simply said, "Installed the permanent license key. The temp had a limit of three concurrent connections."

Sam didn't talk to me for the next couple of weeks. Since he wasn't very talkative in the first place, I wasn't certain, but I thought I'd offended him. Then a surprising thing happened. Sam called me and asked me to point "that test from the other week" at the development environment and to bring the results upstairs when it was done.

When I got upstairs with the results, Sam said to me, "Impressive work the other week. It took me over 20 hours to track down the license key thing. The tests we ran looked like a memory leak, too…except that the memory counters were showing tons of free memory. Anyway, from now on, why don't we look at weird results together?"

From that time on, Sam demanded that management assigned me to all of his projects. He'd frequently ask me to design and run tests that I didn't completely understand, but that would result in massive performance improvements within a day or two. I'd often call him and say, "I've got some odd-looking results here, would you like to have a look?" Sometimes he'd tell me why I was getting weird results, sometimes he'd want to take a look, and other times he'd ask me to run the test again in an hour, but he never again dismissed my results as a tool problem. And I never again announced the cause of a performance issue before confirming my suspicions with Sam.

Of course, the beauty here is that Sam came to see me as a valuable resource to help him architect better-performing applications with less trial and error on his part. In retrospect, I only wish Sam had been more talkative.

Can't Handle the Load? Change the UI

Very shortly after the "memory leak that wasn't" incident, it was decision time for the financial planning application. The application was functioning, but we simply did not believe that we could improve the performance enough to handle the Super Bowl commercial–inspired peak. I hadn't been included in the discussion of options until at least two weeks after both the client and the development team had become very concerned. I'm not exactly sure why I was invited to the "what are we going to do" meeting with the client that day, but it turned out that whoever invited me, intentionally or accidentally, was probably glad they did.

The short version of the problem was that the application gave all indications of being completely capable of handling the return user load, but that, if the projections were close to being correct, there was no way the architecture could handle the peak new user load generated by the Super Bowl advertising campaign. What I didn't know until I got to the meeting on that day was that we'd reached the point of no return in terms of hardware and infrastructure. The application was going to run in the existing environment. The question now was, what to do about the usage peak generated by the marketing campaign?

For about 30 minutes, I listened to one expensive and/or improbable idea after another get presented and rejected. The most likely option seemed to be to lease four identical sets of hardware and find a data center to host them, which was estimated to cost enough that every time it came up, Ted shook his head and mumbled something about not wanting to lose his job.

Finally, I spoke up. I pointed out that there were really only two things that we couldn't handle large numbers of users doing all at once. One was "Generate your personalized retirement savings plan," and the other was "Generate your personalized college savings plan." I also pointed out that for someone to get to the point where those plans were relatively accurate, they'd have to enter a lot of information that they probably didn't have at their fingertips. I then speculated that if we redesigned the UI so that those options weren't available until users had at least clicked through to the end of the questionnaire (as opposed to making it available on every page of the questionnaire, virtually encouraging folks to click the button after each piece of information they entered so they could watch the charts and graphs change), that might reduce the number of plan generations enough to get through the marketing campaign. I further commented that we could put the plan generation links back on each page after the campaign was over.

The looks of shock and the duration of stunned silence lasted long enough that I actually became uncomfortable. Eventually, a woman I didn't know started scribbling on a sheet of paper, then pulled out a calculator to do some calculations, then scribbled some more before very quietly saying, "It might just work." Everyone turned their stunned stares to her when Ted asked her what she'd said. She repeated it, but added, "Well, not *exactly* what he said, but what if we...."

To be honest, I partly don't remember what she said, and I partly never understood it, because she seemed to be speaking in some secret financial planning language to Ted. Regardless of the details, as soon as she was done explaining, Ted said, "Do it!" and everyone started smiling and praising me for solving the problem.

A few weeks later, I got a new build with a modified UI and usage model to test. It took a couple of iterations of minor UI modifications and tuning, but we achieved our target load. I found out much later that the marketing campaign was a success and that the system held up without a glitch. In fact, the campaign went *so* well that a big bank bought the company, Ted got a promotion, and of course, the big bank had their developers rebuild the entire application to run on their preferred vendor's hardware and software.

The obvious beauty here is that the project was successful and that the solution we came up with was not prohibitively complicated or expensive. The less obvious beauty lies in the often-overlooked value of involving people with several different perspectives in problem solving work groups.

It Can't Be the Network

As it turned out, the eVersity project was canceled before the application made it into production (and by canceled, I mean that client just called one day to tell us that their entire division had been eliminated), so we never got a chance to see how accurate our performance testing had been. On the bright side, it meant that the team was available for the client-server to Web call-center conversion project that showed up a couple of weeks later.

The first several months of the project were uneventful from a performance testing perspective. Sam and the rest of the developers kept me in the loop from the beginning. Jim, the client VP who commissioned the project, used to be a mainframe developer who specialized in performance, so we didn't have any trouble with the contract or deliverables definitions related to performance, and the historical system usage was already documented for us. Sure, we had the typical environment, test data, and scripting challenges, but we all worked through those together as they came up.

Then I ran across the strangest performance issue I've seen to this day. On the web pages that were requesting information from the database, I was seeing a response time pattern that I referred to as "random 4s." It took some work and some help from the developers, but we figured out that half of the time these pages were requested, they returned in about .25 seconds. Half of the rest of the time, they'd return in about 4.25 seconds. Half of the rest of the time, in 8.25 seconds. And so on.

Working together, we systematically figured out all the things that weren't causing the random 4s. In fact, we systematically eliminated every part of the system we had access to, which accounted for everything except the network infrastructure. Feeling good about how well things were going, I thought it was a joke when I was told that I was not allowed to talk to anyone in the IT department, but it wasn't. It seems that some previous development teams had blamed everything on the IT department and wasted a ton of their time, so they'd created a policy to ensure that didn't happen again.

The only way to interact with the IT department was for us to send a memorandum with our request signed by Jim, including detailed instructions, to the VP of the IT department through interdepartmental mail. I drafted a memo. Jim signed it and sent it. Two days later, Jim got it back with the word "No" written on it. Jim suggested that we send another memo that described the testing we'd done that was pointing us in the direction of the network. That memo came back with a note that said, "Checked. It's not us."

This went on for over a month. The more testing we did, the more convinced we were that this was the result of something outside of our control, and the only part of this application that was outside our control was the network. Eventually, Jim managed to arrange for a one-hour working conference call with the IT department, ostensibly to "get us off their back." We set everything up so that all we had to do was literally click a button when the IT folks on the call were ready. Out entire team was dialed in on the call, just to make sure we could answer any question they may have had.

The IT folks dialed in precisely at the top of the hour and asked for identification numbers of the machines generating the load and the servers related to our application from the stickers their department put on the computers when they were installed. A few minutes later they told us to go ahead. We clicked the button. About five minutes of silence went by before we heard muffled speaking on the line. One of the IT staff asked us to halt the test. He said they were going to mute the line, but asked us to leave the line open. Another 20 minutes or so went by before they came back and asked us to restart the test and let them know if the problem was gone.

It took less than 10 minutes to confirm the problem was gone. During those 10 minutes, someone (I don't remember who) asked the IT staff, who had never so much as told us their names, what they had found. All they would say is that it looked like a router had been physically damaged during a recent rack installation and that they had swapped out the router.

As far as we knew, this interaction didn't make it any easier for the next team to work with this particular IT staff. I just kept thinking how lucky I was to be working on a team where I had the full help and support of the team. During the six weeks between the time I detected this problem and the IT department replaced the damaged router, the developers wrote some utilities, stubbed out sections of the system, stayed late to monitor after-hours tests in real time, and spent a lot of time helping me document the testing we'd done to justify our request for the IT department's time. *That* interaction is what convinced me that performance testing could be beautiful.

It's Too Slow; We Hate It

With the random 4s issue resolved, it was time for the real testing to begin: user acceptance testing (UAT). On some projects, UAT is little more than a formality, but on this project (and all of the projects I've worked on since dealing with call-center support software), UAT was central to go-live decisions. To that point, Susan, a call-center shift manager and UAT lead for this project, had veto authority over any decision about what was released into production and when.

The feature aspects of UAT went as expected. There were some minor revisions to be made, but nothing unreasonable or overly difficult to implement. The feedback that had us all confused and concerned was that every single user acceptance tester mentioned—with greater or lesser vehemence—something about the application being "slow" or "taking too long." Obviously we were concerned, because there is nothing that makes a call-center representative's day worse than having to listen to frustrated customers' colorful epithets when told, "Thank you for your patience, our system is a little slow today." We were confused because the website was fast, especially over the corporate network, and each UAT team was comprised of 5 representatives taking 10 simulated calls each, or about 100 calls per hour.

Testing indicated that the application could handle up to nearly 1,000 calls per hour before slowing down noticeably.

We decided to strip all graphics and extras from the application to make it as fast as possible, and then have myself or one of the developers observe UAT so we could see for ourselves what was slow. It confused us even more that the application was even faster afterward, that not one of the people observing UAT had noticed a user waiting on the application even once, and that the feedback was still that the application was slow. Predictably, we were also getting feedback that the application was ugly.

Finally, I realized that all of our feedback was coming either verbally from Susan or from Susan's summary reports, and I asked if I could see the actual feedback forms. While the protocol was that only the UAT lead got to see the actual forms, I was permitted to review them jointly with Susan. We were at the third or fourth form when I got some insight. The comment on that form was "It takes too long to process calls this way." I asked if I could talk to the user who had made that comment, and Susan set up a time for us to meet.

The next afternoon, I met Juanita in the UAT lab. I asked her to do one of the simulations for me. I timed her as I watched. The simulation took her approximately 2.5 minutes, but it was immediately clear to me that she was uncomfortable with both the flow of the user interface and using the mouse. I asked her if she could perform the same simulation for me on the current system and she said she could. It took about 5 minutes for the current system to load and be ready to use after she logged in. Once it was ready, she turned to me and simply said, "Ready?"

Juanita typed furiously for a while, then turned and looked at me. After a few seconds, I said, "You're done?" She smirked and nodded, and I checked the time: 47 seconds. I thanked her and told her that I had what I needed.

I called back to the office and asked folks to meet me in the conference room in 30 minutes. Everyone was assembled when I arrived. It took me fewer than 10 minutes to explain that when the user acceptance testers said "slow," they didn't mean response time; they meant that the design of the application was slowing down their ability to do their jobs.

My time on the project was pretty much done by then, so I don't know what the redeveloped UI eventually looked like, but Sam told me that they had a lot more interaction with Susan and her user acceptance testers thereafter, and that they were thrilled with the application when it went live.

For a performance tester, there are few things as beautiful as call-center representatives who are happy with an application you have tested.

Wrap-Up

In this chapter, I've shared with you a series of formative episodes in my evolution as a performance tester. The fact that these are real stories from real projects that I worked on, and the fact that they were sequential over approximately 14 months, only makes them more powerful.

Several years ago, I learned a technique called critical incident analysis that can be used to identify common principles used on or applied to complex tasks, such as performance testing. I learned about this technique from Cem Kaner and Rebecca Fiedler during the third Workshop on Heuristic and Exploratory Teaching (WHET). We were trying to determine how effective this approach would be in identifying core skills or concepts that people use when testing software, which would then be valuable to build training around.

According to Wikipedia (*http://en.wikipedia.org/wiki/Critical_Incident_Technique*):

> A critical incident can be described as one that makes a significant contribution—either positively or negatively—to an activity or phenomenon. Critical incidents can be gathered in various ways, but typically respondents are asked to tell a story about an experience they have had.

These stories are my critical incidents related to the importance of collaboration in performance testing. In these stories, a wide variety of performance testing challenges were tackled and resolved through collaboration: collaboration with other testers, collaboration with project management, collaboration with clients, collaboration with the development team, collaboration with IT staff, and collaboration with end users. All of my performance testing experiences corroborate what these stories suggest, that collaboration is the cornerstone of beautiful performance testing.

## PART II

Beautiful Process

I believe in rules. Sure I do. If there weren't any rules, how could you break them?

—Leo Durocher

## CHAPTER FIVE

Just Peachy: Making Office Software More Reliable with Fuzz Testing

Kamran Khan

IT WOULD BE OBVIOUS TO SAY THAT MOST READERS have used office software and seen something beautiful in their lives—perhaps even simultaneously. And yet to talk, or even think, about the two together requires a stretch of the imagination. We like beautiful objects for a number of reasons: they are arresting and pleasingly unfamiliar; they distract us from the present moment and etch themselves into our memories. When found in office programs, however, these same characteristics activate opposite emotions. We are not pleasantly surprised by mysterious and complicated features or error messages that attract our attention. In fact, in an ideal world, our office applications would never interrupt us, and they'd be as unremarkable as a common chair or desk. So, why do the usual qualities of beauty turn ugly when they're present in our office software? The answer lies in our expectations of how these programs ought to behave.

User Expectations

The word "office" has many connotations, but chief among them is its association with work. Indeed, the term "office" actually derives from "officium," a Latin word that means performance of a work or task. Although the etymology is a secondary concern, it does remind us of the primary aim of office software: to help us complete our tasks efficiently and without any additional hassle. It is with this very goal in mind that Microsoft redesigned the familiar

Office interface, replacing the existing toolbars and task panes with a new ribbon in the 2007 version. Jensen Harris, a program manager on the Office User Experience team, writes that the ribbon was designed to be "predictable, consistent, and human-designed [rather than] clever and auto-optimized." Above all, it was intended to (emphatically) "Help People Work Without Interference."[1]

It seems paradoxical to describe a radical overhaul as "predictable," but the Microsoft Office interface had become so complex that it was detracting from the larger goal of helping users get their work done in a straightforward manner. By using data collected from its Customer Experience Improvement Program, Microsoft was able to analyze how thousands of users interacted with the programs—from which toolbars they customized to how often they used certain menu items.[2] Summarizing this data, Harris notes that "32% of the total command use" of Office 2003 was comprised of the following five commands, in order of use:

1. Paste
2. Save
3. Copy
4. Undo
5. Bold[3]

Considering the hundreds of functions in the Microsoft Office suite, it's surprising to see that almost one third of all user actions were covered by so small and simple a set. Perhaps more significant, this statistic emphasizes the importance of ensuring reliability in the most basic functions of an office program—and suggests that many users can manage a considerable number of tasks with only a handful of functions.

While the new ribbon-based interface of Office 2007 was making news, online office programs like Google Docs were growing in popularity. The increased use of these programs is indicative of a wider trend toward web applications, but it also highlights the fact that many users are willing to trade advanced functionality for simplicity and ease of use. Taking this concept a step further, a few "distraction-free" word processors that contain very few functions have also attracted users.[4] Although traditional office suites remain popular, these alternatives underscore the importance of providing users with minimal annoyance and reliable functionality. Armed with these features, users can create a wide variety of documents—from the mundane to the, yes, beautiful—without having to pay much attention to their chosen tools.

1. *http://blogs.msdn.com/jensenh/archive/2005/09/15/467956.aspx*

2. *http://blogs.msdn.com/jensenh/archive/2005/10/31/487247.aspx*

3. *http://blogs.msdn.com/jensenh/archive/2006/04/07/570798.aspx*

4. WriteRoom (*http://www.hogbaysoftware.com/products/writeroom*) and Dark Room (*http://they.misled.us/dark-room*) are two such examples.

This brings us back to the question I raised in the first paragraph: why do similar traits in office programs and beautiful objects evoke opposite emotions? In short, beauty cannot be easily reconciled with transparency. An office application with traditionally beautiful characteristics would warrant our attention and detract from the overarching goal of getting work done. Instead, developers and testers of office programs must adjust their notions of beauty and concentrate on creating products that hide their complexity and appear simple and easy to use. It seems appropriate, then, that one of the beautiful solutions for testing office software is a method that shares these same characteristics: fuzz testing (or fuzzing) is a powerful and complex testing technique that allows for creativity despite its apparently simple nature.

What Is Fuzzing?

So, what is fuzzing? Fuzzing is a method of testing programs by randomly altering or corrupting input data. Although the technique has been around for (at least) 20 years, it has become more prevalent during the past decade due to an increased emphasis on security testing and the proliferation of tools explicitly designed for fuzzing. A program can be fuzzed manually or automatically, but the technique is most effective when accompanied by automation and logging.

Why Fuzz Test?

The method is simple—as its definition implies—yet it allows for a variety of elegant solutions to a number of challenging problems that testers and programmers face when developing office software.

Improve Interoperability

One of the most daunting problems facing office software is interoperability with other programs, especially similar office programs. Indeed, the top three commands on the Microsoft Office list—paste, save, and copy—illustrate the importance of being able to use data in other programs and documents. Although rather simple, these basic functions allow for a multitude of operations that users will expect the program to handle gracefully. One of the great things about fuzzing is that it can help simulate a number of these scenarios in an automated manner, making it easier to handle the countless possibilities that interoperability allows for.

There are millions of office documents in dozens of modern and obsolete formats, many of which your program will be expected to support. In some cases you might be able to find documentation about specific file formats, but these references can have their own inaccuracies and omissions. You could also try to keep all the various programs around for testing, but this solution would quickly become unwieldy as you tried to manage all of the hardware, operating systems, and licenses that would be required to run the hundreds of programs that can interact with your software. Fuzz testing offers an elegant and simple solution to this ugly problem and, best of all, does not require nearly the amount of effort it would take to keep track of all those programs. With one technique, you can effectively simulate dozens of other complex applications without the associated hassle—and tap into the beautiful potential of fuzz testing.

Instead of attempting such an unmanageable task, developers can use a fuzzer to create a wide variety of documents to simulate the differences that exist between various applications and program versions. This fuzzing-based method is much more convenient and allows you to exercise some creativity when accounting for the endless combinations of documents, file formats, and office programs. In this sense, fuzz testing is similar to beautiful office programs, which also allow users to be productive and creative by providing reliable and powerful functionality that can be used to create infinite end products. Likewise, it ensures that users will be able to open supported documents in obscure formats just as easily as they would more recent ones. Although there will always be some unsupported formats and files, you can make your software more useful to more people by accepting a wider range of input—even if it's technically invalid or violates a format specification. Like office programs that introduce subtle variations, corruption can also alter files and complicate efforts to support the widest range of documents.

There are a surprising number of ways that normal files can become subtly broken by mere accident: a disk with your old writings may slowly deteriorate in your stuffy desk drawer; the spreadsheet your coworker sent you via email may have been corrupted by an interrupted network connection; or maybe the flash drive you use to save your school reports was yanked out of its slot before you could close your word processor. Just as fuzz testing can help you simulate numerous office programs, it can also help you simulate these broken conditions without forcing you to go to the trouble of actually recreating them. Using a fuzzer for these interoperability and corruption situations is a particularly useful and beautiful technique because it allows you to replace a variety of programs and tools with one simple methodology. With enough of this testing, your program will allow users to work with a wider variety of documents without ever having to think about the complex nature of file formats and interoperability.

Improve User Satisfaction

By making your software more accepting of invalid and varied input, you can avoid a whole host of user complaints and bug reports. These reports are an important channel of feedback, particularly in open source projects, but they vary in quality and usually require further information or reclassification to be useful. For example, many users report problems with specific files and then fail to attach them to the submitted bug entry. This is largely the fault of unintuitive bug-tracking software, but it can also occur due to forgetfulness or unfamiliarity with quality assurance procedures.

No matter the reason, these incomplete reports require developers or testers to add follow-up comments asking for the specified files. Sometimes these requests go unanswered and the issues are ultimately closed due to a lack of information, whereas other times users are unwilling or unable to share their files due to privacy or confidentiality concerns. Even when they do attach the correct files, the bug reporters may not remember the steps they took to trigger the bugs, which keeps developers in the dark about the true nature of the problems.

Though fuzz testing cannot prevent or replace all of these bug reports, it can greatly simplify the process by catching a lot of frustrating import errors, crashes, and hangs before they ever annoy users. Since these issues are often hard to avoid or work around, user productivity can be brought to a standstill until a fix is released. Fuzzing can help reduce the frequency of these incidents and bring much needed simplicity to the reporting of these errors by shifting the burden from end users back to testers and developers. Likewise, it removes the guesswork from the equation by providing developers with the required documents and exact steps for triggering the bugs. Using fuzz testing to obviate bug reports contributes to the goal of developing seamless office programs and maintains the illusion of simple software by not exposing users to complicated bug forms and reports.

Improve Security

By producing invalid and varied input, fuzzing can also help improve the stability and security of format filters—including obscure ones that receive less development and testing. In fact, when the Microsoft Office team released Service Pack 3 for Office 2003, they disabled support for a number of older formats by default to prevent security vulnerabilities in filters that most users would never use.[5] Though this is probably the simplest strategy to protect users and reduce testing burdens, you could instead attempt to make those importers and exporters as stable and robust as the more common ones for those few users who do require them. Even if you decide that the required effort is not worth it, you can quickly make some substantial improvements by fuzzing a smaller set of sample documents to simulate a wider variety of files, as mentioned earlier.

Modern office programs contain a number of entry points that can be targeted by malicious users—from those dozens of formats that were previously mentioned to powerful macro languages that provide great control over the application and documents. Since much of the input for these programs comes from unknown sources, users may unwittingly expose themselves to viruses and malware simply by opening a file. In response to this threat and to the large number of security vulnerabilities found in Office 2003, Microsoft placed a greater emphasis on fuzz testing while developing its follow-up suite: "Office 2007, especially its file formats, was extensively fuzzed during its development, often with custom-built fuzzers written by the teams responsible for specific file formats."[6]

5. *http://support.microsoft.com/kb/938810/en-us*

6. *http://www.computerworld.com/action/article.do?command=viewArticleBasic&articleId=9038198*

As the Microsoft example illustrates, fuzz testing can be used to find security issues in features before they are released to the public. This preventive testing benefits users, who don't have to upgrade as often to patch security holes, and developers, who can avoid emergency releases that fix security threats. Fuzzing can help contribute to more stable and secure releases that satisfy both users and developers by making it easier to prevent these vulnerabilities from slipping into releases in the first place.

Fuzz Testing

Although fuzzing does not strictly require any setup, some preparation can make the technique much more effective.

Preparation

To get the best results from fuzz testing, you need a representative set of samples to use with the fuzzer. If you don't already have a comprehensive set of documents, you should look for samples in your own bug tracker. These files are important because they have likely caused problems in the past—they are attached to bug reports, after all—and they may cause further trouble with some simple fuzzing.

Furthermore, these documents are already "known" to the developers in the sense that they can be easily retrieved and referenced with little effort. For example, if you use Bugzilla, you can add a quick statement about the original file when reporting new issues, such as: "The upcoming document is a fuzzed version of attachment 123 from bug 456." Bugzilla will automatically link the "attachment 123" and "bug 456" text to the previous issue and existing file, making it easier for developers to consult them for further information if necessary.

Using fuzz testing to take advantage of this automatic management is also an elegant way to avoid problems with storing and tracking samples offline. Each file uploaded to the bug database gets a unique number that can be used to clearly and consistently reference it later on. Since the documents are already in the database, you also don't need to worry about any privacy or confidentiality restrictions that so often apply to documents personally sent to developers by users and companies. These files are usually restricted to a small set of developers, making them more difficult to track and consult when testing. Once you've exhausted your own bug database, you can turn to other bug trackers—especially those of similar products—and search engines that support searching by file type or extension. You can also create some of your own samples to test newer or less represented features to make sure there is reasonable test coverage.

Using existing bug files is only one of the many creative and simple ways in which you can use fuzzing to complement and build upon existing testing practices. For example, with these samples you can generate fuzzed files that trigger bugs and then write unit tests to prevent regressions and catch bugs in similar code. Fuzz testing is easy to set up and likely won't require many (if any) changes to your core application, especially if you already have a framework for functional testing or a command-line mode that allows for easier automation. You can also use the technique in conjunction with code coverage efforts to improve the scope and breadth of your testing.

General Fuzzing

Equipped with just a general fuzzer and some sample documents, you can quickly start creating variant files that simulate the behavior of other office applications and random corruption. I began fuzz testing with zzuf,[7] a multipurpose input fuzzer that can change random bits of a file to meet many simulation needs. I used it with Gnumeric, an open source spreadsheet program similar to Microsoft Excel, and a handful of spreadsheet files that fellow developers had been using to test the program. In only two steps, I was able to fuzz an existing document and see how Gnumeric handled the altered input:

```
1 zzuf < original_spreadsheet.xls > fuzzed_spreadsheet.xls
2 gnumeric fuzzed_spreadsheet.xls
```

This is the most basic form of fuzz testing: taking some input, corrupting or altering it, and then using it for testing. Of course, this is a simple example that doesn't take into account the intricacy of file formats, but it's a quick and fairly effective start. The first command, for example, will randomly fuzz 0.4% of the file (the default ratio) without any regard for keeping certain structures intact, like the file header. I was able to trigger a number of bugs using this method of testing, but to effectively simulate dozens of applications and versions you'll need to use more sophisticated techniques and a lot more sample documents. Like good office software, zzuf hides its complexity by default, allowing you to write simple and effective tests with minimal effort.

As you continue testing, you can start to use the more advanced features of multipurpose fuzzers like zzuf to gain greater control over fuzzing output. To address the file headers problem that I mentioned earlier, for instance, you can protect byte ranges to make sure the document is properly detected by the relevant importing routines. Similarly, you can prevent certain characters from being altered and disallow other characters from being inserted into the input data to bypass existing sanity checks in the code. The 0.4% ratio that is used by default is also configurable, allowing you to experiment with the amount of corruption and variation you'd like to introduce to the files.

Using these features and an assortment of documents collected from bug databases and the Web, I've tested Gnumeric with hundreds of thousands of altered files. By using zzuf's beautiful mix of simplicity and power, I have been able to create those many thousands of files from far fewer samples. To automate this testing, I use a shell script that invokes the fuzzing and importing/exporting commands, while also performing basic monitoring of exit codes and error

7. *http://caca.zoy.org/wiki/zzuf*

messages to detect bugs. This method of testing has proven effective at triggering a wide variety of bugs in Gnumeric's format filters, particularly the Microsoft Excel (*.xls*) plug-in.

Some of the first fuzzing bugs that I found and reported were crashes that occurred in the early stages of the Excel importer—in basic sheet and row code. By using zzuf's defaults, I was able to identify a number of general problems that would affect many Excel files rather than just a select few. One nice thing about this technique is that it provides quick gains without requiring a lot of testing effort. As you fix these common problems, you begin to build up robustness that prevents more generic errors, making it increasingly difficult to trigger bugs with the existing settings. In beautiful fashion, zzuf guides this rapid progression by providing sensible defaults that later give way to more complex methods and features. Running these fuzzers, testers become like users of office programs who quickly master basic commands before moving on to advanced techniques that make them even more productive. When your fuzz testing stops finding bugs, it's time to start using the more advanced features of your fuzzer to make your testing effective once again.

With a lot of the general problems fixed, I was able to find bugs in more localized functions by decreasing the fuzzing ratio. This change made it easier to find more specific bugs, including those in minor spreadsheet elements like chart error bars and particular plot types. Finding these bugs is encouraging because it signals that your code is becoming more stable and is allowing the altered input to get further into the importers and exporters. By monitoring the results of fuzz testing, you can gather a great amount of feedback about the stability of the code you're testing and the effectiveness of the fuzzing. This feedback can help direct future testing efforts and alert you to techniques that have lost their effectiveness. While analyzing logs of testing runs, I noticed that zzuf's default xor fuzzing, which randomly sets and unsets bits, was no longer as effective as it once was. To look for remaining bugs, I added support for zzuf's individual set and unset methods and was able to find a number of crashes that did not show up in the combined xor testing.

Although I have found bugs in a variety of spreadsheet formats, my testing has been most effective with the Excel format because of its complexity and binary makeup. In contrast, more modern file formats—like Office Open XML (*.xlsx*) and OpenDocument Spreadsheet (*.ods*)— use ZIP compression to archive the contents of XML-based files. These container formats make fuzzing more difficult and require extra steps before you can effectively test with them. For example, to work around the compression problem, you have to use an unpacking utility or unpacking code to extract the archive files before running the fuzzer. You also need to be more diligent about protecting characters that form the markup tags and avoiding invalid XML characters. When you start finding more specialized cases like this, it may be time to shift your testing energy from general fuzzing to more customized fuzzing for these more involved formats and features.

Custom Fuzzing

Once the effectiveness of your general fuzzing begins to wane, you can start writing customized fuzzers to probe deeper into formats and features. Custom fuzzing allows you to go beyond the limits of general fuzzing by integrating specific knowledge about applications and file formats into the testing routines. Before you write your own custom fuzzer, however, you should check for an existing one that may serve your needs—or at least one that could potentially serve as the basis for your own. For example, Jesse Ruderman of Mozilla fame has written a JavaScript fuzzer (jsfunfuzz) that has found security vulnerabilities in both Firefox and Opera.[8]

Inspired by the success of jsfunfuzz, I wrote my own custom fuzzer to test Gnumeric's formula and function parser to make sure it could handle as many valid and invalid combinations as possible. Starting with a list of built-in function names (e.g., sum and pi) and operators (e.g., + and -), I wrote a program to generate thousands of tab-separated cells with randomized values and function parameters. This fuzzer has uncovered dozens of bugs—from crashes and hangs to memory leaks—with many of them being reducible to compact, and rather aesthetic, test cases. The great thing about this type of fuzzing is that you can create a wide variety of input that would otherwise be impossible to generate manually by using some basic rules and constraints for the fuzzing output.

Using this fuzzer, I was able to discover one of my favorite bugs: a crash triggered by a mere three characters, ={}. This seemingly benign expression was enough to crash Gnumeric's powerful and complex parser due to some missing error checking. Finding this bug was a bit surprising because the matching braces were inserted by a function that was actually designed to generate random strings rather than mathematical operators. By combining simple rules and elements, you can create a fuzzer that produces beautifully complex output and locates bugs in surprising and unexpected ways.

Another great aspect of this custom testing is that it guards against many bugs that can easily be triggered by accident. With paste being such a frequently used command, it's safe to assume that random text is going to be inadvertently inserted into a cell or formula at some point. Likewise, spreadsheets will be edited by novice and expert users alike, with both groups attempting to make your software work to their needs.

New users might misuse functions and pass invalid arguments as they attempt to learn the proper syntax. Looking through bug reports that I've filed in the past, I noticed a number of fixed test cases that could have been easily encountered by users making typing mistakes or forgetting to fill in function arguments:

- `=countblank({1})`
- `=ddb(,,2^50,)`
- `=r.phyper(1.0e+65,,,)`

---

8. *http://www.squarefree.com/2007/08/02/introducing-jsfunfuzz/*

I should point out that these test cases were cleaned up a bit before I submitted them to the bug tracking system, but they were all originally found by the custom fuzzer. When reporting the issues, I attempted to make the examples as simple as possible to aid developers in debugging and fixing the issues.

In contrast to inexperienced users, expert users are more likely to try to mix various functions to create powerful function combinations. The following examples are test cases that could represent failed attempts at creating complex function calls from disparate parts:

- `=areas(sumx2py2())`
- `=harmean(transpose(D144:E222)` [only one closing parenthesis]
- `=opt_rgw(0,35/45,-1,2/5/2008,F182,2/5/2008,K36)`

These examples—and indeed much of the output generated by this custom fuzzer—will appear nonsensical to those familiar with spreadsheets, but that's part of the power and appeal of fuzzing. It will produce beautifully compact, three-character crashing expressions right next to complicated function calls that are nested to 10 levels. It makes it easier to develop reliable software by finding bugs that could easily surprise users who accidentally type or paste some text, only to crash the program. This testing also helps to account for differences between function implementations in various spreadsheet programs, some of which could lead to unexpected or empty arguments being passed to the underlying parser.

Random Fuzzing

In contrast to generic and customized fuzzing, random fuzzing works with unstructured or irregular input. One of the bugs I found while testing Gnumeric was a crash triggered by an overly long input line from a text file. Though it sounds like a buffer overflow, it was actually caused by the invocation of a message box that warned when Gnumeric was truncating data to fit the current worksheet. The problem is that the program was actually attempting to display the warning message while converting the file on the command line—where no GUI was present.

Though I was using structured input when I found the bug, the crash could have been triggered just as easily with a long line of completely random data. At some point in your fuzz testing, make sure to throw in this sort of randomized test to broaden your coverage and to help identify any biases that you may have introduced to your testing through your collected samples and customized fuzzers. Many users will attempt to open unexpected files with your program, so this testing will help make sure that sensible error handling is in place.

Two common ways that these unexpected files can be imported is through inadvertent clicks in a file chooser and through attempts to open unsupported files that are believed to be supported. If the program fails under these circumstances, users will likely be confused and unaware of the true cause of the problem and may just assume that your program is generally unreliable. This sort of testing is beautiful because it helps cut down on confusing problems, and because it doesn't even require any specific files—it can be used with any input. It is also largely free of the sort of predictability that can make other fuzzing techniques less effective.

Limitations

It's very easy to overlook details and introduce biases when you're already familiar with a program or file format. For example, your custom fuzzer may always properly end function calls with a closing parenthesis, making it impossible to find bugs that rely on mismatched parentheses. As I mentioned earlier, the Microsoft Office team spent a considerable amount of time fuzz testing Office 2007, but they still missed security vulnerabilities:

> A good example of something testing didn't spot during Office 2007's development—not to mention the even earlier work on Office 2003—was the bug in Excel's file format disclosed by the July [2007] security bulletin MS07-036. The vulnerability, which existed across the Office line [...] was [...] "in the way Excel handles malformed Excel files." It was the first bug in a core Office 2007 application's file format.[9]

One way to avoid this problem is by making continual changes to your fuzzers to generate more test cases and to remove existing biases that could affect the output. To get a better idea of where to start looking, you can use code coverage tools to help identify missing test branches. With this added knowledge, you can add relevant samples or alter fuzzing routines to exercise the neglected code.

While using my custom formula fuzzer, I have made a number of additions and changes to correct initial oversights. Despite this maintenance, it no longer triggers many bugs and is mainly used to monitor for regressions that may have been introduced to the code. After you use fuzz testing for a while, finding bugs will become the exception rather than the rule, which is a good sign that your code base is becoming more stable and robust.

Although fuzz testing is great for identifying obvious problems like hangs and crashes, it's less useful for determining correctness. Your program may not crash or hang on an input line, but it still may be handling the error improperly—which will be difficult or impossible to tell from the techniques described earlier.

Future Considerations

So, what comes next? As the Excel vulnerability illustrates, it's hard to tell when you have fuzzed certain parts of your program enough. Once you reach diminishing returns, though, you should start fuzzing other parts of the program, like the user interface and scripting and macro languages, to make sure they're as stable and reliable as other features. Likewise, new features will create opportunities to extend existing fuzzing tools or develop new ones. By monitoring incoming bug reports, you can notice and correct the omissions that make your

9. *http://www.computerworld.com/action/article.do?command=viewArticleBasic&articleId=9038198*

fuzzing less effective. In fact, this is exactly how I noticed a missing function in my formula fuzzer: a user submitted a bug report that included a function that I had failed to include in my testing. After adding it to the list, my custom fuzzer triggered a crash that I had previously missed.

In addition to monitoring your own project, be on the lookout for new tools that can assist you in your testing. I have done most of my fuzzing with zzuf, but it contains a number of limitations that bias my testing. For example, it cannot add or remove bytes or truncate input, which makes it more difficult to truly simulate certain forms of corruption. Integrating new fuzzing tools and techniques will help you overcome these deficiencies and likely uncover further bugs.

Fuzz testing is a great technique to make office software more reliable and useful. It allows for creative and elegant solutions to many complicated problems that developers and testers face, including those of interoperability, security, and stability. It also fittingly mirrors office software, in the sense that both present simple facades that hide their complexity and allow for countless variations by offering powerful functions. By adding fuzzing to your existing testing practices, you can help ensure that users receive a reliable product that conforms to a different standard of beauty—one based on the simplicity and straightforwardness that users expect from office software.

## CHAPTER SIX

Bug Management and Test Case Effectiveness

Emily Chen
Brian Nitz

I have deep faith that the principle of the universe will be beautiful and simple.

—Albert Einstein

WHY SHOULD A QUALITY ASSURANCE (QA) ENGINEER CARE how "beautiful" a test and bug management system is? Although no one understands exactly what beauty is, there does seem to be a useful relationship between beauty, simplicity, and truth. When this relationship is applied in mathematics and the physical sciences, it is often known as Occam's Razor. It assumes that beautiful and simple explanations of natural phenomena are more likely to be true than ugly and convoluted ones. Sir Isaac Newton put it this way: "We are to admit no more causes of natural things than such as are both true and sufficient to explain their appearances." Although we can find examples of this principle being applied in structured programming, object-oriented design (OOD), and design patterns, beauty and simplicity aren't yet common considerations in bug management or QA test design. In this chapter we discuss how to manage bugs and measure test case effectiveness. We hope you will find this approach to be more beautiful, simple, and true than the more common haphazard QA approaches, which often stray from the scientific method and rely a bit too much on luck.

Bug Management

The following sections explain bug management.

The First Bug Found

The Smithsonian National Museum of American History has part of an engineering notebook on display. The notebook's terse handwritten notes bring to light some arcane details of the operation of Harvard University's Mark II electromechanical computer. Page 92 of this notebook, shown in Figure 6-1, displays typical engineering notes from September 9, 1947:

```
1525 Started Mult+Adder Test.
1545 Relay # 70 Panel F
(moth) in relay.
First actual case of bug being found.
```

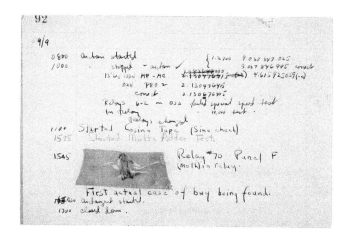

FIGURE 6-1. The first bug found

The Smithsonian's notes alongside this page mention that the term "bug" was used in engineering at least as far back as Thomas Edison's time. But this moth made for a very good story often told by Admiral Grace Hopper, inventor of the COBOL language and one of the computer engineers who worked on the Mark II. This bug became part of computing history. Moths are far too big to become wedged inside individual gates of modern microprocessors, but software bugs haven't gone away. This particular bug report doesn't describe the symptoms, but it contains two important details that are unfortunately lacking in many contemporary bug reports:

- The bug is closely associated with the test procedure (presumably the test procedure that revealed this bug).
- When the root cause was found, it was explained along with a detailed attachment. A yellowed piece of cellophane tape still holds the remains of a two-inch moth to the margin of this bug report!

Why is it important to attach the root cause to the bug report? If I find a bug in my system and fix it, can't I just close the bug? Who cares what the root cause was? The answer to this question is becoming obvious as more organizations embrace open source software. If a bug is found and fixed in a specific distribution, the patch for that bug should be submitted upstream so that other distros downstream from the patch can benefit from the fix. But because of stability requirements, other distros might be stuck with a product based on a branch before this patch was submitted. The bug report should be the place to look for the root cause, the patch(es), and other information that could be useful to anyone trying to backport the fix to another branch. Sadly, these details are rarely available in open source bug tracking systems.

It Isn't "Just a Bug"

An unfortunate legacy of Harvard's moth is that the word for an annoying but "mostly harmless" little creature became embedded in the language of computer science. This cute little word can cause us to underestimate the size and severity of problems that can be caused by software defects, and has almost certainly caused software companies to under-invest in QA and bug management.

For example, what do the following occurrences have in common?

- Two ASCII characters are used to represent a four-digit numeric value, and several hundred billion dollars are spent fixing this problem.
- A space probe crashes into the surface of the planet Mars and is lost.
- Several patients are killed when a user interface caching issue in a radiotherapy machine causes them to receive almost 100 times the prescribed dosage of radiation.
- Mortgage defaults are summed as independent variables under the mistaken assumption that there is no statistical relationship between one mortgage default's probability and that of another. This mistake overestimates the stability of certain financial instruments and eventually contributes to a global economic crisis.

Each of these problems can be traced to a bug. As more aspects of our lives become dependent on the safe and correct operation of software, we must take bugs seriously…even if we have to come up with another term for software defects. Monsters? Demons? For the remainder of this section, we will try to use the word "defect" in place of "bug" to help remind us that we aren't always dealing with a cute little creature.

The First Step in Managing a Defect Is Defining It

If you know your enemy and yourself, you need not fear the result of many battles.

—Sun Tzu
The Art of War, 6 BC

A beautiful defect tracking system should be a conduit for information between the end user, support person, developer, and QA engineer. It should help these people collaborate on a defect's solution. In order to do this, the defect tracking system should maintain crucial bits of information and discourage unnecessary or incorrect information. The important aspects of a defect can be broken down into the kinds of questions a detective would ask when investigating a case: who, what, when, where, and why?

Who?

A beautiful defect tracking system must serve many kinds of users. A defect report is a communication channel between the person who discovered the defect and the person with the expertise to fix it. All defect tracking systems should track *who* logged the defect, *who* fixed the defect, and *who* verified that the defect has been fixed. A beautiful defect tracking system should organize details according to the role of the user, possibly hiding information that isn't relevant to a particular role. The developer needs to know how to reproduce the defect in the correct source code base. A QA person is interested in associating the bug in an existing or new test assertion. But the software user is most interested in whether the defect exists in his system and, if so, whether a patch, upgrade, or workaround exists for the defect.

It is also important to remember that a defect's priority and severity are subject to individual biases. One person might decide that a defect is a Priority 3 because it occurs on only one type of hardware, but for the person whose data center relies on that hardware, it is a Priority 1. It is up to the QA engineers and developers to triage end-user-reported defects and adjust priority and severity according to their organization's defect policy.

For some kinds of bugs, it is now possible to track how frequently the bug has been hit. An ideal defect tracking system would automatically look for a duplicate when a defect is logged and increment the "vote" for that defect. Votes would be used along with Priority and Severity ratings to determine which defects should be fixed first. The Bug Buddy application[1] used on the GNOME project and Mozilla's breakpad[2] attempt to automate the logging of crash bugs. However, because stack traces can vary depending on architecture and other factors, it is still necessary for a human to intervene and determine whether the logged defect is a duplicate of an existing defect.

---

1. *http://library.gnome.org/devel/bug-buddy/stable/welcome.html.en*

2. *http://code.google.com/p/google-breakpad/*

What?

A beautiful defect report should begin with a concise description of a defect's symptoms as well as the conditions necessary for reproducing the defect. Minimally it usually consists of the following:

Description
    A concise description of the defect.

Detailed description
    This should contain enough details to allow someone else to reproduce the defect. For example:

- Software revision (code base)
- Operating system environment
- Hardware
- Other prerequisites
- Test case to reproduce (when the tester does this, one thing is expected to happen, but instead this unexpected thing happens)

> **N O T E**
>
> It is unfortunate that, even though way back in the 1940s Harvard's engineers knew to associate bug #1 with its test case, in 2009 most tools still rely on ad-hoc association between defect and test case.

Priority
    According to published defect policy, how important is it? Usually P1 is most important and P4 or P5 are least important.

Severity
    What is the impact of this defect? This can be related to defect priority but isn't exactly the same thing. For example, a defect that causes a user interface to crash may be a high severity (because it is a crash), but if the defect is seen only in rare environments, it may be deemed a low priority.

When?

The same tools and processes are used to track defects throughout a product's life cycle. However, the granularity of "a typical defect" changes during a product life cycle. For example, unit-level defects found early in product development can usually be traced directly to the source code where they reside. But a defect reported by an end user in a deployed product might appear only when components from many code bases interact with each other or run with particular hardware. Defects found late in a product life cycle are also much more expensive to fix than bugs found before a product release. Therefore, as we will discuss later, it is important to distinguish which bugs were found during QA testing and which bugs were found after product release.

Where?

Where do bugs live? Software bugs are associated with the unique combination of software components that comprise a system. A beautifully simple defect tracking system could be designed around the assumption that each defect in the executable object code can be traced back to a few lines of source code. For small or proprietary projects, which are typically confined to a single code base, this kind of system would work well because there is a clear one-to-one relationship between each defect and the source code that contains the defect. But when a defect is found in a public open source defect tracking system, it isn't always obvious which code base the defect lies in. The defect may have been logged by someone unfamiliar with the code. For most real-world systems, there is neither an automatic nor a robust mapping between the defect report and source code revision.

Since bugs can span several layers of the software stack, bugs can also span several projects and code bases. Although it is useful for the end user or support person to track such "distribution bugs" in a separate defect database, it is also necessary to pass appropriate information into the upstream defect databases so that the component's domain experts can focus on their aspect of the problem. Unfortunately, once a defect is passed upstream, it becomes difficult for distribution end users and support staff to continue to track the progress of the defect, especially in relation to their product. Just because a Nautilus NFS interaction bug is marked as fixed in *bugzilla.gnome.org*[3] doesn't mean that fix has been integrated into your distribution, and there is no easy way for the end user or support person to determine this. Therefore, there is significant duplication of effort in defect logging, defect tracking, and testing, which fails to take full advantage of open source collaboration.

To a developer, it is clear that a defect lives in the source code

Tools such as Bugs Everywhere[4] operate on the purist concept that, since bugs ultimately reside in the source code, defect tracking should live alongside the code and use the same revision control system (e.g., CVS, SVN, Mercurial). This does have significant advantages, especially for small systems where the entire code base can live within one revision control system. When a defect is fixed, both the patched source code and updated defect report are checked into the revision control system, and the correspondence between the defect state and the defect report state are correctly and automatically propagated to branches of the source tree without requiring the developer or software QA person to maintain an ad-hoc set of cross references in the source tree and the state in the defect database. Systems such as Bugs Everywhere and

---

3. *http://bugzilla.gnome.org/show_bug.cgi?id=47942*

4. *http://bugseverywhere.org/be/show/HomePage*

Bugzilla are used in upstream components where defects are confined to a single code base (see Figure 6-2).

Distro 1	Distro 2	Distro 3
Mozilla	Firefox 2	Firefox 3
Java 1.4	Java 1.6	Java 1.6
GNOME 2.6	GNOME 2.20	GNOME 2.24
Xsun	X.Org	X.Org
S10u5 kernel	OS2008.05 kernel	OS2008.11 kernel

Upstream bug tracking systems usually confined to single code base

FIGURE 6-2. Upstream bug-tracking system confined to single code bases

To an end user/support person, defects live in the system or distribution

As projects grow and mature, components interact with components in different code bases. The relationship between code and defect becomes more difficult to track because the person who discovers the defect is further from the code. Organizations try to solve this problem with internal distribution-centric defect databases.

The problem here is that defect databases designed to support end users of a corporate product (distribution) have a weak relationship with the code bases of individual components that interact to generate the defect (Figure 6-3). Open source community developers who are domain experts in component code bases might not have access to distribution-centric databases. Defect information communication between the community and inside the corporate firewall is inefficient, or sometimes nonexistent.

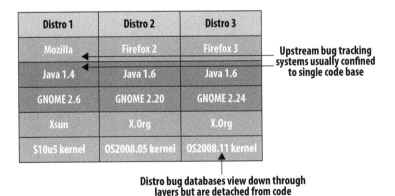

FIGURE 6-3. Distro bug databases are detached from code

A better approach would be to allow the individual code-centric defect tracking systems to do what they do best and pull only the *minimum* information necessary to track the defect. This information would be pulled into a local meta bug database as keys that link back to the original defect in community project databases. For example:

Minimal key pull
> (upstreambugdb, bugid) → key to full defect in upstream database.

Defect key pull with additional fields for convenient local review and sorting
> (upstream bugdb, bugid, synopsis, priority, severity) → key to full defect in upstream database.

This reference database can be made available to the community for viewing and tagging bugs. Tags and fields added to this meta bug database do not have to correspond to fields in the original database. This approach allows community members to create arbitrary tags that categorize bugs from multiple databases into role, project, or individually defined sets without adding to the complexity of upstream defect databases. This thin "metabug" abstraction layer can be enhanced to improve a company's QA support, as well as its ability to contribute meaningful defect data to the open source development community.

One approach to multi-code-base defect tracking. Although no perfect "beautiful defect tracking system" exists today, relatively minor changes in the tools and processes used for defect tracking can have a significant impact on software quality. It is possible to add some Python glue to existing defect tracking systems and build a metadefect tracker that helps users see and organize defects that reside in multiple code bases. Bugjuicer is one such metadefect tracker (Figure 6-4). In the example search shown in Figure 6-5, the end user has found possible duplicates for a particular defect without knowing exactly where in her application stack the defect is located. She searches in the default defect database for the module (Bugjuicer automatically associates the appropriate default defect database with each module). He also searches the distribution and the X Server defect databases. The results come back in a convenient list with links from each defect reference back to its location in its home defect database.

**Bugs can span multiple layers,
distros, and code bases**

Distro 1	Distro 2	Distro 3
Mozilla	Firefox 2	Firefox 3
Java 1.4	Java 1.6	Java 1.6
GNOME 2.6	GNOME 2.20	GNOME 2.24
Xsun	X.Org	X.Org
S10u5 kernel	OS2008.05 kernel	OS2008.11 kernel

**Bugjuicer can search and tag bugs across
multiple layers, distros, and code bases**

FIGURE 6-4. Bugs across multiple layers, distros, and code bases

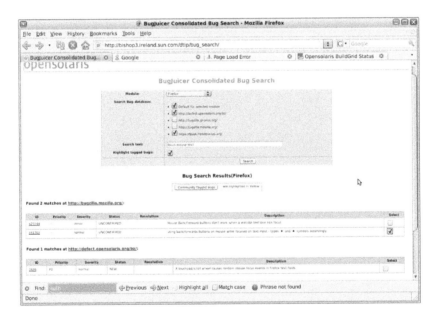

FIGURE 6-5. Bugjuicer bug search

Tags

If the user finds bugs upstream or in the distribution database that are particularly relevant to his problem (bug or metabug), he can apply tags to these bugs (Figure 6-6) so they can be tracked together in a "tag cloud" or "tag set" (Figure 6-7).

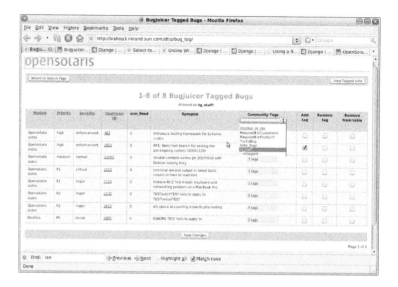

FIGURE 6-6. BugJuicer tag set

FIGURE 6-7. Tagged defect sets (tag clouds)

Tagged Defect Sets (Tag Clouds): Why?

Defect reports often contain multiple hypotheses describing theoretical root causes. But when a defect is closed, the validated root cause should be highlighted. If the developer and QA engineers have followed the scientific method, a closed defect should reference the following:

- The code base the defect resides in
- The hypothesized root cause
- A description of the fix and/or a link to the source code patch
- A test case proving that the root cause of the defect has indeed been fixed

It is also useful to include test cases that disprove or eliminate alternative hypothesized root causes. As Arthur Conan Doyle's Sherlock Holmes character would put it, "When you have excluded the impossible, whatever remains, however improbable, must be the truth."

Test Case Effectiveness

What is so beautiful about testing?

We confess that sometimes it is difficult to see the beauty in software testing. It may be that software QA suffers from a lack of respect and funding because it lacks the superficial glamour enjoyed by other aspects of software development.

While cruising Istanbul's Bosporus channel with other members of the GNOME community last summer, we were asked whether we used Dogtail or Linux Desktop Testing Project (LDTP) for our automated testing. We knew we had evaluated these tools, but we were embarrassed to admit that we didn't know exactly why we didn't rely on them. The exact reason had to do with stability, performance, and the probe effect. But in general, automated test tools are never sufficient for desktop or GUI testing. Why is this? Because it is impossible to simulate every possible combination of user actions on a graphical user interface. Think of how many possible ways you could interact with 10 buttons on a screen. There are more than three million possible different orders in which you could click the buttons, and you could single- or double-click on each button. You could even drag after clicking. Fortunately, some of the low-level behaviors of buttons on a GUI are in well-tested libraries, and other behaviors are prevented. But you can see where a brute-force automation testing methodology is apt to fail.

Fortunately, real users can provide a representative sample of likely workflows that can be fed into test design. Alpha and beta releases with a good feedback mechanism are crucial to good desktop testing.

Execution of many well-defined test cases is critical for effective testing of complex systems, such as the OpenSolaris desktop. However, executing all test cases does not guarantee that a system is sufficiently tested. Many other factors also determine whether test engineers have performed well and whether test cases were effective in measuring the quality of the software being tested.

What is the Test-Case Effectiveness (TCE) metric? TCE is a method for measuring the effectiveness of test cases. A certain number of defects are always found as a side effect of software testing. A "side-effect defect" is a defect that is found during testing but isn't the direct result of a failed assertion in a written test case.

The rationale is that these side-effect defects are not explicitly covered by existing QA test cases, and they need to be examined for the conditions that triggered the bugs. New test cases can then be developed and executed in future test cycles.

Since TCE measures how effective QA test cases are in identifying bugs compared to other means, it can be used to track test coverage over time.

The formula is very simple:

$$TCE = (Nt / Ntot) * 100 \%$$

where Nt is total bugs found by QA and Ntot is the sum of total bugs found (Nt) and the number of test escapes.

Test escapes are bugs found outside the normal QA test cycle. Full coverage with no test escapes gives a TCE = 1.00 (100%), so higher is better.

The goal is to improve TCE by minimizing the number of test escapes with more effective test cases.

Capturing the Impact of Bug Severity

To reflect the severity of bugs found by QA and through test escapes, we can use a weighted TCE, with a weight given to each bug's priority. Bug priority is a weight assigned to a bug that indicates the relative importance of fixing the bug.

The weighting reflects the quality of bugs found by QA test cycles and test escapes.

For example, if we assign the following weights to different priority bugs:

P1= 10, P2 = 8, P3 = 6, P4 = 3, P5 = 1

and QA finds 5 P1 bugs, and test escapes are 15 P3 bugs:

$$TCE(weighted) = 5 \times 10 / (5 \times 10 + 15 \times 6) = 50 / 140 = 0.35 \ (35\%)$$
$$TCE(unweighted) = 5 / (5 + 15) = 5 / 20 = 0.25 \ (25\%)$$

the *weighted* TCE metric reflects that QA is finding more high-risk and damaging bugs, even though overall quantity is low.

Analyzing Test Escape Bugs

To analyze the test escape bugs, allocate each bug into one of the following cause categories:

- Misfiled bug
- Incomplete test case
- No test case
- Test execution problem
- Incorrect test case
- Incorrect functional specification (where a functional specification actually exists!)

Then, determine the corrective action for the test escape, as listed in the following table.

Cause	Corrective action[a]
Misfiled bug	Move bug to correct state (e.g., product/category/subcategory). Need to highlight bug-filing guidelines and educate reporter about how to correctly file bugs.
Incomplete test case	Review functional area that the test case is for. Enhance and redesign the test cases.
No test case	Implement test cases based on functionality that caused the bug.
Test execution problem	Review procedural steps or hardware/software dependencies.
Incorrect test case	Review functionality being tested. Has it changed since the test case was written?
Incorrect functional specification	Contact designer/developer. Examine functional specification review process. Is it too vague?

a. The category with the highest count is the most problematic, so a further corrective action would be to find out why so many bugs appear in that category.

Case Study of the OpenSolaris Desktop Team

The desktop QA team is responsible for the quality of all the desktop applications included with OpenSolaris. These applications include open source projects from many communities, including GNOME, Mozilla, Compiz, Pidgin, etc. OpenSolaris is on a six-month release schedule, but a development build is released to the community every two weeks. Due to the frequency of releases and to ensure high quality, the desktop QA team adopted a formal test process with a focus on functional testing. The QA team was responsible for the test plan and the design of test cases. Many of the test cases come from open source communities. For example, most of the test cases for Firefox are from the Mozilla community, which uses a test case management tool called Litmus.

For most of the desktop applications, although 100% of the test cases are executed, there are still bugs filed out of the normal QA test cycle. The QA team tracks the TCE trend at every build in order to measure and improve the effectiveness of the test cases over the course of development of an OpenSolaris release. The following sections outline an example of how to measure and improve the test cases' effectiveness.

Assumptions

For the OpenSolaris desktop project, we classify all bugs submitted by non-QA engineers as test escapes, excluding the following:

- Enhancement
- Localization (L10N) OS-related
- Hardware
- Device drivers
- Globalization (G11N)
- Build
- "Cannot reproduce"
- "Not a bug"
- Duplicates

The Process of Calculating the TCE Metric

1. Use Bugzilla from the OpenSolaris community (*http://defect.opensolaris.org/bz/*) to gather bug lists directly:
   a. Select product "gnome" and "mozilla" from "Development" classification.
   b. Select "build on bugzilla" for each build.
2. Examine the bug list that is returned to check whether any of the bugs are to be excluded (see the earlier section "Assumptions" for a list of the excluded categories).
3. Analyze each valid bug and determine which category best describes the root cause.
4. Generate the TCE metric:

   $$TCE = (Nt / Ntot) * 100 \%$$

5. Calculate the number of *each* P1, P2, P3, P4, P5 bug.

   Multiply the quantity of *each* P1, P2, P3, P4, P5 bug by its corresponding weighted values, where the weights are the following: P1 = 10, P2 = 8, P3 = 6, P4 = 3, P5 = 1.
6. Calculate Nt, the sum total of *each* weighted P1, P2, P3, P4, P5 bug found during a test cycle.
7. Calculate test escapes, the sum total of *each* weighted P1, P2, P3, P4, P5 bug found *outside* a test cycle.
8. Calculate Ntot = Nt + test escapes.
9. Calculate TCE = (Nt / Ntot) * 100%.

Using the process just shown, we now gather defect data and perform causal analysis from build 108 to build 112. Let's take build 110 as an example. First, we generate the bug list for build 110 by using the OpenSolaris Bugzilla bug tracking application, and then we will get a bug list (Figure 6-8).

16 bugs found.

ID	Sev	Pri	OS	Assignee	Status	Resolution	Summary
7281	cri	P2	Solaris	Brian.Cameron@sun.com	FIXINP		[Elisa] sporatic core dump when closing elisa
7105	maj	P2	Solaris	stephen.browne@sun.com	REOPEN		[tjds] gconfd dies in labeled workspaces
7769	nor	P2	OpenSol	jeff.cai@sun.com	ACCEPT		Evolution reports an error when merging a contact (snv_110)
7667	nor	P3	Solaris	jeff.cai@sun.com	REOPEN		gnome-keyring-* is whining on my console
6865	nor	P3	Solaris	qa-mozilla-firefox@defect.o...	ACCEPT		Two Application windows will be loaded on gnome panel
7860	nor	P3	Solaris	qa-gnome-gconf@defect.opens...	ACCEPT		"pfexec gedit" fails because of something in my user environment
6962	nor	P3	Solaris	Brian.Cameron@sun.com	ACCEPT		gnome-terminal can not remember $PWD when open a new tab
7952	nor	P3	OpenSol	jeff.cai@sun.com	ACCEPT		Evolution hangs at 100% CPU when going offline-online
7050	nor	P3	Solaris	elaine.xiong@sun.com	ACCEPT		When use Ekiga it fail to see the change of buddy's status
7131	nor	P3	OpenSol	qa-gnome-applications@defec...	NEW		magnifier crash on the DTU of sunrayserver
7748	min	P3	OpenSol	jerry.tan@sun.com	ACCEPT		totem dies in the face of five minute fridays...
6858	nor	P4	Solaris	dkenny@opensolaris.org	ACCEPT		[vermillion] short cut key F11 does not work on evince
6960	nor	P4	Solaris	qa-gnome-applications@defec...	NEW		when you add the application to panel through the lauch, the applications on the panel before disappear.
6187	nor	P4	Windows	qa-gnome-applications@defec...	NEW		Disk Usage Analyzer - Treemap Chart does not show directories
7133	nor	P4	Solaris	elaine.xiong@sun.com	ACCEPT		Ekiga crashes down when configuring Ekiga using keyboard navigation
7169	min	P4	OpenSol	qa-gnome-applications@defec...	NEW		[Xvnc] Date failed to show in gdm when connected by Xvnc

16 bugs found.

FIGURE 6-8. OpenSolaris build 110 bug list

We use the same search rule to generate the defect lists from other OpenSolaris development builds, 108–112. After performing TCE analysis on the bug lists, we generated the following table.

Build ID	**Bug logged each build**	**Escaped bugs**	**Analyze test escape bugs**	**TCE value (weighted and unweighted)**
Build 108	Total 4 bugs: 4 P4 bugs	1 escaped bug: 1 P4 bug	Incomplete test case	TCE(weighted)=75% TCE(unweighted)=75%
Build 109	Total 10 bugs: 1 P2 bug 6 P3 bugs 3 P4 bugs	0 escaped bugs	NA	TCE(weighted)=100% TCE(unweighted)=100%
Build 110	Total 16 bugs: 3 P2 bugs 8 P3 bugs 5 P4 bugs	5 escaped bugs: 1 P2 bug 4 P3 bugs	Incomplete test case No test case Test execution problem	TCE(weighted)=63% TCE(unweighted)=69%

Build ID	Bug logged each build	Escaped bugs	Analyze test escape bugs	TCE value (weighted and unweighted)
Build 111	Total 20 bugs: 1 P2 bug 7 P3 bugs 11 P4 bugs 1 P5 bug	2 escaped bugs: 1 P3 bug 1 P5 bug	Test execution problem No test case	TCE(weighted)=92% TCE(unweighted)=90%
Build 112	Total 8 bugs: 2 P2 bugs 4 P3 bugs 2 P4 bugs	1 escaped bug: 1 P2 bug	No test case	TCE(weighted)=83% TCE(unweighted)=87%

The trend of TCE graphics according to the table from build 108 to build 112 is shown in Figure 6-9.

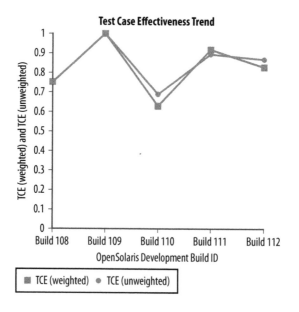

FIGURE 6-9. Test case effectiveness trend

In the graph, the TCE value for build 110 is slightly lower compared to other builds. Our goal, therefore, is to improve test case effectiveness by analyzing each of the escaped bugs in build 110.

In total, 16 bugs were filed: 11 bugs were found by QA during the test cycle, and 5 were escaped bugs. Bug 6962—"6962 P3 normal gnome-terminal can not remember $PWD when open a new tab"—is a typical escaped bug, and so we will review it as an example.[5]

This bug was reported outside the formal QA test process by someone outside the QA team. So, we classified it as an "escaped bug."

In the process of analyzing the root cause of this escaped bug, we reviewed the set of GNOME test cases and found that none of the existing test cases covered this bug. So the test escape cause is "No test case" because the bug was found during ad-hoc testing after the test cycle.

Corrective action

In the bug 6962 example, the corrective action was to review the test cases for the GNOME terminal and design a new test case based on the feature that caused the bug.

The outcome of this corrective action will be new cases and modifications to existing cases.

Here we gave an example of analyzing bugs across five consecutive builds. Our goal is to continually track the TCE trend graphically. The TCE method is designed to give the QA team better visibility into test case effectiveness before products are released. With this approach, the QA team can identify test case problems and correct the testing process before releasing the system.

Conclusions

In this chapter, we have shared with you how to manage bugs and measure test case effectiveness. We started with basic concepts and explained how we implemented them on the OpenSolaris platform. These are real stories from real projects that we worked on. We continue work on those projects and improve the process during each release cycle of OpenSolaris. The proposed technique can be applied within any project testing management model. We hope you will find this approach to be more beautiful, simple, and accurate than commonly used, haphazard QA approaches.

Acknowledgments

We are grateful to Derek Rafter for his great effort in introducing the TCE method on OpenSolaris. Thanks to Nigel Simpson for his detailed reviews and comments on this chapter.

---

5. *http://defect.opensolaris.org/bz/show_bug.cgi?id=6962*

References

Chernak, Y. 2001. "Validating and Improving Test-Case Effectiveness." *IEEE Software*, 18(1): 81–86.

Kidwell, P. A. 1998. "Stalking the Elusive Computer Bug." *Annals of the History of Computing*, 20: 5–9.

McPhee, N. "Therac-25 accidents," *http://www.morris.umn.edu/~mcphee/Courses/Readings/Therac_25_accidents.html*.

Smithsonian National Museum of American History. "Log Book With Computer Bug," *http://americanhistory.si.edu/collections/object.cfm?key=35&objkey=30*.

Tzu, Sun. *The Art of War*. Trans. Lionel Giles. *http://www.gutenberg.org/etext/132*.

## CHAPTER SEVEN

Beautiful XMPP Testing

Remko Tronçon

AT MY FIRST JOB INTERVIEW, ONE OF THE INTERVIEWERS ASKED ME if I knew what "unit testing" was and whether I had used it before. Although I had been developing an XMPP-based instant messaging (IM) client for years, I had to admit that I only vaguely knew what unit testing was, and that I hardly did any automated testing at all. I had a perfectly good reason, though: since XMPP clients are all about XML data, networks, and user interaction, they don't lend themselves well to any form of automated testing. A few months after the interview, the experience of working in an agile environment made me realize how weak that excuse was. It took only a couple of months more to discover how beautiful tests could be, *especially* in environments such as XMPP, where you would least expect them to be.

Introduction

The *eXtensible Messaging and Presence Protocol* (XMPP) is an open, XML-based networking protocol for real-time communication. Only a decade after starting out as an instant messaging solution under the name Jabber, XMPP is today being applied in a broad variety of applications, much beyond instant messaging. These applications include social networking, multimedia interaction (such as voice and video), micro-blogging, gaming, and much more.

In this chapter, I will try to share my enthusiasm about testing in the XMPP world, and more specifically in the Swift IM client (*http://swift.im*). Swift is only one of the many XMPP implementations out there, and may not be the only one that applies the testing methods described here. However, it might be the client that takes the most pride in beautiful tests.

So, what do I consider to be "beautiful testing"? As you've probably discovered by now, opinions on the subject vary greatly. My point of view, being a software developer, is that beauty in tests is about the *code* behind the tests. Naturally, beautiful tests look good aesthetically, so layout plays a role. However, we all know that *true* beauty is actually found within. Beauty in tests is about simplicity; it's about being able to understand what a test (and the system being tested) does with a mere glance at the code, even with little or no prior knowledge about the class or component they test; it's about robustness, and not having to fix dozens of tests on every change; it's about having fun both reading *and* writing the tests.

As you might expect, there is a lot of code in the text that follows. And since I'm taking inspiration from Swift, which is written in C++, the examples in this chapter were written in C++ as well. Using a language like Ruby or Python probably would have made the tests look more attractive, but I stand by my point that true beauty in tests goes deeper than looks.

XMPP 101

Before diving into the details of XMPP implementation testing, let's first have a quick crash course about how XMPP works.

The XMPP network consists of a series of interconnected servers with clients connecting to them, as shown in Figure 7-1. The job of XMPP is to route small "packets" of XML between these entities on the network. For example, Alice, who is connected to the wonderland.lit server, may want to send a message to her sister, who is connected to the realworld.lit server. To do that, she puts her message into a small snippet of XML:

```
<message from="alice@wonderland.lit/RabbitHole"
         to="sister@realworld.lit">
  <body>Hi there</body>
</message>
```

She then delivers this message to her server, which forwards it to the realworld.lit server, which in turn delivers it to her sister's client.

Every entity on the XMPP network is addressed using a *Jabber ID* (JID). A JID has the form *username@domain/resource*, where *domain* is the domain name of the XMPP server and *username* identifies an account on that server. One user can be connected to the server with multiple instances of a client; the *resource* part of the JID gives a unique name to every connected instance. In some cases, the resource part can be left out, which means the server can route the message to whichever connected instance it deems best.

The small packets of XML that are routed through the network are called *stanzas*, and fall into three categories: *message* stanzas, *presence* stanzas, and *info/query* stanzas. Each type of stanza is routed differently by servers, and handled differently by clients.

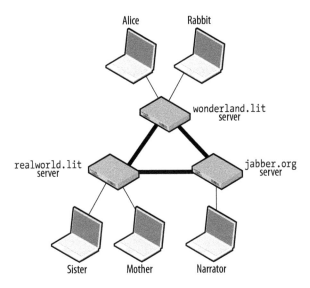

FIGURE 7-1. The decentralized architecture of the XMPP Network; clients connect to servers from different domains, which in turn connect to each other

Message stanzas

Provide a basic mechanism to get information from one entity to another. As the name implies, message stanzas are typically used to send (text) messages to each other.

Presence stanzas

"Broadcast" information from one entity to many entities on the network. For example, Alice may want to notify all of her friends that she is currently not available for communication, so she sends out the following presence stanza:

```
<presence from="alice@wonderland.lit/Home">
  <show>away</show>
  <status>Down the rabbit hole!</status>
</presence>
```

Her server then forwards this stanza to each of her contacts, informing them of Alice's unavailability.

Info/query (IQ) stanzas

Provide a mechanism for request/response interactions between entities, typically used to query or change information on a given entity. For example, Alice could be interested in knowing what client version her sister is using. She therefore sends the following stanza to her sister:

```
<iq type="get" id="aad8a" ❶
    from="alice@wonderland.lit/RabbitHole" to="sister@realworld.lit/Home">
  <query xmlns="jabber:iq:version"/> ❷
</iq>
```

❶ The unique identifier of the stanza is used to match an incoming IQ result to the original IQ request.

❷ An empty child element (or *payload*) in a specific namespace indicates what type of information is requested (in this case, software version information).

Upon receiving this request, her sister's client immediately responds with the name and version of her client software:

```
<iq type="result" id="aad8a" ❶
    from="sister@realworld.lit/Home" to="alice@wonderland.lit/RabbitHole">
  <query xmlns="jabber:iq:version"> ❷
    <name>Swift</name>
    <version>1.0</version>
  </query>
</iq>
```

❶ The `id` attribute of the response matches the one from the request.

❷ The response's payload contains the result of the query.

Stanzas carry information in their *payloads*, which are added as child elements of the stanza. For example, a message can have a `body` payload containing the body text of the message. Different types of payloads are handled differently. By using XML namespaces for payloads, the XMPP protocol can easily be extended to support a virtually unlimited amount of information types, without having to worry about conflicting payload element names. For example, many of the early XMPP protocol extensions (including the software version protocol used in the examples) use the `query` payload. By using namespaces such as `jabber:iq:version`, entities know which type of protocol they are dealing with when they receive a `query` payload, and they know how to interpret the payload.

This section only scratched the surface of XMPP, just enough to get you through the rest of this chapter. If you want to learn more about how XMPP works and what you can do with it, have a look at [XMPP TDG] (see "References" on page 102), or visit *http://xmpp.org*.

Testing XMPP Protocols

One of the important aspects of an XMPP application, be it client or server, is the actual implementation of the XMPP *protocols*. Every XMPP implementation needs to at least implement the XMPP core protocols, as standardized by the IETF in [RFC 3920] and [RFC 3921]. These protocols provide the basic building blocks for XMPP, describing how an XMPP connection is set up, and what you can send over it. On top of the core protocols, the XMPP Standards Foundation created an ever-growing list of *XMPP Extension Protocols* (XEPs). These specifications describe how to extend the core protocol for very specific features, ranging from simple things such as requesting the software version of another client (standardized in [XEP-0092]), up to complex protocols for negotiating audio/video conference calls between clients, transferring files, and so on.

This text focuses on testing the functionality of XMPP protocol implementations, answering questions such as, "Does my client correctly respond to incoming requests?", "Does my client send the right requests at the right time?", "Can my client handle this specific response on this request?", and so on. We start out by looking at the most simple request-response protocols, after which we gradually move up the ladder to more complex protocols. While the complexity of the protocols increases, the level at which the tests are written becomes higher as well, moving from very specific unit tests up to full system tests. Although testing is mainly described from the perspective of a client developer, most of the approaches used here apply to server testing as well.

Unit Testing Simple Request-Response Protocols

Many of the XMPP protocols are simple: one side sends an IQ request, the other side receives the request, processes it, and responds with an IQ result. An example of such a simple request-response protocol is the software version protocol illustrated earlier. An implementation of this protocol consists of two parts:

- The *initiator* implementation sends a software version request and processes the corresponding response when it comes in.
- The *responder* listens for incoming software version requests and responds to them.

These implementations are typically implemented locally in one class for the initiator and one for the responder.[1] Example 7-1 shows how a VersionResponder class is instantiated in a client to respond to incoming software version requests. All this class does is listen for an incoming IQ query of the type jabber:iq:version, and respond with the values set through setVersion. The class uses the central XMPPClient class to send data to and receive data from the XMPP connection.

EXAMPLE 7-1. Using VersionResponder to listen and respond to software version requests

```
class MyClient {
  MyClient() {
    xmppClient = new XMPPClient("alice@wonderland.lit", "mypass");
    versionResponder = new VersionResponder(xmppClient);
    versionResponder->setVersion("Swift", "0.1");
    xmppClient->connect();
  }
  ...
};
```

Since the implementation of request-response protocols is local to one class, *unit testing* is a good way to test the functionality of the protocol implementation. So, let's see how we can unit test the VersionResponder class.

---

1. Some implementations are even known to put both responder and initiator implementations in one class. Don't try this at home, kids!

First, we need to make sure we can create an isolated instance of Responder. The only dependency this class has is the XMPPClient, a class that sets up and manages the XMPP connection. Setting up and managing a connection involves quite some work, and in turn brings in other dependencies, such as network interaction, authentication, encryption mechanisms, and so on. Luckily, all VersionResponder needs to be able to do is send and receive data from a data stream. It therefore only needs to depend on a DataChannel interface, which provides a method to send data and a signal to receive data, as shown in Example 7-2. This interface, implemented by Client, can be easily mocked in our unit test.

EXAMPLE 7-2. Abstracting out data interaction in a DataChannel interface; the XMPPClient class is a concrete implementation of this interface

```
class DataChannel {
  public:
    virtual void sendData(const string& data) = 0;
    boost::signal<void (const string&)> onDataReceived; ❶
};
```

❶ The signal onDataReceived has one string parameter (and no return value). When the signal is emitted, the string argument containing the data received will be passed to the connected slot method.

Now that we have all the ingredients for testing our VersionResponder, let's have a first attempt at writing a unit test. Example 7-3 shows how we can test the basic behavior of the responder, using a mock data channel to generate and catch incoming and outgoing data, respectively.

EXAMPLE 7-3. Testing VersionResponder using raw serialized XML data

```
void VersionResponderTest::testHandleIncomingRequest() {
  // Set up the test fixture
  MockDataChannel dataChannel;
  VersionResponder responder(&dataChannel);
  responder.setVersion("Swift", "1.0");

  // Fake incoming request data on the data channel
  dataChannel.onDataReceived(
    "<iq type='get' from='alice@wonderland.lit/RabbitHole' id='version-1'>"
      "<query xmlns='jabber:iq:version'/>"
    "</iq>");

  // Verify the outcome
  ASSERT_EQUAL(
    "<iq type='result' to='alice@wonderland.lit/RabbitHole' id='version-1'>"
      "<query xmlns='jabber:iq:version'>"
        "<name>Swift</name>"
        "<version>1.0</version>"
      "</query>"
    "</iq>",
    dataChannel.sentData);
}
```

On first sight, this unit test doesn't look too bad: it's relatively short, easy to understand, structured according to the rules of unit testing style, and isolates testing of the protocol from the low-level network aspects of XMPP. However, the beauty of this test is only skin-deep, as the test turns out to be pretty *fragile*. To see this, we need to look at how XMPP implementations generate the response to a request.

Whenever an XMPP client generates an XML stanza, it typically constructs the XML of the stanza by building up a structured document (e.g., using a *Document Object Model* [DOM] API), and then *serializes* this document into a textual XML representation, which is then sent over the network. In Example 7-3, our test records exactly the serialized XML stanza generated by the responder being tested, and then compares it to a piece of XML that it expects. The problem with this approach is that the same XML element can be serialized in different correct ways. For example, we could have switched the order of the from and type attributes of the <iq/> element and still have a logically equivalent stanza. This means that the smallest change to the way stanzas are serialized could break *all* tests.

One solution to avoid the fragility caused by XML serialization is to ensure that serialized stanzas are always in *Canonical XML* form (see [XML-C14n]). By normalizing away nonmeaningful properties such as attribute order and whitespace, this subset of XML ensures that two equivalent XML stanzas can be compared in a stable way, thus solving the fragility of our tests. Unfortunately, since XMPP implementations typically use off-the-shelf XML implementations, they often have no control over how XML is serialized, and as such cannot make use of this trick to compare stanzas.

The solution most XMPP implementations take to verify responses is to check the structured DOM form of the response instead of comparing the serialized form. As shown in Example 7-4, this means that our VersionResponder no longer uses an interface to send raw data, but instead depends on a more structured XMLElementChannel interface to send and receive stanzas as XML element data structures.

EXAMPLE 7-4. Testing VersionResponder using the structured XML representation; this test is no longer influenced by changes in the way the XML stanzas are serialized for transferring (e.g., different attribute order, extra whitespace)

```
void VersionResponderTest::testHandleIncomingRequest() {
  // Set up the test fixture
  MockXMLElementChannel xmlElementChannel;
  VersionResponder responder(&xmlElementChannel);
  responder.setVersion("Swift", "1.0");

  // Fake incoming request stanza on the stanza channel
  xmlElementChannel.onXMLElementReceived(XMLElement::fromString(
    "<iq type='get' from='alice@wonderland.lit/RabbitHole' id='version-1'>"
      "<query xmlns='jabber:iq:version'/>"
    "</iq>"));

  // Verify the outcome
  ASSERT_EQUAL(1, xmlElementChannel.sentXMLElements.size());
  XMLElement response = xmlElementChannel.sentXMLElements[0];
```

```
    ASSERT_EQUAL("iq", response.getTagName());
    ASSERT_EQUAL("result", response.getAttribute("type"));
    ASSERT_EQUAL("id", response.getAttribute("version-1"));
    ASSERT_EQUAL("alice@wonderland.lit/RabbitHole", response.getAttribute("to"));
    XMLElement queryElement = response.getElementByTagNameNS(
        "query", "jabber:iq:version");
    ASSERT(queryElement.isValid());
    XMLElement nameElement = queryElement.getElementByTagName("name");
    ASSERT(nameElement.isValid());
    ASSERT_EQUAL("Swift", nameElement.getText());
    XMLElement versionElement = queryElement.getElementByTagName("version");
    ASSERT(versionElement.isValid());
    ASSERT_EQUAL("1.0", versionElement.getText());
}
```

A downside of this test is that it is slightly less appealing than the one from Example 7-3. For this one test, the fact that it has become less compact and readable is only a small price to pay. However, suppose now that we also want to test the case where the user didn't provide a version to the version responder, in which case we want to send back "Unknown version" as a version string. This test would in fact look exactly like Example 7-4, except that the call to setVersion will pass an empty string instead of "1.0", and the test would compare the version to "Unknown version". Needless to say, this is a lot of duplicated code just to test a small difference in behavior, which will only get worse the more complex our protocol is (and hence the more tests it needs).

A first part of the duplication lies in checking whether the responder sends an <iq/> stanza of type result, whether it is addressed to the sender of the original stanza, and whether the identifier matches that of the request. This part can be easily factored out into a "generic" responder base class and tested separately.

A second problem with our test is the fact that we need to analyze the structure of the XML to extract the values we want to test. The real underlying problem here is the fact that our tests are testing two things at once: the *logic* of the protocol (i.e., *what* it should respond) and the *representation* of the responses (i.e., *how* the request and response is represented in XML).

To separate the logic from the representation in our test, we adapt our VersionResponder to work on a high-level IQ data structure, which in turn contains high-level Payload data structures representing the payloads they carry. Using these abstract data structures, we can now focus on testing the VersionResponder's functionality, without worrying about how the IQ and Payload data structures are actually represented in XML. The resulting test can be seen in Example 7-5.

EXAMPLE 7-5. Testing the logic of VersionResponder; the actual (XML) representation of the stanzas sent and received by VersionResponder are no longer explicitly present in this test, making the test resistant against changes in representation

```
void VersionResponderTest::testHandleIncomingRequest() {
    // Set up the test fixture
    MockIQChannel iqChannel;
    VersionResponder responder(&iqChannel);
```

```
  responder.setVersion("Swift");

  // Fake incoming request stanza on the stanza channel
  iqChannel.onIQReceived(IQ(IQ::Get, new VersionPayload()));

  // Verify the outcome
  ASSERT_EQUAL(1, iqChannel.sentIQs.size());
  const VersionPayload* payload =
    iqChannel.sentIQs[0].getPayload<VersionPayload>();
  ASSERT(payload);
  ASSERT_EQUAL("Swift", payload->getName());
  ASSERT_EQUAL("Unknown version", payload->getVersion());
}
```

The conversion from the VersionPayload structure to XML can now be tested independently, as illustrated in Example 7-6. Although this test still isn't very attractive, the clutter coming from the representational part no longer impacts the tests for the more important behavioral part of the protocol.

EXAMPLE 7-6. Testing the conversion of VersionPayload to XML

```
void VersionPayloadSerializerTest::testSerialize() {
  // Set up the test fixture
  VersionPayloadSerializer serializer;
  VersionPayload payload;
  payload.setVersion("Swift", "1.0");

  // Serialize a payload
  XMLElement result = serializer.serialize(payload);

  // Verify the serialized element
  ASSERT_EQUAL("query", result.getTagName());
  ASSERT_EQUAL("jabber:iq:version", result.getNamespace());
  XMLElement* nameElement = queryElement->getElementsByTagName("name");
  ASSERT(nameElement);
  ASSERT_EQUAL("Swift", nameElement->getText());
  XMLElement* versionElement = queryElement->getElementsByTagName("version");
  ASSERT(versionElement);
  ASSERT_EQUAL("1.0", versionElement->getText());
}
```

In this section, we discussed how to test a simple IQ-based request/response protocol. In our first attempt, we tested the protocol at the lowest level possible, by analyzing the actual data sent over the wire. Subsequent versions tested the logic of the protocol at a higher, more structured level, up to the point where the logic of the responder was tested independently of the actual representation of the data sent over the network. Although it might seem overkill to separate the XML parsing and serializing from the actual data structure for a simple protocol like the one shown here, it makes testing the more complex (multistage) protocols from the next sections a lot cleaner.

Unit Testing Multistage Protocols

So far, the class of protocols we have considered was rather simple: one side sent out a request, the other side responded, and we were done. Although many of the XMPP protocols fall within this category, there are several others that consist of multiple iterations of these request-response cycles. These protocols start by doing a request, and then take subsequent steps based on the response of previous requests. Testing these types of protocols is the focus of this section.

Besides person-to-person conversations, XMPP also allows users to join chat "rooms" to communicate with multiple people at once. Whenever a user wants to join such a *multiuser chat* (MUC for short), an IM client needs to detect the MUC rooms that are available on a server and present this list to the server. Obtaining this list requires a chain of multiple *service discovery* (often called *disco* in the XMPP world) requests. For example, let's assume Alice wants to get a list of all the available rooms on the wonderland.lit server. She starts by requesting all the available services of her server, which is done by sending a disco#items request to the server:

```
<iq type="get" id="muc-1" to="wonderland.lit">
  <query xmlns="http://jabber.org/protocol/disco#items"/>
</iq>
```

The server then responds with the list of all its services:

```
<iq type="result" id="muc-1"
    from="wonderland.lit" to="alice@wonderland.lit/RabbitHole">
  <query xmlns="http://jabber.org/protocol/disco#items">
    <item jid="pubsub.wonderland.lit"/>
    <item jid="rooms.wonderland.lit"/>
  </query>
</iq>
```

Alice now needs to determine which one of these services provides chat rooms. She therefore sends a disco#info request to each service, asking them which protocols they support:

```
<iq type="get" id="muc-2" to="pubsub.wonderland.lit">
  <query xmlns="http://jabber.org/protocol/disco#info"/>
</iq>

<iq type="get" id="muc-3" to="rooms.wonderland.lit">
  <query xmlns="http://jabber.org/protocol/disco#info"/>
</iq>
```

The first service responds:

```
<iq type="result" id="muc-2"
    from="pubsub.wonderland.lit" to="alice@wonderland.lit/RabbitHole">
  <query xmlns="http://jabber.org/protocol/disco#info">
    <feature var="http://jabber.org/protocol/pubsub"/>
  </query>
</iq>
```

This service seems to support only the PubSub protocol (feature), which is not what Alice was looking for. The second service, however, responds with the following feature list:

```
<iq type="result" id="muc-3"
    from="rooms.wonderland.lit" to="alice@wonderland.lit/RabbitHole">
  <query xmlns="http://jabber.org/protocol/disco#info">
    <feature var="http://jabber.org/protocol/muc"/>
  </query>
</iq>
```

Bingo! Now that she found the MUC service, all she needs to do is ask for the list of rooms, which is done using another disco#items request:

```
<iq type="get" id="muc-4" to="rooms.wonderland.lit">
  <query xmlns="http://jabber.org/protocol/disco#items"/>
</iq>
```

This request results in the list of all the MUC rooms on the rooms.wonderland.lit server (in this case, a tea party and a room for discussing croquet):

```
<iq type="result" id="muc-4"
    from="rooms.wonderland.lit" to="alice@wonderland.lit/RabbitHole">
  <query xmlns="http://jabber.org/protocol/disco#items">
    <item jid="teaparty@rooms.wonderland.lit"/>
    <item jid="croquet@rooms.wonderland.lit"/>
  </query>
</iq>
```

As you can tell from this scenario, a lot of stanzas are going back and forth. Things become even more complex if you take into consideration that every step can result in an error response from the responding entity. Testing this protocol therefore involves multiple tests, for determining whether our client can handle every type of response from the server, both successful and unsuccessful. Luckily, because of the high level at which we test our protocols, creating a test for one scenario can be very compact and straightforward. For example, a test for the "happy," error-less scenario described earlier is shown in Example 7-7.

EXAMPLE 7-7. Testing RoomDiscoverer

```
void RoomDiscovererTest::testDiscoverRooms() {
  // Set up the responses
  itemsResponses["wonderland.lit"] = ❶
    DiscoItems("pubsub.wonderland.lit", "rooms.wonderland.lit");
  infoResponses["pubsub.wonderland.lit"] = ❷
    DiscoInfo("http://jabber.org/protocol/pubsub");
  itemsResponses["pubsub.wonderland.lit"] = ❸
    DiscoItems("blogs@pubsub.wonderland.lit", "croquet@pubsub.wonderland.lit");
  infoResponses["rooms.wonderland.lit"] = ❹
    DiscoInfo("http://jabber.org/protocol/muc");
  itemsResponses["rooms.wonderland.lit"] = ❺
    DiscoItems("teaparty@rooms.wonderland.lit", "croquet@rooms.wonderland.lit");

  // Set up room discoverer
  RoomDiscoverer discoverer(channel);
```

```
    // Execute room discovery
    discoverer.discoverRooms();

    // Test results
    ASSERT(discoverer.isFinished());
    StringList rooms = discoverer.getDiscoveredRooms();
    ASSERT_EQUAL(2, rooms.size());
    ASSERT(rooms.contains("teaparty@rooms.wonderland.lit"));
    ASSERT(rooms.contains("croquet@rooms.wonderland.lit"));
}
```

❶ Specify the response to a disco#items request for the top-level wonderland.lit domain. In this case, two items are returned: pubsub and rooms.

❷ Specify the response to a disco#info request for the pubsub service. In this case, respond with the namespace of the PubSub protocol.

❸ Specify the items belonging to the pubsub service. These are added to test whether RoomDiscoverer doesn't pick up items from non-MUC services.

❹ Respond that the rooms service supports MUC.

❺ Specify the list of items (i.e., rooms) of the MUC service.

The test specifies what responses should be sent for both disco#info and disco#items queries directed to specific JIDs. The RoomDiscoverer (which is the class that is responsible for discovering rooms) is then put in action, after which the test checks whether it indeed discovered both MUC rooms (and didn't accidentally include the PubSub service items). Not only is the test simple, but the auxiliary methods used by this test (including the fixture setup and tear down) can be kept very simple as well, as can be seen in Example 7-8.

EXAMPLE 7-8. Setting up the RoomDiscovererTest fixture

```
void RoomDiscovererTest::setUp() {
  channel = new MockIQChannel();
  channel->onSendIQ.connect(bind(&RoomDiscovererTest::respondToIQ, this, _1)); ❶
}

void RoomDiscovererTest::tearDown() {
  delete channel;
}

void RoomDiscovererTest::respondToIQ(const IQ& iq) {
  ASSERT(iq.getType() == IQ::Get);
  if (iq.getPayload<DiscoItems>()) {
    ItemsResponseMap::const_iterator response = itemsResponses.find(iq.getTo());
    ASSERT(response != itemsResponses.end());
    channel->onIQReceived(iq.createResponse(new DiscoItems(response->second)));
  }
  else if (iq.getPayload<DiscoInfo>()) {
    InfoResponseMap::const_iterator response = infoResponses.find(iq.getTo());
    ASSERT(response != infoResponses.end());
    channel->onIQReceived(iq.createResponse(new DiscoInfo(response->second)));
```

```
  }
  else {
    FAIL("Unexpected IQ");
  }
}
```

❶ Whenever an IQ is sent, pass it to `respondToIQ`, which will respond to it.

In this section, I showed how you can apply the high level of testing described in the previous section on more complex multistage protocols. Because the tests aren't cluttered by low-level protocol representational details, the tests can focus on testing the actual logic of the protocol, allowing the number of tests to grow without compromising the beauty of the protocol test suite.

Testing Session Initialization

By looking at both the single- and multistage request/response protocols from the previous sections, we covered most of the XMPP protocols out there. Although the level of testing for these protocols was already rather high, some protocols are still so complex that even testing at the level of "abstract" payloads results in too much clutter for a beautiful test. These are typically protocols that have a complex state diagram, and possibly even require user input during the process. We therefore bring in a higher level of testing: *scenario testing*.

One of the most complex protocols in XMPP is *session initialization*. Session initialization in an IM client involves creating a connection to the server; negotiating parameters of the connection (e.g., using stream compression for lower bandwidth consumption, encrypting the stream for better security, and so on); and finally authenticating with the server (typically involving sending a username and password to the server). Which parameters to negotiate with the server depends on what features the client and the server support, and also on the user preferences of the client. For example, a server might not support stream encryption; depending on whether the user has stated that he only wants to communicate over an encrypted connection, the client should either report an error or fall back on an unencrypted connection, respectively.

Testing all the possible code paths in session initialization requires a concise way of describing a session initialization scenario. Example 7-9 shows such a scenario test where the client encrypts the connection. By introducing helper methods describing what the client is supposed to send and what the server would send in response, we can clearly see how the encryption scenario is supposed to happen. It is easy to create scenarios for error conditions such as the server not supporting encryption (as shown in Example 7-10), and even to test the client's reaction to failing network connections (shown in Example 7-11). Moreover, creating these helper methods doesn't require all that much code, as they involve only setting expectations and responses on payloads, which can be written at the same level as the sections before.

EXAMPLE 7-9. Testing session encryption negotiation

```
void SessionTest::testStart_Encrypt() {
  Session* session = createSession("alice@wonderland.lit/RabbitHole");
  session->setEncryptConnection(Session::EncryptWhenAvailable);
  session->start();

  sessionOpensConnection();
  serverAcceptsConnection();
  sessionSendsStreamStart(); ❶
  serverSendsStreamStart(); ❷
  serverSendsStreamFeaturesWithStartTLS(); ❸
  sessionSendsStartTLS(); ❹
  serverSendsTLSProceed(); ❺

  ASSERT(session->isNegotiatingTLS());

  completeTLSHandshake(); ❻
  sessionSendsStreamStart(); /* (*) Immediately after the handshake, the
    stream is reset, and the stream header is resent in an encrypted form. */
  serverSendsStreamStart();

  ASSERT(session->isConnected());
  ASSERT(session->isEncrypted());
}
```

❶ Before sending XML elements over the stream, the client initializes the stream by sending an opening <stream> tag. All subsequent elements are children of this element. When the connection is closed, the closing </stream> tag is sent.

❷ Similar to the client, the server also starts the stream by sending a <stream> tag.

❸ Immediately after sending the opening stream tag, the server sends a list of all the features it supports. In this case, it announces support for stream encryption using StartTLS.

❹ The client sends a <starttls/> element to request the server to encrypt the connection.

❺ The server responds with a <proceed/>, indicating that the TLS negotiation (or *handshake*) can start.

❻ Fake a successful TLS handshake.

EXAMPLE 7-10. Testing session failure due to the server not supporting encryption

```
void SessionTest::testStart_ForceEncyptWithoutServerSupport() {
  Session* session = createSession("alice@wonderland.lit/RabbitHole");
  session->setEncryptConnection(Session::AlwaysEncrypt);
  session->start();

  sessionOpensConnection();
  serverAcceptsConnection();
  sessionSendsStreamStart();
  serverSendsStreamStart();
  serverSendsStreamFeaturesWithoutStartTLS();
```

```
  ASSERT(session->hasError());
}
```

EXAMPLE 7-11. Testing session failure due to a failing connection

```
void SessionTest::testStart_FailingConnection() {
  Session* session = createSession("alice@wonderland.lit/RabbitHole");
  session->start();

  sessionOpensConnection();
  serverAcceptsConnection();
  sessionSendsStreamStart();
  serverSendsStreamStart();
  closeConnection();

  ASSERT(session->hasError());
}
```

With scenario-based testing, it is possible to test the most complex class of protocols, covering all their corner cases. Although many of the corner cases of each "stage" in such protocols can be tested separately in isolation, scenarios are still needed to test the interaction between the multiple stages of the protocol.

Automated Interoperability Testing

By using unit tests to test our protocols in isolation (without a real network connection to an XMPP server), we were able to test all corner cases of a protocol while keeping our tests clean, simple, fast, and reliable. However, an XMPP client doesn't live in isolation; its purpose is to eventually connect to a *real* XMPP server and talk to *real* clients. Testing an XMPP client in the real world is important for several reasons. First of all, it allows you to check the functionality of your application at a larger scale than the local unit testing, ensuring that all the components work together correctly. Second, by communicating with other XMPP protocol implementations, you can test whether your interpretation of the protocol specification is correct. Finally, by testing your client against many different XMPP implementations, you are able to ensure interoperability with a wide collection of XMPP software. Unless you are developing a dedicated client to connect to only one specific server, testing interoperability with other clients and servers is very important in an open, heterogeneous network such as XMPP.

Because IM clients are driven by a user interface, testing interoperability between two clients is typically done manually: both clients are started, they connect to a server, an operation is triggered through the user interface of one client, and the other client is checked to determine whether it responds correctly to the operation. Fully automating UI-driven features is very hard.

Testing client-to-server interoperability is somewhat easier than testing client-to-client communication. By creating a small headless test program on top of the client's XMPP protocol implementation, we can test whether the basic XMPP functionality of the backend works correctly, and even test complex protocols such as session initialization in action. For example, consider the test program in Example 7-12. This program logs into the server, fetches the user's contact list (also called the *roster*), and returns successfully if it received the roster from the server. By running this program, we can test whether most parts of our XMPP client's backend work: network connection, session initialization, stream compression, stream encryption, sending IQ requests, notifications of IQ responses, and so on.

EXAMPLE 7-12. A test program to connect to a server and request the roster; the JID and password of the account are passed through the environment

```
XMPPClient* xmppClient = NULL;
bool rosterReceived = false;

int main(int argc, char* argv[]) {
  xmppClient = new XMPPClient(getenv("TEST_JID"), getenv("TEST_PASS"));
  xmppClient->onConnected.connect(&handleConnected); ❶
  xmppClient->connect();
  return rosterReceived;
}

void handleConnected() {
  GetRosterRequest* rosterRequest = new GetRosterRequest(xmppClient);
  rosterRequest->onResponse.connect(bind(&handleRosterResponse, _1, _2)); ❷
  rosterRequest->send();
}

void handleRosterResponse(RosterPayload*, optional<Error> error) {
  rosterReceived = !error; ❸
  xmppClient->disconnect();
}
```

❶ When connected (and authenticated), call `handleConnected`.

❷ When a response for the roster request is received, call `handleRosterReceived` with the response and status as arguments.

❸ If there was no error, we received the roster properly.

A program similar to the one from Example 7-12 is run as part of Swift's automated test suite. We use a few different server implementations on every test run, passing the test JID and password of each server through the environment. If `ClientTest` fails due to a bug in a protocol implementation, a new unit test is added and the protocol is fixed. If the bug is due to a certain combination of protocols not being handled properly (either by the client or by the server), a scenario test is added to reproduce the scenario, after which either the client bug is fixed or the client is adapted to work around a specific server implementation bug.

When using automated tests like the one just described, a project is of course always limited to testing against the implementations it has access to. Although it is always possible to test against the handful of free XMPP server implementations out there, testing against implementations from commercial vendors isn't always straightforward. To make it easier for the XMPP community to test their implementations against each other, there has been an initiative to create a centralized place (*http://interop.xmpp.org*) that provides access to test accounts on all server implementations out there, including ones from commercial vendors.[2] This initiative paves the way to easy, automated interoperability testing for XMPP projects.

Diamond in the Rough: Testing XML Validity

When testing the functionality of our protocol in the previous sections, we separated the stanza representation from the actual logic of the protocol to improve the focus of our tests. This split made testing the logic of the protocol straightforward and clean. Unfortunately, testing the representational part that converts the abstract stanzas into XML and back is still tedious and error-prone. One of the things that needs to be checked is whether every variation of the payload transforms correctly to a standards-compliant XML element. For example, for the version payload we used earlier, we need to test the representation of a payload with and without a version number. Conversely, the transformation from XML to a payload data structure needs to be tested for every possible compliant XML element. It would be handy if we could automatically check whether our XML parser and serializer handles all of the possible variations of payloads and stanzas allowed by the protocol standard.

A possible approach for testing XML parsers and serializers is automated *XML validation*. Every protocol specification published by the XMPP Standards Foundation comes with an *XML schema*. This schema describes the syntax and constraints of the XML used in the protocol. For example, it specifies the names of the XML elements that can occur in the payload, the names and types of the attributes of these elements, the number of times an element can occur, and so on. Such XML schemas are typically used to test whether a piece of XML is syntactically valid according to the rules specified in the schema. Unfortunately, the XMPP schemas currently serve only a descriptive purpose, and are only used to document the protocol. This is why using the XMPP schemas in automated processes, such as validity checking, is still mostly unexplored terrain. However, there has been interest lately in making normative XML schemas, which would open up some more possibilities for making the tedious testing of XMPP parsing and serialization more pleasant and, who knows, even beautiful!

Conclusions

In our quest to create beautiful tests for checking XMPP protocol implementations, we started out by testing simple request-response protocols at the lowest level: the data sent over the network stream. After discovering that this form of testing does not really scale well, we abstracted out the protocol to a higher level, up to the point where the tests used only

---

2. Unfortunately, this initiative has currently been put on hold for more urgent matters, but it will hopefully be revived soon.

high-level data structures. By testing protocol behavior on a high level, we were able to write tests for more complex protocols without compromising the clarity of the tests. For the most complex protocols, writing scenarios helped to cover all of the possible situations that can arise in a protocol session. Finally, since XMPP is an open protocol with many different implementations, it's very important to test an XMPP application on the real network, to ensure interoperability with other implementations. By running small test programs regularly, we were able to test the system in its entirety, and check whether our implementation of the protocol plays together nicely with other entities on the network.

The focus of this chapter has mostly been on testing the protocol functionality in XMPP implementations, as this is probably the most important part of quality control in XMPP. However, many other forms of testing exist in the XMPP world besides protocol tests. For example, performance testing is very crucial in the world of XMPP servers. Simple test scripts or programs like the ones described earlier can be used to generate a high load on the server, to test whether the server can handle increasing amounts of traffic. In XMPP clients, on the other hand, testing the user interface's functionality is very important. Although automated UI testing is known to be hard, many complex parts, such as contact list representation, can be unit tested in isolation, which can avoid bugs in vital pieces of client code.

Although it's already possible to write simple, clean, and thorough tests for many aspects of XMPP, there's still a lot of beauty in testing waiting to be discovered. If you have suggestions or ideas, or want to help work on improving testing in the XMPP community, feel free to stop by *http://xmpp.org* and join the conversation!

References

[XML-C14n] Boyer, John. 2001. *Canonical XML (http://www.w3.org/TR/xml-C14n.html)*.

[DOM] Le Hégaret, Philippe. 2002. The W3C Document Object Model (DOM) (*http://www.w3 .org/2002/07/26-dom-article.html*).

[RFC 3920] Saint-Andre, Peter. 2004. *Extensible Messaging and Presence Protocol: Core (http://www .ietf.org/rfc/rfc3920.txt)*.

[RFC 3921] Saint-Andre, Peter. 2004. *Extensible Messaging and Presence Protocol: Instant Messaging and Presence (http://www.ietf.org/rfc/rfc3921.txt)*.

[XEP-0092] Saint-Andre, Peter. XEP-0092: *Software Version (http://www.xmpp.org/extensions/xep -0092.html)*.

[XMPP TDG] Saint-Andre, Peter. Smith, Kevin. Tronçon, Remko. 2009. *XMPP: The Definitive Guide (http://oreilly.com/catalog/9780596157197/)*. Cambridge: O'Reilly.

## CHAPTER EIGHT

Beautiful Large-Scale Test Automation

Alan Page

AUTOMATED TESTING CAN BE MUCH MORE THAN SIMPLY writing and running tests that operate without human intervention. Alas, for many testers, automated testing consists only of the manual generation of test scripts or code that executes some specified test scenario or piece of product functionality. Consideration of the logistics of running the tests is too often an afterthought of the automation process.

Most testers are familiar with the claim that automated testing has the potential to save time. However, in many cases, test automation doesn't actually save the amount of time that testers and their management team have anticipated. In reality, many automation attempts fail because other than the actual test execution, none of the remainder of the process is automatic. For automation to be successful, especially on a large scale, the entire end-to-end process—from the moment the tester completes the authoring of the test until results are analyzed and available for viewing—must be automatic. Without this level of automation, the amount of time testers spend monitoring automation systems will quickly grow out of hand.

When I was young, my parents went to a fireworks stand and bought one of those big packages of fireworks. We eagerly waited until it got dark, and then our family went outside on our patio and began our show. We had quite a variety of explosions and showers of sparks and were generally entertained. It was a bit of a pain sometimes to try to find some of the fuses in the dark, and a few duds disappointed us, but for the most part, we were adequately amused.

A few years later, I attended my first *professional* fireworks show. Not only were the explosions and sparkles huge, but everything ran a million times smoother than our home fireworks show.

People oohed and aahed at the shapes and marveled over how well the show was synchronized to music. There was nothing wrong with our home fireworks show, but the professional show—due to the size, complexity, and how smoothly it ran—was truly beautiful.

A system where testers spend the majority of their time monitoring progress, examining errors (aka "duds"), and pushing tests and their artifacts from one stage to the next is far from beautiful. Beauty occurs when the entire system reaches a point of automation at which the tester can concentrate on what they do best: testing software.

Before We Start

For this topic, a few words on the approach to automation are in order. These days, there's a bit of a controversy in the testing world centered on when automated tests help test teams and when they stop teams dead in their tracks. Testers are worried about what to automate and how much to automate. Test managers are worried about showing ROI on the investment they've made on automation tools and in writing the tests, and in leveraging their automation investment to the fullest potential.

These testers and their managers often struggle as they try to determine how much of their testing effort they should automate. I have an answer to this dilemma that works for every test team, a metric they can use to make sure they are automating the right amount of tests. The metric is the same for every team, and unlike most metrics, it is always correct. *You should automate 100% of the tests that should be automated*. The metric itself is simple (albeit inherently un-actionable); the difficulty lies in determining exactly *which* tests to automate. Product architecture, stakeholders, schedule, and many other factors can help lead test teams to the correct automation decisions. I see many automation attempts fail because testers spend too much time automating (or attempting to automate) behaviors or scenarios where automation simply isn't worth the effort in the first place. Likewise, test automation efforts also can fail when testers fail to automate tasks that are clearly prime targets for automation. Deciding which tests to automate is extremely difficult and up to the test team and stakeholders to determine for their particular situation (and fortunately for the attention span of the reader, far beyond the scope of this chapter).

Also, note that for the sake of this essay, I'm referring to testing performed by an independent test team. Automation is the perfect and commonly acceptable solution for developer-written unit tests. The difficult decisions about what tests to automate typically occur in areas such as end-to-end scenarios or advanced GUI manipulation, or other areas where a human set of eyes and a brain are sometimes the most efficient oracle for determining success.

What Is Large-Scale Test Automation?

On a small software product, it may be possible for a single tester to write and run automated tests from his desk and report results via email or by manually updating a web page or spreadsheet. Testers are also likely responsible for entering bugs for any issues discovered by the tests, and verifying that resolved bugs are fixed. For a system to be capable of handling thousands of tests or more distributed across hundreds of machines, the system must, at every step—from the moment test authoring is complete to the point where results are available—be completely automatic. Manual support for automated testing can take a significant amount of testing time away from the test team. Before we discuss implementation and architecture details of such a system, it will be helpful to discuss the workflow and the life of tests in an automation system.

The Basics of a Test Automation System

Even the bare necessities of a beautiful automation system enable efficiencies from end to end, but automation systems come in all shapes, sizes, and ranges of splendor. For all test teams that use automated tests, some basic steps are common. Figure 8-1 shows a basic automation test workflow.

FIGURE 8-1. Automated test life cycle workflow

Somewhere at or near the beginning of testing, a tester will write one or more automated tests. Testers may create *test suites* (a set of tests targeting a particular area or small feature) as well. They may write scripts, such as JavaScript, or create a compiled binary written in a language such as C# or C++. At some point in the process, the tests inevitably execute and a process (or person) tracks test results (e.g., "Pass" or "Fail"). Once the test results are available, the tester enters newly discovered errors into the bug tracking system, and may cross-reference fixed bugs to ensure that the relevant tests are now correctly passing.

The problem with the basics is that there are numerous scenarios where manual intervention may be necessary. Once the tester writes his tests, it may be his responsibility to copy the scripts or binaries (along with any needed support files) to a network share where other testers can access them. In other cases, the tester may be responsible for running the tests himself, analyzing the results, and reporting. Often, the tester is also responsible for entering bugs to correspond with failed tests, and verifying that bugs resolved as fixed truly are fixed.

A Beautiful System

The end-to-end automation process can certainly be more eye-catching. Let's look at what a more sophisticated automation system and process might look like.

Once the tester completes the authoring of their code or script, they check it into a source control management system (SCM), where an automated build process builds the tests. Once the building process is complete, the system copies tests and support files to a common location where testers (as well as the tools that make up the automation system) can access them. Configuration of the systems used for running the tests happens automatically. The deployment to these machines and subsequent execution occurs automatically. A common database stores all test results for easy reporting and analysis. Finally, the system automatically records test failures in the bug database.

Even in a system such as this, there are many stages where nonautomated tasks can begin to monopolize a tester's time. I've personally seen many test teams create thousands of automated tests thinking that they will save massive amounts of testing time, but end up spending countless hours on the work surrounding those same automated tests. Indeed, on many teams, the testers spend so much time babysitting tests and analyzing test results that they have little time left for actual testing.

The First Steps

The first step for success is simple: write great tests. Many test teams set themselves up for failure by holding the quality bar for their test code to much lower standards than their product code. Teams that write poor tests in an effort to save time almost always end up putting a large effort into maintaining their tests and investigating failed tests.

Test code must be easily maintainable. Whether the tests are going to be around for 10 days or 10 years, on a large team, chances are that someone other than the author will have to read, debug, or modify the code at some point. On many teams I've observed, once authoring of an automated test and integration of that test into the system are complete, that test remains in the system forever (unless, of course, the team removes the component under test from the product). Whether or not the "once a test, always a test" concept is appropriate (as well as mitigation techniques for the issue) is a topic for a different essay.

Code reviews and static analysis of the test code are also important. Hardcoded paths to test servers or hardcoded usernames and passwords are frequent causes of fragile tests, as are hardcoded resource strings that fail the first time the test runs on non-English builds. Tools or scripts that analyze source code at or extremely close to compile time are essential for detecting many common programming errors such as these.

Finally, it's critical that test code is under source control and builds in a central location. Source control eases maintenance by enabling testers to investigate an entire history of changes to test code, overlaying infrastructure or "collateral" (noncode files used by the tests, such as media files or input data). Frequent builds or continuous integration are just as applicable to test code as they are to product code. Central builds allow the latest tests to run on every build of the production code, and ensure that tests are available from a central location. If testers build their own tests and are responsible for copying the tests to a server, mistakes are eventually bound to occur. A central build also enables the embedding of consistent version information into every test. Version information greatly simplifies debugging when tests suddenly begin to fail or behave differently than expected.

Test Infrastructure Is Critical

All of the statements in the previous section apply directly to test infrastructure and tools. Chances are that if your team has a system similar to the one described in this essay, the development of at least some parts of the system occurs in-house. Moreover, these testing tools need to be inherently reliable and trusted. I have watched test teams struggle with poor tools and spend time writing workarounds for poor implementation only to have their workarounds break when someone finally gets around to updating the tools.

To that end, code reviews, unit testing, and acceptance testing are critical for all major pieces of a test infrastructure. Nobody wants to use a test tool that wastes testers' time, but nearly everyone wants to use tools that are intuitive, reliable, and just work.

Test Collateral

Another mistake that many teams make is mismanagement of their test collateral. By collateral, I mean data files, documents, add-ins, and any other bits of data used by the tests. It is vital to ensure that all of these files are under source control, but even more critical to guarantee that these files are available in a location that satisfies two key criteria. First, the files must be available to the automated testing system. For example, files on a share accessible to the test team members might not be available to the automation system if it has different access rights on the network. Second, the collateral files need to be stored in a nontemporary location. Sustained engineering or maintenance teams cringe when they inherit tests that attempt to copy collateral from a server or share that doesn't exist anymore.

Mitigation for this issue can include setting up a permanent server for test collateral or using a database to store all collateral items. Regardless of the solution, including a plan for handling test collateral is essential to ensure the robustness of the overall automation system.

Automated Tests and Test Case Management

As the number of test cases grows from hundreds to millions, test case management becomes a critical element of the overall system. In order to track what every test is doing and which tests are passing and failing, all tests need an associated unique identification number. At the very least, assigning test ID numbers enables tracking of test results across a number of testing configurations and scenarios, but it can also enable tracing of requirements or user stories to the tests that verify these requirements or stories.

Unique IDs assigned to individual test cases are a minimum requirement, but implementing a larger set of attributes associated with the test enables a much larger set of functionality.

Table 8-1 shows a small excerpt of test case IDs and samples of associated attributes in a test case management system.

TABLE 8-1. Example test case management identification attributes

Test case ID	Test binary or script	Command line	Configurations	Tags
10001	perfTest.dll	/entry:perfTestOne	All	Performance; Core
10002	perfTest.dll	/entry:perfTestTwo	Main	Performance
11001	scenarioTest.exe	/Persona:Peggy	Main	Scenarios
11002	scenarioTest.exe	/Persona:Carl	Mobile	Scenarios
12001	Applications.js		All	Applications
13002	filesysBVT.dll	/entry:createFileTests /full	Main	FileSystem; BVT
13023	filesysBVT.dll	/entry:usbStorageTests	USBStorage	FileSystem; BVT; USB

A brief explanation of the fields in Table 8-1 follow:

Test case ID

This is a globally unique identifier assigned to each test. It's not necessary for the numbers to be sequential, but they must be unique. On large systems, a method for automatically assigning unique IDs is necessary. The sidebar "Breaking It All Down" on page 109 explains some common methods for generating IDs.

Test binary or script

Automated tests generally "live" in a binary (EXE or DLL) or a script such as JavaScript, QuickTest Pro, PowerShell, or Python. The system (or harness) that is responsible for running the tests uses the binary or script name when executing the tests.

Command line

The test system uses the command line along with the binary or script name in order to run the test. This enables customization, such as adding data references for data-driven tests, or enables the isolation of single tests within larger test files so they can run independently.

Configurations

Early in planning for a software application or system, the team will define the configurations where the software will run. The configurations may be based on common installation scenarios, languages, or compatible platforms. For example, a team building a web portal and service may decide that valid test platforms are the last two versions of Internet Explorer and Firefox, and the latest versions of Chrome, Safari, and Opera. It's likely that not every test will need to run on every platform. For some test teams, the excitement of test automation encourages them to run *every* test on *every* build. In the end, what these teams find is an abundance of redundant test and an automated test pass that takes far too long to complete to be helpful. Smartly tagging tests using pair-wise or other methods of matrix reduction for determining test configurations is a smarter way to deploy large-scale automation.

Tags

Tags are an optional method of describing additional metadata about the test. With tags in place, both the test run and the reporting of results are easily customizable. Running all "performance tests," for example, is simple if all performance tests are tagged as such. With multiple tags, it's also just as easy to view all results with similar customizations, or to drill down into special areas. Example queries could be "from all tests, view just performance tests" or "from all File System tests, show BVT tests, except for those run on Windows XP".

BREAKING IT ALL DOWN

For test automation authors, it often makes architectural sense to create several tests within one test binary. One of the most common approaches is to write test cases in a library (a *.dll* on Windows), and use a "test harness" to run the tests within the DLL.

For managed (e.g., C# or VB.NET) test binaries, attributes are a commonly used method:

```
[TestCaseAttribute( "Checkout Tests", ID=1)]
public TestResult BuyItems()
{
    TestResult.AddComment("executing Checkout Tests: Buy One Item");
    //implementation removed ...
    return TestResult.Pass;
}
[TestCaseAttribute( "Checkout Tests", ID=2)]
public TestResult BuyItems()
{
    TestResult.AddComment("executing Checkout Tests: Buy Zero Items");
    //code removed ...
    return TestResult.Pass;
}
```

The harness (or "runner") for managed code uses .NET Reflection to discover and run the tests in the library. Unit test frameworks such as NUnit and MSTest use this method to execute tests embedded in managed libraries.

Native (e.g., C or C++) binaries can use an alternate method of assigning tests to internal library functions. One somewhat common method is to embed a table within the library containing function addresses and other information about the test:

```
struct functionTable[] =
{
    { "Checkout tests: Buy one Item", 101, BuyItems, 1 },
    { "Checkout tests: Buy invalid number of items (0)", 102, BuyItems, 0 },
    { "Checkout tests: Buy negative number of items (-1)", 103, BuyItems, -1 },
    { "Checkout tests: Buying Scenario_One", 104, BuyingScenarioOne, 0 },
    // ...
};
```

The layout of the structure in this simple example contains four elements. They are:

Test description

A plain-text description of the test (likely used in logging and reporting).

Test ID

Unique identifier of the test.

Function pointer

Address of the function that the harness should call for this test.

Optional parameters

Value for the harness to pass to the function specified in the function pointer. This allows the test author to create one test function that, depending on a parameter, executes multiple test cases.

In the structure listed here, the description of the first test is "Checkout tests: Buy one Item," the Test ID is 104, the function called by the harness is BuyItems, and the parameter passed to the function is the value 1. There are, of course, multiple methods for implementing a test harness in native code, but this approach is simple and likely common.

A simple method that native code test harnesses can use to obtain information about tests in a library is for each test library to have an entry point that dumps the test IDs and entry points for all tests. Other than being useful for those wanting a quick method for determining which tests are in a binary, automation tools can manually parse this data in order to create test cases in a test case manager directly from the descriptions and unique IDs within a test binary:

```
void PrintFunctionTable()
{
    // display descriptions, entry points, test ID and parameters
    // for functionTable
}
```

There's one remaining hurdle to address. In a large system with hundreds of test libraries written by dozens of testers, it's virtually impossible to guarantee that test IDs will be unique across the test binaries or scripts. In the code excerpts shown earlier, for example, the managed function "Checkout Tests" and the native function "Checkout tests: Buy one Item" are both assigned the same ID.

One solution is to assign a bank of test IDs to each tester. As long as testers only use the IDs assigned to them, there's no problem. The usefulness of this solution fades quickly as testers come and go on a project, and as test libraries are shared between teams. A much better solution, of course, is an automated solution. One way to accomplish this is to use a test harness or a similar tool and take steps such as the following in order to assign unique IDs to every test across an entire product:

1. Obtain the embedded test information from a library using the techniques described earlier (Reflection for managed code or a function table for native code).

2. Create new unique IDs for each test in the library.

3. Store a mapping of the library name, original ID, and unique ID in a database (see Table 8-2). The ID mappings enable uniqueness of IDs across a large system with minimal impact to the individual testers' authoring needs.

TABLE 8-2. Table with mapping of local IDs to global IDs

Library name	Local ID	Unique ID	Command line (samples)
buyTest.dll	1	1000001	harness.exe buyTest.dll/id:1
buyTest.dll	2	1000002	harness.exe buyTest.dll/id:1
shoppingTest.dll	1	1100001	nHarness.exe shoppingTest.dll 1
shoppingTest.dll	2	1100002	nHarness.exe shoppingTest.dll 2
shoppingTest.dll	3	1100003	nHarness.exe shoppingTest.dll 3

The example here implies that there are (at least) two test harnesses in use by the test team, and that they use different command lines to execute tests. Much more metadata about the tests (e.g., target module, test history) is often included in the test metadata.

The point of thoughtful, planned test case management is to save time at later stages of the automation process. If there's a failure in a test, giving a tester even 30 minutes to "dig in" to the failure and get more details is just too long. When there's a failure, you need to know exactly which test failed, what component it was testing, what caused the failure, and what kind of test was running. Otherwise, you may as well shrug your shoulders and say, "I don't know, boss, something went wrong." You can't expect to run millions of tests and keep everything in order without careful preparation and organization of the test data.

The Automated Test Lab

Tests need a place to run. Whether it's 10 machines in an office or hundreds of machines in an offsite data center, careful planning of the lab, including a test deployment strategy, is crucial. For efficiency reasons, it makes sense to run tests in parallel across a bank of test machines rather than sequentially on a single machine. If compatibility is a concern on the test team, or if a variety of environments are required for any other reason, the number of machines needed to complete automated testing in a reasonable amount of time grows quickly.

An efficiently configured test lab requires that there are enough machines available to allow the automated tests to complete in a reasonable amount of time while not having so many computers that machine utilization is too low. Test labs require computers, space, power, and cooling. To best offset the cost of running the test lab, the machines in an automated test lab should be as busy as possible. In addition to effectively using the machines in the test lab for running automated tests, another tactic is to use the machines in the lab to run extended versions of tests, stress tests, or specific customer scenarios between runs of the automated test pass.

Deploying the Test Bed

The test lab will likely contain both physical machines and hosted virtual machines. Deploying virtual machines is usually as simple as copying the appropriate virtual hard drives to the host system. For physical machines, installing a fresh version of an operating system plus updates and any necessary test applications is too time-consuming for practical test automation. If testing requires a fresh operating installation to be in place, a more efficient approach for the task of OS and application installation is via a disk-imaging tool that can quickly write an image of an operating system plus relevant applications to disk. Any time computers in the lab are being *prepared* for testing is time that they are *not* testing. Going through a 2-hour installation process in order to run a 10-minute test is something that few people would consider efficient. Minimizing test bed preparation time is a key part of increasing lab efficiency.

Other Considerations

Outside of the scope of testing technology but still necessary in order to deploy a successful test lab are plans for maintenance, power, and cooling. A well-planned and well-organized lab will save time if there are ever any problems with computer hardware or networking that need investigation. It's also certainly possible to house the test lab in a remote location. If this is the case, the lab should include remote control power strips or a 24-hours-a-day service-level agreement in the off chance that a machine hangs so hard during testing that normal means of rebooting are not possible.

Test Distribution

Once the computers in the test lab are prepared, the next piece (and possibly the most significant piece of the overall system) is to deploy and execute the tests. If you've invested in a test lab filled with hundreds of test machines, you want to make sure machine utilization is high—i.e., reducing as much as possible the amount of time those machines are idle, waiting for the instruction to run tests.

The flow chart in Figure 8-2 describes what decisions in test distribution may look like.

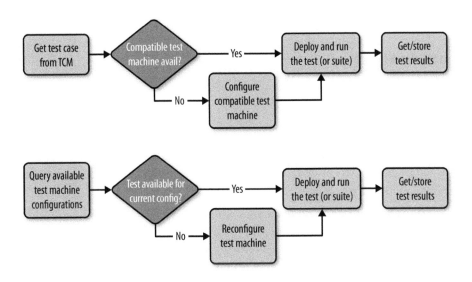

FIGURE 8-2. Test distribution flow chart

Depending on implementation, the first step is to take an inventory of either the test cases or the configurations available for testing. When starting with test cases, the next step is to begin deploying operating system and application configurations to test machines. When starting with available configurations, the secondary step is matching un-run test cases with the current set of machine configurations. In general, the former works a bit better when testing on a known smaller set of configurations, whereas the latter is slightly more convenient when dealing with a larger number of configurations.

One or more machines (sometimes called *test controllers*) are in charge of distributing the tests to the waiting machines in the test labs. These machines implement a connection system using sockets, message queues, or another multi-machine-aware synchronism mechanism.

Once preparation of the test computer is complete, the system copies the test to the target machine and the test executes. A test controller waits for the test to complete (or hang or crash), and then obtains the logfile from the test computer. The controller can parse the logfile for results directly, but more often it sends the logfile back to the test case manager or to another computer for parsing and analysis.

Yet another thing to consider in an automation system is a mechanism for knowing when the test has completed. Waiting a fixed time is risky, as tests will take a varying amount of time to complete on different systems. On the other hand, simply allotting a large amount of time for a test to complete usually means that test machines are idle for extended lengths of time. For tests that pass, the simple solution is for the test harness to signal the controller when the test process exits. Additionally, associating a maximum time length for tests will trigger the controller to obtain results and crash log information from the test machine if the test does not complete (i.e., the harness does not signal completion) within the specified time.

Failure Analysis

If your tests are doing anything interesting, some of them are bound to fail. Some of the failures will be because of product bugs, and others will be due to errors in the tests. Some failures in related areas may be due to the same bug or, if you are running a single test on multiple configurations, it may fail in multiple (or all) configurations. If the same test (e.g., "verify widget control activates menu items") fails on both Windows XP and Windows Vista, failure analysis can analyze logfiles or other test collateral. If it determines that the same issue causes both, it can report only one failure.

If a team has a lot of tests and any significant number are failing, the test team can end up spending a lot of time investigating failed tests—so much time, in fact, that they have little time left for actually testing. The unfortunate alternative to this *analysis paralysis* is to simply gloss over the failure investigation and hope for the best (a practice that often ends with a critical bug finding its way into a customer's hands).

The solution to this predicament is to automate the analysis and investigation of test failures. The primary item that enables analysis to work effectively is to have consistent logging implemented across all tests. Matching algorithms implemented by the failure analysis system can look for similarities in the logs among failed tests and identify failures potentially triggered by the same root cause. The failure analysis system can also analyze call stacks or other debugging information automatically for any tests that cause a crash.

When tests fail, the system can either create a new bug report or update an existing report, depending on whether the failure is a new issue or already known (see Figure 8-3). An excellent return on investment for large-scale test automation requires integration in all stages of the automation, check-in, and bug tracking systems. A successful solution greatly reduces the need for manual intervention in analyzing test results and failures.

Reporting

From management's point of view, test results may be the most important artifact of the test team. Current and relevant test results are another key aspect of an automation system, and it is critical that test results are current, accurate, and easily available.

The role of an automation system in reporting is to ensure that the items in the previous paragraph are possible. Tracking and tagging of test results is imperative. For any new failures (automatic failure analysis should filter errors found in previous testing), information about

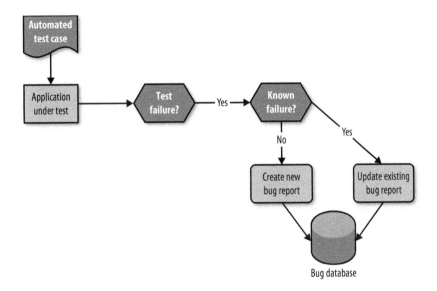

FIGURE 8-3. Automated failure analysis

the failure such as call stacks and logfiles need to be readily and quickly available so that diagnosis of the issue by the tester is as efficient as possible.

THE TRUTH ABOUT TEST RESULTS

Every team I know of that runs automated tests also tracks test results closely. Most of these teams have goals to reach or exceed, and a specified pass rate by the end of a milestone or by the time of release. For example, they may have a goal of passing 95% of their tests, or passing 100% of their "priority 1" test cases.

When teams tell me this, I always follow up by asking them what they do if they don't reach their goal. I ask, "What do you do if you're at a milestone exit, and your pass rate is only 94%?" They inevitably answer, "Oh, it depends on the failure. If the errors blocking us from reaching our goal don't meet the bar, we go ahead and move on." This, I suppose, is better than telling me that they just stop running that test (which is, unfortunately, something else I've heard in my career).

So, what is a reasonable goal for test pass rates? The answer is right in front of you. Rather than aim for a magic number, what you really want is to investigate 100% of the failures and ensure that none of those failures are serious enough to block the release. Of course, if you have a high pass rate, you will have fewer failures to investigate, but I see nothing special in reaching a magic pass rate number or letting the pursuit of that number drive your testing.

Putting It All Together

Once the whole package is together, test automation truly begins to become a benefit to testing. Testers can focus on one thing only: writing fantastic automated tests. These are tests that don't require constant maintenance, and tests that always generate meaningful actionable results. Figure 8-4 shows one description of the entire automation system described here.

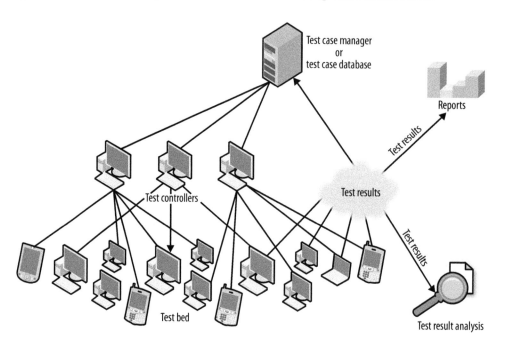

FIGURE 8-4. Large-scale test automation

Of course, if your automation system isn't at this level of maturity, you shouldn't expect it to get there instantly. The implementation of the details, as well as the relevant cultural changes, won't happen overnight. As with any large-scale change, changing and growing a little at a time is the best approach to turn an inefficient system into a beautiful one. Start by writing better tests; poor test automation is one of the biggest obstacles to automation success. Also make sure that test scripts and code are part of a source control system, and that tests go through some sort of continuous integration process to ensure some level of test quality and consistency.

Then, set up a test lab for running automated tests. Start working out a way to distribute tests to these machines and execute the tests. Then, begin gathering and aggregating simple high-level test results. Next, find a way to log test failures in the bug database. After that, investigate how you can automatically investigate failures and separate new failures from known failures. Finally, look for any other areas where testers are investing significant time and energy keeping the system running, and find a way to automate those tasks.

Before you know it, you will have a beautiful system. As it improves, testers on your team will have more and more time to do what they are best at, and something that they were (hopefully) hired to do in the first place: *test software*. Otherwise, despite thousands of automated tests and testers who are perpetually busy, you actually may not end up with a well-tested product. And that would be a sad ending to what should be a beautiful story.

## CHAPTER NINE

Beautiful Is Better Than Ugly

Neal Norwitz
Michelle Levesque
Jeffrey Yasskin

NOTE

"Beautiful is better than ugly" is the first line of The Zen of Python.[1] The Zen captures the guiding principles of the Python community, both in developing the language and creating beautiful applications with it.

IMAGINE THAT YOU'RE WRITING A PIECE OF CODE and hit a strange bug. You spend all day trying to isolate what could be going wrong, only to discover that you didn't *make* a mistake. Your code works perfectly. In fact, the problem isn't with your code at all; the problem is a bug in the compiler or interpreter that you're using. Yuck! It wouldn't take many days like this before you abandoned this flaky programming language in favor of something more stable. Stability in the programming languages we use is something that most of us take for granted, but it doesn't just happen automagically. The Python interpreter is made up of code just like any other piece of software, and it is equally vulnerable to mistakes and bugs. So how do you keep the programming language stable enough that these types of problems don't happen? Moreover, how do you ensure correctness in an organic environment where the language will

1. *http://www.python.org/dev/peps/pep-0020/*

inevitably grow and change? Where patches will come from people you don't know who could be living anywhere on the globe? This task would be nearly impossible without the help of a comprehensive set of tests and a strong testing philosophy, so it's no wonder that Python has both. As Python[2] has grown and become more complex, so too have its testing practices evolved in order to handle these complexities. We now use more sophisticated techniques such as reference leak testing, automated continuous builds, Valgrind,[3] and Coverity[4] or Klocwork[5] to supplement standard testing. Every one of these techniques helps add to our confidence that each release of Python is at least as stable as the last, and makes it easier for new contributors to submit patches with confidence.

The Value of Stability

Python is a community-operated project. It grows, changes, and improves only as fast as its volunteer contributors[6] are able to commit patches. Patches can be as small as a one-line fix to documentation. As some people leave the project, others step in to take their places, and this continuous cycle of new developers and casual submitters is what keeps Python alive.[7] Thus the project's very existence depends on keeping the barriers to entry low so that those who have a limited interest in contributing to Python aren't scared away.

Comprehensive tests not only protect Python against mistakes that could be made by new contributors who are unfamiliar with the code base, it also helps lower the barrier to entry for these new contributors. It is much more reassuring to make a change to a complex code base if you're able to run tests against your change and satisfy yourself that your change did not break anything. When you make a change, you can just run the test suite, and if it passes, you can be reasonably sure that you didn't break other parts of the system. This can be used not only when committing, but also during development: make a small change, run the tests, write a bit more, run the tests again. Changes that cause tests to fail are rolled back.

This allows Python to maintain a stable build philosophy: *if the tests are passing, you can check out from head and get a working Python.* This stability is necessary for Python to be taken seriously. To maintain this philosophy, Python uses a variety of testing—static and dynamic—which in combination allows people to be reasonably certain that the tests will catch most errors. In addition, bug fixes must be accompanied by a test that failed before the application of the fix but passes thereafter. This is the rule, and although it is not always followed, we have found it to be a valuable one and try to stick with it.

2. *http://www.python.org/*

3. *http://www.valgrind.org/*

4. *http://www.coverity.com/*

5. *http://www.klocwork.com/*

6. *http://www.python.org/dev/committers*

7. *http://www.vimeo.com/1093745*

The Python community has found this process so important that they're currently in the process of moving toward a pre-commit system so that even committers will be unable to check in changes until all of the tests pass. This shows that the tests aren't there simply to prevent inexperienced coders from making newbie mistakes; as Python grows in size, scale, and complexity, testing can catch errors made even by veteran members of the core developer team. This was influenced by the fact that several core Python developers work at Google, which has a pre-commit system. Once we experienced the benefits of this policy, we knew it would be useful in Python as well.

The use of testing in Python development extends beyond just tests that are in Python's code base itself. When changes to the language are made, they may accidentally break backward compatibility (because we update the tests). If Python applications that use the language have a comprehensive series of tests, then in many ways these become tests of the Python language as well. In that way, Python's tests extend beyond just its own code base and out to every test ever written in Python.

Ensuring Correctness

The obvious—though not only—purpose of testing is to find bugs. First, each developer runs most of the tests before submitting. Why only "most"? The entire test suite, including all the options, takes over an hour to run.[8] Most developers won't wait that long before checking in. The tests we ask developers to run[9] take at most seven minutes, a length of time most developers are willing to wait. We prefer to get them to run a slightly less complete set of tests rather than ask them to run the whole thing and have them ignore that request.

But, since the whole test suite does provide value on top of the smoke tests, we need some way to run them.

The Buildbot System

The Buildbot system[10] tests every check-in on many platforms. It runs on all of the active branches (currently 2.6, trunk [2.7], 3.1, and py3k [3.2])[11] on roughly 15–20 different architectures, and we're about to add even more systems.[12] The machines are donated, and we're always looking for more diversity. When any buildbot sees a build or test failure, it sends

---

8. *http://docs.python.org/dev/results/*

9. *http://www.python.org/dev/faq/#how-to-test-a-patch*

10. *http://buildbot.net/trac*

11. *http://www.python.org/dev/buildbot/*

12. *http://snakebite.org/*

email to the python-checkins mailing list.[13] In theory, after submitting a change, a developer pays extra attention to her email to see if she has caused any problems.

Since most developers are on an x86, running Linux or Mac OS X, and compiling with gcc,[14] this serves to make sure that Windows and other minority platforms stay stable. We have a subset of "stable" platforms, and we don't release new versions of Python until those buildbots pass all their tests.

Sometimes buildbots catch really subtle problems that would have caused real problems for users. Back in January of 2008, r60086[15] introduced:

```
char sign = reverse ? -1 : 1;
```

into the implementation of `mmap.rfind()`. On most platforms this works, but on platforms where chars are unsigned, it would break. Few developers actually use such systems, so we probably wouldn't have caught the problem until it broke a user's program. Fortunately, there *were* buildbots on a few systems with unsigned chars, which correctly failed. After some random changes trying to fix the problem,[16] we successfully identified and fixed it a week later with r60346.[17] Since we knew when the buildbots had started failing, only a few changes could possibly have caused the problem. If we'd waited for a user to find the problem, that person would have had to file a bug, a developer probably would have had to binary search for the offending change, and the whole process would have taken much longer and been much more painful for everyone. With the buildbots' early warning system, we knew exactly where to look for the problem, and no users had to suffer at all.

Refleak Testing

The primary implementation of the Python interpreter is written in C, which means it needs some way to release memory. Python manages memory with reference counting[18] and has a collector for cyclic garbage. If the C code increments an object's reference count without decrementing it, you get a particular kind of memory leak that we call a reference leak, or "refleak." To detect this, Python's debug build[19] keeps track of the total number of references. A debug build is a special way of compiling Python that aids in various types of debugging. Debug builds include a lot of extra information and assertions that are not part of the normal release builds. This makes debug builds slow, and they consume more memory. Since the

13. *http://mail.python.org/pipermail/python-checkins/*

14. *http://gcc.gnu.org/*

15. *http://mail.python.org/pipermail/python-checkins/2008-January/064885.html*

16. *http://mail.python.org/pipermail/python-checkins/2008-January/065197.html*

17. *http://mail.python.org/pipermail/python-checkins/2008-January/065228.html*

18. *http://docs.python.org/extending/extending.html#refcounts*

19. *http://www.python.org/dev/faq/#how-do-i-create-a-debug-build-of-python*

debug build keeps track of the number of references, the test suite can run each test several times in a row and compare the total number of references after each run. Even without a reference leak, the number of references may go up for the first run or two because of cached objects, but if the number keeps increasing after several runs, especially if it goes up by the same number in each run, you have a reference leak.

Approximately twice a day, we run the test suite in this mode to find newly introduced refleaks. We'd like to run it more often since refleaks are much easier to track down when you know the exact change that introduced them, but it takes nine times as long as the ordinary test suite, so twice a day is a reasonable compromise.

The current results are at *http://docs.python.org/dev/results/make-test-refleak.out*, and the script that runs the test suite in various modes is at *http://svn.python.org/view/python/trunk/Misc/build .sh?view=markup*.

Doc Testing

The Python documentation is written using restructured text (reST)[20] and converted to HTML, and malformed reST can produce broken HTML. Like any other build, we need to ensure that the docs build correctly. We do this automatically twice a day in the same script that runs the test suite. The most recent build of docs is at *http://docs.python.org/dev/*.

There is an additional benefit of updating the docs often: many users find problems in the development versions of the docs. Once we began updating the online docs nightly, doc bugs didn't have to wait for release to be found and fixed. Overall, users have access to more accurate documentation and are happier.

Like the code, Python docs are managed for stability. We strive to ensure that the development version of the docs always produces proper documentation. To insulate users from the occasional problems that arise, there is always a golden release version of the docs as well. This version of the docs is always vetted and in a known good state.

Release Testing

Finally, there are always bugs that the automated tests miss. To find these bugs, we release a series of alphas, betas, and release candidates before releasing a major version of Python.[21] As a rule of thumb, you find about the same number of bugs with each order-of-magnitude increase in the number of users. Before releasing the alpha, few people other than core developers use that version Python. With the alpha release, adventurous users try it out and report bugs. More people try the beta release, and lots of people try the release candidates.

20. *http://docutils.sourceforge.net/rst.html*

21. *http://www.python.org/dev/peps/pep-0101/*

Each of these stages finds lots of bugs without alienating people who want a more stable product.

Table 9-1 lists the download numbers from *http://www.python.org/webstats/*.

TABLE 9-1. Number of Python downloads

Version	Release date	Downloads
2.6a1	01-Mar-2008	19,377
2.6a2	03-Apr-2008	19,746
2.6a3	08-May-2008	37,466
2.6b1	18-Jun-2008	26,434
2.6b2	17-Jul-2008	56,137
2.6b3	20-Aug-2008	25,916
2.6rc1	12-Sep-2008	28,831
2.6rc2	17-Sep-2008	26,312
2.6 release	01-Oct-2008	2,722,887
2.6.1 release	04-Dec-2008	2,869,104
2.6.2 release	15-Apr-2009	51,194

Bug fix releases (e.g., 2.6.1 and 2.6.2) also go through rigorous testing with a no new feature policy. Only bug fixes are allowed in micro releases.[22]

Dynamic Analysis

Valgrind is a dynamic analysis[23] tool. This means that it analyzes an application while the application runs. The memcheck tool that is part of Valgrind detects memory leaks and errors, including invalid memory reads and writes. Using dynamic analysis is very powerful because it can find issues that are otherwise hard to detect. For example, a memory access might happen only once in a million times and doesn't always cause a noticeable problem. Such an issue can be detected with little effort when using Valgrind.

Python has used dynamic analysis tools for over 10 years, to minimize the amount of memory leaked. Memory leaks can be very detrimental to applications, as they can effectively create a denial-of-service (DoS) issue. Although Python can't prevent an application from harming itself, it can certainly strive to not leak any of its own structures. Even small leaks can become catastrophic if they occur frequently in a long-running server.

---

22. *http://www.python.org/dev/peps/pep-0006/* and *http://www.python.org/dev/peps/pep-0102/*

23. *http://en.wikipedia.org/wiki/Dynamic_code_analysis*

The Python interpreter should never crash, and preventing illegal memory operations is one important step in providing a robust runtime and avoiding an entire class of security exploits.

The first time dynamic analysis tools were run, they reported many errors. Over time, we fixed all of these. Before each release, we run the standard Python test suite under the tools, and typically there are few new errors, due to the way Python is developed. Generally, new features have comprehensive tests that catch problems before the dynamic analysis tools have a chance to find them. When there was a massive upheaval of code in the transition from Python 2 to Python 3, we ran Valgrind periodically to ensure that at each stage there weren't too many errors. Since we've been running these tools and fixing the problems, stability and robustness have not been a problem for Python. Even as Python's use has grown by orders of magnitude, there has not been an order of magnitude more problems reported by users, due to our focus on testing and use of tools.

Several large companies that are heavy users of Python have run their own independent code audits for security issues. They have found a handful of issues each time, but not many. This is due in part to Python's use of static and dynamic analysis tools, as well as the Python community's commitment to testing.

Much more recently, in 2008, Fusil[24] was introduced. Fusil is a fuzzer that calls public functions with semi-random arguments with constraints based on the interface. Based on these API parameters, it will stress test using values that might cause a problem and verify that the system doesn't crash. For example, `audioop.findmax()` didn't check its second argument for a negative value, causing a crash. Fusil tried to call it:

```
audioop.findmax(''.join(chr(x) for x in xrange(256)), -2392392)
```

and discovered a crash, which was fixed in r64775.[25] Fusil can find cases like this with minimal programmer effort, which gives us the huge benefit of spending time fixing problems rather than auditing code to find problems. Fuzzing is not a substitute for a security review, but it can provide valuable information to determine the likely threats to an application.

Static Analysis

Static analysis[26] is a technique in which a program analyzes source code to find potential problems. It is similar to an automated code review.[27] Lint and compiler warnings are two examples of static analysis. Static analysis can be used to find style issues, but the main reason to use it is to find subtle problems. Often these problems can occur in uncommon situations, such as error conditions (i.e., the worst possible time to make a bad situation worse).

24. *http://pypi.python.org/pypi/fusil/*

25. *http://svn.python.org/view?view=rev&revision=64775*

26. *http://en.wikipedia.org/wiki/Static_code_analysis*

27. *http://en.wikipedia.org/wiki/Code_review*

For example, static analysis can find invalid memory uses or memory leaks in error-handling code. Very often, the problems it finds can lead to crashes in conditions that rarely happen or that are hard to reproduce. By contrast, dynamic analysis is good for finding problems in code that already has test cases. Static analysis is a nice complement and finds problems in code that *isn't* executed. This can make systems far more robust, even when unexpected conditions arise.

Static analysis also can be used to find unreachable code. It typically looks at inter-procedural issues in addition to the intra-procedural problems that compilers typically flag as warnings.

Python uses many different tools for static analysis. Compiler warnings have been used for a long time, and they help avoid platform dependencies and ensure that Python works on as many platforms as possible.

Even tools such as grep, awk, cut,[28] and (gasp!) Perl can be used to find problems. Python has a C API[29] that allows programs to call into it. For this to work, the C API should prefix all identifiers with some variation of "Py" in order to prevent name conflicts. Every once in a while APIs that were meant to be internal and didn't have the "Py" prefix have mistakenly been made available publicly. Such misnamed functions can be easily found by looking in the generated library using `nm library | egrep -v Py ....` This is much easier than parsing the code.

There are several static analysis tools, both open source and proprietary, available for many languages. Python is primarily implemented in C and Python. Coverity and Klocwork have run their tools over the C parts of the Python code base. We also use pychecker[30] and pylint[31] on the Python parts of the code to find problems and fix them before anyone ever has a chance to notice.

One might think it wasteful or redundant to use multiple tools for the same task. However, we have found that although about half of the problems are found by both tools, the other half are distinct. After running Coverity and fixing about 50 problems, another 50 distinct problems were found by Klocwork. Using multiple tools helps find as many problems as possible.

When calling a C function from Python, Python wraps the arguments in a tuple. The C function then needs to parse this tuple into C-native ints and chars that it can operate on. To make this easier, we provide a function called `PyArg_ParseTuple()`[32] that operates a lot like the C `scanf()`[33] function. One example call looks like the following:

28. *http://en.wikipedia.org/wiki/Unix_utilities*

29. *http://docs.python.org/extending/index.html*

30. *http://pychecker.sourceforge.net/*

31. *http://www.logilab.org/857*

32. *http://docs.python.org/c-api/arg.html*

33. *http://en.wikipedia.org/wiki/Scanf*

```
static PyObject *string_replace(PyStringObject *self, PyObject *args) {
    Py_ssize_t count = -1;
    PyObject *from, *to;
    if (!PyArg_ParseTuple(args, "OO|n:replace", &from, &to, &count))
        return NULL;
    ...
}
```

If from, to, or count has a different type than the format string claims, PyArg_ParseTuple could write garbage to memory and cause a crash or, worse, a security vulnerability. We ought to have enough unit tests to cover this on any particular platform, but types can change on different platforms, which would make porting harder. For example, on a 32-bit platform, Py_ssize_t is 32 bits, so the program will work even if someone uses the format string character for an int or long. On a 64-bit platform, Py_ssize_t will be 64 bits, but ints will still be 32 bits, and longs can be either 32 or 64 bits. These inconsistencies would cause Python to break on only some developers' machines or, worse, on only some users' machines after we've released. To make sure Python works regardless of the platform, we can also use static analysis to check that all uses of PyArg_ParseTuple use exactly the right types. Fortunately, gcc already has a very similar analysis pass to check the arguments to printf() and scanf(). One of the Python developers modified this pass in gcc to also check uses of PyArg_ParseTuple, which found a couple of problems and gave us assurance that no more were lurking in the code base.

Conclusions

As Python has evolved from a small, obscure language to one used in production by companies all across the globe, we have striven to maintain a stable and reliable product despite huge growth in developers and language complexity. Without a strong suite of tests, Python never would have been able to manage this growth while maintaining its high bar for stability.

We were lucky that we adopted strong testing practices early on. It's much easier to encourage newcomers to write comprehensive tests when they're entering into a community in which it's already a fundamental part of the culture. It's just what we do here.

We believe that we've found a good balance that reinforces comprehensive testing practices without adding unnecessary hurdles that might discourage contributors, but this balance has evolved and changed as necessary throughout Python's life cycle. We also now run a large number of tests in the background that contributors might not even be aware of. Our buildbots help us to catch problems on less common platforms, and continuous refleak checkers help identify those problems early. We run both static analysis tools (such as Coverity and Klocwork) and dynamic analysis tools (such as Valgrind and Fusil) for even more comprehensive coverage. Each and every one of these testing tools has proven its worth and caught problems that otherwise would have been put in front of real users. Despite these sophisticated tools, however, we still rely on basic unit tests; it is this whole suite of varied types of tests that has allowed us to preserve Python's stability.

We're always looking for more people who are interested in helping out and joining our community of developers. There's always a list of bugs that need fixing[34] or features that users would like to see. If you're interested, you should send us a patch. Just remember to include a test.

---

34. *http://bugs.python.org/*

CHAPTER TEN

Testing a Random Number Generator

John D. Cook

ACCORDING TO THE CLASSICAL DEFINITION OF BEAUTY, something is beautiful if it exhibits both complexity and unity. Professor Gene Veith explained this idea in an editorial by describing two kind of paintings:[1]

> In painting a black canvas has unity, but it has no complexity. A canvas of random paint splatterings has complexity, but it has no unity.

Michelangelo's painting of the Sistine Chapel ceiling has rich detail along with order and balance. It exhibits complexity and unity. It is beautiful.

Some works of beauty are easy to appreciate because both the complexity and the unity are apparent. I would say the Sistine Chapel falls in this category. However, other works require more education to appreciate because it takes knowledge and skill to see either the complexity or the unity. Modern jazz may fall into this latter category. The complexity is obvious, but the unity may not be apparent to untrained ears. Tests for random number generators may be more like modern jazz than the Sistine Chapel; the complexity is easier to see than the unity. But with some introduction, the unity can be appreciated.

1. Veith, Gene Edward. "Acquired taste," *World Magazine*. February 29, 2008.

What Makes Random Number Generators Subtle to Test?

Software random number generators are technically *pseudo*random number generators because the output of a deterministic program cannot really be random. We will leave the "pseudo" qualification understood and simply speak of random number generators (RNGs). Even though the output of an RNG cannot actually be random, there are RNGs that do a remarkably good job of producing sequences of numbers that for many purposes might as well be truly random. But how do you know when the output of an RNG is sufficiently similar to what you would expect from a true random source?

A good RNG leads us to believe the output is random, so long as we look only at the output and don't restart the sequence. This is our first hint that RNGs are going to be subtle to test: *there is a tension in the requirements for an RNG.* The output should be unpredictable from one perspective, even though it's completely predictable from another perspective. Tests must verify that generators have the right properties from the perspective of user applications while not being distracted by incidental properties.

The idea of what constitutes a good RNG depends on how the RNG is applied. That is why, for example, a generator may be considered high-quality for simulation while being considered unacceptable for cryptography. This chapter looks at tests of statistical quality and does not address tests for cryptographical security.

Suppose we are asked to generate random values between 3 and 4. What if we wrote a program that always returned 3? That would not satisfy anyone's idea of a random sequence, because something "random" should be unpredictable in some sense. Random values should jiggle around. So next we write a program that yields the sequence 3, 3.1, 3.2, ..., 4, 3, 3.1, 3.2, ... in a cycle. The output values move around, but in a predictable way. We shouldn't be able to predict the next value of the sequence. The output values should spread out between 3 and 4, but not in such a simple way. Thinking about this leads to another reason RNGs are subtle to test: *there's no way to say whether a particular value is correct.* We cannot test individual values; we have to look at things like averages.

Even when we look at averages, there are still difficulties. Suppose the output of a random number generator is supposed to have an average value of 7, and the first output value is 6.5. That's OK, because the sequence does not (and should not) always return 7; it should just average to 7 in the long run. Should the next value be 7.5 so that the average is correct? No, that would make the second value predictable. So should the average work out to 7 after three outputs? No, then the third value would be predictable. We can never require the average to be exactly 7 after any fixed number of outputs. What we can say is that as we average over longer and longer output sequences, the average should *often* be *close* to 7. The weasel words "often" and "close" are the heart of the difficulty. These terms can be made precise, but it takes work to do so.

Since we must write tests that verify that certain things happen "often," we have to quantify what we mean by "often." And we cannot simply say "always." This brings up a third reason why testing RNGs is subtle: *any test we write will fail occasionally*. If a test never fails, then it demonstrates a predictable attribute of our random number sequence. So not only *can* our tests fail from time to time, they *should* fail from time to time!

What are we to do if it is impossible in principle to write tests that will always pass? Ultimately, some subjective judgment is required. However, we can do better than simply printing out a list of output values and asking a statistician whether the sequence looks OK. It all goes back to the terms "often" and "close." These two concepts are often traded off against each other. We can decide what "often" means and then pick the corresponding notion of "close." If we want tests that should only fail around once in every 1,000 runs, we can pick a definition of "close" to make that happen. But only on average! Even a test that fails on average once every 1,000 runs may fail twice in a row.

Uniform Random Number Generators

It doesn't make sense to ask for a program that generates random numbers without some further information. What kind of numbers: integers or floating-point? From what range? Should all values be equally likely, or should some values be more likely than others? In statistical terms, we need to know what distribution the numbers should follow. Only then can we test whether software satisfies the requirements.

The most fundamental RNG produces values from the unit interval[2] with all values equally likely. This is called a uniform RNG. When people say they want random numbers but give no further details, this is often what they have in mind. This is the most important random number generation problem because, once it is solved, we can bootstrap the solution to solve other problems. In other words, the grand strategy for generating random numbers is as follows:

1. Generate random values uniformly distributed in the interval (0, 1).
2. Transform those values into whatever other distribution you need.

The first step in this grand strategy is the hardest part. Fortunately, this problem has been solved for most practical purposes. There are uniform RNG algorithms, such as the Mersenne Twister,[3] that have been extensively studied by experts. These algorithms have good theoretical properties and have been through empirical gauntlets such as George Marsaglia's DIEHARD battery of tests.[4] It's very easy to *think* you have created a good RNG when you haven't, so

---

2. Generators are inconsistent as to whether the end points should be included. In my opinion, excluding both end points causes the lest difficulty. But some generators include one or both end points.

3. Matsumoto, Makoto, and Takuji Nishimura. "Mersenne twister: a 623-dimensionally equidistributed uniform pseudorandom number generator," *ACM Trans. Model. Comput. Simul.* Vol. 8, No. 1 (1998).

4. Gentle, James E. *Random Number Generation and Monte Carlo Methods*. Springer, 1998.

most of us should use a uniform RNG that has been vetted by experts. Implementations of these standard algorithms are easy to find.

Although most people will not need to come up with new *algorithms* for uniform random number generation, more people may need to come up with new *implementations* of standard algorithms, and of course these implementations will need to be tested. For example, you may need to test a port of a standard algorithm implementation to a new programming language. In that case, you could generate, say, a million values from the original generator, then set the same seed values in the new generator and verify that you get the exact same sequence of outputs. This is an exception to the rule that there are no deterministic tests for random number generators.

Most testers will be concerned with the second step of the grand strategy: testing code that transforms uniform random sequences into sequences with other distributions. Although very few people develop their own uniform generators, many people have reasons to develop custom nonuniform generators.

Nonuniform Random Number Generators

Suppose you want to decide how many cashiers to hire for a grocery store. If shoppers arrived at regular intervals and all took the same amount of time to check out, this would be a simple problem. But in reality, shoppers do not arrive like clockwork. Nor do they all take the same amount of time to check out. Some shoppers dart into the store for a pack of gum, whereas others come to stock up on a week's worth of provisions for a family of eight.

There is an entire branch of mathematics called *queuing theory* devoted to studying problems like how many cashiers a grocery store needs. Often, queuing theory assumes that the time needed to serve a customer is exponentially distributed. That is, the distribution of service times looks like the function e^{-x}. A lot of customers are quick to check out, some take a little longer, and a few take very long. There's no theoretical limit to how long service may take, but the probability decreases rapidly as the length of time increases, as shown in the first image that follows. The same distribution is often used to model the times between customer arrivals.

The exponential distribution is a common example of a nonuniform distribution. Another common example is the Gaussian or "normal" distribution.[5] The normal distribution provides a good model for many situations: estimating measurement errors, describing the heights of Australian men, predicting IQ test scores, etc. With a normal distribution, values tend to clump around the average and thin out symmetrically as you move away from the middle, as shown in the second image that follows.

---

5. The normal distribution was not so named to imply that it is "normal" in the sense of being typical. The name goes back to the Latin word *normalis* for perpendicular. The name has to do with a problem that motivated Carl Friedrich Gauss to study the distribution.

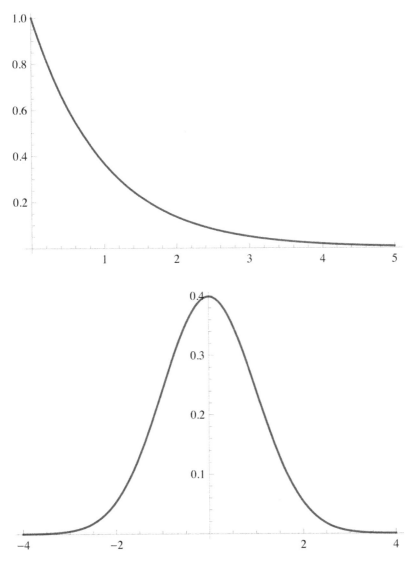

Software is readily available to generate random values from well-known distributions such as the exponential and the normal. Popular software libraries have often been very well tested, though not always. Still, someone using an RNG from a library would do well to write a few tests of their own, even if they trust the library. The point is not only to test the quality of the library itself, but also to test the user's *understanding* of the library.

One of the most common errors along these lines involves misunderstanding parameterizations. For example, the normal distribution has two parameters: the mean μ and standard deviation σ. It is common for people to specify either the standard deviation σ or the variance σ^2. If the documentation says an RNG gives samples from a normal (3, 8) distribution, does that mean the standard deviation is 8 (and the variance is 64), or does it mean the standard deviation is $\sqrt{8}$ and the variance is 8?

To make matters worse, some of the most common differences in parameterization conventions don't show up when using default values. For example, the standard deviation for a normal distribution defaults to 1. But if $\sigma = 1$, then $\sigma^2 = 1$ as well. Some people even parameterize the normal in terms of the precision, $1/\sigma^2$, but that also equals 1 in this case. A test using default values would not uncover a misunderstanding of the parameter conventions. The exponential distribution is similar. Some folks parameterize in terms of the mean μ, and others use the rate $1/\mu$. Again the default value is 1, and so any confusion over whether to use mean or rate would be masked by the default parameterization.

No library is going to contain every distribution that every user would want. The C++ Standard Library, for example, provides only seven distributions, but there are dozens of distribution families in common use. New distributions that may be unique to a particular problem are invented all the time. Many people have to write custom nonuniform random number generators, and there are common techniques for doing so (inverse CDF transformation, accept-reject algorithms, etc.).

A Progression of Tests

If a nonuniform random generator has a high-quality uniform random number generator at its core, the main thing to test is whether the generator output has the correct distribution. Fortunately, tiny coding mistakes often result in egregious output errors, so simple tests may be adequate to flush out bugs. However, some bugs are more subtle, and so more sophisticated tests may be necessary. The recommendation is to start with the simplest tests and work up to more advanced tests. The simplest tests, besides being easiest to implement, are also the easiest to understand. A software developer is more likely to respond well to being told, "Looks like the average of your generator is 7 when it should be 8," than to being told, "I'm getting a small p-value from my Kolmogorov-Smirnov test."

Range Tests

If a probability distribution has a limited range, the simplest thing to test is whether the output values fall in that range. For example, an exponential distribution produces only positive values. If your test detects a single negative value, you've found a bug. However, for other distributions, such as the normal, there are no theoretical bounds on the outputs; all output values are possible, though some values are exceptionally unlikely.

There is one aspect of output ranges that cannot be tested effectively by black-box testing: boundary values. It may be impractical to test whether the endpoints of intervals are included. For example, suppose an RNG is expected to return values from the half-open interval (0, 1]. It may not be practical to verify that 1 is a possible return value because it would only be returned rarely. Also, if algorithm incorrectly returned 0, but did so rarely, it may not be detected in testing. These sort of boundary value errors are common, they can be hard to detect via testing, and they can cause software to crash.

Mean Test

One of the most obvious things to do to test a random number generator is to average a large number of values to see whether the average is close to the theoretical value. For example, if you average a million values from a normal random generator with mean 4 and standard deviation 3, you'd expect the average to be near 4. But *how* near?

For the special case of the normal distribution, there's a simple answer. The average of a sequence of independent normal values is itself a normal random value with the same mean. So if we average a million samples from a normal with mean 4, the average will have a normal distribution with mean 4. But the standard deviation of the mean is smaller than the standard deviation of the individual samples by a factor of $1/\sqrt{n}$, where n is the number of samples. So in this example the average of our samples will have standard deviation $3/\sqrt{10^6} = 0.003$. An important rule of thumb about normal distributions is that samples will lie within 2 standard deviations of the mean about 95% of the time. That means if we take a million values from a normal random number generator with mean 4 and standard deviation 3, we would expect the average to be between 3.994 and 4.006 around 95% of the time. However, such a test will fail about 5% of the time. If you'd like your test to pass more often, make your criteria looser. For example, samples from a normal distribution are within 3 standard deviations of the mean 99.7% of the time, so testing whether the average of a million samples is between 3.991 and 4.009 will fail in only about three out of every thousand tests.

In summary, the way to test samples from a normal random number generator with mean μ and standard deviation σ is to average n values for some large value of n, say $n = 10^6$. Then look for the average to be between $\mu - 2\sigma/\sqrt{n}$ and $\mu + 2\sigma/\sqrt{n}$ around 95% of the time, or between $\mu - 3\sigma/\sqrt{n}$ and $\mu + 3\sigma/\sqrt{n}$ around 99.7% of the time.

In practice, exactly how often the tests fail might not be important. If there's a bug that throws off the average of the random values, it's likely your tests will fail every time. These kinds of errors are usually not subtle. Either the tests will pass most of the time or fail nearly every time. I cannot recall ever wondering whether a test was failing a little too often.

How do you test an RNG that doesn't produce a normal distribution? How would you test, for example, an exponential RNG? There's a bit of magic called the central limit theorem that says if we average enough values, any[6] distribution acts like a normal distribution. For an exponential distribution with mean μ, the standard deviation is also μ. If we average a million samples from that distribution, the average will very nearly have a normal distribution with mean μ and standard deviation μ/1,000. As before, we can test whether the average falls between two or three standard deviations of what we expect.

The central limit theorem provides a better approximation for some distributions than others. The more the distributions start out looking something like a normal distribution, the faster the averages will converge to a normal distribution. However, even for distributions that start out looking nothing like a normal, the averages start to be approximately normal fairly quickly.[7] However, as was mentioned earlier, we can often get by without paying too close attention to such details. Suppose you expect your test to fail about 5% of the time, but instead it fails 10% of the time. In that case you probably do not have a bug that is throwing off the average. And if the test fails every time, a bug is a more plausible explanation for the failure than any subtle behavior of the averages.

The only case that is likely to cause problems is if the distribution being tested does not even have a mean. For example, the Cauchy distribution looks something like a normal distribution, but goes to zero more slowly as you move away from the middle. If fact, it goes to zero so slowly that the mean value does not exist. Of course you can always take the average of any number of samples, but the averages are not going to settle down to any particular value. In that case, the central limit theorem does not apply. However, you could do something analogous to a mean test by testing the *median*, which always exists.[8]

Variance Test

The mean test can flush out certain kinds of coding errors. However, it is easy to write incorrect code that will pass the mean test: always return the mean! For example, suppose an RNG is supposed to return values from a normal distribution with mean 4 and standard deviation 9. Code that always returns 4 will pass the test. Code that returns normal random values with mean 4 and *variance* 9 would also pass the mean test. The latter is more subtle and more likely to occur in practice.

The combination of a mean and variance test gives much more assurance that software is correct than just the mean test alone. Some software errors, such as the standard deviation–variance confusion just mentioned, leave the mean unaffected but will throw off the variance.

Incidentally, it is a good idea to use widely different values for mean and standard deviation. Suppose software swapped the values of the mean and standard deviation parameters on input.

6. Certain restrictions apply. See your probability textbook for details.

7. If you really want to know the details of how quickly the averages converge to the normal distribution, look up the Berry-Esséen theorem.

8. See *http://www.johndcook.com/Cauchy_estimation.html*.

Testing with samples from a normal with mean 7 and standard deviation 7 would not uncover such a bug. Testing with samples from a normal with mean −2 and standard deviation 7 would be much better because −2 is an illegal value for a standard deviation and should cause an immediate error if parameters are reversed.

Just as the mean test compares the mean of the samples to the mean of the distribution, the variance test compares the variance of the samples to the variance of the distribution. Suppose we compute the sample variance of some large number of outputs from an RNG; say, one million outputs. The outputs are random, so the sample variance is random.[9] We expect that it will "often" be "near" the variance of the distribution. Here we return to the perennial question: how often and how near?

As with testing the mean, the answer is simplest for the normal distribution. Suppose an RNG produces values from a normal distribution with variance σ^2. Let S^2 be the sample variance based on n values from the RNG. If n is very large, then S^2 approximately has a normal distribution with mean σ^2 and variance $2\sigma^4/(n-1)$.[10] As before, we apply the idea that anything with a normal distribution will lie within two standard deviations of its mean 95% of the time.

For example, suppose we're testing the variance of samples from a generator that is supposed to return values from a normal distribution with mean 7 and variance 25 (standard deviation 5). The mean value 7 is irrelevant for testing the variance. Suppose we compute the sample variance S^2 based on 1,000 values. Then S^2 should have mean 25 and variance $2 \cdot 5^4/999$. This would put the standard deviation of S^2 at about 1.12. Thus we would expect S^2 to be between 22.76 and 27.24 about 95% of the time.

If the random number generator to be tested does not generate values from a normal distribution, we fall back on the central limit theorem once again and gloss over the nonnormality. However, the use of the central limit theorem is not as justified here as it was when we were testing means. Typically, sample variances will be more variable than the normal approximation predicts. This means our tests will fail more often than predicted. But as before, we may not need to be too careful. Coding errors are likely to cause the tests to fail every time, not just a little more often than expected. Also, the tests in the following sections do a more careful job of testing the distribution of the samples and have a solid theoretical justification.

Just as some distributions do not have a mean, some distributions do not have a variance. Again, the Cauchy distribution is the canonical example. Calculating the sample variance of Cauchy random numbers is an exercise in futility. However, the following tests apply perfectly well to a Cauchy distribution.

---

9. See *http://www.johndcook.com/standard_deviation.html* for how to compute sample variance. If you just code up a formula from a statistics book, you might be in for an unpleasant numerical surprise.

10. This isn't the way this result is usually presented in textbooks. More precisely, $(n-1)S^2/\sigma^2$ has a $\chi^2(n-1)$ distribution, that is, a chi-squared distribution with $n-1$ degrees of freedom. But when n is large, we can approximate the χ^2 distribution with a normal and obtain this result.

Bucket Test

Suppose an RNG passes both the mean and the variance test. That gives you some confidence that the code generates samples from *some* distribution with the right mean and variance, but it's still possible the samples are coming from an entirely wrong distribution.

To illustrate this potential problem, consider two generators. The first returns values from an exponential distribution with mean 1 (and hence standard deviation 1). The second returns values from a normal distribution with mean 1 and standard deviation 1. The mean and variance tests could not detect an error that resulted in calls to the two generators being swapped. What kind of test could tell the two generators apart? You could count how many values fall into various "buckets," or ranges of values. For example, you could count how many output values fall between −1 and 0, between 0 and 2, and greater than 2. The difference between the distributions will be most obvious in the bucket of values between −1 and 0. The exponential generator will have *zero* values in that bucket, whereas the normal generator will have about 19% of its values in the same range. Usually we would be looking for more subtle cases where all buckets would have some values and the only question is whether some buckets have too many or too few samples. (What we call "the bucket test" here is commonly known as the chi-square (χ^2) test.[11] And some people use the term "bin" where we use "bucket.")

Here's how to do a bucket test. Divide your output range into k buckets. The buckets should cover the entire range of the output and not overlap. Let E_i be the expected number of samples for the ith bucket, and let O_i be the number of samples you actually observe. Then, compute the chi-square statistic:

$$\chi^2 = \sum_{i=1}^{k} \frac{(O_i - E_i)^2}{E_i}$$

If this value is too large, that says the observed counts are too different from the expected counts and so maybe our generator does not follow the right distribution. If this value is too small, that says the expected counts agree too well with the expected values and don't have enough random variation.

The description here leaves several questions unanswered. How many buckets should you use? Where should you put them? How do you know when χ^2 is too large or too small?

First we consider the number of buckets. If there are too few buckets, the test is not very demanding and errors could go undetected. On the other hand, if there are too many buckets, then we do not expect to find many samples in each bucket and the theoretical requirements of the test are not met. A common rule of thumb is that the expected number of samples in

11. Knuth, Donald E. *The Art of Computer Programming, Vol. 2: Seminumerical Algorithms*, Third Edition. Addison-Wesley, 1998.

each bucket should be at least five.[12] This is no problem because we are *generating* our data rather than collecting it. We can determine our number of buckets first, then choose the number of samples n so large that we expect well more than five samples in each bucket.

Next, how do we decide where to place the buckets? We could arbitrarily decide on, say, 10 buckets and pick the boundaries so that we expect an equal number of samples in each bucket. For example, if we wanted to test a Cauchy random number generator, we could use the Cauchy distribution function to find cutoff values x_i for $i = 1, 2, 3, \ldots, 9$ so that we expect 10% of the samples to be less than x_1, 10% between x_1 and x_2, 10% between x_2 and x_3, on up to 10% of the values greater than x_9.[13] Also, if you are particularly interested in some region, you could make that one of your buckets. For example, if someone is concerned that there are too many values greater than 17 for some generator, you could make a bucket for values greater than 17.

Finally, we address the range of values we should expect. If we have b buckets, the statistic χ^2 has a chi-square distribution with $b-1$ degrees of freedom. Since we're generating our samples and can have as many as we want, we might as well make b fairly large. (Remember to make the number of samples n large enough so that each bucket is expected to have at least five samples.) Then we can approximate the chi-square distribution by a normal and not have to consult tables to find a typical range of values. For large b, a chi-square distribution with $b-1$ degrees of freedom has approximately the same distribution as a normal distribution with mean $b-1$ and variance $2b-2$. Then we can use the same rules as before regarding how often a normal random variable is within two or three standard deviations of its mean.

Kolmogorov-Smirnov Test

One shortcoming of the bucket test is that it is "chunky." It is possible that a random number generator puts approximately the expected number of samples in each bucket and yet the samples are not properly distributed within the buckets. For example, suppose the bucket boundaries were at $m + 1/2$ for several integer values of m. If a bug in the random number generator causes all floating-point values to be rounded to the nearest integer, all samples would land exactly in the middle of the bucket. The counts in each bucket would not be affected by such a bug, and if the generator were otherwise correct, the bucket test would pass most of the time.

We would like a more fine-grained test of how the random samples are distributed. Here's one way to proceed. Take a large number of samples n. For each sample x_i we can compare the actual proportion of samples less than x_i to the proportion of samples we would expect to have

---

12. Knuth, Donald E. *The Art of Computer Programming, Vol. 2: Seminumerical Algorithms*, Third Edition. Addison-Wesley, 1998.

13. In case you're curious: $x_i = \tan(\pi(0.1\ i - 0.5))$.

seen. In other words, we will compare the *empirical* distribution function with the *theoretical* distribution function. The empirical distribution is defined as:

$$F_n(x) = \frac{\text{the number of } x_i \text{ values} \leq x}{n}$$

and the theoretical distribution function $F(x)$ is the theoretical probability of the RNG returning a value no greater than x. We want to look at the differences between $F(x)$ and $F_n(x)$. In short, we want to do a direct comparison of the theoretical and empirical distribution of values. This is the idea behind the Kolmogorov-Smirnov (K-S) test.[14]

To carry out the test, we calculate two numbers:

$$K^+ = \sqrt{n} \max_{\infty} \left(F_n(x) - F(x) \right)$$
$$K^- = \sqrt{n} \max_{\infty} \left(F(x) - F_n(x) \right)$$

Aside from the factor $\sqrt{n}$, the number K^+ is the maximum amount by which the empirical distribution exceeds the theoretical distribution. Similarly, K^- is the maximum amount by which the theoretical distribution exceeds the empirical distribution, multiplied by $\sqrt{n}$. If the theoretical and empirical distributions were to line up perfectly, K^+ and K^- would both be zero. It would be almost impossible for K^+ or K^- to be zero in practice, and values near zero are suspicious. At the other extreme, if the theoretical and empirical distributions do not line up well, either K^+ or K^- would be large and indicate a problem. So what would be suspiciously small and suspiciously large values of our statistics?

With the previous test, we appealed to the central limit theorem to reduce our problem to a normal distribution. That's not going to work here. We're going to pull a rabbit out of the hat and give range values without saying where they came from. For large n, we expect K^+ to be between 0.07089 and 1.5174 around 98% of the time. How large does n need to be for this to hold? Values of n that you would want to use for testing, say $n = 1,000$, are more than big enough. Donald Knuth's book gives more details concerning the K-S test, such as an explanation of where the range values come from and how to find your own values based on how often you want the test to pass.

If the K-S test usually passes, this is strong evidence that the transformation from uniform to nonuniform random values was implemented correctly. In that case, if the uniform RNG is trustworthy, then the nonuniform generator is trustworthy. Of course it is possible that a bug could still slip through the process, but this is unlikely. If the K-S test fails, examining the values of x that determine K^+ and K^- could help developers locate the bug in the RNG.

---

14. Knuth, Donald E. *The Art of Computer Programming, Vol. 2: Seminumerical Algorithms*, Third Edition. Addison-Wesley, 1998.

Conclusions

Tests for evaluating RNGs can exhibit complexity as well as unifying order. Such tests are beautiful by the classical definition of beauty. RNGs are complex because they are deterministic programs that must give the illusion of being nondeterministic. Tests of RNGs are at least as complex as the generators they validate. These tests are complex because we can seldom say anything absolute about how the RNG should behave. We have to be content with statements about how they should *usually* behave.

There are several unifying principles in testing random number generators:

- Tests boil down to saying some statistic should often be inside a certain range. The more demanding your idea of "often" is, the wider your range must be.

- Nonuniform RNGs transform the output of uniform RNGs. If you have confidence in your uniform RNG, you only have to test the distribution properties of your nonuniform RNG. The more subtle properties of randomness are inherited from the uniform RNG and do not need to be as carefully tested.

- Precise analysis of random sequences requires advanced statistics, and yet we can get a lot of mileage out of one simple observation: samples from a normal distribution are often within two or three standard deviations of their mean.

- We do not have to look too closely at how often tests pass. Correct generators usually pass tests, and buggy generators usually fail.

## CHAPTER ELEVEN

Change-Centric Testing

Murali Nandigama

THE BEAUTY OF TESTING IS FOUND NOT IN THE EFFORT but in the efficiency. Knowing what should be tested is beautiful, and knowing what is being tested is beautiful. In this chapter we discuss some techniques that are associated with efficient testing methodologies. Testing activity encompasses all aspects of a software development life cycle, be it one of the traditional waterfall, incremental, or spiral models, or the modern agile and test-driven development (TDD) models.

One of the recent project management trends is to set up continuous integration frameworks where changes are frequently integrated into the source code, the product is built, and a large part of existing tests are run to validate the correctness of code change. Although this concept was akin to the exhaustive testing methodology of the old school that was deemed as very difficult, recent advances in hardware configurations and reduced cost make this approach financially feasible. But in most common scenarios, the project would not have sufficient test cases in place to provide 100% code coverage. So, if a change is made in parts of the code that have no coverage with the existing test suite, the effectiveness of this approach becomes questionable, as the code coverage is less than 100%. Whether this approach is the best strategy or whether one should apply a change-centric testing approach is the main issue we are going to examine in this chapter.

Change-centric testing is a methodology in which the impact of the code change and the effects its propagation has on the state space of an executable are captured, and test cases that are guaranteed to cover the cumulative change effects are executed. Along with change-centric tests, we should also execute a small set of general functional and integration tests to ensure the overall correctness of the code base. This approach also highlights the areas of the code where no coverage is provided by the existing test cases, and thus opens up the possibility for targeted test development.

In the example shown in Figure 11-1, an executable has many methods in its state space. The methods in the black shade represent the actual change in the code. The gray-shaded methods represent the secondary change in the executable, since they depend on the methods that changed, and the lighter gray-shaded methods represent the third-order change impact. Other than those methods, the state space of the executable remains unaffected. So, ideally, if we can identify the test cases that are going to test the marked change, we have tested all the changes.

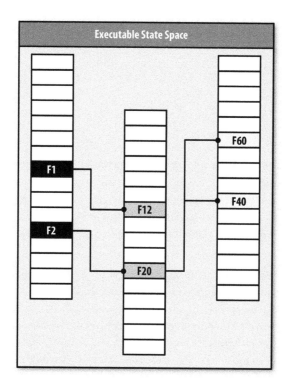

FIGURE 11-1. Change propagation in an executable state space

This approach is many times more efficient than always running all the tests on the executable for every change or running a large static test list on every change without regard to whether the test set is actually touching and testing the change made to the code base.

How to Set Up the Document-Driven, Change-Centric Testing Framework?

For new projects it is a fairly easy task to set up a document-driven, change-centric testing process. In many typical projects, most of the functional specifications draw requirements from the market requirements document (MRD) or product requirements document (PRD) and/or from user interface mockups or wire frames that are generated from the PRD specs. Let us annotate various artifacts in the UI mockups and make sure that these annotations are carried forward into the functional specifications. Look at the example in Figure 11-2, which describes a sample project for data operations.

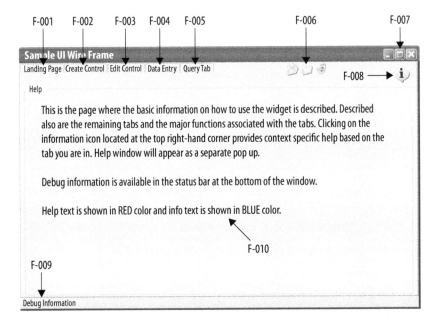

FIGURE 11-2. Sample wire frame for a graphical user interface

In this example, a sample UI wire frame is created with five tabs, three file operation controls, and three window operation controls. An information bubble is provided at the top right-hand corner of the panel for each tab, and the bubble displays context-specific help as per the requirement. Additionally, a debug window is provided at the bottom part of the panel instead of the regular status bar.

All the major functional areas of the application are tagged with sequential key words. Each of those functionality triggers may perform one or more tasks, and all of them would be tagged using the main tag as the root identifier, for example, F-008001, F-008002, and so on.

When use cases (or functional test cases) are developed for each functionality, they would be annotated to identify the area for which the test case scenario is developed.

Whenever corresponding code that is related to the functionality is checked in, the appropriate identification tag should be used as part of the check-in message into the source code control system.

Under this scenario, not only can QA execute unit tests, smoke tests, nightly tests, functional tests, and/or basic acceptance tests (BATs) on the executable, but they can make sure that all tests corresponding to the functionality tags that can be queried from the source code control system log are executed as well.

Whenever a bug is found in the development cycle or in the maintenance cycle, the developer should mention the functionality tag as part of the check-in log so that QA can query for changes based on tag values and make sure that the corresponding tests are executed. Any tests that are developed to verify the fix should also follow the same nomenclature.

This is a very simple and high-level abstract of the change-centric testing process. This approach is a document-driven process and ideal for getting into the practice of change-centric testing on a new project.

But in reality, software development life cycles are much more complex. There could be carryover code from previous projects. There could be open source libraries that are customized for the product in-house. And there could be third-party modules that are used as part of the executable.

In addition, agile development methodologies such as XP and Scrum use an iterative development process and may not even have complete or frozen requirement documents, high-level design documents, and wire frames upfront.

How do we accomplish change-centric testing in such scenarios?

Change-Centric Testing for Complex Code Development Models

In complex multiyear, multiperson software development life cycles, we usually start with an existing code base as well as preexisting test suites. Also, it is very common that there is no clear map of test cases to source files. A lot of teams actually do not have any documentation or any form of retrievable media in place that identifies what parts of the executable are touched by a given test case in the test repository.

However, many teams follow standard naming conventions and divide the source code and test code into hierarchical directories, as shown in Figure 11-3, to provide some heuristics of tests to source association at a higher level.

But this association may not be a true representation of test suites to features association in the executable. So, running a batch of test suites based on code change in a given code module is at best guesswork and does not guarantee a good change-centric testing approach.

```
|   |   |   |-- nsXULMenuAccessibleWrap.h              |   |   |   |-- feeds.xml
|   |   |   |-- nsXULTreeAccessibleWrap.cpp            |   |   |   |-- pageInfo.css
|   |   |   `-- nsXULTreeAccessibleWrap.h             |   |   |   |-- pageInfo.js
|   |   |-- other                                      |   |   |   |-- pageInfo.xul
|   |   |   |-- Makefile.in                            |   |   |   |-- permissions.js
|   |   |   |-- nsAccessNodeWrap.cpp                   |   |   |   `-- security.js
|   |   |   |-- nsAccessNodeWrap.h                     |   |   |-- safeMode.js
|   |   |   |-- nsAccessibleRelationWrap.h             |   |   |-- safeMode.xul
|   |   |   |-- nsAccessibleWrap.cpp                   |   |   |-- sanitize.js
|   |   |   |-- nsAccessibleWrap.h                     |   |   |-- sanitize.xul
|   |   |   |-- nsApplicationAccessibleWrap.h          |   |   |-- sanitizeDialog.css
|   |   |   |-- nsDocAccessibleWrap.h                  |   |   |-- sanitizeDialog.js
|   |   |   |-- nsHTMLImageAccessibleWrap.h            |   |   |-- softwareUpdateOverlay.xul
|   |   |   |-- nsHTMLTableAccessibleWrap.h            |   |   |-- tabbrowser.css
|   |   |   |-- nsHyperTextAccessibleWrap.h            |   |   |-- tabbrowser.xml
|   |   |   |-- nsRootAccessibleWrap.cpp               |   |   |-- test
|   |   |   |-- nsRootAccessibleWrap.h                 |   |   |   |-- Makefile.in
|   |   |   |-- nsTextAccessibleWrap.h                 |   |   |   |-- alltabslistener.html
|   |   |   |-- nsXULMenuAccessibleWrap.h              |   |   |   |-- browser_alltabslistener.js
|   |   |   `-- nsXULTreeAccessibleWrap.h             |   |   |   |-- browser_bug304198.js
|   |   |-- xforms                                     |   |   |   |-- browser_bug321000.js
|   |   |   |-- Makefile.in                            |   |   |   |-- browser_bug356571.js
|   |   |   |-- nsXFormsAccessible.cpp                 |   |   |   |-- browser_bug386835.js
|   |   |   |-- nsXFormsAccessible.h                   |   |   |   |-- browser_bug405137.js
|   |   |   |-- nsXFormsFormControlsAccessible.cpp     |   |   |   |-- browser_bug409481.js
|   |   |   |-- nsXFormsFormControlsAccessible.h       |   |   |   |-- browser_bug413915.js
|   |   |   |-- nsXFormsWidgetsAccessible.cpp          |   |   |   |-- browser_bug416661.js
|   |   |   `-- nsXFormsWidgetsAccessible.h           |   |   |   |-- browser_bug419612.js
|   |   `-- xul                                        |   |   |   |-- browser_bug420160.js
|   |       |-- Makefile.in                            |   |   |   |-- browser_bug423833.js
|   |       |-- nsXULAlertAccessible.cpp               |   |   |   |-- browser_bug424101.js
|   |       |-- nsXULAlertAccessible.h                 |   |   |   |-- browser_bug427559.js
|   |       |-- nsXULColorPickerAccessible.cpp
|   |       |-- nsXULColorPickerAccessible.h
|   |       |-- nsXULFormControlAccessible.cpp
```

FIGURE 11-3. Source and tests organization

Steps to Change-Centric Testing

So, how can we create a change-centric testing baseline for this type of project?

1. Understanding the caller–callee dependency between the functions/methods in the executable.

   This step involves generating the call graph of the executable state space after running all automated, manual, and ad-hoc test cases that are available in your project.

   Storing the data generated from caller–callee dependencies in a retrievable format to query the data store to identify the change propagation impact.

2. Understanding the mapping of source files to test cases and code coverage.

   This step involves generating the test case to source file/function mapping and storing the data in a retrievable format.

   At the end of the exercise, we have a many-to-many mapping between test cases and source files and functions.

   Identifying the gaps in coverage after the execution of all test cases in the project.

   Developing a targeted test development plan based on the gap analysis from the code coverage analysis.

Understanding the caller–callee dependency and test case to source file mapping

To understand the impact of change propagation across the executable, one needs to have a clear understanding of the caller–callee relations among the various methods in the executable.

Call graph generator tools would provide extraordinary help in generating this type of information.

To understand the use of call graphs to determine the impact of change, let us look at Figure 11-4.

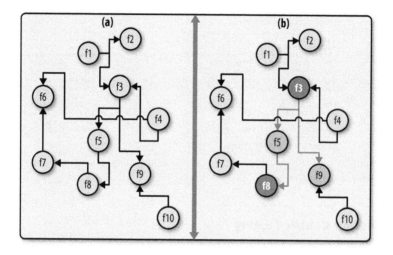

FIGURE 11-4. Call flow diagram

Let us consider the illustration in Figure 11-4(a) as the static caller–callee relation between the methods in a sample executable. Methods f2 and f3 make use of the functionality in method f1, methods f5 and f9 use functionality from f3, and so on. At the same time, methods can inherit functionality from more than one parent method and also share their functionality with more than one method downstream.

In Figure 11-4(b), we see that method f3 has been changed. Since method f3 has been changed, all subsequent methods that call method f3 and their children have potential impact on their behavior due to the change introduced in the method f3, even if they have not changed themselves. However, based on empirical data analyses, it can be safely assumed that a third-degree separation from the actual change can be safe, as any consequences of the change in method f3 would have been caught when testing the functionality of the changed method and all methods associated with it by two degrees of separation.

So, in theory, if we can identify and run test cases that touch the code in methods f3, f5, f9, and f8, we could account for the impact of change that is caused in the executable by modifications to f3.

Generating the call graph of caller–callee functions in the executable

A lot of experienced testers are very familiar with static code analysis tools. There are many commercial as well as open source static code analyzers on the market (*http://en.wikipedia.org/wiki/List_of_tools_for_static_code_analysis*).

However, in order to generate a reliable caller–callee function graph, we should be using dynamic binary analysis (DBA) and instrumentation tools.

One of the widely used open source DBA tools is Valgrind. There is a Valgrind extension that is of particular interest to us: Callgrind. Callgrind generates a reliable and comprehensive call graph from a debug or optimized build of an executable.

Make sure that you have set up the Valgrind environment on the test box properly before you execute the Callgrind extension. Callgrind generates an output file in the form of a text document.

With the help of the KCachegrind tool, the Callgrind output can be converted into a visual display.[1]

Example 1

Let us say that your program is called "foobar" and you have 20 test cases in your test base.

Now, we execute the following command:

```
valgrind -tool=callgrind ./foobar test1
```

This generates an output file *callgrind.out.pid*, where the "pid" is a number. This number will be unique for each run that you perform.

So, if you create a batch file that has 20 lines, each calling a separate test case as the argument for your executable, you would end up with 20 *callgrind.out.pid* files.

Executing the command `callgrind_annotate callgrind.out.pid` generates a test output file that contains two parts. The first part is the output header information, and the second part, which is of interest to us, would be formatted like this:

```
--------------------------------------------------------------------------
Ir                      file:function
--------------------------------------------------------------------------
3,437,648               foobar.c:main [/home/your/path/project/foobar]
2,525,400               testframework.c:DrawCircle [/home/your/path/project/foobar]
703,261                 foobar.c:Draw [/home/your/path/project/foobar]
...
```

---

1. For more details on how to execute Callgrind and KCachegrind tools, see the following resources: *http://valgrind.org/*, *http://kcachegrind.sourceforge.net/cgi-bin/show.cgi/KcacheGrindCalltreeFormat*, *http://kcachegrind.sourceforge.net/cgi-bin/show.cgi/KcacheGrindIndex*, *http://kcachegrind.sourceforge.net/cgi-bin/show.cgi/KcacheGrindInstallation*, and *http://www.stanford.edu/class/cme212/profiling.pdf*.

This information, as seen in the example, is presented in a three-column format. Column one is the number of times the call is made. Column two is the *file:function* to which the call is made. And column three is the path to the file.

So, in short, for each test *X*, we know the list of file/function calls that are made to execute the test case.

This data will finally generate a many-to-many mapping between test cases to source files. In this scenario, all tests that provide code coverage on a given source file above a specific code coverage percentage that you decide is relevant should be considered as target tests that cover the given source file.

If this information is stored in any suitable relational format, we can query for the list of test cases that touch a given file or function. Or alternatively, we can query for all Files:Functions that are touched by a given test case.

Understanding the change impact

The use of the KCachegrind tool on the cumulative *callgrind.out* data would generate call graph visualizations from the *callgrind.out.pid* files, and this visual information is very useful to understand the change impact dependencies.

There are various output formats for the KCachegrind tool, including the "dot" file format, which is human-readable. Dot files are used as input to the Graphviz tool, a popular graph visualization tool. Dot-file data can be stored in a database where programmatic queries can find the caller–callee dependencies.

Based on the caller–callee dependencies, we should be able to identify how far a change impact is going to propagate. In general, we would have three types of functions in the executable:

- Source functions
- Sync functions
- Pipe functions

A *source function* is one that is called by many other functions in the executable, and it is not dependent on other function calls in the executable, except for the OS calls and third-party shared libraries that are not part of your executable source code. So, a change made in this function has a lot of potential secondary impact on all the functions that are calling it.

A *sync function* is not called by any other function in the executable, but it makes calls to many other functions in the executable. Any change in any of the functions that it is depending on could potentially result in a behavior change for this function. So, a change made in this function theoretically has no propagation impact.

A *pipe function* makes calls to other functions, and some other functions make calls to this function. Therefore, a pipe function is impacted by changes in the functions to which it makes calls and also can potentially impact downstream functions due to its behavior change.

So, with the help of call graph generation, we should be able to identify major source functions, and pipe functions as well as sync functions.

This exercise should be periodically performed on the executable to identify any major changes in the function behavior.

We will use this information in the change-centric testing shown later in "Example 3" on page 152.

But the key question that we have to come back to is this: how do we identify test coverage gaps in the executable? If we do not have a comprehensive test suite that provides 100% code coverage, then the data generated in "Example 1" on page 149 would have gaps that don't account for portions of the code change.

Understanding the code coverage and gap analysis

Code coverage is one of the good tools available in the arsenal of QA teams. There are many articles in print and online that debate the merits of code coverage. However, code coverage can also reliably provide the map/gap of source files to test cases, and that is what we are interested in obtaining for the purpose of change-centric testing (see *http://en.wikipedia.org/wiki/Code_coverage#Software_code_coverage_tools*).

For the purpose of illustration, we would be looking at a C/C++ code base and associated tests and identifying the source files to test cases mapping.

As described earlier in Figure 11-3, we already have some kind of rough mapping between the source modules to test suites by looking at the directory structures. As described in "Example 1" on page 149, we have also generated the test case to File:Function mapping for the existing test cases. However, we have not yet found the coverage gaps that would create blind spots in our change-centric testing approach.

Now, let us create an instrumented build for the executable.

For most of the C/C++ projects, an instrumented build can be created by adding the following lines to your build configuration file:

```
export CFLAGS="-fprofile-arcs -ftest-coverage"
export CXXFLAGS="-fprofile-arcs -ftest-coverage"
export LDFLAGS="-lgcov -static-libgcc"
```

Once the instrumented build is created, we can perform multiple test runs that use only the specific set of test suites that are designed to test a specific module in the code base. This will generate a rough heuristic of test suites to code coverage mapping. If we have 20 test cases in the test suite to test a feature X in the application foobar, and those 20 test cases are providing, say, 60% code coverage, then any change made in the remaining 40% of code in the module is not testable using the test suite in any test approach. So, the alternatives are to perform ad-hoc testing and hope that the change is tested and validated, or write a new test case, since we already know that this part of the code is not testable using the existing test suite.

Example 2

Look at the Firefox browser instrumentation and test cases execution example from *https://wiki .mozilla.org/QA:CodeCoverage*.

Once an instrumented module is tested using the planned test cases that are designed to cover the module, we will be able to understand the extent of code coverage provided by the test cases on the given module. This exercise provides the covered areas of the code base for the module as well as the untested portions of the module.

On a periodic basis, a report can be generated with the details of source code coverage that has been generated by executing the test suite to monitor the changes in the coverage gaps.[2]

Example 3

Source files *file1.cpp*, *file2.cpp*, and *file3.cpp* are modified in the last 24 hours and the changes are checked into the source code control system.

The batch file/cron job, which runs on a daily basis, runs a `diff` command on the source tree with respect to the revision that was used yesterday, and would generate a text report that not only shows the list of source files that are changed but also the lines of source that have changes.

Armed with this data, we can identify the list of test cases that should be run to validate the change, as described in "Example 4" on page 153.

What Have We Learned So Far?

We know how to generate caller–callee dependencies among the functions in the source code of the executable using dynamic binary analysis, with the help of the Valgrind tool suite.

We also have identified the test case to source files mapping from the Callgrind tool. To do this, we need a debug or optimized build where build symbols are preserved for generating useful call graphs.

We have identified the source, sync, and pipe functions in the source code using the KCachegrind tool.

We have generated an instrumented executable using gcov.

We also have generated the extent of cumulative code coverage after executing all tests at once on the executable to identify covered areas of code and code gaps.

From the source code control system, we have identified the list of changed files in the last 24 hours, as well as details of the changed code.

---

2. Script used in Mozilla to convert a code coverage HTML report into a CSV file that can be used for programmatic analysis. See *http://wiki.mozilla.org/Firefly*.

Armed with this data, we can generate an effective change-centric test suite that has the highest probability of testing the changes in the code base.

Example 4

Source files *file1.cpp*, *file2.cpp*, and *file3.cpp* are modified in the last 24 hours, and the changes are checked into the source code control system.

The batch file/cron job, which runs on a daily basis, runs a `diff` command on the source tree with respect to the revision that was used yesterday, and would generate a text report that not only shows the list of source files that are changed, but also the lines of source that have changes.

From the code coverage data, we have identified that:

- *file1.cpp* has 80% coverage
- *file2.cpp* has 30% coverage
- *file3.cpp* has 100% coverage

Scenario 1

Function 1 in *file1.cpp* is modified. It is a source function, and five other functions make a call to it. This data is obtained from the call graph we generated earlier.

We have test cases that touch the source *file1.cpp*, and the source file coverage details show that the tests are covering the code block that belongs to Function 1.

We have existing test suites to validate this primary code change. We also identified the test cases corresponding to the source files that contain the five functions that are calling Function 1. We made sure that specific functions have been covered by the test cases that map to respective source files and flagged all those functions that do not have code coverage for future test development. We then continued the process for the functions that are making calls to these five functions that have indirect change impact.

Scenario 2

Function 2 in *file2.cpp* is modified, and it is a sync function. This data is also obtained from the call graph we generated earlier.

There is low coverage on this file, 30%, and the tests that are generating this coverage are not touching Function 2.

Even though we do not have a test case in place to validate this change, the risk of failure is contained within this function. However, we flagged this scenario to develop test cases to validate this change as soon as possible, depending on the project priorities.

Scenario 3

Function 3 in *file3.cpp* is modified, and it is a pipe function. It makes calls to three functions, and four other functions make a call to it.

We have test cases that touch the source *file1.cpp*, and the source file coverage details show that the tests are covering the code block that belongs to Function 1.

We have existing test suites to validate this code change. We also identified test cases corresponding to the source files that contain the four functions that are calling Function 3. We made sure that the specific functions have been covered by the test cases that map to respective source files and flagged all those functions that do not have code coverage for future test development. We then continued the process for the functions that are making calls to these four functions that have indirect change impact.

This way, we have generated a list of test cases that can test the change. We have also identified potential gaps in the test suites that miss testing certain parts of change, which we would not have identified without this approach.

As usual, this change-centric test list has to run in conjunction with a static list of limited functional test cases that are meant to cover the overall behavior of the application.

Conclusions

Change-centric testing is not a difficult task to accomplish. Once there is a good understanding of the extent of coverage provided by the existing test suites, the call graph dependencies in the executable, and the details of change made to the source code in a given interval, it will become a trivial task to generate a dynamic list of tests that test the change. Empirical experiments on large code bases have shown that the list of bugs that slipped detection is much shorter, and a lot of test cycle time is saved in this approach. This approach is beneficial when the existing "run all tests on a nightly basis" takes more than few hours to complete. With a change-centric testing approach, the size of the test suite that needs to be run on a nightly basis can be reduced dramatically.

Also, a change-centric testing approach provides a good insight into gaps in code coverage versus daily changes in the code base. This is a useful input for targeted test development.

However, this approach does not advocate that you stop running full-cycle system tests periodically. Full-cycle system tests need to be run at regular but longer intervals instead of daily or nightly intervals.

## CHAPTER TWELVE

Software in Use

Karen N. Johnson

I stood in the ICU at my mom's bedside, thinking, "Don't cry, not now." I told myself I'd cry later on when I was alone. I didn't want to disrupt what was already chaos around me by becoming hysterical. I wanted to think clearly about what was going on. And I knew once I started crying, I would not be able to stop.

So I kept swallowing deeply, trying not to cry. My mom was lying in the hospital bed, hooked up to multiple devices. Her eyes were closed tight; she seemed to be in a deep sleep. I had the feeling that she was many miles away from me, but I was standing only inches from her side.

My mom had fallen and within 48 hours a brain injury had erupted deep inside her head that required emergency neurosurgery. Now post-surgery, she was in what the nurses and doctors refer to as a nonresponsive state. Her condition was unclear and her status considered unstable.

The neurosurgical ICU at Brigham and Women's Hospital in Boston is shaped in an arc, with each patient in a small alcove of her own. Each patient has her own nurse who stays within a few feet of the assigned patient at all times. That day an assortment of doctors, specialists, and family members streamed through the arched pathway, disappearing into the separate alcoves. A sense of urgency hung in the air. It occurred to me that each alcove had not only a patient but also a family and an event that had taken place. Everyone in the ICU has a story, a drama unfolding, and a family in panic and wait mode.

I was about as alone with my mom as one can be in a busy ICU. I looked up and around at all the equipment. There were tubes, wires, and unknown devices. All the equipment looked pretty scary. I started reading the labels on the devices for distraction. Labels, I thought, will give me something to focus on. Reading labels will keep me from crying. The labels had company names printed on them, names such as Abbott Labs, Hospira, and Baxter. I knew each of these companies. I knew people who had worked at each of these companies. Gee, *I'd* worked at these companies. Memories of past projects and people began to trickle through my mind, a welcome distraction.

One tube in particular caught my eye. It was a feeding tube. It distressed me to see my mom's name on that tube. She'd always said that if she ever needed to be on a feeding tube, we should just…. I didn't want to think about that. I moved closer to the tube, my eyes following it from the fluid in the sterile bag hooked on an IV pole winding its way down to my mom. "Total parental nutrition" was the medical description of the fluid being pumped. I'd worked on that type of medical device and the computer software that directs it in building the right composition of fluids for the patient. If the dosage of the fluids or the mix of fluids is not correct, the patient can die.

I realized this was software I'd tested.

A Connection to My Work

Three weeks later, with my mom's situation stabilized as much as possible, it was time for me to go home to Chicago. My mom's condition had improved. She'd moved from the ICU to a regular hospital room, and then on to a rehabilitation center. Her progress had gone well, but she had a long way to go for a full recovery. I knew upon my return to Chicago I would once again have to seek work. Sometimes work finds me, and sometimes I find it. It's been that way since I left my full-time employment almost three years ago and became an independent consultant.

Once I was settled back into my home office, I contacted people I knew and in general looked for work. I got an unexpected phone call from a local company that I sometimes contracted jobs through. Was I available for some validation work? The contract company told me that the client had asked for me by name. The reason they'd asked for me was based on my previous experience with medical software. I had a good hunch which client it was, based on the contracting company. Who's looking for me? And what's the work?

The answer was, "The product is a total parental nutrition (TPN) product, and they need someone who can ensure the software testing has been robust enough. Are you interested?"

A few phone calls and a signed contract later, I was paired with a pharmacist to work on reviewing the software testing of a TPN product. A product just like what my mom was now dependent on for staying alive. When someone's in a hospital or rehab center, it's hard to know which device is being used on any given day, especially when the device isn't at the patient's bedside but is instead used at the medical lab offsite or down a hallway in a hospital lab where the IV bags of solutions are built before being dispensed to the patient.

So I don't know for certain whether the software I've tested in this area is the exact software that was used to build the solutions that kept my mom alive. But for me, the experience of seeing her hooked to a device that could easily and may possibly have been the same device with the same software that I tested had an effect on me.

If you've never tested medical software or worked with medical devices, you might want to believe that the testing and the overall development process is more rigorous than it is for any other type of hardware or software. But it isn't, necessarily.

The truth is there is not much difference between the software testing that takes place on medical software and other software. Yes, there are mountains of documentation, internal audits, and a final stamp of approval from the Food and Drug Administration (FDA). But when you peel back the formality and the perceived rigor, testing medical software relies on people and their abilities just as much as any other software or product. There is no special magic behind the testing of medical software; the quality of a product comes from the talents and ability of the team.

I think back to an earlier experience I had testing medical software. The personal conviction, common sense, and pure integrity of a couple of people in particular on the team made the difference. I was an individual contributor on that team, and I am fortunate to have seen integrity in action, which is clearly one of the more beautiful sights to see. For me, in more than two decades of working with software and watching technologies come and go, it is the people that always make the difference. Just because it is beauty that cannot be seen on a canvas nor heard at a symphony doesn't make it less beautiful. I believe it is a story to be told.

From the Inside

It was just a few years ago when I heard about the need for a software tester on a project with two people I had known for some years. It sounded like an unusual project; a project that I might be able to sink my teeth into. It was testing the software that communicates to and directs a medical device. I'd never worked with software that could so immediately affect a person. I recall asking what the worst-case scenario was if the software didn't perform correctly. The answer "patient death" made me open my eyes wide and think hard about accepting the work.

After all, it wasn't but a couple of years earlier that I had been working on an e-commerce site that sold groceries. On that team we occasionally made lighthearted jokes on stressful days that the worst that could happen was a customer would be missing his milk and bread. Before accepting the new project, I recall thinking that there would probably be no lighthearted days on this one. That was a good general realization to have before beginning work.

On a personal level, I knew one of the leads, Michael Purcell, from previous work experience, but I had never worked with him directly on a project. His reputation and work ethic are well known. I'd admired his work from afar, and the chance to work with him on a project appealed to me. Even more appealing was the prospect of being paired directly with him.

The second person I knew was Ed Young. I'd hired him some years before. I remember thinking that even if the work would be intense, I could relax in one regard: I knew I could rely on Ed and Michael. Ethically, I could trust both of them; there was simply no way either person would ship a product he didn't believe was ready. And I also knew that they would listen carefully and closely to anyone working on the project, regardless of the person's stature or employment status. I've seen projects before where contractors were treated poorly and their input barely listened to. There would none of that with Ed and Michael leading.

I wanted to be on this team.

I was given the title of Study Author, as about half of my time would be writing and the other half devoted to hands-on testing. This was a perfect pairing of tasks for me.

In some ways I was part of the entire team working toward ensuring that the product was ready for market. In other ways, I worked alone, which has always suited me well. Although several testers were focused on specific, discrete parts of the product suite, my focus was to be broader. I would test alone, away from the other testers, and test from a wider perspective with a more holistic approach, while the other testers would focus on specifics and details. I sat near the team, but we rarely had the same schedule. Ed and a test lead spent time together coordinating activities while Michael and I coordinated our own efforts. And yet we communicated as an entire team frequently.

Notably, on every project I've worked on that I would consider successful, constant communication was always a contributor.

I was paired with Michael and functioned in several ways as his right hand. We talked candidly then and we talk candidly now about what my strengths are and are not. Michael is a tough but honest critic, and this includes his ability to critique his own work and strengths. Michael and I agreed that one of my strengths was my ability to write. My past experience writing validation documents that could stand up to an FDA audit would be critical. And Michael's ability to edit my writing proved to be another perfect pairing. (In fact, as a personal request, Michael was my preview editor of this chapter.)

We recognized that Michael knew the product better than I did, but we also believed I had a more comprehensive testing background compared to his engineering background.

It's interesting that physical beauty often includes a sense of harmony and symmetry. These pairings—testing and writing, testing knowledge versus engineering knowledge, low-level specific component testing versus high-level general system testing—brought symmetry to our work. These were forms of checks and balances.

Many times, Michael would explain his testing ideas to me, and at least two things would take place during these exchanges. One was that I was slowly and in detail learning about the product. And the second was that we would use the strengths, insights, and experiences we each had while we took turns raising challenging questions. Questions such as: How could we test better? What else can we do to challenge the product? What else can we do to gain faith that the product will work well in production?

One of the subtlest aspects of working on a project is the atmosphere. It doesn't seem to be something that is discussed often. It seems we are more engrossed by the technology or the tools or the raw skills of the people, not to mention how often we focus on the deadlines. And yet it's the atmosphere on a project that I believe contributes to my ability to do my best work. Working with Michael I've always felt like I can muse out loud, share my thoughts—really brainstorm without recrimination. I can go out to the far edges and toss ideas out. And of course, after chatting over ideas, we do toss a fair amount of them out. But I think that in order for team members to generate test ideas, they need wide-open space to explore what might be possible before they can lasso those ideas into reality.

And so, this is how we worked. We worked together; we worked alone. We constantly reverted back to guiding questions and challenged each other and our ideas. We kept plodding on, doing our best.

And yet, something was missing.

Adding Different Perspectives

There was a day when the three of us, Michael, Ed, and I, were talking in a hallway. We were talking about how each of us felt pretty certain there were still defects in the product. Even though the test team had been diligent in testing, something was missing. Where was our confidence and conviction that the product was ready? We each had the sense that there were issues still lurking. It was more than a hunch; we each knew of a few bugs that hadn't been consistently reproduced and corrected. Each of the testers felt the same: the product wasn't ready yet.

How could we solve the problem?

From a business perspective, Ed worked to get the approvals and financing needed to implement our new ideas. It's easy not to think about what efforts Ed had to work through with management, because he gracefully kept those concerns from draining our energies. Michael and I remained focused on the testing efforts.

Like many complex problems, it took more than one solution. First, we added a different approach to testing. We wanted an opportunity to follow through on our hunches where issues remained. A new team of testers would be brought in to execute testing in an exploratory approach while the existing testers who had been working with prepared written test scripts would continue. The plan was to keep the scripted testers executing the test scripts that would be required for the FDA audit before product launch and to have the second team find what was missing. The second team of testers would be trained, fed hunches, and would primarily function as exploratory testers.

Once the decision to bring in more testers was made, the urgency on the project picked up pace. A training room was turned into a makeshift test lab. The room had several rows of workbenches with computers. The computers had the needed mix of operating systems and software already in place. Arrangements were made so that the new test team could have the training room without disruption for several weeks.

Unfortunately, the computers were all desktop models and cabled such that moving any equipment required cutting cable wraps. The workbenches were narrow and the spaces between the computers limited, so keeping a notebook alongside a computer was difficult. The room was never designed for working such long days, and the days were long. It was a windowless room with limited unused space. And by having so many of the computers working so many hours per day, the room could get hot and sticky, even though it was winter.

Still, the room had energy. Every person working there, whether all day or for brief bursts of time, knew they were there for a reason. The work was clear. When the software you're testing is responsible for what dose a patient receives and death is a very real risk, there is a sense of purpose that's difficult to articulate but a feeling and sensation that hangs in the air each day.

The exploratory testers were hired quickly. They had less time to learn the product than the scripted testers, but they received more personal interaction from various members of the team who were anxious to get them up to speed. Before long, there was a testing frenzy taking place, with both teams of testers working to get the product in shippable shape.

Another solution we came up with was to build and use a scientific test lab that would be equipped with the medical devices and the computers for testing, which would more closely simulate real use. The science lab would require space and equipment that hadn't been planned previously. The theory was that we would rigorously exercise the software using yet another test strategy. Instead of focusing on details and purposely looking to discover issues at the micro level, the testing planned for the science lab was designed to find issues at a more macro level. We needed time to explore all the components together.

Another solution was to carve out time to purposely test from a multiuser perspective. We knew that in a busy medical lab multiple people would be using the software in bursts of activities. We wanted to test resource contention, file-sharing issues, and periods of stress on the system in specific ways that we believed would mimic real-life use. I had previous experience testing software in multiuser scenarios, and even though my experience was not related to medical software, that background was helpful in the planning process.

Exploratory testing, stress testing, multiuser testing, and real-life simulation are all different ways of exploring software. By altering focus, different views and issues can be found and exposed. In our case, none of these approaches were frivolous or far-fetched; in fact, each form of testing was designed to be as practical and realistic as we knew how to make it.

Exploratory, Ad-Hoc, and Scripted Testing

Cem Kaner first introduced the term "exploratory testing" in the book *Testing Computer Software* (Wiley). In his use of the term, he offered an approach that emphasized the value of testing as a brain-engaged, thoughtful process, as opposed to testing by executing prescriptive test scripts. Since then, software testing expert James Bach has devoted more than a decade to teaching, writing, and presenting on the topic of exploratory testing. The following is a definition of exploratory testing taken from James's website:

> The plainest definition of exploratory testing is test design and test execution at the same time.

With exploratory testing, test charters are written to focus testing and provide a strategy for a test session. Session-based exploratory testing adds the concept of defining a length of time for the session. Testing is executed in sessions where the focus remains primarily, if not exclusively, on the test charter. Within a test session, a tester can explore, create ideas, and execute these ideas, providing a sense of test coverage and confidence. And when it's not possible to finish all of the ideas in one test session, additional test sessions can be planned. Exploratory testing takes discipline.

There are elements from this definition posted on Wikipedia (*http://en.wikipedia.org/wiki/Exploratory_testing*) that are worth reflecting on:

> Exploratory testing seeks to find out how the software actually works, and to ask questions about how it will handle difficult and easy cases. The testing is dependent on the tester's skill of inventing test cases and finding defects. The more the tester knows about the product and different test methods, the better the testing will be.

The second group of testers used several different approaches to testing, including, but not limited to, exploratory testing. For their exploratory testing, the testers executed focused sessions. I think one important differentiator between ad-hoc testing and exploratory testing is focus. The testers were trained on the product and had access to everyone on the team, but were then left to their own thinking process to create test ideas, investigate, test, and discover. The exploratory testing was certainly reliant on the thinking and skills of the testers.

As testers completed test sessions, they would discuss their findings, resolve their questions, and report defects. Those post-execution conversations determined whether additional testing was needed and shaped those next steps. Those conversations provided valuable learning sessions—learning for the testers as well as for the other people on the team.

James Bach uses the term "debrief" to describe a conversation that can be held after testing that helps draw out information from the tester. He offers a debriefing checklist on his website at *http://www.satisfice.com/sbtm/debrief_checklist.htm*. These post-execution conversations that we held did not follow James's checklist of ideas. Instead, the questions and conversations were more specifically tailored according to the tester, the topic, the findings, and the overall context of what was taking place and what metrics the team was interested in maintaining.

There is no advantage in departing from the formality of scripted testing to adopt exploratory testing without adapting as needed. There is beauty in finding your own path, in understanding what is needed and applying what makes sense.

Another alternative to prescriptive test scripts and exploratory testing is ad-hoc testing. Ad-hoc testing is often confused with exploratory testing, but there are essential differences between the two.

James's site offers the following clarification of the difference between ad-hoc and exploratory testing:

> Exploratory testing is sometimes confused with "ad hoc" testing. Ad-hoc testing normally refers to a process of improvised, impromptu bug searching. By definition, anyone can do ad-hoc testing.

With ad-hoc testing, testers execute test ideas as the ideas tumble into their heads. The core advantage of ad-hoc testing is that everyone can test. Each tester's primary ideas have an opportunity to be explored. But this might be where the advantage of ad-hoc testing ends. Most people untrained in testing run out of ideas rather quickly, and so, after a short burst of test session, they're done. Untrained testers often cannot repeat the steps they took to find a defect. And with ad-hoc test sessions, testers bounce from one area of an application to another area; it is hard to understand what's been tested and what remains to be tested.

But ad-hoc testing has its advantage in generating energy, especially when it's executed in "bug bash" sessions. We used this tactic on our project as well. Someone on the team would share an idea about where a defect might remain, and then all the testers would pursue that idea for a short period of time. As people tested, they would talk out loud, and impromptu brainstorming would take place. Everyone had ideas. One benefit of having the second team of testers and a separate test room was having the chance to explore ideas and to participate in unplanned test activities. If one person shared an idea, everyone in the room could jump in and add to or extend the idea in some way.

Other tests sessions were executed when a tester was paired with someone on the team for a conversation and generating ideas about potential issues. Some of those ideas came from the scripted testers who had either a suspicion about a defect or had encountered an issue but had not been able to replicate the defect. Those ideas were shared in conversations before testing, and that same spirit of collaboration continued post-execution. The scripted testers were encouraged to share their test ideas with the exploratory testers. The scripted testers could continue the required test execution work, and the exploratory testers could work on hunches.

And yet another type of testing took place when the exploratory test team looked at the scripted tests for a particular area of the product and generated more ideas after reading the scripts. In part, the test scripts provided training through having such detailed test steps written out. By reviewing the scripts, testers could extend their ideas based on whether those tests would include different data or different permutations, or sometimes they would just provide food for thought. Is that ad hoc? Is that exploratory? Each of these approaches to testing had its positive impact. Bugs were being found and repaired, and our confidence was rising.

Multiuser Testing

I have a vision in my mind about performance and multiuser testing. The vision certainly applies when test automation is being used, but also when manual multiuser testing takes place. I envision multiple test automation scripts running at the same time, each script simulating multiple users performing a set of activities. I see each script running like a bar of color, like radio frequency waves. The scripts run like music, in a crescendo, the peaks coming close together, almost colliding and creating spikes, and at times running wildly with different peaks and lulls in a cadence of their own. I think of it especially when I hear full symphonic pieces of music, the sense of harmony, of working together.

Each instrument adds to the overall symphonic effect, just as each manual tester adds to the overall impact on the system under test. Even a single manual tester alters the environment by simply being on the system. It takes the entire orchestra to achieve some sounds, just as it takes a multitude of scripts or manual testers to achieve a production load simulation. The activity is no longer about one tester, but rather is about what is achieved as a collective.

Multiuser testing is not the same as performance testing per se. Performance testing is often focused primarily on transaction timings. In the case of multiuser testing, our goal was not about timings, but instead focused on what happens when multiple people execute a specific activity at the same time. Overall, the multiuser test ideas were about preventing data corruption, record contention, duplicate records, or system crashes.

The test concepts were sobering reminders of the importance of thoroughly testing a medical device. Although a test condition might have been, "Let's check race conditions on editing a patient record," underneath that test condition was a possibility that two lab technicians could edit a patient's record at the same time and cause either corrupted data or leave patient data in such a state that an inaccurate patient prescription could be created—and should the prescription be dispensed to the patient, that patient could die. Such was the case with nearly every test condition in the multiuser area of testing, and the potential consequences were chilling.

One advantage of having the exploratory testers in one physical room was that we could coordinate multiuser tests more easily. We'd speculated about a few issues in this area, but we didn't gather proof of how ugly it could be until we had the ability to orchestrate multiple people with multiple PCs running through multiple tests. We had accumulated a collection of ideas, and now we had the means to execute.

Michael crafted a set of multiuser tests before the exploratory testers joined the project. I had worked with multiuser testing previously, and we had discussed ideas. Our collection of ideas was centered on making sure patient data and patient prescriptions would not collide and could not be corrupted. Since the application prevented more than one instance running on one computer, it had not been possible to easily plan or conduct this type of testing by any one tester alone at his desk with only one computer. We did have a small test lab with multiple workstations, where some multiuser tests had been attempted, but not with this much focus or attention and not with the ease of access to multiple computers and multiple testers whose activities could more readily be orchestrated.

The test suite grew significantly as team members added new ideas and "what if" scenarios. The test execution sessions had energy. One idea would spawn another, and that one yet another. Everyone had ideas and everyone contributed. The opportunity to brainstorm had been revived. No longer was testing disengaged from thinking, as is often the case with executing prescriptive test cases. Testing in the makeshift test lab had a professional atmosphere focused on finding and sharing ideas. When an intelligent group of people gathers together and is given the time and space to explore, the desire to come up with great ideas and to be a strong contributor flourishes. In contrast, isolated, solitary, mechanical test execution reduces brain engagement by virtue of the need to execute and prove that the test script was not varied in the execution process.

Upstairs, the scripted testers plodded along. Piles of executed test scripts stacked up with their traditionally daunting impression that everything had been tested. But the energy and the ideas flowing in the training room made it apparent that all the test ideas had not been thought of before and were not captured by the test scripts. Rather than viewing the test scripts as defective or inadequate, the general sense of the team was that the software and the devices offered more permutations and possible flaws than might ever be tested, found, or addressed.

We might want to believe that all the testing has been executed, every bug has been found, and perfect software has been achieved, especially when it comes to a medical device. But perfection is not reality. Instead, assurance is found in knowing that a product works well and that, even without perfection, beauty exists.

With the mix of testing activities taking place, we were in fact finding issues. And in finding more flaws, our confidence that we were seeing the product more accurately increased. Better to find defects and argue about what needed to be addressed than not find the defects before shipping.

Most of the multiuser tests were executed with someone standing at the front of the room and explaining the test. Each tester would try out the software to make sure they understood what was being discussed and how to execute what was needed. The person leading the test would then orchestrate the testers to discover "what would happen if...?"

The testers worked through multiple executions with the same goal until we had good answers to the following questions:

- Did each tester understand what she needed to do?
- Was the test conductor satisfied that the timing and execution had achieved the goal?

- Had the test been executed enough times to conclude what the results were?
- Were any issues discovered?

In addition to the multiuser testing, testing was run to ensure that a busy medical lab with a volume of data, patients, and prescriptions would be ready to handle the anticipated load. At a high level, we knew what the correct responses should be: no duplicate records, no race conditions, no data corruption, and no system hangs. Beyond that, no tester needed specifically written expected results to know when something was wrong.

These tests were later turned into formal test scripts. What had been exploratory at the start became repeatable scripts. The value of turning the testing into repeatable scripts was the assurance that this form of multiuser testing would be executed any time the software was released in the future. This is an aspect of working with regulated software: test scripts deemed as essential for one release cannot be dismissed for the next release without a review and explanation. It had become clear to us that this form of testing needed to remain as part of the overall product testing for all future releases.

We couldn't ensure the creativity and energy of the future testing, but we could ensure that multiuser testing would be considered essential. To have a team able to function in such a way that it can achieve something no one person can achieve alone is, to me, the beauty of teamwork. For each of these sessions I participated in, and the multiuser testing sessions in particular—even when the testing found no issues—the sense of teamwork had immeasurable positive and lasting effects.

The Science Lab

Most of the testing throughout the project took place with just the software, and a smaller amount of the testing took place with the software and the medical devices paired together. But Michael felt that the full product couldn't be validated without a realistic workout, and that workout would be bringing all the components together in a lab with multiple days of heavy full usage.

Michael was in the process of designing what, to this day, I still think of as "the science lab." The intention of the lab was to pair computers with the medical devices. Once the lab was assembled, we paired the exploratory testers and the scripted testers for simulated use of the medical devices and the software in a scenario that mimicked real life as closely as possible. The lab testing days were planned as the final formal testing of the product.

Michael had planned every aspect of the science lab with some assistance from me. It was no simple task to think through, order, and arrange computers, software, cabling, workbenches, medical devices, more cabling, fluids, IV bags, tubing, printers, and labels. The room was also equipped with a laminar flow hood, which is a workbench designed to be partially enclosed to minimize contamination of the fluids being worked with. It can be loud when the air filtration is running, and it also takes up considerable space and adds some complexity to working with the devices. But Michael felt that the flow hood was necessary, as most labs would have a flow hood and some, if not all, patient prescriptions would be built inside a flow hood. Each tester would be trained to work with it. For the computers, the network connections had to be configured, as did the software. For the medical devices, each device required some assembly and calibration before use.

Then it was time to assemble the lab, and we spent several days doing this together. I recall Michael's practical suggestion for the lab assembly days: wear jeans and bring a pocketknife if you own one. We cracked open the boxes for computers and the medical devices. I learned more about the devices while configuring the equipment. As we set up, we discussed the logistics of the coming days.

The day we finished setting up the lab, I stood at the door and looked back to see how everything looked. The lab was a large rectangular room with concrete walls. The back wall had a large sink and a long counter. In the middle of the room were two long worktables with two rows of carefully configured devices. Overhead, a long wire-framed tunnel loomed with countless cables running from devices to computers and from devices to printers. The computers were configured. The printers had paper. The devices had been calibrated and there were rows of fluids ready for use. The laminar flow hood had been set up and configured. The lab looked clean, organized, and ready.

At the end of the day, I taped a paper sign from the inside of the glass door. The sign had the project name and a short list of who to call for access to the room. We shut the lights off. Michael headed out for the day. I recall standing for a short time outside the lab door, peering through the glass, ready for the coming days of testing.

Simulating Real Use

A test execution plan was laid out for the testing days at the science lab. The core of the plan simulated multiple full days of real-as-possible use of not just the software, but also the software that worked with the devices and the devices that generated the solutions. We wanted to test what might be thought of as "end to end" testing, at least as far as we could take the simulation. After all, we didn't have patients. But we wanted the testing to be comprehensive and holistic. We also had an underlying desire to see the software and the devices working in harmony for multiple hours and days in a row. And although we weren't trying to stress-test either the software or the devices (this had been done previously), we did want testing to span full and hearty days of work.

Unlike many days on the project when people would work alone, the testing days at the science lab were very much a team exercise. Everyone had a role, and each person knew what work she needed to execute. Prior to the days in the lab, we'd mapped out a plan. We briefed everyone on the team and discussed the plan multiple times in advance, to both smooth out the plan and to incorporate ideas and feedback from the team. We wanted to be ready to rock and roll when we hit the lab.

Two teams were planned. Each team represented a technical configuration that would be used in production, the theory being that each team would mimic a medical lab with a specific computer, software, and medical device configuration. The overall lab would be busy, printers would have other prescriptions in the queue, fluids would need to be replaced, tubing that would get a heavy workout would need to be flushed and possibly changed. We planned the days to be busy, robust, and even a bit hectic in spots, just as a medical lab might be.

Each team had multiple patient prescriptions to fulfill, with each prescription representing a variation we wanted to address. And, of course, that itself could be a deviation from real use. Perhaps on an ordinary day in an actual medical lab there wouldn't be this much variation of prescriptions.

Understanding, knowing, and designing testing around real-life scenarios can be challenging. To know how a product will be used in the field by actual users means you have to gain insights from the user perspective. It can be particularly challenging if the product has never been released to production.

Even on products that are already in production, finding out what users really do with the software can be difficult. In the case of a web application, it might be possible to get that information from server logs. In the case of medical devices, we can't just ask a hospital or a lab for their production logs. Sensitive patient data is well protected (understandably) by the Health Insurance Portability and Accountability Act (HIPAA) and other regulations.

But what if we're not interested in the patient data? What if we just want to do the best possible testing and we believe having insight into field use will give us that? I've wanted to shout this question to some unknown group of medical doctors and lab specialists, but the short answer is that I've never seen that dilemma solved.

It would be great to have the test lead of each medical device paired with a medical practitioner to see real-life events unfolding and learn how a device or software is used under stressful, tight timing, and intense situations when the need is critical.

I envision a wonderful pairing: an opportunity for testers to better understand a product's use and for an end user to be able to give insight to a tester in a way that no requirement document or any use case could ever impart. Why isn't this just viewed as a practical, grounded solution? And why would the software testing community and the actual medical practitioners not be encouraged to make this happen?

Instead, as testers, we earnestly try to create scenarios we believe are realistic. But what do we know when we're sitting in an office surrounded by office workers and far away from the setting a product will be used in? We do the best we can.

In life, we don't know when a memory is being created. It isn't until time passes and we see the events that stay with us become the memories that we keep. I can recall the days in the science lab vividly in memory.

It seemed that everyone on the team was just a bit nervous, a bit anxious, and more willing to help each other than ever. There was an atmosphere that's hard to describe. Maybe a collection of words is the best way to describe those days in the science lab: serious, intent, stressful, exciting. It also seemed that we wanted each person to be able to execute what was needed. The sense of camaraderie was strong. We moved together. If one person needed a break, the whole team would have to wait. We arrived together, we worked together, we ate lunch together, and we couldn't wrap up for the day unless the whole team was ready.

The days in the lab were long. People made mistakes. We documented what we did. We had two team members on hand who did not execute but were there to collect documentation and review materials as they were generated. I think we each knew that we would have to uncover something truly significant in order for these days to be repeated. We hoped we were long past that part of the product cycle.

Instead of testing the software in small, focused areas, and thinking about the software from a technical perspective, designing simulated real-life scenarios has the beauty of stringing multiple aspects of usage into full-length scenarios. There was a hope, and certainly an intent, that full-length scenarios would flush out defects not found until this type of simulated usage was executed.

After all, this is how the product would be used.

Testing in the Regulated World

In 2001, my boss Jim Kandler explained how to test software in a regulated world. His explanation to me (referring to the FDA) was: tell them what you going to do, do it, and then prove you did it. "Gee, that's it?", I can recall thinking. But it's a lot harder to do than it sounds.

What Jim meant by "tell them what you going to do" is this: document the process. Document it for multiple people—the team who will execute the process, the company so that they know the team has a process, and of course, for the FDA. I was taught that an FDA auditor will review the process documentation as one of the first parts of an audit and then ask for evidence that you've followed the process. Some of the other documents they request first are defect reports, the trace matrix, and the final validation report.

What I've found is that detailing the process you believe the team follows is harder than it sounds when you get down to the nuances, not to mention the exceptions that occur in real life.

In the regulated waterfall approach to software development that I've seen, requirements are drafted. Requirements are from a business perspective, the patient perspective, the customer perspective, and from a systems point of view. Often people write them without thinking about testing or about how they are going to prove the requirement. Often people write them without a software tester's involvement.

The requirements evolve into design specifications, and since the business analyst often cannot address the technical implementation, the design is usually written by development. One of the classic issues is that development often writes design specifications ahead of time, so they haven't yet hit the roadblocks of implementing the ideas. The design gets written ahead of time, ahead of knowledge, and then the documents go through a chronic revamp process, which leaves the documents in a state that is less than helpful.

It seems to me that when unregulated software is being developed, open conversations about possible remaining bugs are fairly common. Conversely, when the product undergoes FDA scrutiny, those open conversations are less easy to have for political reasons. For regulated products there is a formal process for documenting, reviewing, and resolving defects. But even with a regulated product, there is tremendous momentum in getting a product to ship. To announce late in the process that more tests could be done or that possible defects exist creates unsettled circumstances. Everyone knows that if critical bugs are found, those bugs need to be fixed. Opening up the code requires reexecuting numerous test cases and possibly extensive product release documentation adjustments. The cost can be significant. Pressure mounts. It's exactly a condition in which creating and asking to execute additional testing can be difficult. And it is exactly a condition under which more testing should be done—especially on products that have such critical outcomes.

Nonemployees are rarely part of the FDA audit at the end of the product development cycle. The lead person who works with the FDA to move the product through the audit is carefully selected. The lead person needs a mixture of regulatory experience, product experience, and enough knowledge about the team to assemble whatever additional information is needed rapidly and with confidence. I've never witnessed a hands-on tester pulled into the process.

In 2001, one of my first training experiences was being sent to FDA auditor training. My boss, Jim Kandler, wanted me to understand firsthand what an FDA auditor was trained to look for. Beyond the papers, if I were an FDA auditor myself, I'd want to talk to the testers from the team. I'd want to hear directly from the people who touched the software and got to know the product. I would not want to be left with a designated spokesperson.

What happened behind the doors of the FDA audit for this particular product, I will never know. I know the product is in use on the market.

At the End

On the last day of testing at the science lab, we lingered about. Most of us were working as contractors. We knew once the testing was done we'd roll off the project and likely never work as a team again. This is part of a contractor's work: projects end and people move onto other projects. Some people keep in touch, some don't. I like the frequent change. I like being on a project long enough to see what works and what doesn't. I like to get to know people. I like to see products launch and be used.

The days in the science lab were some of the last project days for the contractors. The overall product release moved forward with activities such as final validation documents, manufacturing considerations, and delivery details before final product launch.

I wasn't prepared to see a total parental nutrition product used to care for a family member. But I'm grateful that in this imperfect world, people do their best to create products that matter. And each of those products needs people who can test.

## CHAPTER THIRTEEN

Software Development Is a Creative Process

Chris McMahon

MOST OF THE WELL-KNOWN SOFTWARE DEVELOPMENT QUALITY PROCESSES come to us from the manufacturing industry. ISO9000, Six Sigma, and Lean all come from the assembly line, as does CMM to a certain extent. They are certainly all effective in the environments in which they were conceived.

And yet for every software business that succeeds in improving quality by these means, any number of others fail to get any benefit, regardless of how much they spend implementing the systems. At the same time, there are any number of highly successful software businesses and software products that succeed even though they follow no accepted quality processes at all.

A number of us in the software testing and development community have begun to suspect that we have been applying processes to the analysis of quality in software development that do not map to the actual work that we do. A few of us go further and suggest that software development, although it has roots in computer science and engineering, is now fundamentally a creative process, not a manufacturing activity or an engineering discipline at all. When we try to analyze and evaluate what we are doing, we are using the wrong tools when we look to manufacturing and engineering.

A software tester who goes about his work as if he were inspecting widgets on an assembly line is almost certainly not adding much value to the project. But a software tester who goes about his work as if he were editing a manuscript, or reviewing a book or a work of art, or as if he were on stage for a performance, is probably a valuable member of the team.

Agile Development As Performance

High-performing agile teams manifest the same attitude toward their work that performing artists do, although the literature of agile development has yet to absolutely refute the manufacturing/engineering paradigm that agile teams' behavior undercuts. On a high-performing agile team, anything that needs doing is done by the whole team: if there is development to be done, the whole team helps; if there is testing to be done, the whole team helps; if the stories need work, the whole team works on them. Could that be any more different than an assembly line or a factory floor? High-performing agile teams resemble theater troupes (where everyone has a role to play) and performing musical groups (where everyone is an expert on a particular instrument) more than they do manufacturing organizations.

In the past I was a successful performing musician. I was a bass player. A music teacher I once knew, when referring to our jazz band, said, "In regard to rhythm, the drummer is the judge, but the bass player is the policeman." On an agile team, the product owner or customer is the judge. But as a software tester, I want the developers to write great code to be sure that the story is done as well as it can be done. If there's a bug, I want to help get it fixed, and if the story isn't right, I want to help make it right. As a bass player, I want the soloist to sound as good as she can, and I want the performance to be fantastic. If the singer misses a note, I know how to cover it, and if the timing goes wrong, I know how to bring it back into line. It is hard to describe this work as quality control, and yet there is a relationship there we can exploit.

It's a remarkable thing to bring a performer's attitude to bear on a software development project. On Thursday nights I play for a purely amateur but quite good jazz band, and there is absolutely no difference in my attitude or in my approach to the work when I stop testing software and go make music with my jazz band. Some time ago I wrote, "As a dedicated tester (on an agile team), it is your business to zoom around the project looking for high-risk items to investigate." Two years later, I would rephrase that: your business is to listen carefully to what is happening around you, advance your own work in that context, but listen especially hard to find the places where a problem might happen soon, and find a way to prevent it if you can. We bass players do exactly that all the time.

The biggest difference between performing music and performing software is that when performing music, everything happens all at once at the same time. I suspect that improvements in software development tools in the coming decades will eventually provide a similar experience for software development teams. Compile-build-test-deploy cycles get shorter every day. I can clearly imagine developing and testing software using specialized tools in real time according to a story, exactly the same way that a jazz band cooperates on stage to manifest a particular song, with all the members of the team interacting and moving forward together, according to a shared plan.

Practice, Rehearse, Perform

Agile teams say, "In two weeks we need to ship running tested features to our users." Bands say, "In two weeks we need to perform well-rehearsed songs for a paying audience." Not only are these very similar goals for creative teams, but the underlying processes that agile software teams and bands undergo in order to be able to perform reliably are also similar.

For one thing, excellent software creators have to practice their craft. Musicians, of course, practice scales and techniques suitable for their instruments. Developers have practiced such disciplines as Design Patterns and Code Kata in various languages, and have contributed code to open source projects subject to scrutiny and criticism by their peers. Testers have examined the function of general systems, and have acquainted themselves not only with the literature and practice of their craft, but also with code, overall quality processes, user experience principles, design principles, and the like.

For another thing, excellent software creators have to rehearse. Musicians get together before the performance to work with each other to get a shared understanding of how the performance will be executed. Software creators do "spikes," short projects to explore the best way to approach a feature. Software creators review each other's work, from the first requirements to the code itself to the actual product before release. Testers, of course, have an important role as critical voices in any review. Testers often find themselves in a position to direct the pace of a project, because they are involved in so many aspects simultaneously, just as a bandleader directs the pace of the whole band's rehearsal before the performance. When testers do find themselves directing the pace of a project, it is important that they not be a bottleneck. Testers should be in a position to improve inputs to the testing work (code, deployment) as well as output from the testing work (bug reports, documentation, training).

And finally, both musicians and software creators have to perform. Musicians have an audience, but software creators have users, or customers, or clients. These are the people we have to please in order to continue working in our field. If we don't make the audience happy, we surely won't be performing very long. (Or getting paid very much.) As Steve Jobs said: "Real artists ship."

I presented this argument once to someone I didn't know well, who objected that musical performances leave no functioning artifacts behind in the way that software development does, and that therefore my argument is essentially flawed. I countered: record albums, music videos, sheet music for others to perform, soundtracks. He countered that a recording session is fundamentally different from a live performance.

It is certainly true that a recording session is different than a live performance *from the point of view of the audience*. From the performer's point of view, it is merely a difference in kind, rather than a difference in essence. Just as a software creator is always aware of the users, the performer is always aware of the audience. A recording session is still a performance, although the tools in use are different and the nature of the team is different, just as writing code with Vim is different from writing code with Emacs, just as writing in Ruby is different from writing in C, just as creating mainframe systems is different from creating web applications. The fundamental processes are the same, as is the nature of the audience.

Evaluating the Ineffable

If we fully accept that software development is a fundamentally creative process, we are free to apply analytical and critical tools not from engineering and manufacturing but from the liberal arts. Elsewhere I have written the beginning of some scholarly analysis on the subject, but this book is not for scholars: this book is to inspire practitioners.

Now and then I am a professional writer. Once I was working on a really difficult software testing project, but I had found a fantastic and unique approach to the situation, and I had committed myself to writing a feature article on the subject. But I couldn't make the article work. The software project itself was not yet complete, and my personal situation was extremely stressful at the time. My editor saved the article. He guided my thinking, suggested an outline, suggested a path to the conclusion, and it turned out to be one of the best articles of my career as a writer.

As a software tester, I want to help the project in the same way that editor helped me. I want to help the project go forward smoothly, and I want to make sure it goes smoothly in the future. If the problem consists of small things, I help fix them, and if the project is having a problem even seeing how to get to the end, I want to help guide it there. As a software tester, it is not my part to criticize the subject or focus of the work; it is my job to facilitate the work in the way that a good editor does. Again, it is hard to describe this work as quality assurance, and yet there is a relationship there we can exploit.

Two Critical Tools

The editor in question was Brian Marick, one of the authors of the Agile Manifesto. Marick wrote an intriguing piece some time ago called "Six years later: What the Agile Manifesto left out." (See "References" on page 179.) In it he discusses four values not mentioned in the Agile Manifesto: skill, discipline, ease, and joy.

Skill and discipline are necessary, of course, but less interesting for the purposes of this chapter, because there are arguably objective and defensible (even if poorly executed) ways to measure both skill and discipline.

Of far more interest are ease and joy. The only possible way to evaluate the ease and joy on a software development project is with purely aesthetic criteria. Could we discuss 99.9999% ease in any sort of rational sense? Or a maturity model for joy? Of course not; it is ludicrous on the face of it.

And yet Marick values ease and joy so highly that he continues to speak about them in conference keynotes, and to write about them. But how to evaluate them? Critical tools from philosophy and psychology seem very promising.

The New Criticism was a highly influential movement in literary criticism from the 1940s to the 1960s. Although less popular today, I like to use the New Criticism as an example, because the criteria for deciding the value of a work's aesthetic is so easy to describe: a work is valuable to the extent that it has unity, complexity, and intensity. Ease could be evaluated in this way.

Every aspect of the project should be easy. From writing code and checking it in, to running unit tests continually, to building and deploying test environments and production environments, all the tools and processes should be ready to hand and ready to use without undo attention on extraneous detail. Thus ease should be unified across the project. To the extent that ease is not unified, the project lacks value.

Complexity is necessary but must be managed. In high-functioning software teams, agile or not, complexity is managed by abstract layers of tools. There are tools in place to make the complexity of a large code base easy to manage, tools in place to run tests, tools in place to deploy environments, and even more tools in place that manage other tools to make even larger operations as easy as possible. Complexity is a given; the ability to manage complexity with ease is a sign of a high-functioning team. To the extent that complexity is not managed, the project lacks value.

Intensity is everywhere on a software project. When I test software (or on the rare occasion when I develop software), it takes full, intense concentration to be effective. Distractions like "yak shaving" cause critical failures. From the other side, the user experience of great software should also be an intense experience. Software creates ease to the extent that it supplies an intense experience not hampered by inconvenience or defects. To the extent that intensity is diluted by distractions (both in the development process and in the user experience), the project lacks value.

Evaluating joy requires a different set of tools. I suggest joy could be evaluated by using well-known psychological approaches. Although the field is small, the psychological work focused on joy is important enough to have been explicitly covered by the *New York Times* in an article in 1998 (see "References" on page 179).

But as Marick has pointed out, discussing joy in the context of a software development project is often difficult. We software workers should not be here just to have a good time. We need to be productive! And serious! There is no place for joy on a software project!

But perhaps there should be. As the *Times* article points out,

> [P]sychology journals have published 45,000 articles in the last 30 years on depression, but only 400 on joy…. It was not always like that. When psychology began developing as a profession,

it had three goals: to identify genius, to heal the sick and to help people live better, happier lives. Over the last half century, however, it has focused almost entirely on pathology, taking the science of medicine, itself structured around disease, as its model.

So much effort in the field of software development has been devoted to emphasizing negative aspects of the work. Just for example, consider how much time, effort, and money have been spent tracking defects. The promised payoff for tracking defects is the ability to analyze trends in the nature of defects reported and fixed—but I know of no one who has actually had any great success doing this.

Instead of spending all that time and money working on tracking defects, what if we had spent it on *preventing* defects or on *fixing* defects? Software development would be a much more joyful place.

Of course, there are teams working today that have no need to track defects because they simply fix them as they are identified. The few defects that exist on such teams have very short lives. Although the people working on such teams certainly seem happier to me when I talk to them than people working on less-agile teams, I know of no psychological profiles of such teams. I would encourage interested readers to create them.

Software Testing Movements

More interesting consequences come about when we acknowledge that software development is a fundamentally creative process and not in any way related to manufacturing or engineering. For example, when we become free to question the state of the practice, we are also free to change the state of the practice.

Good software testers do not validate function. Their tools do that for them. Good software testers make aesthetic judgments about the suitability of the software for various purposes, exactly as does the editor of a book or the leader of a band or the director of a play. Good software testers supply critical information about value to people who care about that value, in a role similar to that of a book reviewer or a movie critic.

Great software testers make aesthetic judgments about the suitability of entire approaches to software development itself. Consider the genesis of the Watir and Selenium tools for testing web applications. These are great examples of successful ongoing projects that were started in reaction to the poor state of the software testing practice at the time, and that are more and more defining the state of the software testing practice today and into the future.

In the late 1990s there were almost no free software testing tools, especially for user-interface and browser-based testing. And the proprietary tools available would (and still do) frequently break down in the face of a real UI. James Bach's article "Test Automation Snake Oil" (1999) and Bret Pettichord's article "Hey Vendors, Give Us Real Scripting Languages" (2001) are good examples of the prevailing attitude at the time (see "References" on page 179). Emotions often ran high.

Pettichord had been teaching a "Scripting for Testers" course with Brian Marick, using a simple browser controller in Ruby called IEC, written by Chris Morris. I tried out IEC a couple of times, and it was always pretty broken. But after Paul Rogers spent a few weeks rewriting the whole framework from scratch and renamed it "Watir" (Web Application Testing In Ruby), it suddenly became a serious tool for serious work. I am proud to have been one of the first (maybe the very first, I'm not sure) serious users of Watir. On at least two occasions I have easily and successfully used Watir to diagnose the failures of commercial test automation tools.

At about the same time that Watir was getting off the ground, Jason Huggins was building an internal time-and-expenses project at ThoughtWorks, a well-known Chicago software consulting business. He wanted to test his code, but no tool would do what he wanted. He devised an ingenious hack: open the browser in an iframe, and inject JavaScript into the page to manipulate the page elements. ThoughtWorks agreed to release Jason's hack as open source, and the Selenium project was born. Bret Pettichord was involved in that release as well.

Finally, Ward Cunningham, probably most well known for inventing the wiki, devised a simple and ingenious tool called Fit as a way for business users to specify the internal functions of code. In many cases these business users are testers, or are at least aided by professional testers as they tell the software what it should do by means of Fit.

The pace of development of tools for writing software has always far outstripped that of tools for testing software. But by automating the repetitive checking of proper function in the applications under test, Watir, Selenium, and Fit allow the professional software tester to keep up with that pace. The craft of software testing may now advance along with, and in concert with, the craft of software development. All these tools are improving quickly, and continue to gather new users and new maintainers.

The Beauty of Agile Testing

Pettichord wrote another well-known article, "Four Schools of Software Testing." The existence of Watir, Selenium, and Fit brought about what is generally recognized as a fifth school, "Agile Testing," which always advocates a very high level of test automation and usually acknowledges the value of manual examination of the application by skilled testers.

The promise of great test automation has always been to free testers from the drudgery of the repetitive checking of proper function. But if the repetitive checking of proper function is automated, what then is a software tester to do?

For one thing, the tester can become an expert in the design and implementation of system test frameworks. This involves programming, but programming these sorts of system test frameworks is nothing at all like application development. Programming a beautiful test automation harness requires an understanding of the system under test as well as an understanding of what sort of tests are most likely to be written, and what sort of testing is most likely to be valuable to the project, and what sorts of tests are most likely to be maintainable into the future as the application being tested undergoes changes. It is fascinating and rewarding work, and has been a big part of my own career.

An agile tester is also certainly an aesthetic critic. With the test automation examining the dusty corners of the application, the tester is free to evaluate with a critical eye the new features, incoming stories, overall suitability for purpose, and perhaps even the software development process itself.

QA Is Not Evil

There is a faction among software testers that strongly resists having the term *quality assurance* applied to their work. These testers do not want to be associated in any way with "quality police" functions such as maintaining handoff procedures and quality gateways and other obstructive practices that have their roots in factory floors and assembly lines, but which are historically associated with the term *software quality assurance*.

But testers are uniquely positioned to be facilitators of good process. Testers are sometimes the only members of the team, for instance, that are acutely aware (before release, at least) of any mismatch between the software requirements and the software implementation. Testers are often the members of the team most widely read on the subject of software development practice. Testers are often the members of the team with the best understanding of the overall state of the project.

The thing about great movie directors and great bandleaders and great critics is they are great only to the extent that they are appreciated by their colleagues and by their audience. This is the classic mistake of traditional software quality assurance work: those workers appointed themselves the arbiters of quality on software development projects without any support from the teams they worked with or from the users who needed the software. In an aesthetic software development process, QA work is about guiding the software development process to increase success and criticizing the software development process constructively rather than obstructing the process and becoming "damage to be routed around."

On an agile team, process is a very malleable thing. Agile teams have frequent retrospectives, and every retrospective is an opportunity for the team to change their own software development process. After a year or two or three of agile retrospectives, a given team's process is certainly going to be unique, and with experienced quality assurance people as part of the team, the team's process will almost certainly be far more efficient than it was at the beginning.

Beauty Is the Nature of This Work

It is popular among people who think, talk, and write about the process of software development to construct analogies to describe the work. They say "Software development is like..." and "When we do software development, it is as if we were doing...".

There are no such analogies in this essay. It is very clear: developing software is not *like* the work of a performing artist; developing software *is* the work of a performing artist. Evaluating software quality is not *like* evaluating an artistic performance; it *is* evaluating an artistic performance. This is not theory; this is really how high-performing software development teams go about their work. We can make great improvements to our own work when we acknowledge this.

I very much hope that the software development community as a whole, and software testers in particular, not only admit but celebrate the fundamentally aesthetic process of creating software. Whether we recognize it explicitly or not, this is the reason we can talk about Beautiful Testing at all.

References

Bach, J. 1999. "Test Automation Snake Oil." *http://www.satisfice.com/articles/test_automation _snake_oil.pdf.*

Hall, T. 1998. "Seeking a Focus on Joy In Field of Psychology." *New York Times*, April 28, Science section. *http://www.nytimes.com/1998/04/28/science/seeking-a-focus-on-joy-in-field-of-psychology .html.*

Marick, B. 2007. "Six years later: What the Agile Manifesto left out." *http://www.exampler.com/ blog/2007/05/16/six-years-later-what-the-agile-manifesto-left-out/.*

Marick, B. 2008. "Agile Development Practices keynote (text)." *http://www.exampler.com/blog/ 2008/11/14/agile-development-practices-keynote-text/.*

Pettichord, B. 2001. "Hey Vendors, Give Us Real Scripting Languages." *http://www.stickyminds .com/sitewide.asp?ObjectId=2326&ObjectType=COL&Function=edetail.*

Pettichord, B. 2007. "Schools of Software Testing." *http://www.io.com/%7Ewazmo/papers/four _schools.pdf.*

## CHAPTER FOURTEEN

Test-Driven Development: Driving New Standards of Beauty

Jennitta Andrea

Beauty As Proportion and Balance

THE DEFINITION OF BEAUTY IS SUBJECTIVE, contextual, and ever-changing. Throughout history, groups develop their own qualitative and quantitative standards for beauty, guided by a complex set of forces, including economy, geography, and culture. Despite this diversity, there is notable consistency in the fundamental elements of physical beauty. One common element is proportion. A recurring ratio of 1:1.618—the divine proportion—is found in faces universally judged as beautiful, and occurs repeatedly throughout the natural world (Huntley 1970). There appears to be a generalized attraction to things that are proportional, unified, balanced, coherent, and harmonious.

Humans are naturally inclined to reestablish harmony when the status quo is disrupted. The Diderot Effect (McCracken 1988) describes the domino effect of change triggered by the introduction of an inconsistency, such as when French philosopher Denis Diderot received the gift of a new robe. The elegant red robe clashed with his humble, cluttered office, causing him to completely redecorate until the office matched the elegance of the robe.

These two perspectives on beauty—*proportion* and *balance*—can be applied to software methods. A software method is a collection of elements: activities, practices, roles, tools, and work products. A beautiful software method unifies the proportion of the elements through their sequence, tempo, and size, guided by a complex set of forces, including criticality, complexity, and team composition (Cockburn 2002).

The elements of a software method are interdependent. Changing one practice in isolation tends to have a ripple effect on other practices; project smells (Andrea et al. 2002) alert us when practices become disjoint. Beautiful software methods follow the chain reaction of smells until the interdependent practices are brought into harmonious balance.

Agile: A New Proportion and Balance

The originators of the Extreme Programming (XP) agile method believe that if a practice is worth doing, then it should be done early, often, and intensely—turn the dial past maximum (Beck 2000). On the surface, XP looks familiar because it contains the standard set of practices. In reality, no practice has been left unchanged. Two key catalysts for XP's domino effect of change are *small releases* and *test-driven development*.

XP's concept of a small release is to deliver *running, tested features* to the user community on a regular basis to maximize business return on investment and to respond to timely feedback with strategic product adaptation (Jeffries 2002). The small release dictates the underlying *proportion* for agile software development. Everything—requirements, design, development, integration, testing, and review—must be condensed in order for an entire cycle to fit into a short, fixed-sized iteration (typically two weeks). Physical distance between people and conceptual distance between roles must disappear so that interactions are timely, continuous, collaborative, and concrete. Development practices must be highly focused and disciplined so that the software is simultaneously stable and malleable.

Small releases require us to reestablish *balance* within the whole software development process through the following interdependent practices: stories, face-to-face communication, co-located team, on-site customer, automated test driven development, continuous integration, refactoring, and collective ownership.

Test-Driven Development

The remainder of this chapter focuses specifically on automated test-driven development (TDD) as a means to facilitate *frequent delivery of running, tested features* within a small release. Quality is intensely proactive and grounded in business value. Table 14-1 illustrates a summary of the TDD red-green-refactor cycle.[1]

---

1. This summary is expanded into the full TDD process in Table 14-2, and discussed later in this chapter.

TABLE 14-1. Simplified TDD process (red-green-refactor)

	Author	Developer
Red	1. Create Example	
	2. Execute Example	
		3. Execute Example
		4. Create unit tests
		5. Execute unit tests
Green		6. Write system code
		7. Execute unit tests
		8. Execute Example
	9. Execute Example	
Refactor		10. Refactor system code
		11. Execute Example and unit tests

Red (steps 1–5)

One or more automated functional tests (Examples) define the completion criteria for a user story. The reference to "red" indicates that the Example fails when executed because the relevant system code does not exist yet. Unit tests are written to drive the detailed design and implementation of the code. Unit tests also fail at this point.

Green (steps 6–9)

Developers focus on writing the system code needed to make each unit test pass. Tests are run frequently at this stage to provide feedback on their progress. The reference to "green" indicates that the unit test passes when the relevant system code is in place. Examples pass when all related unit tests pass. At this point, another Example can be introduced, or technical debt can be paid down through refactoring.

Refactor (steps 10–11)

At any stable point—i.e., when all tests are passing—the system code can be restructured without changing the public interfaces or behavior. The tests are run after every discrete refactoring step to ensure that they are all still "green."

Reordering process steps to perform test specification prior to development is a radical concept, producing significant short-term and long-term benefits. However, if this concept is introduced in isolation, many other parts of the development process will become imbalanced. In order to achieve enduring success, we must bring interdependent practices into balance with TDD. This chapter focuses on a balanced approach to TDD, with permanent trustworthy requirements, testable designs, powerful tools, and new team collaborations.

Examples Versus Tests

TDD has turned out to be an unfortunate name. When the phrase "test-driven development" is taken at face value, the specification activity is in danger of being confused with a testing activity. Functional requirement specifications begin to resemble detailed test scripts (see Figure 14-2 later), which are difficult to understand and maintain. Alternative terms have been proposed to focus attention on specification rather than testing, such as Examples,[2] Behaviors,[3] and Expectations (Hendrickson 2009). During an open space session at the 2008 Agile Alliance Functional Testing Tools program workshop,[4] a group of practitioners developed the "TDD Triangle" (Figure 14-1) to clarify our terminology.

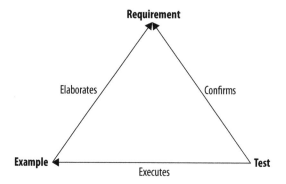

FIGURE 14-1. The "TDD Triangle"

A Requirement is a general statement describing how the system is expected to behave (aka feature or business rules). The Requirement is expressed in the vocabulary of the business domain. For example, in the domain of a video store point-of-sale system, one requirement is:

> The *Catalogue* contains the list of all unique *Movie Titles* that the *Video Store* currently offers for purchase or rental.

Requirements are anchoring points for TDD. An Example (also known as acceptance test, story test, or functional test) elaborates a Requirement with concrete explanations of how the system will behave under specific conditions. Examples are expressed in the vocabulary of the business domain, and typically have a three-part structure: precondition + action = postcondition, often expressed in the form, "Given the system is in state X when we do Y, we expect the outcome to be Z." The following Examples elaborate the video store requirement:

2. *http://www.exampler.com/*

3. *http://behaviour-driven.org/*

4. *http://tech.groups.yahoo.com/group/aa-ftt/*

Success Example

Given the *Movie Title "Star Wars"* is not already in the *Catalogue*, when we add it, then we expect *Star Wars* to be available in the *Catalogue*.

Duplicate Error Example

Given the *Movie Title "Star Wars"* is already in the *Catalogue*, when we add it, then we expect a *Duplicate Movie Title Error*.

A test is the act of *executing* an Example against the real system to *confirm* the requirement has been met. A test can be run many times, each of which is a record of what happened during a particular execution, for example: "Duplicate Error Example passed on July 2, 2009 with build 1.3 in the Qual environment." An Example can be used as a test, but not all tests are Examples (e.g., nonfunctional or exploratory tests).

The shift is subtle: an Example becomes a test when it is executed, but first and foremost the purpose of an Example is to elaborate the Requirement.

Readable Examples

It is essential that an Example can be clearly understood by a number of different audiences:

Nontechnical subject matter experts

These people verify that the Example is a correct and complete specification.

Technical team

These team members use Examples to drive their design and coding work. Toolsmiths read an Example to automate it; programmers read an Example to develop correct system code; operations support reads an Example to fix or enhance a specific part of the system.

A readable Example is all of the following (Andrea 2005):

- Declarative: expresses "what," not "how"
- Succinct: includes only what is necessary
- Unambiguous: two people understand it the same way
- Autonomous: stands alone; does not depend on other Examples
- Sufficient: full coverage in minimal scenarios
- Locatable: organized and searchable

In Figure 14-2, the sample labeled "Test Script" is a traditional detailed functional test script, which is *not* what we are aiming for as a requirement specification: the tactical user interaction details obscure the business rule that needs to be expressed (in other words, the "how" eclipses the "what").

1. Test Script

1. Start at the Maintain Catalogue page
2. Page title should be: Video Store Admin–Maintain Catalogue
3. Click the Add New Title button
4. Page title should be: Video Store Admin–Add New Title
5. Enter text "Star Wars" into the field labeled Title
6. Select Science Fiction from Category selection list
7. Click the Save button
8. Page title should be Video Store Admin–Maintain Catalogue
9. Message should be "New title successfully added"
10. Title should be listed as:

Title	Category	# Copies	# In Store
Aladdin	Children	4	2
Star Trek	Sci Fi	1	1
Star Wars	Sci Fi	0	0
Toy Story	Children	0	0

11. ...
12. ...
13. ...

2. Domain-Specific Language

1. Add Movie Title (Star Wars, Sci Fi)
2. Verify Catalogue:

Title	Category	# Copies	# In Store
Aladdin	Children	4	2
Star Trek	Sci Fi	1	1
Star Wars	Sci Fi	0	0
Toy Story	Children	0	0

5. Add Movie Title (Star Wars, Sci Fi)
6. Verify Add Movie Title message ("Error: The movie title Star Wars already exists")

3. Declarative, Behavior-Driven

1. **Given** catalogue contains: Star Wars, Sci Fi
2. **When** add movie title: Star Wars, Sci Fi
3. **Then** catalogue unchanged
7. **And** message: "Error: The movie title Star Wars already exists")

FIGURE 14-2. Toward readable specifications

Creating a Domain-Specific Testing Language (DSTL) makes this same script more readable, provided the vocabulary of the specification is declarative and is expressed as business domain goals and real-world objects. In Figure 14-2, line 1 of the DSTL is equivalent to lines 1–8 of the Test Script. Although this is a significant improvement, the reader must still piece together the business rule from these high-level statements.

Adding simple structuring statements to a DSTL brings us another step closer to a beautiful specification. The declarative, behavior-driven Given/When/Then style shown in Figure 14-2 helps express the business rule more clearly. Specifications like this can be captured in many different formats: tabular, textual, graphical (e.g., various UML notations), workflow storyboard, UI wire frame, etc. The key is to find the format that best expresses the concepts within the business domain.

Permanent Requirement Artifacts

Examples are permanent artifacts that elaborate Requirements; Stories are transient artifacts used to subdivide, prioritize, and plan the incremental development of the system. Our challenge is to end up with a coherent big picture of system requirements as we incrementally build it out of small, potentially disjointed stories, each of which may add new Examples and/or modify existing ones.

Figure 14-3 reflects the choice made to implement the success story of a particular feature in the first iteration. The story is shaded in gray to remind us of its transient nature. The righthand side of the diagram is the first increment of the permanent artifact containing the feature description (Requirement) seamlessly integrated with the corresponding Example.

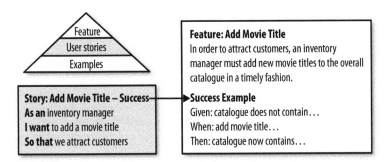

FIGURE 14-3. Iteration 1 requirements artifacts

Figure 14-4 illustrates building up the permanent specifications incrementally (shown here in the style supported by Concordion[5]). The initial success scenario is enhanced with a number of "what if" questions that link to further business rule descriptions and their corresponding Examples. Regardless of the size or ordering of the Stories used to plan the work during the project, the final requirements artifact needs to integrate Requirements and Examples in a coherent fashion. This is indeed a new standard of beauty for software requirements.

Testable Designs

Unlike other forms of specification, TDD directly influences the software's design; if properly practiced, TDD ensures that the design is highly testable (Meszaros 2007). A testable system makes it easy for people and tools to:

- Set the starting state for the system/component and all dependent systems/components
- Control environmental factors, such as date and time
- Completely isolate the system/components from its dependents
- Trigger an action on the system/component
- Control responses from dependent systems/components
- Access all direct and indirect (side effect) outcomes

5. *http://www.concordion.org/*

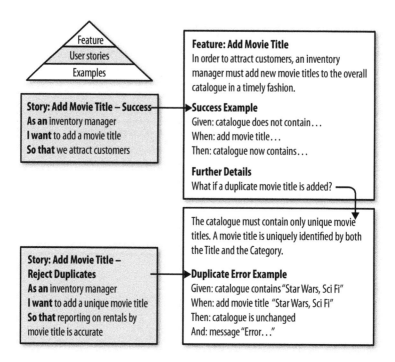

FIGURE 14-4. Iteration 2 requirements artifacts

Designing a system for this type of flexibility, controllability, isolatability, accessibility, and repeatability involves new design strategies.

A typical three-tier architecture (Figure 14-5) is nicely layered, but often awkward to test. Control and validation typically are limited to the UI and database layers. It is impossible to substitute external components (operating system functions or third-party systems) because they are directly referenced throughout the code.

In contrast, a design that emerges from the TDD approach (Figure 14-5) is modular, with exposed interfaces and plug-in points to enable substitutions (e.g., mocks). When proper attention is paid to features supporting traceability (e.g., logging of inputs, intermediate steps, and results), the system itself facilitates automated testing, exploratory testing, and production support. Testing can be performed easily at any level. This is indeed a new standard of beauty for software architecture and design.

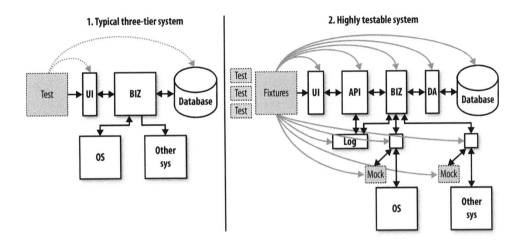

FIGURE 14-5. Toward a testable design

Tool Support

The numerous criticisms about the wastefulness of automating Examples argue they are bad tests in the sense that they rarely uncover new problems or errors of omission (Marick 2008). This goes back to the TDD misnomer, which confuses this practice with testing. TDD expects Examples to be automated to ensure that the requirements are trustworthy; automation is how we guarantee the specification is accurate over the entire life of the system. This is in sharp contrast to most other specifications, which become out of sync with the system as soon as development begins.

Automated Examples are subject to a high set of standards. Compared to production code, automated Examples must be:

- More correct
- Maintained as long or longer
- More readable
- Easier to write
- More easily and safely maintained
- More locatable

These statements are startling, and absolutely true. Automated Examples must be "more" than production code to eliminate the temptation to treat them as optional when pinched for time. Tools supporting automated Examples must also be "more" than development tools and testing tools to permit us to meet the high standards placed upon Examples.

The Agile Alliance Functional Testing Tools (AAFTT) workshops and discussion group give voice to the community of practitioners that need tools to support TDD. A beautiful TDD tool is one that offers the following core features to support the variety of roles engaged in the full process, shown in Table 14-2.

TABLE 14-2. Full TDD process

	Author	Reader	Automator	Developer
Red	1. Create Example			
	2. Execute Example			
	3. Version control Example			
		4. Find Example		
		5. Review Example		
		6. Execute Example		
			7. Create DSTL	
			8. Execute Example	
			9. Version control DSTL	
		10. Review Example and DSTL		
				11. Execute Example
				12. Create unit tests
				13. Execute unit tests
Green				14. Write system code
				15. Execute unit tests
				16. Execute Example
				17. Version control system code
	18. Execute Example			
		19. Execute Example		
Refactor				20. Refactor system code
				21. Execute Example and unit tests

Author

First and foremost, the author (SME, analyst, tester) requires a powerful development environment with the types of features commonly provided by modern software development tools: code completion, dynamic syntax validation, refactoring, and version control (including branching and merging of the functional test and supporting DSTL code). Rich support for a DSTL is essential. The format of the specification language and the look and feel of the tool should be accessible to the variety of nontechnical participants.

Reader

The reader (SME) must be able to comprehend Examples quickly to gain a clear, unambiguous understanding of system capabilities. The reader requires Examples to be well organized and easy to find through browsing or searching. Navigation and dynamic searching to and from other Requirements artifacts are required.

Executors

Many different roles execute the Examples at different times, and for different reasons; we must be able to execute the Examples from a number of different environments:

- Authors run Examples in the TDD tool as they create the Example.
- Developers/automators run Examples in their development environment as they create system code.
- Readers run Examples from a desktop tool (such as a browser) to sign off on the requirement specification.
- Other roles can use automated Examples to enhance their work. For example, marketing and sales could run Examples to set up demo data and ensure that the system is stable before giving a presentation.

The tool must support arbitrarily grouping the Examples together into suites, either statically or dynamically based on metadata (e.g., priority, failures, functional area). It is also necessary to be able to debug the Example from any of the execution environments and navigate seamlessly between the Example, the DSTL, and the system code.

Result consumer

The result consumer (programmer, tester, operational support, release manager, etc.) is interested in the fine-grained details about whether an individual Example passed or failed, why it failed, and where it failed. They want to be able to navigate from the failure to the specific line in the Example, and then directly to the specific line in the system code. Recording the history of test results provides valuable progress and trend information.

Report consumer

The report consumer (Scrum master, project manager, release manager, compliance officer, auditor, etc.) is interested in aggregated test results in order to track progress and ultimately make a go or no-go decision.

All of these core features, and more, define the new standard of beauty for TDD tool support.

Team Collaboration

XP takes the notion of an incremental and iterative life cycle to the extreme, as shown in Figure 14-6. The individual aspects of beauty described previously are brought together to form a powerful, sustainable synergy.

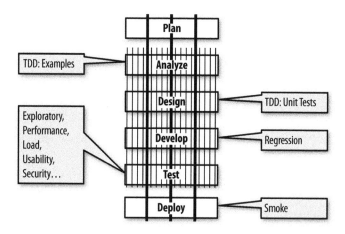

FIGURE 14-6. XP Incremental and iterative life cycle

The vertical lines extending from Plan to Deploy mark three separate iterations. An iteration starts with lightweight planning to identify the stories on which to focus during the next time box. It finishes with running, tested stories that can be deployed to a Qual environment for further testing.

The shorter vertical lines extending from Analyze to Test indicate multiple stories within an iteration. An individual story goes through its own software development life cycle: analyze, design, develop, and test. All the while, it is continuously integrated with the rest of the evolving system.

The callout notes highlight opportunities for proactive and continuous quality, encompassing all process steps and multiple team roles in close collaboration:

Analyze

> Writing and automating Examples requires collaboration between a multitude of roles, each providing a different perspective and skill: subject matter expert, business analyst, tester, toolsmith, technical writer, and user experience designer.

Design

> Developers and testers collaborate closely during unit test-driven development. The testable design makes automated, semi-automated, and manual testing highly effective and efficient; nothing should be difficult to test.

Develop

> The automated test suite is run frequently during development to ensure that no unexpected side effects were introduced by an incremental change or code refactoring step. A new sense of courage and control is experienced.

Test

> In stark contrast to other approaches, at the beginning of the test phase, XP testers receive code that is stable and known to conform to the current set of requirements. With TDD's proactive approach to quality, testers are able to focus their skill and energy on exploratory, integration, and nonfunctional testing.

This level of team collaboration, courage, and continuous testing defines a new standard of beauty for overall product quality.

Experience the Beauty of TDD

Beauty is in the eye and the heart of the beholder. An outside observer would likely find Diderot's renovated office to have been a vast improvement over its scruffy, untidy predecessor. However, Diderot was unhappy with the end result, and wrote "Regrets on Parting with My Old Dressing Gown"[6] because he was financially and emotionally drained from the *unexpected* domino effect of change triggered by his new red robe.

The Diderot Effect theory comes from studies of consumer behavior and upward mobility. It serves as a warning about the unintended consequences of upgrading one item in isolation. Let this chapter be a similar warning for teams deciding to embrace TDD: this decision involves much more than simply selecting an automated test tool. The team must be committed to supporting significant changes within each and every role, and must be willing to let go of their comfortable old ways:

- Requirement specifications look different and require more discipline than ever before. The reward is an unprecedented level of specification trustworthiness.

- All levels of system design and the act of writing code are directly influenced by the TDD practice.

6. *http://fr.wikisource.org/wiki/Regrets_sur_ma_vieille_robe_de_chambre*

- The pace of work is regulated by the iteration length and the red-green-refactor cycle.

- A new breed of powerful tools support and facilitate cross-functional, cooperative work.

- Role collaborations form a richer and more interconnected network. In particular, the tester role is engaged earlier, and the tester's work is enriched and more effective.

TDD can be a truly beautiful experience when the team is committed to achieving the correct proportion and balance for their particular context.

References

Andrea, J., G. Meszaros, S. Smith. 2002. "Catalog of XP Project 'Smells.'" The Third International Conference on Extreme Programming and Agile Processes in Software Engineering, XP2002, May. Alghero, Sardinia, Italy.

Andrea, J. 2005. "Brushing Up On Functional Test Effectiveness." *Better Software Magazine*, November/December, 26–31.

Beck, K. 2000. *Extreme Programming Explained: Embrace Change*. Boston: Addison-Wesley.

Cockburn, A. 2002. *Agile Software Development*. Boston: Addison-Wesley, 113–172.

Hendrickson, E. 2009. "From the Mailbox: Fully Automated GUI Testing?" *http://testobsessed .com/2009/05/18/from-the-mailbox-fully-automated-gui-testing/*.

Huntley, H. E. 1970. *The Divine Proportion: A Study in Mathematical Proportion*. New York: Dover Publications.

Jeffries, R. 2004. "A Metric Leading to Agility." *http://www.xprogramming.com/xpmag/jatRtsMetric .htm*.

Marick, B. 2008. "Position statement for functional testing tools workshop." *http://www .exampler.com/blog/2008/07/09/position-statement-for-functional-testing-tools-workshop/*.

McCracken, G. 1988. *Culture and Consumption: New Approaches to the Symbolic Character of Consumer Goods and Activities*. Bloomington, IN: Indiana University Press, 118–129.

Meszaros, G. 2007. *xUnit Test Patterns: Refactoring Test Code*. Boston: Addison-Wesley.

## CHAPTER FIFTEEN

Beautiful Testing As the Cornerstone of Business Success

Lisa Crispin

IN MARCH OF 2009, DURING HIS "TRAVELS IN SOFTWARE" TOUR, Brian Marick visited our team. He interviewed several of us about our experiences working together as an agile team for more than five years. I've been a tester on this team since it adopted Scrum in 2003. When Brian's interview with me was almost over, he remarked, "We've talked for an hour and you haven't mentioned testing." That made me laugh, but it was true. I'd spent all the time talking about how we work together to deliver more business value in better ways. When I first thought about the term "beautiful testing," this synergy is what came to my mind.

People try to quantify testing in various ways. What about its qualities? I imagine that most people don't associate the words "beautiful" and "testing" in the same sentence. For me, the beauty of testing lies in the team's absolute commitment to quality, to doing the right thing, and to doing things right. My team at ePlan Services Inc. focuses on testing to help the business achieve healthy growth. To paraphrase Elisabeth Hendrickson, we don't see testing as a phase. It's an integral part of software development, equal in value to coding. Everyone on the team drives themselves to deliver the highest quality software possible, which means everyone on the team does a beautiful job of testing.

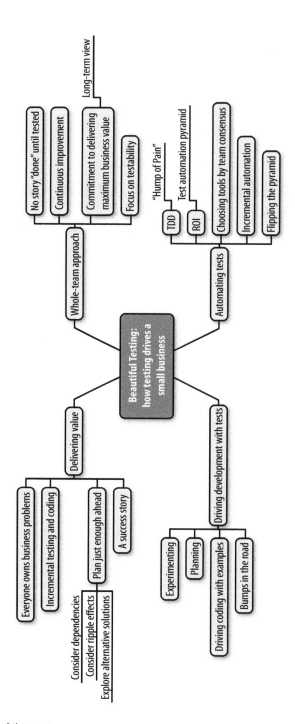

FIGURE 15-1. Mindmap of Chapter 15

My team's commitment to driving development with tests, not only with test-driven development (TDD) at the unit level, but also at the business-facing level, helped make our company a profitable and fast-growing business. Our software includes processes and features that outshine our competitors. We release new business value to production every two weeks. We work side-by-side with our business experts and customers, contributing our own ideas for business solutions. We have automated 100% of our regression testing, and these tests allow us to refactor and implement new functionality fearlessly. If you've never experienced this situation, I can tell you that it's incredibly freeing and empowering. Our team is confident that we can come up with a good solution every time.

Beautiful testing is undramatic. It's life on an even keel. It's confidence that we can deliver every sprint and not mess up. Nobody has to die.

Here is a success story that I hope will inspire you to think differently about testing. It isn't an afterthought or a safety net. It's a solid foundation for beautiful code, happy development teams, and happy customers.

The Whole-Team Approach

From the first Scrum sprint, our mission was to produce the best code we could. We were fortunate to have management who believed a focus on quality, rather than speed, would pay off in the long run. We committed to driving development with tests, not only at the unit level with TDD, but at higher levels too. Inspired by ideas from Brian Marick, Robert "Uncle Bob" Martin, and others, we asked our customers for examples of desired behavior for each theme (aka epic or feature set) and story, and turned these into executable business-facing tests that also guided coding. We worked to automate 100% of our regression tests so that we could devote plenty of time to end-to-end, exploratory testing.

No Story Is "Done" Until It's Tested

In our early sprints, I was daunted to hear programmers say during the scrums, "I'm done with Story XYZ," when I knew that code hadn't been tested, had no automated tests, and was not "done" in any true sense. I raised this issue at the first sprint retrospective. We wrote on our storyboard, which at the time was a big whiteboard, "No story is done until it's tested," and then we lived by this rule.

Since our team was new to TDD, we wrote task cards for writing unit tests until they became an ingrained habit and part of every coding task. We also had a column on our storyboard where we indicated whether high-level tests had been written for the story. Coding task cards weren't moved into "Work in Progress" until the high-level acceptance tests were available on the wiki.

Continuous Improvement

Our most important tool was the retrospective we had at the beginning of every sprint. This was a great chance to solve testing issues. Like many (if not most) teams, we felt the pain of testing being squeezed to the end of the iteration. Testing tasks, especially the test automation tasks, were being carried over to the next iteration.

In our retrospectives, we came up with some rules for ourselves to help address these issues:

- All high-level acceptance tests must be written up on the wiki, usually in a list or bullet-point form, by day four of the two-week iteration.
- The team must focus on completing one story at a time.
- A story must be ready for the testers to test by day four of the iteration.
- No new functionality can be checked in on the last day of the iteration.

These rules have become a natural part of our process. Anytime we find testing tasks lagging behind coding, we check to see whether we've neglected our guidelines or need new ones. We challenge ourselves to set the bar higher. In our early days doing continuous integration, our goal was a stable build by day 12 of the iteration. Now we have a stable build every day. Reaching such a goal was a thrill, and testing continuously along with coding got us there.

Every six months we set our team goals. For example, when we decided to measure unit test coverage, we set a goal to select a tool and get a baseline of coverage. For the next six months, our goal was to achieve 70% coverage. When we met that, we set a new goal for the next six months to improve it to 73%. Every sprint, we evaluate our progress and experiment with new ideas or approaches as needed. Is our test coverage good enough? Are there more production support requests than usual? Is there a performance problem in production? At one time, the ability to release on any day, not just the end of the sprint, seemed like an unachievable dream. Now we can respond quickly to any business emergencies, or help the business take advantage of opportunities, by releasing mid-sprint if desired. We can take the time we need to think through every business problem and come up with a good solution. That's a lot prettier than hacking quick fixes into a scary code base.

Delivering Maximum Business Value

Our company's business model depended on implementing the right software in a timely manner. We were a small startup that wasn't yet profitable. Our team had to find ways to optimize the company's return on the software investment.

Some organizations turn to agile development because they think it will let them "go faster." Agile values and practices will allow you to deliver business value more frequently, but only if you take the long view. For example, learning TDD is a big investment, but having good automated test coverage and well-designed code allows the team to deliver features more quickly.

Focusing on Testability

Our legacy application was unstable and buggy. We were determined to start producing high-quality software. Since we had no automated regression tests in late 2003, I wrote manual test scripts for all the critical functionality of the web application. The entire team—including programmers, the DBA, the system administrator, and the Scrum master—spent the last day or two of each two-week sprint executing these manual tests. It's impressive how this activity motivates team members to design code for testability, and to investigate good ways to automate regression testing at different levels.

We were committed to using test-driven development at the unit level, as well as using higher-level, business-facing tests to guide coding. We intended to automate 100% of our regression tests in order to keep technical debt to a minimum, get immediate feedback about whether code changes break something, and allow continual refactoring. Most importantly, automating all regression tests means more time for critical exploratory testing. There's a special beauty in catching an unexpected ripple effect from a new feature in time to correct it well before releasing.

Automating Tests

After a few weeks of research and discussion, the team decided that going forward we'd write all new code in a layered architecture, designed with automated testing in mind. As with many (if not all) teams new to TDD, our programmers found it hard to write unit tests for the legacy code, where business and presentation logic was mixed up with database access. In fact, it was just hard to do TDD, period. Brian Marick refers to this phenomenon as the "Hump of Pain" (see Figure 15-2). As the team became proficient in TDD, the programmers started writing unit tests whenever they changed legacy code, as well as when they coded in the new architecture.

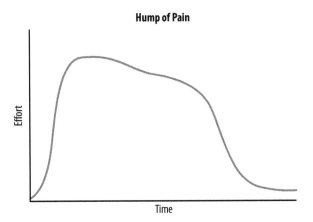

FIGURE 15-2. The Hump of Pain

My team liked Mike Cohn's "test automation pyramid" idea (Figure 15-3). We knew our best return on investment (ROI) would be from automating tests at the unit level. We were keen to do the bulk of our functional test automation "behind" the GUI, and had chosen FitNesse as the tool to accomplish this.

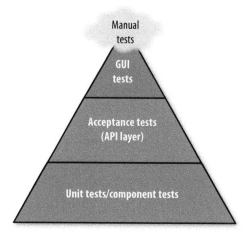

FIGURE 15-3. Test automation pyramid

Our immediate problem was a huge, buggy legacy system where the presentation, business logic, and database layers were intertwined. The fastest way to get some automated regression test coverage was through the GUI. But GUI tests are notoriously brittle and hard to maintain. We had to find good tools to help us achieve a reasonable ROI.

Choosing Tools by Team Consensus

Since our entire development team takes responsibility for quality and for making sure all testing activities are successfully completed for each release, we choose tools as a team. This applies to both development and test frameworks.

Here's an example of one of our team tool decisions. In early 2004, commercial test automation frameworks were not very programmer-friendly. Most used a proprietary scripting language. We're a Java shop, and the programmers don't want to work with another programming language. JUnit was the obvious choice for TDD. We had decided to use CruiseControl for our continuous integration build process, and CruiseControl uses Ant.

I had heard good things about Canoo WebTest, a test framework in which one specifies tests as Ant scripts. WebTest drives tests through a simulated browser, not an actual one, but our thin client layer doesn't experience many browser incompatibilities. We liked the way it reported results with our build output. Everyone on our team was comfortable with this approach, so we went with WebTest for our GUI test automation. It's one of several test automation frameworks we use now.

Amazing new tools come out every week. If practitioners we respect recommend a new tool, and it potentially offers valuable new features, we'll budget time to try it. We always challenge the tools we have and see whether there's something better. If a tool's ROI isn't high enough, we shouldn't keep using it. If a new tool offers more value for the amount of work and expense to get it up to speed, we should switch. We wouldn't abandon existing automated regression tests, but we might start creating new ones in a different framework. Each team member is free to question the tool we're using or propose a new one. It's a team decision whether to try out or adopt a new test tool. The freedom to experiment and share opinions means a better testing infrastructure, and more beautiful testing.

Team tool decisions apply to more than test frameworks. The defect tracking system, the wiki, the voice response technology, all of these choices are a team effort. As we used the pyramid to guide our automation choices, we use agile principles and values to guide our other tool selections. Simplicity, speed and clarity of feedback, and supporting collaboration are among the most important considerations when we evaluate a new addition to our infrastructure.

Incremental Automation

When you start with no automated tests, achieving a goal of 100% regression test automation means beginning with baby steps. While the programmers were busy mastering TDD, I started building an automated GUI smoke test suite to replace our laborious manual regression testing.

I asked our customers for a prioritized list of the critical areas of our application that must always work. Each sprint, I added a few WebTest scripts. A teammate helped me configure our build process to automatically run the tests. With each iteration, we spent less time executing manual regression scripts. After about eight months, we no longer had to do any manual regression testing on the old code, and had automated tests at both the unit and GUI level for each new story. That was a beautiful feeling.

At first, the WebTest scripts ran in the continuous build process along with the few JUnits we had. As we got more WebTest scripts and more JUnit tests, we moved the WebTest scripts, which are much slower than unit tests, to a "nightly" build.

Flipping the Pyramid

Like many new teams, our test automation triangle was upside down. To borrow a term from Patrick Wilson-Welsh (*http://patrickwilsonwelsh.com/?s=pyramid&sbutt=Go*), we needed to flip our test triangle right side up.

As soon as the programmers had traction on TDD and some bandwidth to devote to a new layer of tests, it seemed like time to start using FitNesse for functional testing. I went to a programmer and asked, "Will you help me write FitNesse tests for this story you're working on?" He did, found it easy to do and useful, and told the rest of the team. After a few more iterations, each programmer had tried FitNesse and found it worthwhile. We started writing task cards for FitNesse tests for every story that was "FitNesse-able."

As we built up suites of FitNesse regression tests, our test automation pyramid started to change shape. For a period of time it became more of a diamond than a triangle, bulging out in the middle FitNesse layer. As more and more code was implemented with TDD in the new architecture, the unit level base of the pyramid outgrew the upper layers. We kept writing WebTest smoke test scripts as well, but they were an ever-smaller percentage of our regression tests.

As of April 2009, we have 3,864 unit tests, 474 FitNesse tests, and 99 WebTest scripts. We've flipped our test automation pyramid the right way around. Each "test" contains many assertions, so this multiplies out to many thousands of automated regression tests.

These tests are run in multiple continuous builds. The build that runs the JUnit tests takes about eight minutes. This build may go several days without failing, or it might fail multiple times a day; it depends on the stories underway, and whether someone's doing a big refactoring or working on code used in multiple areas. The person who "broke the build" jumps right into fixing it, and if he needs help, the team is ready.

Complete feedback from the functional and GUI tests, which we call the "full build," takes a couple of hours. Generally, regression tests will be caught several times during the sprint. We're happy those bugs aren't making it out to production, and we fix them immediately. Every two hours, we know whether or not we have a stable, releasable build. This is invaluable.

No automated test suite is foolproof, but this safety net affords us the ability to refactor as needed and implement new code without fear of unexpected consequences. It keeps our technical debt to a manageable level. We have time to do manual exploratory testing and learn about possible ripple effects.

We also have a few dozen Watir test scripts, which add to our regression safety net, but more importantly, they help us do more exploring than we could with only manual keystrokes.

To set up a scenario for manually testing in the UI, we can run a script or two that sets up the appropriate test data, gets us to the right screen, and saves us many hours of tedium and time. We can get through many more scenarios than we could with 100% manual testing.

Driving Development with Tests

Mastering TDD at the unit level seemed more straightforward than learning how to use business examples and business-facing tests to guide development. FitNesse was clearly a good tool for this purpose, but figuring out the right approach involved lots of trial and error.

Experimenting

We found that FitNesse tests were really easy to write. In our zeal to turn business examples into executable tests, the product owner (PO) and I got carried away. Our team had a difficult, high-risk theme coming up that involved complex algorithms and had a hard deadline. The PO and I spent days writing executable FitNesse tests for different parts of this theme, well ahead of the team starting on the stories for those features.

When the first iteration of working on the theme began, the programmers' reaction to our detailed FitNesse tests was: "Huh?" They couldn't see the forest for the trees. The complex, highly detailed test scenarios didn't give them a "big picture" of what they needed to code. In addition, the test design wasn't compatible with the code's architecture.

We had to back up, provide some "big picture" examples, and rewrite all the FitNesse tests, but our team learned a good lesson. We now write only high-level acceptance test cases in advance of coding. We don't start writing detailed, executable tests until someone picks up one of the coding task cards.

There's no prescription you can follow for knowing when to write tests, how many tests to write, and how detailed they should be. Every team has to experiment together and find out what works.

Planning

My team sees testing and coding as two parts of one software development process. It's impossible to separate beautiful testing and beautiful coding. When we plan at the theme or epic level, we consider testing as well as coding. Can we write FitNesse tests for these stories? Do we need new data to test with? Is our current test environment adequate? Do we need to work with any third parties? Theme and story estimates include time for testing activities. During iteration planning, we write test task cards alongside development task cards. We use the Agile Testing Quadrants (Figure 15-4) to help us think of all the types of testing, when we need to do them, and what tools we'll need.

When we start a new project or theme, we usually start by working through examples, mocking up prototypes, and thinking about high-level tests that will guide development. These are among the tests in Q2. The Q1 tests are a given, since we'll use TDD, but it's easy to forget about Q3 and Q4 when we're planning. It might take advance planning to implement the right tools for activities such as performance testing, and we have to be sure to budget enough time for adequate exploratory testing.

We're fortunate that Steve, our product owner, gets what he calls "advance clarity" about each story from all the business stakeholders. He writes up their conditions of satisfaction and goes through his own checklist for each story, and considers things such as legal issues, impact on third parties, and whether any new reports are needed. He often writes a few high-level test cases. He understands that we use tests to drive coding, and helps us prepare for these tasks

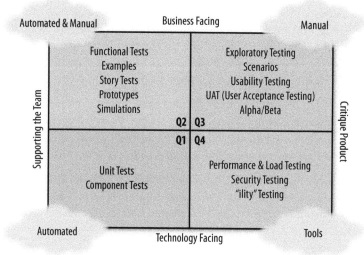

FIGURE 15-4. Agile Testing Quadrants

by giving us real-life examples that we can turn into executable tests. Such strong collaboration between the business and technical teams is part of beautiful testing.

When a complex theme is coming up, we hold hour-long brainstorming sessions where we and the customers work through example scenarios on the whiteboard and think about the best way to design the system. Everyone on the team feels free to ask questions and contribute ideas. It's sometimes a tester who comes up with a simpler solution than the product owner had proposed.

Driving Coding with Examples

Regression tests at the GUI level were a key to our success, especially early on. Once we no longer had to devote time to manual regression testing, we were able to start using FitNesse to convert examples of desired system behavior into tests that drive development.

As mentioned earlier, our product owner supplied us with useful real-life examples that we could turn into executable tests. These were in the form of either whiteboard drawings or Excel spreadsheets. We turned these into executable FitNesse tests, such as the one seen in Figure 15-5.

Also as mentioned earlier, we consider testing when we plan big new themes. Some new features might be straightforward to code but not so easy to test. During sprint planning, we write task cards for all testing tasks. Here's a typical set of task cards for a story to process an incoming loan payment:

Test two payments in the same day.

Loan Processing Fixture									
take loan in the amount of	1000	with interest rate	6.0	frequency	Monthly	and term	1	year with loan origination date	10-01-2005
check	periodic payment is	86.07							
post payment	1	of	86.07	on	10-31-2005				
post payment	2	of	86.07	on	10-31-2005				
receive payment	1	of	86.07	on	11-01-2005				
receive payment	2	of	86.07	on	11-01-2005				
settle and confirm payment	1								
settle and confirm payment	2								
check	interest applied for	1	is	5.10					
check	principal applied for	1	is	80.97					
check	principal applied for	2	is	86.07					
check	loan balance is	832.96							

FIGURE 15-5. Example FitNesse test

- Write high-level test cases for applying loan payment interest and principal
- Write FitNesse test cases for applying loan payment interest and principal
- Write FitNesse fixtures to automate tests for applying loan payment
- Write Canoo WebTest tests for processing loan payment
- Manually test processing loan payments

Have I mentioned that anyone on the team can sign up for any testing task? Because our application is so testing-intensive, even though we have two testers for five programmers, the programmers often pick up testing tasks, such as writing FitNesse tasks. And it's not unusual for them to use FitNesse tests for their own test-driven development.

Bumps in the Road

Of course, there are bumps in our automation road. Even after five years, a hard-to-solve problem can trip up our team. Here's a recent example. We had fallen behind almost two years in our version of FitNesse, and finally upgraded to the latest version. The new version no longer produced HTML result files, and the parser used by our continuous build to produce test results was no longer of any use.

I spent days trying to get the new version integrated with our continuous build, but couldn't produce the right result files. At the same time, a teammate was converting our continuous build processes from CruiseControl to Hudson. In the end, we worked together to get the FitNesse suites running as part of the Hudson build processes. My main contribution was to get help from the testing community in the form of a Hudson plug-in for FitNesse and a stylesheet to get the results into the necessary format. My teammate, a system administrator and programmer, did the heavy lifting. Neither of us could have succeeded as quickly working independently.

Our team gives the same attention to automated test design as we do to production code design. Good coding and design practices are as essential to test scripts as to any production code. We continually refactor our tests to minimize our maintenance costs. If there's a change in functionality, good test design means that updating the tests is a simple task.

Our investment in test design pays off multiple ways. Our automated tests provide incontrovertible documentation of the system behavior. Often, one of our business people will come over with a question such as, "I can't remember how the interest portion of a loan payment is calculated if a loan payment was skipped." I can run a FitNesse test to show conclusively how the functionality is implemented. That saves hours of discussion about "I thought we designed it to work this other way."

Delivering Value

When Brian Marick interviewed me for "Travels in Software," he asked me an interesting question: "What would you go back and tell your 2003 self?" The most important thing I wish I had known back when our team first implemented Scrum was that we really needed to understand the business inside and out. Not only the parts of the business automated in our software, but all the manual operations, accounting, marketing, and sales—everything that makes the business succeed.

Everyone Owns Business Problems

A year into agile development, our team effectively used TDD to produce robust, stable code. We were automating 100% of our regression tests, and devoting significant time to exploratory testing. Too often, though, we failed to deliver the exact functionality the customers wanted. We missed or misunderstood requirements, especially in areas outside the main application, such as accounting. We sometimes missed ripple effects that changes in one part of the system had on other, seemingly unrelated parts.

Problems not caused by software defects also troubled us. Application users made mistakes that had to be corrected with manual data changes. How could we make the system more "foolproof," and could we provide software to allow users to unravel their own messes? How could we maximize the ROI of the software we delivered every two weeks?

We decided to budget time to study the business more closely. Sitting with our customers as they performed their daily processing, we found simple software solutions that could save them hours of time every week and reduce the possibility of manual errors. For example, adding some information to an existing screen was easy to do and saved significant research time. Software to perform some complex calculations, which up to then had been done manually, took a couple of iterations to deliver. Because the business people are able to make more accurate operations, they don't come to us as often needing manual corrections in the database. Understanding the entire accounting system, not just the parts done by the application, was critical to ensuring that accounts balance correctly.

Here's another example of what I learned when I dedicated extra time and effort to learning the business. I worked at ePlan for more than five years without understanding that money moved among five different accounts. It's critical that the cash balances of these accounts balance every day. Learning this allowed me to "get" why our accountant might get a bit nervous when one account is out of balance by half a million dollars. Understanding the money movement, we could write the correct code to make sure money was withdrawn from and deposited to the correct accounts every day. It might seem obvious now, but it took us several years to achieve this level of understanding. Now we can help the business take stock accurately every day.

Incremental Testing and Coding

We've always tried to break work into small chunks, and focus on completing one small piece of functionality at a time. Another thing I'd tell my 2003 self is to commit to delivering less. We all want to satisfy our customers, but we have to be realistic. Working in small increments has made us much more efficient. We break complex stories into what we call "steel threads." The first "thread" is an end-to-end slice of the most basic functionality. We build each subsequent "thread" on top of the completed ones. Each thread is testable. Often the functionality is usable even before all the threads are finished.

Here's an example. We recently had a theme that involved uploading, parsing, and validating a file, creating data and persisting it in the database, and then processing the data. Testers, programmers, and customers mocked up the system on a whiteboard. The UI consisted of four screens. Our first UI "thread" was to display each screen, with some hardcoded data and buttons to navigate from one screen to another. There wasn't any business value yet, but we could show it to the customers to make sure they liked the flow, and write an automated end-to-end GUI test. We added functionality to each screen incrementally, completing testing and test automation for each small "thread" and building on that for the next increment.

Another "thread" was to parse and validate the uploaded file. We wrote FitNesse test cases for the parsing and validation, then wrote and tested the code without needing the UI at all. Then, we specified tests for creating the data and inserting it in the database and wrote that code. We tackled the code to process the data the same way. Those slices of functionality could be completed independently of the UI slices. By the time all the code was in place, we had time for end-to-end exploratory testing, with scripts to help set up the scenarios for manual testing. The exact functionality the customers needed was delivered quickly and defect-free. This incremental approach leads to the most elegant solution.

Plan Just Enough Ahead

If I tell you, "Don't plan your stories and themes too far in advance of when you will actually start developing them; priorities may change, and you want the information fresh in your minds when you start working on the stories," it doesn't sound like I'm talking about testing.

That's because I can't separate testing out from coding. Practices and principles that improve testing usually improve coding, and vice versa.

Our development team's depth of business knowledge makes planning more efficient. We can provide useful input when the business starts to plan a new feature. We can ask good questions that help them flesh out their requirements. We often suggest alternative solutions that might cost less to develop. We can help business experts decide whether a particular functionality will have a good ROI, so that we don't waste time planning features that don't deliver enough value.

A Success Story

When our team first implemented Scrum, the business had about 500 customers, wasn't profitable, and was in danger of going under because we couldn't deliver what our customers needed. As of this writing, we have well over 3,000 customers, we've been profitable for a couple of years, and in spite of the current unhealthy economy, we're growing steadily. Guiding development with tests, combined with our domain knowledge, helps ensure that we produce the right software. Our tests were designed to ensure that we code the right features the right way, and as a bonus, they also provide a super safety net. Our team's long-term commitment to designing software the right way helps us deliver value quickly and frequently. Our business stakeholders can count on our team's ability to change and grow our product, delighting existing customers and attracting new ones. Our beautiful team approach to testing and coding means joy and satisfaction for our team, our business, and our customers.

Post Script

I wrote the first draft of this chapter as a tester for ePlan Services Inc. I subsequently accepted an opportunity at Ultimate Software Group. I'm pleased to report that my experiences thus far with my new team echo my experiences at ePlan.

At the time I joined them, Ultimate had been doing Scrum for four years, and was delivering four production releases per year with 28 (!) Scrum teams. My new team is committed to driving development with tests at the unit and acceptance level. We work hard with the product folks to understand how our clients will use our software. Seeing the process work so similarly to what my team at ePlan did is a huge affirmation.

The common threads are the teams' focus on the customers' needs and on delivering what they want at the right time. Driving the coding with tests and examples helps ensure that our code base will accommodate all future changes. The business has confidence that new software features are delivered on time and continue to produce value.

## CHAPTER SIXTEEN

Peeling the Glass Onion at Socialtext

Matthew Heusser

I don't understand why we thought this was going to work in the first place.

—James Mathis, 2004

It's Not Business...It's Personal

I'VE SPENT MY ENTIRE ADULT LIFE DEVELOPING, TESTING, and managing software projects. In those years, I've learned a few things about our field:

- Software testing as it is practiced in the field bears very little resemblance to how it is taught in the classroom—or even described at some industry presentations.
- There are multiple perspectives on what good software testing is and how to do it well.
- The previous point means that there are no "best practices"—no single way to view or do testing that will allow you to be successful in all environments—but there are rules of thumb that can guide the learner.[1]

---

1. I am a member of the context-driven school of software testing, a community of people who align around such ideas, including "there are no best practices." See *http://www.context-driven-testing.com/*.

Beyond that, in business software development, I would add a few things more. First, there is a sharp difference between *checking*,[2] which is a sort of clerical, repeatable process to make sure things are fine, and *investigating*, which is a feedback-driven process.

Checking can be automated, or at least parts of it can. With small, discrete units, it is possible for a programmer to select inputs and compare them to outputs automatically. When we combine those units, we begin to see complexity.

Imagine, for example, a simple calculator program that has a very small memory leak every time we press the Clear button. It might behave fine if we test each operation independently, but when we try to use the calculator for half an hour, it seems to break down without reason.

Checking cannot find those types of bugs. Investigating might. Or, better yet, in this example, a static inspector looking for memory leaks might.

And that's the point. Software exposes us to a variety of risks. We will have to use a variety of techniques to limit those risks. Because there are no best practices, I can't tell you what to do, but I can tell you what we have done at Socialtext, and why we like it—what makes those practices beautiful to us.

Our approach positions testing as a form of risk management. The company invests a certain amount of time and money in testing in order to get information, which will decrease the chance of a bad release. There is an entire business discipline around risk management; insurance companies practice it every day. It turns out that *testing for its own sake* meets the exact definition of risk management. We'll revisit risk management when we talk about testing at Socialtext, but first, let's talk about beauty.

Tester Remains On-Stage; Enter Beauty, Stage Right

Are you skeptical yet? If you are, I can't say I blame you. To many people, the word "testing" brings up images of drop-dead simple pointing and clicking, or following a boring script written by someone else. They think it's a simple job, best done by simple people who, well…at least you don't have to pay them much. I think there's something wrong with that.

Again, the above isn't critical investigation; it's checking. And checking certainly isn't *beautiful*, by any stretch of the word. And beauty is important.

Let me explain.

In my formative years as a developer, I found that I had a conflict with my peers and superiors about the way we developed software. Sometimes I attributed this to growing up in the east coast versus the midwest, and sometimes to the fact that my degree was not in computer

---

2. My colleague and friend Michael Bolton is the first person I am aware of to make this distinction, and I believe he deserves a fair amount of credit for it.

science but mathematics.[3] So, being young and insecure, I went back to school at night and earned a Master's degree in computer information systems to "catch up," but still I had these cultural arguments about how to develop software. I wanted simple projects, whereas my teammates wanted projects done "right" or "extensible" or "complete."

Then one day I realized: they had never been taught about beauty, nor that beauty was inherently good. Although I had missed a class or two in my *concentration* in computer science, they also missed something I had learned in mathematics: an appreciation of *aesthetics*. Some time later I read *Things a Computer Scientist Rarely Talks About* (Center for the Study of Language and Information) by Dr. Donald Knuth, and found words to articulate this idea. Knuth said that mathematicians and computer scientists need similar basic skills: they need to be able to keep many variables in their head, and they need to be able to jump up and down a chain of abstraction very quickly to solve complex programs. According to Knuth, the mathematician is searching for truth—ideas that are consistently and universally correct—whereas the computer scientists can simply hack a conditional[4] in and move on.

But mathematics is more than that. To solve any problem in math, you *simplify* it. Take the simple algebra problem:

$$2X - 6 = 0$$

So we add 6 to each side and get $2X = 6$, and we divide by 2 and get $X = 3$. At every step in the process, we make the equation simpler. *In fact, the simplest expression of any formula is the answer.* There may be times when you get something like $X = 2Y$; you haven't solved for X or Y, but you've taken the problem down to its simplest possible form and you get full credit. And the best example of solving a problem of this nature I can think of is the *proof*.

I know, I, know, please don't fall asleep on me here or skip down. To a mathematician, a good proof is a work of art—the stuff of pure logic, distilled into symbols.[5] Two of the highest division courses I took at Salisbury University were number theory and the history of mathematics from Dr. Homer Austin. They weren't what you would think. Number theory was basically recreating the great proofs of history—taking a formula that seemed to make sense, proving it was true for F(1), then proving if it was true for any F(N), then it was also true for F(N+1). That's called proof by induction. Number theory was trying to understand how the elements

---

3. Strictly speaking, I have a bachelor's degree in mathematics with a concentration in computer science.

4. "Conditional" is a fancy word for an IF/THEN/ELSE statement block.

5. I am completely serious about the beauty of proofs. For years, I used to ask people I met with any kind of mathematics background what their favorite math proof was. Enough blank stares later and I stopped asking. As for mine, I'm stuck between two: the proof of the limit of the sum of $1/(2^N)$ for all positive integers, or Newton's proof of integration—take your pick. (Rob Sabourin is one notable exception. I asked him his favorite, and he said he was stuck between two....)

of the universe were connected (such as the Fibonacci sequence, which appears in nature on a conch shell), or how to predict what the next prime number will be, or why pi shows up in so many places.

And, every now and again, Dr. Homer Austin would step back from the blackboard, look at the work, and just say, "Now…there's a beautiful equation." The assertion was simple: beauty and simplicity were inherently good.

You could tell this in your work because the simplest answer was correct. When you got the wrong answer, your professor could look at your work and show you the ugly line, the hacky line, the one line that looked more complex than the one above it. He might say, "Right there, Matt. That's where you went off the rails."[6]

By the end of the semester, we could see it too. For that, I am, quite honestly, in his debt.[7]

Of course, you can learn to appreciate beauty from any discipline that deals in abstraction and multiple variables. You could learn it from chess, or chemistry, or aerospace engineering, or music and the arts.[8] My experience was that it was largely missing from computer science, at least in the 1990s. Instead of simplicity, we celebrated *complexity*. Instead of focusing on value to customers, more senior programmers were writing the complex frameworks and architectures, leaving the junior developers to be *mere implementers*. The goal was not to deliver value quickly but instead to develop a castle in the sky. We even invented a term, "gold plating," for when a developer found a business problem too simple and had to add his own bells and whistles to the system, or perhaps, instead of solving one problem and solving it well, he created an *extensible framework* to solve a much larger number of generic business problems.

Joel Spolsky would call this person an "architecture astronaut," in that they get so abstract, they actually "cut off the air supply" of the business.[9] In the back of my mind I could hear the voice of Dr. Austin saying, "Right there—there—is where your project went off the rails."

Ten years later, we've learned a great deal. We have a growing body of knowledge of how to apply beauty to development; O'Reilly even has a book on the subject. But testing…testing is inherently ugly, right? Aside from developer-facing testing, like TDD, testing is no fun at best and rather-have-a-tooth-pulled-with-no-anesthetic at worst, right?

No, I don't think so. In math we have this idea of *prima facie* evidence, that an argument can be true on its face and not require proof. For example, there is no proof that you can add one to both sides of an equation or double both sides and the equation remains true. We accept

---

6. No pun on Ruby intended. I am a Perl hacker.

7. Him, and Dr. Kathleen Shannon, and Dr. Mohammad Mouzzam, and Professor Dean Defino, and Professor Maureen Malone.

8. My coworker and occasional writing partner, Chris McMahon, has a good bit to say about testing as a performing art. You should check out…oh, wait, he has his own chapter. All right, then.

9. *http://www.joelonsoftware.com/articles/fog0000000018.html*

this at face value—prima facie—because it's obvious. All of our efforts in math build on top of these basic prima facie (or "axiomatic") arguments.[10]

So here's one for you: boring, brain-dead, gag-me-with-a-spoon testing is *bad* testing. It's merely checking. And it is not beautiful. One thing we know about ugly solutions is that they are wrong; they've gone off the rails.

We can do better.

Come Walk with Me, The Best Is Yet to Be

This phrase is very common and I am unsure of its origins. I believe I first read it in the collected poetry of my grandmother, Lynette Isham. My favorite poem of hers included this line: "Once there was music in my heart. Then I met you...and I heard the words."

This was about her son, my father, Roger Heusser. I don't know about testing, but that's some of the most beautiful prose I have ever read. I had to put it in print.

For our purposes, let's look at software risk management as an investment of time and resources to find problems before those problems become angry customers. James Whittaker, the author of *How To Break Software* (Addison-Wesley), took that idea one step further to say that customers don't want to pay a tester a salary; they want testing to be performed, and are willing to pay for it.[11] This makes testing, at least in theory, a naturally outsourceable function.

No, I'm not suggesting that your team outsource testing.[12] At Socialtext, we develop and test software in parallel (more about that later) and do informal collaboration instead of handoffs. Outsourcing, as an alternative, usually involves "passing off" software to a test team and waiting for results, only to get a hundred bug reports dropped in your lap. Generally speaking, that is neither effective nor efficient—and certainly not beautiful.

I am suggesting that *management wants testing to have happened*, and wants the results of that testing to be presented in a way they understand. How we do that is up to us. Let's start with that ugliest of false dichotomies: manual or automated testing.

---

10. In fact, most of geometry is built on top of the idea that parallel lines never intersect. The proof of this basic rule? You won't find it. Anywhere. It's prima facie. If you can figure it out, give me a call; we could probably win at least a million dollars. I am completely serious.

11. *http://blogs.msdn.com/james_whittaker/archive/2008/08/20/the-future-of-software-testing-part-1.aspx*

12. If your organization simply does not view development or testing as a core competence—perhaps if you are not a software company—it might a good idea for you to find a partner that does have that competence and wants to develop a symbiotic relationship with you. (See my M.S. thesis at *http://www.xndev.com/CS/CS692/TheOutsourcingEquation_ABIT.doc*.)

Automated Testing Isn't

It's very tempting to speak of "automated testing" as if it were "automated manufacturing"—where we have the robot doing the exact same thing as the thinking human. So we take an application like the one shown in Figure 16-1 with a simple test script like this:

1. Enter 4 in the first box.
2. Enter 4 in the second box.
3. Select the Multiply option from the Operations drop-down.
4. Press Submit.
5. Expect "16" in the answer box.

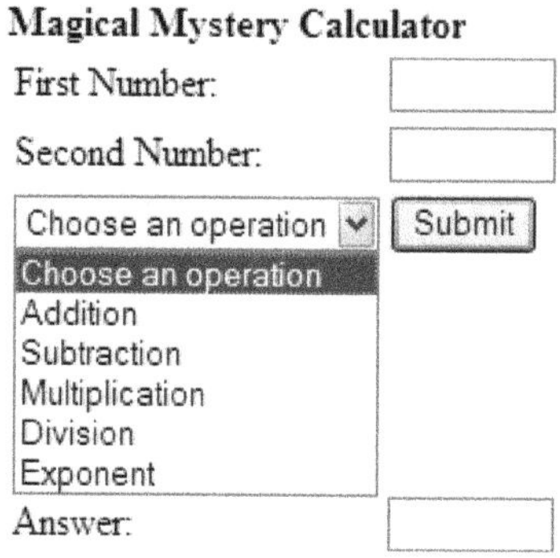

FIGURE 16-1. A very simple application

We get a computer to do all of those steps, and call it automation. The problem is that there is a hidden second expectation at the end of every test case documented this way: "And nothing else odd happened."

The simplest way to deal with this "nothing else odd" is to capture the entire screen and compare runs, but then any time a developer moves a button, or you change screen resolution, color scheme, or anything else, the software will throw a false error.

These days it's more common to check only for the exact assertion. Which means you miss things like the following:

- An icon's background color is not transparent.
- After the submit, the Operations drop-down changed back to the default of Plus, so it reads like "4 + 4 = 16".
- After the second value is entered, the cancel button becomes disabled.
- The Answer box is editable when it should be disabled (grayed out).

- The operation took eight seconds to complete.
- The new page that is generated has the right answer, but the first value entered is zeroed out. In other words, it now reads 0 + 4 = 8.

A thinking, human tester would notice these things in an instant. A computer will not. So an "automated test" is simply not the same thing as having a human being running the test. Moreover, say the requirements allow 10 seconds for the result. A human can notice that the simple multiplication is just barely within tolerance, and might experiment with large numbers or complex operations in order to find other errors. A computer cannot do that.

So we find several different root causes of bugs, which could be found by different methods.

Into Socialtext

Before I could introduce Socialtext, I needed to introduce our work environment and lay out the fundamental issues involved when we test. At Socialtext, we have a number of different defects, with different root causes, that need to be found (or prevented) using different technical strategies. Without those precepts, we'd be making assumptions about the mission of our team (find bugs? or report status?), our goals (100% automation of all tests?), and what metrics are appropriate (number of tests? statement coverage?).

I did a simple check in the Socialtext Bug database and found the following rough categories of bugs (Table 16-1).

TABLE 16-1. Defect categories and examples

Category of defect		Examples
Untestable or rendering	9	Exported PDF has incorrect font; widget headers do not preserve padding; tag lookahead does not keep up with typing
Browser compatibility untestable or rendering	9	Workspace pulldown has no scrollbar on IE6
Catchable by computer-based browser execution and evaluation	19	Delete tag; tag does not go away
Catchable by reasonably light slideshow	7	All files list is incorrectly sorted for a complex sort
Special characters, exception-handling, internationalization	13	Special characters (@$==, copyright or trademark, etc.) in fields do not render correctly on save
Appliance installs or upgrades	8	Appliance upgrade fails
Backup, restore, import, export	3	Import of old (<3 releases back) workspace fails
Usability issues	9	Tab order, spelling, too many clicks to use, "make this UI like other dialogs"

Category of defect		Examples
Any kind of test	8	Icons render as "X" on latest build; open or save fail on latest build; home page of app fails on latest build
Background/batch processes	4	Automatic emails are going off too often/not often enough/incorrect
Complex interactions of software	7	Two specific widgets, used together, can corrupt each other (out of dozens); cannot perform a specific operation twice in a row
Performance	4	Twitter-like signals take > 1 minute to display
Total	**100**	

We could argue the importance of the different categories of defects; for example, you could argue that test automation should include special cases, or complex interactions, or "any kind of test," or that appliance upgrades should be automated and count as "automatable defects." You could argue that some of the rendering could be caught by automation, and that we could have software that opens a socket, downloads a PDF, and then does some sort of compare against a PDF generated last week.

In any event, I submit that this defect breakdown shows that an application will fail in many different ways, and test strategy needs to address those different ways through a variety of approaches, or a balanced breakfast. Now I would like to tell you about how we find those bugs at Socialtext.

But...What Do You Make?

Oh, excuse me. At Socialtext we make software that allows people to have conversations instead of transactions. Think Facebook, or blogging, or Twitter—but inside your business and secure. Our initial product offering was a wiki, which enables a sort of corporate intranet that can be edited by anyone at any time, using a simple markup language or even an MS Word–like editor.

Figure 16-2 shows a simple wiki page: a user story for a new feature.

To change the page, the user clicks the Edit button, which brings up the page shown in Figure 16-3.

Notice that this editor is very similar to Microsoft Word, with its buttons for bold, italics, headers, add a link or image, and so on. The text also appears formatted on-screen. A literal-text inspection could find the right words on the page, but they could be missing formatting or have other font problems. Simply testing the editor itself is a nontrivial testing problem.

FIGURE 16-2. Viewing a wiki page

FIGURE 16-3. Editing a wiki page

Socialtext's wiki software is built out of open source components, with a Linux (Ubuntu) operating system, Apache web server, Postgres database, and Perl programming language—essentially a LAMP stack.[13]

Software Process at Socialtext

Socialtext follows a development process inspired by Extreme Programming. The basic unit of work is a "story," which is an extremely lightweight requirements document. A story contains a brief description of a feature along with examples of what needs to happen to consider the story completed; we call these examples "acceptance tests" and describe them in plain English. The purpose of the story is to create a shared mental model of what work will be done and to have a single point of reference and expectations. Of course, each story is embodied in a Socialtext wiki page; we tag stories with "Needs Review," "In Dev," "In QA," or "Awaiting Signoff" to create an informal workflow and indicate progress of the work.

We do not expect our stories to be complete, as requirements change over time. Instead, we try to make our stories *good enough* for the developers to begin work, and declare them "good enough" when the story review process reaches the point of diminishing returns.

We do not expect our stories to be correct—but we do have a review process to make them *better*.

We do not expect our stories to be unambiguous, as English is a vague and ambiguous language itself—but having concrete examples certainly helps.

A story describes a complete feature, but that feature may not itself be marketable or saleable. So we collect a series of stories in an iteration, and timebox those iterations at two weeks in length. We are not dogmatic about iteration length, and allow a three-week iteration around the Christmas holiday. Figure 16-4 illustrates some of the activities that happen during a typical iteration and the order in which they happen.

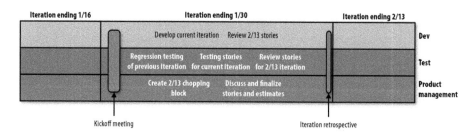

FIGURE 16-4. Iteration progression overview

13. Linux, Apache, MySQL, Perl: LAMP.

Ideally, developers finish stories and get to "code close" on the Wednesday of the second week of the iteration that begins on a Monday. Regression testing takes about two days, and on Monday, everyone starts on the next iteration. This assumes that the testers find no bugs in regression testing and that the developers are always on time. And, I am sure, that theory might sell a lot of books. Our experience has been that it's common for regression testing of the previous iteration to run into the next. That's OK because the devs haven't handed off any stories yet. (When that happens, one of the biggest problems we face is straddling the iterations, which is when developers and testers are fixing and finding bugs in the previous iteration while attempting to kick off and develop the current one.)

When you consider that, at this point, product management is working on stories for the next iteration, you realize that the team is working on three iterations at once. You may ask how this is beautiful (more about that later), but one explanation is that it is a pipeline, not a waterfall.

What We Actually Do

Let's follow a story—specifically, Edit Summaries. First, a product manager gets an idea. He notices that customers are using our "Recent Changes" feature heavily, but want to know if the change is important ("Matt modified the vacation policy") or minor ("Matt made spelling and grammar changes to the contracting policy"). Edit Summaries would allow the user to create a summary that shows up when people are looking at revision history (what's new) or a user's stream of actions. It's a killer feature, and product management says we have to have it in order to sell to Acme Corporation, so they draft a story. The story looks something like Figure 16-5.

Story Overview

T-Shirt Estimate	S
Points	2
Estimator(s)	Shawn Devlin , Jeremy Stashewsky
Dependencies	Tech Story: NLW logs events to database
Lead Dev	Jeremy Stashewsky
Lead QA	Matt Heusser
Priority	2
Customer	Adina Levin
Comments	(1 for UI changes and 1 for backend changes)
Notes	

The user-interface will include a check box and text box for the user to enter an optional, brief edit summary. The summary is intended to convey the changes made (eg "fixed spelling" or "increased vacation policy by one week." That summary is recorded on the save event, and will be displayed along with the event where events appear, such as the user's profile or activities widget. Summaries will also appear as an new column when user's click revisions (page history.) Future work includes having the summaries appear any time a list of pages is show, such as search results, pages tag list, what's new, etc. This is described in Story: Users' edit summaries appear in the list view snippets

FIGURE 16-5. Details on a story

The story starts out with a customer, who is the business sponsor (probably a product manager), and a description of a feature. At this point the story is only a paragraph of text; no one has been assigned. The product manager, developers, architect/coach, and occasionally QA meet to discuss the overall size of the story, implementation details, and story tests. We record our estimates in terms of points, which are ideal engineering half-days for a developer to implement. Due to pairing, vacation, interruptions, and so on, the ideal is never realized; we track the actual number of points accomplished and use that to predict future performance, a notion known as "iteration velocity."

During this process, the product management team might create mockups. For example, the Edit Summary dialog should like Figure 16-6.

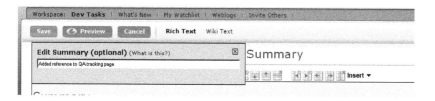

FIGURE 16-6. An Edit Summary mockup

One more thing about the actual requirements for Edit Summaries before we move on. You'll notice that once the Edit Summaries go in, it is not clear how the user will get them out. There are other stories that specify that Edit Summaries can appear in revision history, in Recent Changes, in a user's activity stream as updates, and as micro-blog posts. This story is to *capture* the Edit Summary, and is concerned only with the single dialog box.

The story includes the header, a plain-text description, some sample screen captures, and the acceptance tests.

During the initial cut of the story, the product owner makes a good-faith first attempt to create acceptance tests, which are augmented by developers and testers before any developer writes a line of code. The goal of the story-creation and review process is not to create an exhaustive list; this is not big-testing-up-front (BTUF). Instead, the team is striving to really understand the problem domain, so that when we find a problem later on, the entire team will shrug in agreement that "yup, that's a bug" and be committed to fixing it as a whole team—instead of whining that someone changed their minds or that the requirements weren't right.

Table 16-2 lists some of the acceptance tests for the Edit Summaries dialog. "lando" is Orlando Vazquez, and MRH is Matthew R. Heusser. The tests are stored on a wiki page, and at the end of a working time-block, the worker updates the document with what is completed—but we're getting ahead of ourselves. Notice that these are specifications at the behavioral level of the feature.

TABLE 16-2. Acceptance tests for the Edit Summaries dialog

Test	Dev sign off	QA sign off
User mouses over Save button in either edit mode and a summary UI appears.	lando	MRH
User quickly passes over Save button; summary UI does not appear.	lando	MRH
Move focus (click), either into edit area or entirely away; summary UI disappears.	lando	MRH
Move focus (click) entirely away, mouse over Save again, summary UI appears; click in edit area, summary UI disappears.	lando	MRH
Mouse over Save, UI appears. Move mouse directly to the right, click Cancel. Click Edit. UI should not appear.	lando	MRH
Summary UI maintains content across disappearing and reappearing during editing.	lando	MRH
User enters a summary and clicks Cancel. User clicks edit, and goes to Edit Summary, old summary is gone.	lando	MRH
Superfluous whitespace should be minimized from the Edit Summary; " dog " becomes "dog", etc.	lando	MRH
Entering ":" or ";" in the summary should save and retrieve correctly.	lando	MRH
Summaries persist on st-admin export/reimport workspace.	lando	MRH
Commenting on a page shouldn't change the current Edit Summary.	lando	MRH
User cannot enter > 250 characters in the UI.	lando	MRH
Backend truncates > 250 characters.	lando	MRH
Documentation is updated to include new screen captures.	lando	

This table lists only 15 tests; I'm sure you can think of more. The actual software had 35, including requirements for localization, for an API so programmers can write an Edit Summary without the web browser, and for creating some amount of test automation, which acts as a requirement and is fed into the story estimate.

You'll note that I do not view this as a list of *everything* to test. It is not a list of test cases; it is a list of acceptance tests. These tests have value for communication, to create a shared model of the work to be done, and as examples. As a list of test cases, it is actually pretty weak. It does give the developers a good idea of the expected behavior for Edit Summaries.

At this point the developers had everything they needed to write the code. Orlando called Stash (Jeremy Stashewsky) on the phone and, sharing a shared-editor screen, created the story as a pair. They coded the backend in Perl and, along the way, wrote unit tests in TDD-style to aid in design and testing. A lengthy discussion of TDD is outside the scope of this chapter, but I have asked Lando to say a few words about what he did:

My process while TDD'ing a new story is to first plan some simple unit tests that act almost like a spec of how I would like to see the story work. I write these simple failing tests, and then write the code to make them pass. Then, having implemented the "normal" use-case scenarios, I go on to flesh out the rest of the story tests and edge cases in the same way.

```
# initialize some globals we'll use
setup_tests();

signal_edit_summary: {
    my $hub = setup_page(
        revision_id  => $save_revision_id,
        edit_summary => 'Dancing is forbidden!',
        signal_edit_summary => 1,
    );

    $hub->edit->edit_content;
    my $page = load_page_by_id(hub => $hub, page_id => $page_id);
    is $page->edit_summary, 'Dancing is forbidden!', 'proxy method
works';

    # check that the signal was created
    signal_ok (
        viewer => $user,
        signaler => $user,
        body => "Dancing is forbidden!" (edited Save Page in Admin
Wiki)',
        topic => {
            page_id => $page_id,
            workspace_id => $current_workspace->workspace_id,
        },
        msg => 'normal length edit summary with signal'
    );

    # check that the appropriate events were created
    is_event_count(2);
    event_ok (
        event_class => 'signal',
        action => 'page_edit',
    );
    event_ok (
        event_class => 'page',
        action => 'edit_save',
    );
}
```

After Lando finishes his work, he deletes the page tag "In Dev" and adds a tag called "In QA." The next time a developer looks at the page that tracks this iteration's work, the story has magically moved into the QA queue, and the QA lead (that's me) will pick it up.

Now I check out the latest version of the code and rip through the story tests in all supported browsers: the newest and previous versions of Internet Explorer, Firefox, and Safari. I also try odd combinations of characters, special characters, and, of course, straight text with no spaces.

After story tests, I conduct exploratory testing of the story and related changes.[14] I find that in Internet Explorer, the box appears in the wrong position (in the far right), return the story to "In Dev," and email the developer. Lando fixes the issue, marks it in QA, I retest, and I move the story to customer acceptance.

Occasionally, the problem is big enough to mark, hard enough to fix, and not critical to the success of the story. In that case, the tester will create a Bugzilla (bug tracking) ticket and add it to the story as a note. The product manager can read the bug and determine whether we can ship with the defect or not. The follow-up story, for example, was that summaries are added to revision history. I found that I could add 250 characters of text with no spaces and cause serious scrollbar and margin issues in the revision history page. After a quick huddle, we decided that a) you don't see this issue using the largest words in the English dictionary, b) it should probably be fixed, but perhaps not today, and c) I would create a bug report.

That tests the story once, but we release out to our Software-as-a-Service production server every two weeks, and a minor change to something else can easily ripple. If we retested every acceptance test on every browser every two weeks, the burden would eventually cripple the team. So we do some test automation using a framework we developed called *wikitests*.

Wikitests[15]

A wikitest is a keyword-driven test that drives the browser. With wikitests, each test is expressed as a series of commands in a table, one command per table row. These commands are Selenese, which is near English. They can be read by anyone with a modest programming background, and because they are stored in wiki pages, anyone can view, revise, and save them. In addition, we can build our own commands—for example, `st-login`—which combine common operations. For example, the following tables show the test for Edit Summaries. You'll notice that the first column is the command, and the second and third are parameters. For example, in the first command, `Pt` is the name of the pause variable, and `5000` is the amount

14. On rereading this chapter, I'm a little disappointed in myself that the second half covers very little description of the time and effort we spend on exploratory testing, but I wanted to cover the areas that were most unique, special, and beautiful about Socialtext. Given the list of authors in this book, I expect plenty of coverage of exploratory methods in other chapters.

15. A few years ago, Bret Pettichord was running a class on homebrew test automation where he suggested a style of test automation framework. I would argue that wikitests are among the most advanced known frameworks developed in that style. The framework itself strings together open source and home-development components to create an overall effect. The browser-driver component of the framework is Selenium RC, mostly written by Jason Huggins. `test:www:selenium`, developed by my coworker, Luke Closs, wraps Selenium RC so that it can be driven through the Perl programming language. Other components take Socialtext wiki pages and convert them into Perl commands, which are executed by `test::www::selenium`. Ken Pier manages the ongoing project to create, extend, and maintain wikitests. I have made some modest contributions, developing plug-ins, wikitests commands, and lots and lots of test cases, but the actual credit goes to Ken and Luke. Other contributors include Kevin Jones, Lyssa Kaelher, Shahed Hossain, the aforementioned Chris McMahon, our intern David Ahnger-Pier, and, recently, Audrey Tang.

to substitute. In the second, `st-admin` is the backend command to take an action, `update-page` is the parameter to create a new page, and the third column is the expected result to compare. (If the output said "Unable to create a new page" or something like that, the test would log an error.) The number after `wait_for_element_present_ok` is the number of thousandths of a second to wait, `%%variable_name%%` means substitute a variable for the data, and so on. An abbreviated version of the Edit Summaries test follows.

Comment	Test Case: Edit Summaries		

Comment	Test Case: Edit Summaries—create a page from file	
st-admin	updatepage workspace %%workspace%% email %%email%% page "Edit Summaries %%start_time%%" < %%wikitest_client_files%%wikitest_toc.txt	The "Edit Summaries % %start_time% %" page has been created

Comment	Test Case: Edit Summaries—create one Edit Summary	
open_ok	/%%workspace%%/index.cgi?Edit Summaries %%start_time%%	
wait_for_element_visible_ok	steditbuttonlink	30000
click_ok	steditbuttonlink	
wait_for_element_visible_ok	link=Wiki Text	30000
click_ok	link=Wiki Text	
wait_for_element_visible_ok	wikiwyg_wikitext_textarea	30000
wait_for_element_visible_ok	stsavebuttonlink	30000

Comment	Test Case: Edit Summaries—type the summary	
wait_for_element_present_ok	steditsummarytextarea	30000
click_ok	steditsummarytextarea	
type_ok	steditsummarytextarea	Quick Summary for my friends % %start_time% %
click_and_wait	stsavebuttonlink	

Comment	Test Case: Edit Summaries—create a second Edit Summary	
open_ok	/%%workspace%%/index.cgi?Edit Summaries %%start_time%%	
wait_for_element_visible_ok	steditbuttonlink	30000
click_ok	steditbuttonlink	
wait_for_element_visible_ok	stsavebuttonlink	30000
wait_for_element_visible_ok	link=Wiki Text	30000
click_ok	link=Wiki Text	
wait_for_element_visible_ok	wikiwyg_wikitext_textarea	30000

Comment	Test Case: Edit Summaries—type the second summary	
wait_for_element_present_ok	steditsummarytextarea	30000
click_ok	steditsummarytextarea	
type_ok	steditsummarytextarea	A second summary for a wikitest % %start_time% %
click_and_wait	stsavebuttonlink	
wait_for_element_visible_ok	steditbuttonlink	30000

Comment	Test Case: Edit Summaries—revision history	
click_and_wait	link=3 Revisions	
wait_for_element_visible_ok	link=Back To Current Revision	30000
text_like	qr/A second summary for a wikitest %%start_time%%.+Quick Summary for my friends %%start_time%%/	

Comment	Test Case: Edit Summaries—teardown	
st-admin	purgepage workspace %%workspace%% page edit_summaries %%start_time%%	page was purged

Comment	Test case: Edit Summaries COMPLETED		

A few points about this testing style: all HTML elements have to have an ID name, such as st-save-button-link, and the software runs around, clicking links and looking at values. To find the name of elements, I had to use a tool[16] and "inspect" the user interface—or else collaborate with the developers on names before the code was produced.

Thus the overall process is to create a test case (which is a wiki page), run the test, watch it fail, change something, and try again. In this example, we see several dead stops and retries, as I abandon one test strategy and move to a different one, or perhaps peer into the code to debug it. All in all, it takes me half a day to write automation for a feature that can be tested manually, in all browsers, in an hour. I did not pick this as some sort of extreme example; this problem is typical. Moreover, the wikitest is not sapient; it cannot tell if the Edit Summary dialogue would appear to be too wide, move down suddenly, or be the wrong color. What it does do is allow some amount of basic sanity coverage in a short period of time, which we desire in order to enable many quick iterations.

Wikitest output looks something like this:

```
# st-login: wikitester@ken.socialtext.net, d3vnu111, test-data -
/nlw/login.html?redirect_to=%2Ftest-data%2Findex.cgi
ok 1 - open, /nlw/login.html?redirect_to=%2Ftest-data%2Findex.cgi
ok 2 - type, username, wikitester@ken.socialtext.net
ok 3 - type, password, d3vnu111
ok 4 - click, id=login_btn, log in
ok 5 - wait_for_page_to_load, 60000
#
# comment: Test Case: Edit Summaries
# Set 'pt' to '5000'
#
# comment: Test Case: Edit Summaries - create a page from file, because we can't type
# newlines with type_ok st-admin update-page --workspace test-data --email
# wikitester@ken.socialtext.net --page "Edit Summaries 1234802223"
# < /opt/wikitest_files/wikitest_toc.txt
ok 6 - st-admin update-page --workspace test-data --email wikitester@ken.socialtext.net
    --page "Edit Summaries 1234802223" </opt/wikitest_files/wikitest_toc.txt
ok 7 - open, /test-data/index.cgi?Edit Summaries 1234802223
ok 8 - click, st-edit-button-link
ok 9 - wait_for_condition, try { selenium.isTextPresent('Editing: Edit Summaries
    1234802223') ? true : false } catch(e) { false }, 55000
ok 10 - wait_for_condition, try { selenium.isVisible('st-save-button-link') ? true :
    false } catch(e) { false }, 30000
ok 11 - wait_for_condition, try { selenium.isElementPresent('st-edit-summary-text-area')
    ? true : false } catch(e) { false }, 5000
ok 12 - click, st-edit-summary-text-area
ok 13 - type, st-edit-summary-text-area, Quick Summary for my friends
ok 14 - click, st-save-button-link
ok 15 - wait_for_condition, try { selenium.isElementPresent('st-edit-button-link') ?
    true : false } catch(e) { false }, 30000
ok 16 - click, st-edit-button-link
```

16. Firebug and the Web Developer plug-in are free for Mozilla Firefox. The IE developer toolbar is a good alternative for Internet Explorer.

```
ok 17 - wait_for_condition, try { selenium.isVisible('st-save-button-link') ? true :
    false } catch(e) { false }, 55000
ok 18 - wait_for_condition, try { selenium.isElementPresent('st-edit-summary-text-area')
    ? true : false } catch(e) { false }, 30000
ok 19 - click, st-edit-summary-text-area
ok 20 - type, st-edit-summary-text-area, A second summary for a wikitest
ok 21 - click, st-save-button-link
ok 22 - wait_for_condition, try { selenium.isVisible('st-edit-button-link') ? true :
    false } catch(e) { false }, 60000
ok 23 - click, //a[@id='st-watchlist-indicator'], clicking watch button
ok 24 - wait_for_condition, try { selenium.isVisible('link=3 Revisions') ? true :
    false } catch (e) { false }, 60000
#
# comment: Test Case: Edit Summaries Revision History
ok 25 - click, link=3 Revisions
# comment: Test Case: Edit Summaries teardown
# st-admin purge-page --workspace test-data --page edit_summaries_1234802223
ok 26 - st-admin purge-page --workspace test-data --page edit_summaries_1234802223
#
# comment: Test case: Edit Summaries COMPLETED
1..26
```

If failures occurred, the software would say something like, "It looks like you failed X of Y tests" or "Failed after X tests run." We use a tool, called tap2html, that summarizes the results of tests suites so that we can see success and failure of a 10,000 test-step suite at a glance and drill down into details when needed.

Although we do have some canned test data (for search, watch pages, and so on), each test case is designed to run independently. Wikitests can also be grouped into test sets, so it is possible to make a wikitest that is a series of links to other wikitests. To do regression testing with wikitests, we run a test suite, redirect the output to a file, and search through the file for "not ok", "error", "warning", and other messages. (Yes, we have some scripts that can process the errors and tell us what test cases failed, and a visualizer that takes ASCII text output and converts it into a graphical representation viewed in a browser.)

A Balanced Breakfast Approach

So far, we have acceptance tests, unit tests, and wikitests. We are painfully aware of the bugs that wikitests fail to find, and yet every two weeks we need to do regression testing of all of our features, with a goal of moving code to internal staging within 48 hours of starting regression tests. To do that, we create a candidate test-tracking wiki page. Using the candidate page, we can assign testers to work on different pieces of the software, and report what bug reports have been filed. When the page says "ok", "ok", "ok" for all elements, testing for the iteration is done. ("bz" followed by a number means the tester found a bug.) Let's look at a candidate page, already in progress, and discuss it:

Testing Iteration Ending 2009-01-30:

- test-release status on iteration page: Green

wikitests:

- FF2: **PASS. Widgets tests have been fixed in master but not in 01-30**
- FF3 **in progress** chris. (Thought this was mine. **PASS.**) Ken (It was, I figured I'd take it off your hands. It's snowing here. -C)
    — TC: Hidden Email Address for Public wiki must have a race condition.
- IE7: **PASS mostly** mcchris at step 5941 in TC: Calc Watchlist the database is corrupted and apache-perl crashed. Can not reproduce. Otherwise no errors at all. **update:** Stash suggests that the nlw-error.log record indicates a race condition when saving spreadsheets such that an expected db record does not exist upon a subsequent INSERT.
- IE6: mcchris **PASS**
    — TC: REST Workspace passes on re-run
        — original run encountered a single 502 error. this makes me nervous
    — TC: Hidden Email Address for Public wiki passes run manually. fails b/c of a race condition w/ search results maybe?
    — **All widgets tests failed** Cursory manual examination widgets seem ok but slow as usual.
    — **All Reports tests failed** The reports tables were not in place and we're sending raw sql to the browser when the env is fubar. Following up with Stash/someone. Note: I think I have seen this failure to put reports tables in place before. Will try to figure out why that happens
- Safari: matt the cheshire cast button in test_case_revisions doesn't work, and causes a failure. mcchris says this is a known issue. test_case_preview seems to switch from simple to rich text mode, which isn't possible in safair. Widget tests fail but will be tested manually.

Run Test Case: Gadgets Galore to get one of every Gallery gadget on your Dashboard

Visual Inspection:

link checklist here if desired. template here

- FF2 Pass - Added Slideshow tests for Edit Summaries and changed the Miki Tagging order
- FF3 **PASS (provisional)** Chris
    — multipage export to PDF and to Word failed on my laptop but I believe those are local problems and would like others to confirm.
        — *worksforme* on ff3/linux. --rs
- IE7 **PASS** -chris

- IE6 scotty - **PASS** all fixed
- Safari matt - The automated tests showed I saw some strangeness for Export and upload when editing. So I ran it manually without a pro lem – also upload while editing isn't supported on safari, so I'm not worried.

Socialcalc - matt - I noticed that you can click first background color, then text color, to create an awkward effect, but It's just an awkwardness; I did not file a bug. Also {bz: 2046}

- IE6 - ok
- IE7 - ok
- Safari - ok
- FF2 - ok
- FF3 - ok

People - matt

- IE6 - ok but {bz: 2049}
- IE7 - ok but {bz: 2049}
- Safari - ok but {bz: 2049}
- FF2 - ok but {bz: 2049}
- FF3 - ok but {bz: 2049}

Test My Conversations widgets by creating entries in all three tabs and clicking on all links in entries. Items should open in new pages.

Signals - scotty

- IE6 - ok
- IE7 - ok
- Safari - ok

And so on.

TestRunner is a suite of developer-facing tests. We list it for completeness; if TestRunner is red, something is wrong. Wikitests are the suite of all browser-driving, unattended tests. "Slideshow" blends wikitests and visual inspection, and was invented by Socialtext's product quality manager, Ken Pier. A typical Slideshow run takes about half an hour, and can catch visual bugs that a wikitest would miss. Due to limitations of our test tools, other tests are run manually, such as HTTPS-based access. Because Selenium cannot access HTTPS pages by driving the browser, we sometimes run HTTPS tests manually to make sure the Secure Sockets Layer works correctly. I did not list feature retests, which we do to check the features of the new stories in the new "iteration" branch, to make sure any new changes do not "step on" the code introduced earlier in the cycle, bug reverification in the new branch, or the heavy exploratory methods we do. Most of our exploratory work is tied to a story, but we also conduct exploratory tests on the candidate, and sometimes those charters are tracked on the candidate page.

During candidate testing we also test the upgrade of our software from one version to the next. Because we offer both a hosted version and an appliance, and because we allow customers to upgrade at any time, we have a set of outstanding versions in the field. For some time we had a matrix and tested every combination of the software upgrade to current—and yes, that could very nearly be an entire chapter. Suffice it to say, it needs to be done and done well, and we have tools and eventually developed architectural enhancements to make upgrade testing, if not fun, at least less painful.

SocialCalc, People, and Dashboard are new products. Because the code is so new and the graphics for those products are so complex, the user interface is constantly evolving, and it would be premature for us to invest heavily in wikitests.[17] So we have some wikitests for them that work in some browsers, and we also have a documented test plan. Testing these products means running the wikitests, then also following up by hand with exploration, and finally consulting the test plan to see what you've missed, and perhaps going back to cover those areas. Figure 16-7 shows an excerpt of the Dashboard test plan.

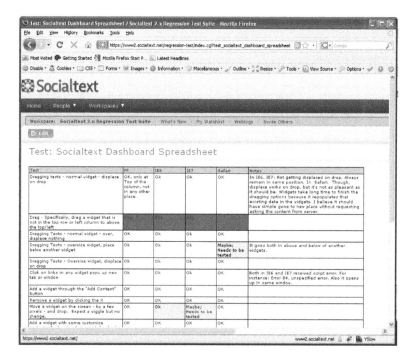

FIGURE 16-7. Socialtext Dashboard test cases

17. Matthew wrote that in March of 2009. By June, we had much more wikitests coverage.

This is an older version; the current version is all white. I kept the red and yellow around to show how a manager can get status at a glance. At the same time, keeping these tests current can take a large amount of time. We strive to have the bare minimum of documented test cases.

Regression and Process Improvement

The stress on a software testing team comes from many directions. If we tried to rerun every test idea every two weeks, the weight would compound. Within a half-dozen iterations the team would be perennially behind. If we tried to automate every test idea, we'd have the same problem—and as I discussed earlier, trying to do automation can lead to blinders about entire categories of defects.

So as odd at it seems, the critical questions in this area are: What do we *not* test? What tests can we *skip*? What tests always seem to pass, we expect to always pass, and provide us only confirmatory value?

These are philosophical questions about truth, the classic problem of induction. As the saying goes, if we are trying to determine the truth of the statement "all swans are white," a million white swans give us less information than a single black one.[18]

Over the past year, we have changed our tactics several times. It's impossible to know anything for sure, but if we spent eight hours per iteration testing features that always worked—and involved a well-isolated piece of the code—well, we had plenty of other techniques to use that could deliver results. We added reviews earlier in the process, changed the iteration schedule by a day or two here or there, and changed the format of our team standup meetings.

Perhaps it's time I told you about our staging tests.

The Last Pieces of the Puzzle

Once the candidate tests pass, the code leaves the test group and is placed in an internal staging environment. We use our own software—the wiki on staging—to essentially run our business.[19] We use it to create project plans, to track the iteration, to do QA tracking, and to create stories, for blogging and communication. That way, staging becomes the final proving ground for our software before it goes into production, and our employees occasionally do find defects or, more likely, usability issues or performance issues that unit and functional testing did not uncover.

---

18. The best book about testing I've read this year is, by far, *The Black Swan* by Nassim Taleb (Random House), and this illustration comes entirely from him, with credit due. Of course, he took it from David Hume, who took it from some ancient Greeks....

19. We do keep some element of sales and accounts payable, etc., on production, which is ever so slightly more stable, and has passed that "final test bed" of staging. Wouldn't you?

Our entire testing puzzle includes feature testing, wikitests, running test plans, exploratory testing, getting feedback from staging, usability, story review, beta programs, logging and log evaluation, and occasional performance research. If we tried to do everything and do it well, our team would swell in size and make the company unviable—or it would simply burn out the staff very quickly. Instead, we have to ask how much is enough and what can we trade out.

Our goal is not to know exactly what the software can do, but instead to provide a rapid assessment of the software that is fit for purpose. A few key questions I haven't mentioned yet are: "What should I be doing right now?" and "Am I done yet?"

Again, those are philosophical questions—questions of aesthetics. I would posit that combinations of the puzzle pieces that look the most beautiful are probably the correct ones.[20] The term for assembling these pieces is something I reluctantly call "test architecture."[21] It turns out that Fred Brooks, the author of the all-time software classic *The Mythical Man-Month* (Addison-Wesley), appears to agree with me. At OOPSLA (the object-oriented software conference) in 2007, he defined the architect role in two halves:

1. First, to serve as an advocate for the customer.

2. In order to do that, to have an understanding of the entire product, end-to-end.

In the day and age of self-organizing, self-governing teams, I find a command-and-control big-designer-style architect to be archaic, but that work of advocating for the customer and understanding the product still needs to be done. Working at a higher level than developers, and with an express goal of finding and fixing flaws in the software, I honestly believe that the testing group has the capability of serving—in the best possible way—as architects of the product. In other words, we *are* testing software, *and* helping to put together the puzzle pieces to create a product that will delight and amaze our customer.

Delighting and amazing the customer through applying our minds and building our skills. Hmm....

Somewhere, in the back of my mind, I see Dr. Homer Austin, my old math professor. And he is smiling.

---

20. This is Occam's Razor restated.

21. Very reluctantly, as the analogy tends to separate the doers from the thinkers, which I believe is dangerous.

Acknowledgments

Of course, I am in debt to my professors at Salisbury University and also Grand Valley. Dr. Roger Ferguson and Dr. Paul Jorgensen both encouraged my interest in testing, and Dr. Paul Leidig encouraged me to write. Chris McMahon brought me into Socialtext, and Ken Pier, Luke Closs, and the rest of the Socialtext team built the testing process before I was even hired; it's been a privilege to work with them. (Ken also provided considerable, insightful peer review of this chapter.) Steve Poling, my friend and fellow technologist, has been encouraging me to write something like this for years.

My wife and children have been wonderful, encouraging, supportive, and understanding. I'd like to thank them most of all.

## CHAPTER SEVENTEEN

Beautiful Testing Is Efficient Testing

Adam Goucher

IN HIGH SCHOOL I WOULD, ON OCCASION, BE ACCUSED OF BEING LAZY. My witty response would invariably be something along the lines of "I'm not lazy; I'm efficient." It is somewhat fitting that I have been consciously pursuing a path of actual efficiency in how I approach my testing activities.

The change from "uncover quality-related information" to "uncover quality-related information *as efficiently as possible*" happened as a result of my rise in seniority at a couple of different organizations and an increased role in the business side of development. It turns out that management, while interested in standard quality information, is really interested in knowing when I/we think the product is ready to ship.

In this chapter I will share my three main methods toward efficient (beautiful) testing: SLIME, scripting, and mindmaps.

SLIME

SLIME (*S*ecurity, *L*anguages, Requ*I*rements, *M*easurement, *E*xisting) is a mnemonic that describes the order in which I conduct testing on a new application, or even a feature, in order from first to last. The key rationale behind the order is to reduce the amount of retesting that needs to be completed. (Being able to see the look on your boss' face when you tell him you are SLIME-ing your application is secondary.)

S: Security

The very first thing I want to think about when testing something is security. Yes, loss of personal information is dangerous, as is being an unwilling participant in something nefarious. But the real reason for testing this first is how ingrained security is into the architecture of your application; if something so deep changes, you have to retest pretty much everything again. Change the database permission scheme? Retest *everything* that interacts with the database. Change how the application interacts with the host operating system? Retest *everything* that interacts with the operating system.

Security tends to be one of the rare categories of tests that have to work in all areas of the application. Granted, "they only can take over the machine through half of the application" is better than through the whole application, but on the whole it is a failure.

Now, I am by no means a security expert, and so this is not a full, detailed vulnerability sweep of the application. If your environment is such that you need deep security testing (health or financial records, for instance), it should be done by someone who knows what she is doing at a very proficient level. Instead, the goal here is to give us a reasonable level of comfort that things are not completely broken. In a web application, these are the sorts of things I am looking for:

Cross-site scripting (XSS)[1]

> When checking for XSS, I look for places where the application trusts the client. Never, ever, ever trust the client. Input should be validated before stored or rendered, as well as encoded whenever possible. When actual HTML, JavaScript, or CSS needs to be stored, whitelists are used instead of blacklists, as they control what is allowed rather than what is disallowed.

SQL injection[2]

> This is another issue of trusting the client. Using raw user input to access your database directly is a Bad Idea. I will either manually correlate database interactions that I can control in the frontend with the actual code or use a script to pull out all the database calls and inspect that. SQL injection is a problem that has a known solution: parameterized SQL and/or diligent escaping so code inspection is a quick and efficient way of identifying this type of problem.

Appropriate permissions

> Can a user of a certain permission class do what they should be able to do? And only what they should be able to do?

---

1. *http://en.wikipedia.org/wiki/Cross-site_scripting*

2. *http://en.wikipedia.org/wiki/SQL_injection*

Information leakage

Can a user access/view/modify information they should not be able to access? Consider a multitenant system with Coke and Pepsi as two of your clients. Clearly, Coke should not be able to see Pepsi's information, and vice versa.

L: Languages

The next letter and layer of testing that is done centers around Languages. Having already tested a product where we put in the ability to treat non-English characters in a non-crash-inducing manner once in my career, I can say from personal experience that this is one area in which it is best to get it right the first time. It is also very deep in your code, as it handles all textual data that flows through your product. To be considered successful, I expect my applications to be able to:

1. Accept any character from any language

2. Store that character

3. Do manipulations with and against it

4. Retrieve that character

5. Display it

This seems daunting, but it is relatively easy to both test and code for.

In Microsoft Windows, the *Charmap* application will display all the characters that are installed on it. If you have one of the many Unicode fonts installed, then you can select the ones that look interesting, copy them to the clipboard, and paste them directly into your application. In OS X, the *character palette* (enabled in the International settings of System Preferences) provides similar functionality.

One thing to remember when using this trick is that the actual content of the test data you use doesn't matter. We care primarily about how the data flows through the system and its manipulations.

Another heuristic that there might be a problem with language support is whether or not things are being encoded as Unicode[3] throughout the system. Two quick checks for this are to 1) check the encoding that the web server tells the browser to use, and 2) check the encoding of storage tables in the database.

---

3. For an introduction to Unicode, see Joel Spolsky's "The Absolute Minimum Every Software Developer Absolutely, Positively Must Know About Unicode and Character Sets (No Excuses!)" at *http://www .joelonsoftware.com/articles/Unicode.html*.

I: requIrements

I admit that the third letter is a cheat to make the mnemonic work. This phase deals with the requirements that caused this testing to actually happen. When people think about testing, this is often where they jump to directly.

This is the *new*, never-been-tested-before stuff. If your application grew a password-reset functionality this release, then this is what is tested. What is not (directly and intentionally) tested is the existing password code. The theory here is that the development team is a conscientious one, testing new code as they go along, and has a large set of unit tests to tell them quickly when they have accidentally broken another part of the product as a result of their changes. This gives us a bit of comfort in ignoring traditional regression testing in favor of what is adding value to the product.

In any case, any time there is a change of code there is always a risk of bug injection or unearthing one that was previously hidden. This risk increases significantly when the nature of the change is initial creation.

M: Measurement

By this point we have a fair degree of confidence that the new components of the product are functioning the way they were intended (from the "I" phase). We can now measure whether they are performing within acceptable limits.

There are a lot of competing (and often contradictory) definitions for types of tests that fall into this category, but this is how I define things:

Load
> Keep loading the constrained resource (CPU, RAM, network bandwidth, etc.) until the system crashes. Fix the crash and repeat until the resource can be fully utilized without causing a crash.

Performance
> This is a specific number, often expressed in terms of X actions per Y time; for example, the number of authentications per minute.

Stress
> Stress tests determine how the system handles load being added, then removed, in different amounts over a period of time. The example I use when teaching is an ATM in a train station. Load is zero when the station is closed, but then ramps up during morning rush hour, again a bit around lunch, and once more during the afternoon rush hour (and sometimes once more in the evening during a sporting event or concert). Resources should be properly accessed and released depending on the load.

Scalability

>Does adding more resources, either in the current system or by adding new ones, allow us to handle a proportional amount of traffic? The increase in performance won't be perfectly linear to the added resources, but should be in the same ballpark.

I also approach the measurement tasks in the order presented here. After all, you can't really do stress testing until your system can handle maximum load.

E: Existing

The last part of the SLIME process is all about the existing functionality and behavior of the product. This is commonly referred to as regression testing, but SLIMR did not sound quite right.

By definition, the code tested here has not changed from the prior release. If it had, it would have been addressed in the "requIrements" step. Because of this, you should be able to accomplish the testing here fairly quickly.

Existing code is also a prime candidate for more extensive automation that would then allow you to spend more time manually testing the code that changed. This is the place to bring in tools such as Selenium or Watir, not during requIrements testing.

SLIME is a useful mnemonic to consider when approaching a new testing task, but it is important to remember that it is a heuristic. That is, it is fallible. If the whole purpose of a release is to address performance concerns, then doing three (or even just two, depending on how you define things) different types of tasks before measuring application performance is actually counter to the goal of providing beautiful, efficient information to the project stakeholders.

Scripting

Most testers think of tools such as QuickTest Pro and Selenium when you mention scripting. Although those are useful tools in their domains, for increasing test efficiency it is hard to beat the power of Python, Ruby, or Perl.

When time is not a concern, you can afford to be religious about your language choice. In testing, time is always a concern, so you have to choose the best one for the task at hand. Here are some of the criteria I use when doing this evaluation:

- Do I know it? If not, can I learn it?
- Does it support all my target platforms?
- Can it interact with the applications components (.NET assemblies, Java JARs)?
- Can it interact with my other tools?
- Can it interact with the database/LDAP/other server?

Once I have decided on a scripting language, there are a number of useful scripts I can create to make me more efficient.

Discovering Developer Notes

There is an adage I have heard on more than one occasion from the developers I am working with: *The code doesn't lie*. Since the code doesn't lie, it is a fantastic resource for quality information. Given the size of today's code bases, it is certainly not efficient to try and read through it all line-by-line, looking for things of interest. Instead, you can create a script that crawls through the code, highlighting things flagged as interesting.

"Interesting" is a rather vague term, and that is intentional because things that are interesting vary from project to project. But here are two things to start your personal list:

TODO (and its variants)
> Most modern IDEs have a shortcut to insert TODO as a comment in the code, the idea being that the developer is leaving himself a note to come back later and do whatever he is indicating still needs to be done. Too often, though, the code that needs to be done isn't done, and it is checked in with the TODO still outstanding. This can lead to a silent accumulation of technical debt and schedule risk.

FIXME (and its variants)
> FIXME is much like TODO but is an indication of an identified bug (or bugs) in an area of code. I have seen FIXMEs as simple as "Should have a better variable name" and as complicated as "This is completely broken and needs to be redesigned."

Both TODO and FIXME are useful constructs, but they need a certain level of visibility in the organization, with corresponding entries in the bug, issue, or project management systems.

LOUD

Testing languages was second only to security in terms of importance in the first part of this chapter. But what if you cannot read another language aside from English? How will you test that you are displaying the correct values to the user in the UI? The short answer is that you can't. At some point in the process you need to be able to trust the people providing you with translations. If you cannot, that is a sign that you need to get a new translator.

What you can do, however, is ensure that all the strings displayed to the user are externalized from the application in some manner rather than being hardcoded in. For example, in Java you can put your translations in resource bundles.

LOUD gets its name from the netiquette of using all capitals to express yelling. To LOUD a string, you modify the English (or any language, for that matter) translations so that:

- All letters are uppercase.
- The first character of each translation is a ^.
- The last character of each translation is a $.

Once LOUDed, you can interact with your application in the normal manner and log bugs when you see something that:

- Is not uppercase.
- Does not start with a ^.
- Does not end in a $.
- Has been LOUDed, but should not have, for example, trademarked product names.
- Has multiple LOUD segments in a single sentence or paragraph. This is a sign that strings are being dynamically generated. Although it may seem more efficient from a programming perspective to reuse the same key throughout the system to refer to a common word, it breaks up the context of the string sent out for translation.

Sure, you could do it by hand, but imagine having to do that to a 10,000-line resource bundle once a week for an entire release cycle. And the next one. And the one after that. That is certainly not a beautiful use of a tester's time. Or anyone else's, for that matter.

Oracles and Test Data Generation

In the testing lexicon, an oracle is a *principle or mechanism by which we recognize a problem*. Data generation is the exact opposite of an oracle. Rather than verify data, data is produced. Sometimes the rules surrounding our oracles and data generation are simple and straightforward. Other times they are algorithmic and/or complicated. Scripting languages excel at both these tasks.

In one company I worked for, the application would create entries in a number of different database tables in a number of different systems as the result of a single workflow. And of course each of those entries had different data integrity and business rules around them. Rather than check each of these manually, I wrote an oracle in Python that would take a transaction ID and then verify that everything was correct across the various systems. Just be careful that you actually know the business rules before you rely on this solely for verification purposes.

Because that system dealt with personal and financial information (it was for car dealers), there were a number of obstacles in terms of what was valid test data. I tried tracking accounts and other such testing information in a spreadsheet and later a wiki, but it never quite worked. Scripting came to the rescue. I created a number of scripts that could reach into the application's database and tell me a valid user for a dealership with a valid credit bureau.

Actually, I combined both of these techniques with a Selenium RC script on the frontend that used valid test data from the database to conduct the UI tests, and would then use the oracle script to verify that the backend data was correct as well.

I would argue that knowing a scripting language is going to be a necessary skill for a successful tester, if it is not already. It decreases the time it takes you to glean information from expansive code bases, efficiently lets you do testing that you might not have been able to without, and it won't forget a validation step.

Mindmaps

When I learned how to test, or more accurately, how to prepare to do testing, it was in a large organization that held onto classic test design ideas. Tests were thought out ahead of time, broken down step-by-step, entered into a system, and then approved by an analyst. Modifications to these tests had to be requested and were infrequent. After that, moving to the fast-paced world of a startup was quite the shock. Change was constant, as was a lack of time available to maintain this sort of detailed script, and I veered toward the complete lack of documentation end of the scale.

Then I started going to testing conferences and noticed that the top testers I respected were all taking notes and organizing their thoughts with a technique I had last used in high school: mindmaps. A couple of years have passed since that epiphany, and mindmaps have quickly become my secret weapon in test efficiency.

A mindmap is a traditional brainstorming tool where ideas branch out from a central idea, getting more and more specific the farther out from the center they are. If you consider the process of traditional test idea generation, it is the same, except that the traditional method is usually captured in a hierarchical manner. The big problem with those structures is that they typically show just the name of the test and not what they are testing. Mindmaps only show what is being tested, which is much more useful information for both testers and their stakeholders.

Since mindmaps are a visual medium, Figure 17-1 is the start of a mindmap for testing a user feature. You can see that, so far, there are three major areas of functionality identified for the feature, with Registration having been flushed out somewhat. A key item to notice is the level of detail that is included, specifically in relation to things such as password validity. Traditional test design would often include a list of valid passwords to test with, and certainly the mindmap structure could be used to replicate that, but mindmaps work best when your base assumption is that your testers can think. They should know what "valid" means in the context of the product's password field. By letting the testers decide which test data to use, they will increase the variability of it, which will go a long way to counter the effects of the Minefield Problem.[4]

---

4. *http://www.satisfice.com/repeatable.shtml*

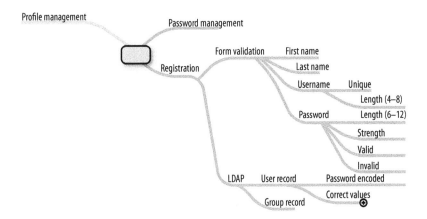

Profile management

Password management

Registration

Form validation

First name

Last name

Username — Unique

Length (4–8)

Password — Length (6–12)

Strength

Valid

Invalid

LDAP   User record   Password encoded

Correct values

Group record

FIGURE 17-1. A mindmap for a user feature

In addition, test documentation is often easier to keep up-to-date using mindmaps. As a tester is executing tests, they will often think of other interesting test ideas. In traditional test management tools, this involves numerous screens and sometimes even a wizard. With a mindmap it is as simple as adding another node to the map.

I have also had success with mindmaps in increasing test coverage by involving the whole team in their development. On one team that I led, we would be given a number of requirements for a particular release, which would then be distributed to the team. Each team member would create a mindmap on their own regarding the feature, and then as a team we would convene and expand on them by adding our own experiences to the table. By collectively building on things created individually, we not only identified any gaps in the testing early on, but also started the knowledge-sharing process that is necessary for any team member to test any component of the project.

This is not to say that mindmaps do not have weaknesses. I have identified three challenges with them that I think teams new to them should be aware of:

Acceptance

Mindmaps are pretty radical to management when first introduced. They almost completely replace the large binder of test cases they can point to and say, "This is what we test." Education around the benefits of not having explicit test data and starting with small feature sets is key in overcoming this hurdle.

Naming and organization

Hierarchical folder-based structures lend themselves nicely to a standardized test-naming convention (e.g., *folder_folder_folder_number*). The organic nature of mindmaps makes that really hard. Similarly, the lack of specific test data at each end node means a one-to-many relationship between ideas and actual data used. The solution to this seems to be to talk in terms of the type or category of tests that are failing rather than specific test names or numbers.

Multiuser

Systems such as Quality Center are designed from the ground up to be multiuser, whereas most mindmap tools are designed to be single user. This has ramifications when you have multiple users trying to modify the same map. The solution to this problem is to make smaller maps based on discrete functionality. Often there are still areas of overlap, but they are minimized.

To me, though, the benefits of mindmaps, especially on the small- to medium-sized teams I have worked with, far outweigh the weaknesses in terms of capturing and organizing test ideas.

Efficiency Achieved

By incorporating SLIME, a multipurpose scripting language, and mindmaps into how I approach testing, I have been able to provide my stakeholders with better and timelier information about the quality of the application I am testing. That, to me (and I suspect to them), could be considered efficient and perhaps beautiful testing.

## PART III

Beautiful Tools

To a man with a hammer, everything looks like a nail.

—Mark Twain

## CHAPTER EIGHTEEN

Seeding Bugs to Find Bugs: Beautiful Mutation Testing

Andreas Zeller
David Schuler

SUPPOSE YOU ARE A TEST MANAGER OF A SOFTWARE PROJECT. You are at the end of a development cycle: all the new features are there, and all the tests have passed. Now is the time for you to decide: *Are you ready for release?*

In principle, everything should be settled, as all tests have passed. However, the fact that all your tests have passed may not mean much if your test suite is not good enough. If your test suite does not properly check the program outcome, for instance, your tests may pass even though the result is wrong. So, how can you check whether your test suite is effective in finding defects? In this chapter, we will explore a simple, elegant, and indeed beautiful way to test the quality of a test suite—namely by *systematically seeding artificial defects* into the program and checking whether the test suite finds them.

Assessing Test Suite Quality

Engineers and managers like to quantify things, and the quality of a test suite is no exception. To measure the quality of a test suite, various *coverage metrics* have been developed and deployed in practice. Best known is *code coverage*, where we check individual statements for whether they have been executed in a test suite. Obviously, if a test suite does not execute a statement, this calls for trouble. Suppose the statement has a bug that triggers a failure each time it is executed.

If the test never reaches that statement, the bug will never be found—at least not during the test.

Besides code coverage, there are more advanced criteria to aim for: *branch coverage* criteria ensure that each branch is taken at least once, and *condition coverage* criteria ensure that each (sub)condition evaluates once to true and once to false. All these criteria are easy to measure and are frequently used as quality targets: "We must reach at least 90% code coverage in all modules!"

Any such test quality metrics are to be taken with a grain of salt, though. The first problem with metrics is that *bugs are not distributed uniformly across a program*. As an example, consider Figure 18-1, showing the defect distribution in the AspectJ compiler, as extracted from the AspectJ version and bug databases. Each class file is represented by a rectangle (the more lines of code, the larger the rectangle). The brightness indicates the *number of defects*: the darker a class, the higher the number of defects fixed in that class. In some AspectJ classes (such as the one BcelWeaver class), up to 32 bugs had to be fixed after release; in others (the white ones), none at all. This uneven distribution is known as the *Pareto effect*: "20% of the modules contain 80% of the defects." Obviously, you would want your test suite to focus on the defect-prone modules rather than spending extra effort on achieving at least 90% coverage in a class that is defect-free anyway.

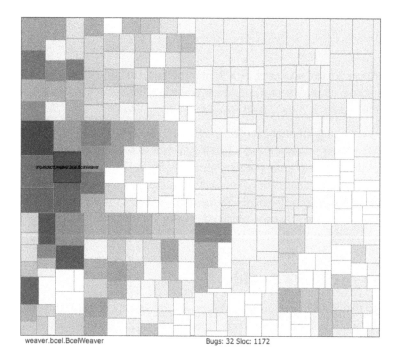

FIGURE 18-1. Defect distribution in AspectJ

The second problem with metrics is that not only are bugs unevenly distributed, but *risk* is, too. In every project there are some modules in which defects have serious consequences—because they are frequently used or because the entire functionality depends on them. Again, you would like to allocate your testing efforts based on this risk, rather than achieving a specific coverage. (If you were testing a commercial airplane, you would also spend much more time on the engines than on the seats.)

As a good tester, you are probably already aware of defect and risk distributions, but here's a third and final problem. Coverage metrics only tell you something about the test execution—but not about the test itself. As an example, consider the JUnit test in Example 18-1: it creates a file, writes a text into it, and then closes it. If anything goes wrong, the file methods will throw some exception, and the test will fail.

EXAMPLE 18-1. An insufficient file I/O unit test

```
import static org.junit.Assert.*;

void testFileWrite()
{
    BufferedWriter out = new BufferedWriter(new FileWriter("outfilename"));
    out.write("aString");
    out.close();
}
```

This is how many systems are actually tested in practice: if it does not crash, it is probably fine. Unfortunately, this is not sufficient, as the test *fails to check the result*. It may well be that the file methods create a wrong file, write some random output, or do nothing at all. With such insufficient tests in place, we may easily achieve 100% coverage of any test criterion but fail to catch even the simplest defect.

What the test *should* do is at least reopen the file and check its contents—but how would we recognize this? How do we determine how well a test does its job? This is an instance of Plato's old problem: "Quis custodiet ipsos custodes?" or "Who watches the watchmen?" Fortunately, there is a way to test a test, a way so simple and straightforward that it can easily qualify as "beautiful."

Watching the Watchmen

A common way to test the quality of quality assurance is to *simulate* a situation in which quality assurance should trigger an alarm. For instance, to test a watchdog, one could check whether the dog actually gives an alarm when facing a (staged) intruder. To test the quality assurance of a clothes company, one could insert a faulty cloth into the production chain and check whether quality assurance finds it. Secure systems are routinely tested using penetration testing, simulating an attack from a malicious source.

In 1971, Richard Lipton adapted this simulation concept to testing. His idea, written down in a paper called "Fault diagnosis of computer programs," was to seed *artificial defects*, called *mutations*, into the software under test, and to check whether the test suite would find them. Such an artificial defect could be to change a constant, to remove a function call, or to negate a branching condition. If the test suite fails to detect the mutation, it would likely miss real defects, too, and thus must be improved.

Looking back to Example 18-1, we could mutate the implementation of the `BuffereredWriter.write()` method such that it does nothing at all—for instance, by inserting a return statement at the beginning of the method. The test in Example 18-1, however, would not detect this mutation, indicating that it would miss real defects, too. (And indeed it would, as we already discussed its inadequacy.) Example 18-2 shows an improved version of the test. This improved version would not be fooled; if `BuffereredWriter.write()` were rendered inoperable, Example 18-2 would immediately detect this mutation.

EXAMPLE 18-2. An improved file I/O unit test

```
import static org.junit.Assert.*;

void testFileWrite()
{
    BufferedWriter out = new BufferedWriter(new FileWriter("outfilename"));
    out.write("aString");
    out.close();

    BufferedReader in = new BufferedReader(new FileReader("outfilename"));
    String contents = in.readLine();
    in.close();

    assertEquals("aString", contents);
}
```

The basic idea of mutation testing is to seed lots of these artificial defects into the program, test them all individually, and focus on those mutations that are not detected—and to systematically improve the test suite until it finds all mutations. This simple approach brings obvious benefits. First, you can truly assess the quality of your tests, and not just measure features of test execution. Second, modules with a high risk—that is, modules where defects have serious consequences—will also exhibit these consequences when mutated, and if none of these consequences is detected, your test suite really needs some improvement. Third, the more similar mutations are to real defects, the more likely you are to also replicate the defect distribution in your program. Mutation testing would solve all these issues, and it is no surprise that as a criterion for assessing test suite quality, mutation testing has been shown to be superior to almost every single metric in existence. Mutation testing frameworks such as Mothra (for FORTRAN programs [DeMillo et al. 1988]) or μJava (for Java programs [Ma et al. 2006]) are publicly available for everyone.

But if mutation testing is so superior, why doesn't everybody use it? In the past years, we have experimented a lot with mutation testing open source software, and we can report that although the basic idea of mutation testing is straightforward, the devil is in the details. There are many issues to address and to overcome. The good news, though, is that we managed to address all these issues.

Efficient Mutation Testing

The first and obvious issue with mutation testing is that it is very time-consuming. After every single mutation, the program must be rebuilt and retested. As the number of mutations can easily go into the thousands, we are talking about several thousand build processes and test suite executions. Obviously, mutation testing requires a fully automated test—and it had better be fast. But also from the side of seeding mutants, there are some techniques to improve efficiency:

Manipulate binary code directly
> By mutating binary code rather than source code, you can eliminate the costly rebuild process after a mutation. The drawback is that binary code can be harder to analyze, in particular for complicated mutation operators (see the next section).

Use mutant schemata
> Traditionally, a mutation-testing framework produces a new mutated program version for every single mutation. However, one can also create a single version in which individual mutants are guarded by runtime conditions.

Ignore noncovered code
> A mutant can impact the program behavior only if it is actually executed. Therefore, one should mutate only statements that are covered by the test suite and run only those tests that exercise the mutation. Such coverage information is easily obtained from a single test suite run.

All these optimizations help in making mutation testing efficient. The next step is to keep the number of mutations down.

Selecting Mutation Operators

The next problem is: how do we mutate a program? There is an infinite number of ways one can mutate a program—replacing constants with constants, variables with constants, array references with variables, operators with other operators, method calls with other calls (or other receivers), conditions with negated conditions, and so on. A number of studies have shown, though, that a very small set of mutation operators can show almost the same effectiveness as a larger set:

Replace numerical constant
> Replace a numerical constant *X* with *X* + 1, *X* − 1, or 0. This also includes pointers (which may thus be set to null).

Negate jump condition
> Replace a branch condition *C* with its negation ¬*C*.

Replace arithmetic operator
> Replace an arithmetic operator with another one, e.g., + with -, * with /, << with >>, and so on.

Omit method call
> Replace a method call *f*() with a constant 0 (or remove it completely if it has no return value).

Such simple mutations are easy to apply on binary code and lead to a small number of mutations. This so-called *selective mutation* is what we used in our experiments.

An AspectJ Example

In our experiments, we applied these mutation operators to medium-sized programs such as the AspectJ core, a 100,000-line Java package with a test suite of 321 unit tests, taking 21 seconds for a single run. We obtained 47,000 mutations, which, using the optimizations outlined previously, were evaluated in 14 CPU hours. This means that if you happen to have a single-core machine, you can run a mutation test overnight; if your machine has eight cores, you can run it during an extended lunch. (And if you're running the latest and greatest, expect even lower times—or larger test and program sizes.)

The AspectJ test suite detected only 53% of the executed mutations. Some of the undetected mutations indicate real trouble. For instance, consider the staticAndInstanceConflict() method (Example 18-3) from the AjProblemReporter class in AspectJ. This method decides whether an error should be reported and eventually reports it to its superclass. However, if we mutate the method such that the call to super.staticAndInstanceConflict() is suppressed, the error reports are suppressed as well.

EXAMPLE 18-3. A mutation that suppresses a method call (the AspectJ test suite does not detect this)

```
public void staticAndInstanceConflict(MethodBinding currentMethod,
        MethodBinding inheritedMethod) {
    if (currentMethod instanceof InterTypeMethodBinding)
        return;
    if (inheritedMethod instanceof InterTypeMethodBinding)
        return;
    super.staticAndInstanceConflict(currentMethod,
        inheritedMethod); // Mutation: suppress this method call
}
```

Unfortunately, the AspectJ test suite does not detect the mutation. Although the test suite checks whether the compiler detects erroneous input, it does not check whether the errors are reported properly. This does not mean that there would be any defects in error reporting, but it means that if there are any defects, the test suite would fail to find them.[1]

Equivalent Mutants

Whenever we find a mutation that is not detected by a test suite, we must add an appropriate test. Sometimes, though, there is no way to write such a test—because the mutation does not change the program behavior at all. Example 18-4 shows such an *equivalent mutant*.

EXAMPLE 18-4. Mutating the result from +1 to +2 makes no difference

```
public int compareTo(Object other) {
  if (!(other instanceof BcelAdvice))
    return 0;
  BcelAdvice o = (BcelAdvice)other;

  if (kind.getPrecedence() != o.kind.getPrecedence()) {
    if (kind.getPrecedence() > o.kind.getPrecedence())
      return +1;   // Mutation: replace +1 with +2
    else
      return -1;
  }
  // More comparisons...
} ...
```

In Java, a compareTo() method compares the method target with another object; it is supposed to return a positive, negative, or zero value depending on whether the target is greater, smaller, or equal to the other object. Every caller of compareTo() will simply check for the sign of the comparison result, including the test. By changing the return value from +1 to +2, we keep the semantics of compareTo()—and the program—unchanged.

(Of course, we could change the test to specifically test for a return value of +1, and thus successfully detect the mutant. But this will not improve our test suite in any way either.)

The problem with equivalent mutants is that they are not as rare as one may think; in an experiment with the Jaxen XPath engine, we found as many as 40% equivalent mutants in a sample of undetected mutants. None of these help to improve the test suite. Assessing the equivalence of mutants is a generally undecidable problem, so it must be done manually—and this is a time-consuming activity, easily taking several minutes to hours per mutant.

Struggling for hours only to find that it is impossible to write a test case is not entirely uncommon in testing. When one wants to improve code coverage, one may find that a

---

1. Does this mean that there are many ways to do something wrong in AspectJ? Yes and no: in our experiments, we assessed only the unit tests, which indeed fail to check for a number of conditions. However, AspectJ also comes with a set of system tests, which may catch several of these mutations.

particular statement cannot be reached. Such dead code, however, means a defect, which is a valuable reward. An equivalent mutant just eats up time.

Worse still, the proportion of equivalent mutants increases as the test suite improves. Suppose that 20% of the 22,000 undetected AspectJ mutants, or 4,400, are equivalent. These equivalent mutants will remain undetected no matter how we improve the test suite. If an extended test suite catches all 17,600 nonequivalent mutants, all of the remaining 4,400 undetected mutants, or 100%, will be equivalent.

Focusing on Impact

In our experiments, we were surprised to find thousands of undetected mutations, out of which an intriguing proportion were equivalent. We wanted to focus on the most valuable mutations, where a "valuable" mutation would be the one that helps improve the test suite most. (Of course, an equivalent mutant would be the least valuable.)

Remember what we said earlier about the risk distribution? We assumed that if some mutation in a component C could impact several other components, then the component C would be *risky*, and the more components impacted, the higher the risk. We want to reduce risk in our test suite. Therefore, we would focus on those undetected mutations that have the *highest impact* on other components. If I can find a mutation that changes the behavior all across my program, but my test suite does not care, I should have a good reason to improve it.

The question was about how to measure the impact of a mutation. So far, we have explored two ways of measuring impact:

Impact on code coverage

If a mutation leads to different execution paths being taken, it has a higher likelihood of changing the program behavior. We therefore count the number of methods in which the coverage changes after a mutation. The more methods, the higher the impact (Grün et al. 2009).

Impact on pre- and postconditions

Every method has a number of conditions that hold for its arguments and its return values. We automatically learn such conditions from executions, and then check whether they are violated after a mutation. The more conditions are violated, the higher the impact of the mutation (Schuler et al. 2009).

Both methods return very good results. Focusing on those mutants with the highest impact yields a low ratio (≤ 3%) of equivalent mutants, yet points to those locations where a defect would cause the greatest damage across the program. The mutation in Example 18-3 for instance, impacts no less than 21 conditions all across AspectJ; in other words, there are 21 places where the behavior changes because of the mutation. Yet it does not trigger a single test—definitely a reason to improve the test suite!

The Javalanche Framework

To conduct our mutation testing experiments, we have built a framework called *Javalanche* for the mutation testing of Java programs. Javalanche implements all the optimizations listed earlier and thus is able to test even medium-sized programs in a reasonable amount of time. Javalanche also supports ranking mutations according to their impact, thus allowing you to focus on those mutations with the highest impact.

The Javalanche framework is publicly available at our website (*http://www.javalanche.org/*). As a framework, Javalanche can easily be extended with additional operators or impact detectors. It is fully automated—we simply use it as a batch tool to run overnight—although a simple Eclipse integration is also available (Figure 18-2). If you are looking for an interactive tool, we also recommend taking a look at μJava, mentioned earlier, where lots of settings can be made interactively.

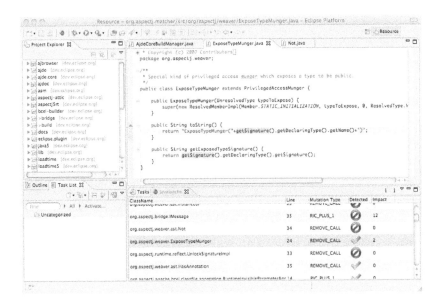

FIGURE 18-2. Javalanche running in the Eclipse environment

Odds and Ends

It was 30 years ago when the first paper on mutation testing was published. Only now, though, does mutation testing come of age. The reasons are manifold:

- Automated testing is much more widespread than it was 10 years ago, and there is no mutation testing without it.

- Computing power keeps on increasing, and we can begin to afford the huge computing requirements imposed by mutation testing.

- Modern test case generators make it fairly easy to obtain a high coverage automatically—but still, the test cases are not good enough.

- We have a variety of dynamic and static optimizations that make mutation testing reasonably efficient, and also highly effective when it comes to improving test suites.

All this implies that mutation testing will become much more commonplace in the future. It is therefore good news that the first scalable mutation testing tools are available for everyone to experiment with—and to experience the beauty of mutation testing.

Acknowledgments

We would like to thank the students and researchers with whom we have experienced beauty in mutation testing. Valentin Dallmeier provided lots of support in invariant learning, binary instrumentation, and invariant detection. Bernhard Grün implemented impact detection on coverage. We also thank the reviewers for their helpful comments on earlier revisions of this chapter.

References

The Mothra framework was the first mutation-testing framework for FORTRAN programs. This overview is well worth a read:

> DeMillo, R. A., D. S. Guindi, K. N. King, W. M. McCracken, and A. J. Offutt. 1998. "An extended overview of the Mothra software testing environment." In *Proceedings of the Second Workshop on Software Testing, Verification, and Analysis*, 142–151. Banff, Alberta: IEEE Computer Society Press.

The μJava framework is much more recent. This short paper gives an overview on its features:

> Ma, Y.-S., J. Offutt, and Y.-R. Kwon. 2006. "MuJava: a mutation system for Java." In *ICSE '06: Proceedings of the 28th International Conference on Software Engineering*, 827–830. New York, NY: ACM.

Our own work on Javalanche is covered in these two papers:

> Grün, B.J.M., D. Schuler, and A. Zeller. 2009. "The impact of equivalent mutants." In *Mutation 2009: International Workshop on Mutation Analysis*, April, in Denver, CO, USA.

> Schuler, D., V. Dallmeier, and A. Zeller. 2009. "Efficient mutation testing by checking invariant violations." In *ISSTA 2009: International Symposium on Software Testing and Analysis*, July, in Chicago, IL, USA.

The preceding two papers, as well as the Javalanche tool itself, are available via our website: *http://www.javalanche.org/*.

## CHAPTER NINETEEN

Reference Testing As Beautiful Testing

Clint Talbert

AUTOMATED REGRESSION TESTING IS NOT GENERALLY THOUGHT to be beautiful. In fact, if automation is successful, it should operate outside of human consciousness; it consists of systems that run thousands of tests after each build without any human interaction at all. Automation is usually associated with the maintenance phase of a well-established project, which is not very sexy. However, when attempting to test web technologies, you find yourself trying to test behaviors and technologies before those technologies have widespread adoption from developers. On the Mozilla project, we are trying to solve this problem by using our automated regression systems as a means for moving regression testing away from its reactive roots to a more forward-looking, anticipatory style of testing.

Our goal is to establish and support openness, innovation, and opportunity on the Internet. We work toward that goal by developing a platform to provide open web technologies in a way that is consistent with the vision of the Internet we wish to create.[1] The most notable example of our work is the Firefox browser, but there are many other products built from the same base; Thunderbird, Komodo, Miro, and Songbird are some of the more well-known examples. These products enable people to do everything from reading email to playing music to developing other applications, but they all share one core commonality: they are all built atop the Gecko web rendering engine.

---

1. See the Mozilla Manifesto at *http://www.mozilla.org/about/manifesto.en.html*.

In the Mozilla platform, UI elements are encoded in XUL, an XML-based markup language. This markup uses JavaScript to enable interaction with those elements, and it uses the same cascading style sheets that your website would use. You might have heard of XML-based HTML—XHTML—which is a cousin of XUL. In fact, you can even write a web page in XUL. So, it isn't too surprising that the same rendering engine is used to render both standard web pages as well as user interface elements in every Mozilla Platform application. This is why the Gecko rendering engine is a critical piece of our support of the open Web, and changes there will drastically affect every downstream application, regardless of whether that application displays web content as its primary function.

Because the rendering engine is one of the most critical components in the Mozilla platform, reference testing, our visual testing framework, is one of the best examples of the way we are using simplicity and extensibility to do anticipatory testing using a regression framework. The reference test framework is a beautiful illustration of the application of these principles to leverage the benefits of automated testing in a more proactive manner. There are three core components that you should understand about reference testing in order to take these lessons and apply them to your own test infrastructure:

- Elegantly solve the problem
- Embody extensibility
- Build community

Reference Test Structure

Before we can talk about extensibility or community, we should cover what the reference tests are and how they work. They are built upon the simple idea that you can use two different snippets of web code to generate the same visual rendering. If there are differences in that rendering, then the test must fail. For example, we can test that an element with a style rule like `<div style="font-weight:bolder">` should have the same effect as the `<div><b>` HTML markup in the reference file (Table 19-1). Both of these should cause the sentence to turn bold.

TABLE 19-1. Testing style rule versus semantic markup

Test	Reference
`<div style="font-weight: bolder">This is bold</div>`	`<div><b>This is bold</b></div>`
This is bold	**This is bold**

So, let's envision that we wanted to test CSS styles and selectors[2] instead of semantic markup. In that case, we could use the CSS selector to control the rendering of our test, while keeping the inline style to control the rendering of our element (Table 19-2). So while the test in Table 19-1 tests the equivalence of CSS style rules to HTML markup, the test in Table 19-2 tests that the class selector and the inline style rule from the CSS subsystem are functioning properly.

TABLE 19-2. Testing class selector versus inline style

Test	Reference

```<html>```
  ```<head>```
    ```<style type="text/css">```
      ```div.headline {font-weight:```
```bolder}```
    ```</style>```
  ```</head>```
  ```<body>```
    ```<div class="headline">```
      ```This is bold```
    ```</div>```
  ```</body>```
```</html>```
	```<html>```
	  ```<body>```
	    ```<div style="font-```
	```weight: bolder">```
	      ```This is bold```
	    ```</div>```
	  ```</body>```
	```</html>```

This is bold	**This is bold**

This test uses the class selector to transform the "This is bold" sentence to a bold font, whereas the reference uses the same inline style that we used in Table 19-1. Could we have used the same reference file from Table 19-1 in Table 19-2? Yes, we could, but that would have potentially tested a different code path. Using CSS style rules for both the test and the reference in Table 19-2 allows us to isolate the test to the CSS subsystem in Gecko, providing us the confidence to know that the class selector is working properly.[3] With this method, we can isolate and test specific behaviors for all the visual web technologies that we support. We currently use reference testing to test HTML, XHTML, CSS, XUL, and Scalable Vector Graphics (SVG).

Reference tests are controlled by manifest files, which can include other manifest files in turn, allowing us to nest these tests throughout the source tree. A manifest file looks like Example 19-1.

EXAMPLE 19-1. Sample reference test manifest file

```
== test1.html test1-ref.html
!= test2.xhtml test2-ref.xhtml
fails-if (MOZ_WIDGET_TOOLKIT=="windows") == test3.html test3-ref.xhtml
```

2. 2CSS 2.1 selectors, *http://www.w3.org/TR/CSS2/selector.html*.

3. Actually, due to the implementation of `<b>` in Gecko, this tests the same code path, but it is the clearest explanation of the principle of reference testing.

The manifest is a very straightforward grammar, and I'm sure you can already see how it works. Each test item is specified by a line of the form:

[<known-failure>] [<http>] <type> <test url> <reference url>

The three required parameters are the type, test URL, and reference URL. The first three lines in Example 19-1 correspond to this, as do most tests in the reference test framework. Here, the first token == or != determines the relationship between the test and the reference, which are the second and third tokens, respectively. The == means that for the test to pass, the renderings must match, whereas the != means that the renderings must be different for the tests to pass.

The *<known-failure>* optional parameter allows us to direct the system on how to expect failures and assertions under different situations. For example, the line in Example 19-1 would expect test3 to fail on Windows and pass on other operating systems. If the test unexpectedly passed on Windows, this would be deemed a failure. Like fails-if, there are other operators to conditionally ignore assertions, skip tests, or mark tests as unreliable. The *<http>* optional parameter indicates that the test should be run over an HTTP server because the test depends on certain HTTP headers or a specific HTTP status.[4]

The framework reads in a manifest and generates a pool of canvas elements for the associated test files and their references. As the test runs, each file is loaded onto a *<canvas>* element in a browser window. The "magic" happens when the document's onload event fires, calling the code shown in Example 19-2. With the first onload event, the test rendering is copied onto a canvas and saved. The second onload event from the reference file drops us into case 2 of the switch statement, copying the reference rendering to another canvas and initiating a call to gWindowUtils.compareCanvases to compare the two canvases.[5]

EXAMPLE 19-2. Image comparison in the reference test framework

```
function DocumentLoaded()
{
    ... Some Housekeeping Stuff ...

    if (gURICanvases[gCurrentURL]) {
        gCurrentCanvas = gURICanvases[gCurrentURL];
    } else if (gCurrentCanvas == null) {
        InitCurrentCanvasWithSnapshot();
    }
    if (gState == 1) {
        gCanvas1 = gCurrentCanvas;
    } else {
        gCanvas2 = gCurrentCanvas;
    }
    gCurrentCanvas = null;
```

4. See the reference test README file at *http://mxr.mozilla.org/mozilla-central/source/layout/tools/reftest/README.txt.*

5. The nsIDomWindowUtils CompareCanvases code, C++, *http://mxr.mozilla.org/mozilla-central/source/dom/base/nsDOMWindowUtils.cpp#611.*

```
resetZoom();

switch (gState) {
    case 1:
        // First document has been loaded.
        // Proceed to load the second document.

        StartCurrentURI(2);
        break;
    case 2:
        // Both documents have been loaded. Compare the renderings and see
        // if the comparison result matches the expected result specified
        // in the manifest.

        // number of different pixels
        var differences;
        // whether the two renderings match:
        var equal;

        if (gWindowUtils) {
            differences = gWindowUtils.compareCanvases(gCanvas1, gCanvas2, {});
            equal = (differences == 0);
        } else {
            differences = -1;
            var k1 = gCanvas1.toDataURL();
            var k2 = gCanvas2.toDataURL();
            equal = (k1 == k2);
        }
        // And then we use the manifest token to determine how to interpret
        // the result of the compareCanvases call....
        ...
```

If the framework determines that the result of the comparison does not match the manifest, then the test is deemed a failure. When a test fails, both the test canvas and the reference canvas are serialized to data URLs in a test log. Using that information, log viewers can render failures visually by superimposing the test image over the reference image for an easy visual comparison of what went wrong.

Reference Test Extensibility

Testing frameworks tend to outlive the applications they test, making extensibility a critical attribute of their design. Extensibility is particularly important for reference testing because it must continue to adapt to the ever-changing open web. Although reference tests like the one in Table 19-1 were all you needed in 1996, today's web pages exhibit far more complex behaviors, and the tests to mimic those behaviors have evolved as well. Reference tests continue to adapt to meet the challenges presented by the Web in order to maintain a comprehensive test suite for the rendering engine.

Asynchronous Tests

The Web is no longer a static playground. Pages modify their DOMs, adding and removing elements and style rules, and the browser must adapt on the fly. To test this behavior, "reftest-wait" tests were developed. In this class of tests, the rendered canvas is not sent to the compareCanvas function when the onload event fires. Instead, the test author uses JavaScript to indicate to the reference test framework when to snapshot the file for comparison. This allows us to craft tests that can make use of the standard onload handler ourselves, as many web pages do (Table 19-3).

TABLE 19-3. Asynchronous reference test

Test	Reference

<pre><!DOCTYPE HTML>
<html class="reftest-wait">
<head>
<style>
body::before {
  content:"Before";
  border:inherit;
}
.cl::after {
  display:block;
  content:"After";
}
</style>
<script>
function fixupDOM() {
  document.body.setAttribute("style",
"border:2px solid red;");
  document.body.className = "cl";
  document.documentElement.className = "";
}
</script>
</head>
<body onload="fixupDOM()">
</body>
</html></pre>
	<pre><!DOCTYPE HTML>
	<html>
	<body style="border:2px solid red;">
	<span style="border:2px
	solid red;">Before</span>
	<div>After</div>
	</body>
	</html></pre>

Before After	Before After

There are two things to notice in this test: the first is the class attribute of the <html> element, and the second is the onload attribute of the <body> element. The "reftest-wait" value of the class attribute on the <html> node instructs the subsystem that this is a reftest-wait test. The reference test subsystem will create a listener to detect when the class attribute's value changes. In the <body> element, we have defined an onload event handler to direct the browser to call the fixupDOM function as soon as the page is loaded. The fixupDOM function changes the style of the body tag, causing the CSS system to automatically generate content, causing the words "Before" and "After" to appear. Note the last line of the fixupDOM function:

```
document.documentElement.className = ""
```

This line clears the class attribute on the <html> tag, signaling the reference test's listener and causing the framework to snapshot the canvas for comparison. If the test failed to clear the reftest-wait value, then the test would time out and be marked as a failure.

The reference file for this test is much simpler. It is a static HTML page that contains markup that will match the test's final state. Because this is a static page, there is no need to have the reftest-wait flag on the reference markup; the reference test system takes the snapshot of the reference rendering as soon as it is loaded. It is useful to keep the reference file as simple as possible in order to be certain that the test is testing what you want it to test, which in this case is CSS-generated content.[6]

Printing Tests

Imagine for a moment that you are at the airport with your self-printed boarding pass, and the barcode on it doesn't scan due to a faulty printout. These days, companies are moving away from paper as more and more content goes online: reservations, receipts, tickets, bills, maps, photos, the list goes on. But if you want a hard copy of any of this information, it is up to you to print it. So, although printing might seem like a problem that has long since been solved, it is actually critically important to modern browsers, and will only grow in importance as more services switch to a "do-it-yourself" model for vital documents.

Printing involves a different type of rendering, from margin settings to pagination to different color models. Even on the simplest of pages, when a print action is taken, the page must be chopped into different sections based on the page settings for the physical paper. For example, if you print on legal paper you'll want a different layout than if you print on an envelope. As websites have grown in complexity, they have also attempted to take control of the way that they are printed from browsers. Web pages can now include printing-specific style rules using the @media CSS rules, and this creates an entirely new domain of page rendering possibilities that must be tested.[7]

The reftest-print class of tests allows us to test various print configurations. The syntax works exactly the same as the reftest-wait asynchronous tests, but the mechanism is quite different (Table 19-4).

---

6. CSS 2.1 generated content, *http://www.w3.org/TR/CSS2/selector.html#before-and-after*.

7. CSS 2.1 @media rules, *http://www.w3.org/TR/CSS2/media.html*.

TABLE 19-4. Printing reference test

Test	Reference

`<!DOCTYPE html PUBLIC "-//W3C//DTD HTML`
`4.01//EN">`
`<html class="reftest-print">`
`<title>Height test</title>`
 	
`<div style="top: 0; left: 0; right: 0;`
`position: fixed; height: 100%; border-left:`
`2em blue solid;">`
`The left border of this box must span the`
`entire page content area.`
`This box must be repeated on the second page.`
`</div>`
 	
`<p style="page-break-before: always;">...`
`</html>`
	`<!DOCTYPE html PUBLIC "-//W3C//DTD HTML`
	`4.01//EN">`
	`<html class="reftest-print">`
	`<title>Height test</title>`
	`<style type="text/css">`
	`  html, body { height: 100%; margin: 0;`
	`padding: 0;}`
	`</style>`
	
	`<div style="height: 100%; border-left: 2em`
	`blue solid;">`
	`The left border of this box must span the`
	`entire page content area.`
	`This box must be repeated on the second page.`
	`</div>`
	`<div style="height: 100%; border-left: 2em`
	`blue solid;">`
	
	`The left border of this box must span the`
	`entire page content area.`
	`This box must be repeated on the second page.`
	`</div>`
	`</html>`

The reftest-print class works like a typical class definition. It defines a specific page layout, forcing the page to render as though it were printed on a set of 3 × 5-inch index cards. Since the purpose of the reftest-print class is to change the canvas size, it must be included in both the test and the reference markup. Unlike the asynchronous test in Table 19-3, there is no need to remove the reftest-print value.

The test in Table 19-4 ensures that the total page height for the root element is calculated properly. By using the height setting of 100%, the total height becomes a function of the root element's height. If calculated correctly, then the test <div> will span onto two pages in the test markup. The ... in the markup is drawn behind the blue box, and is only used to cause the page-break-before CSS-style rule to believe that there is content inside the `<p>` element, thus causing the page break.

The reference case is much clearer: two `<div>`s, each with a 100% height setting, cause the renderer to put one `<div>` on each page.

Invalidation Tests

The most recent addition to the reference test framework's capabilities is invalidation testing. When part of a document changes while the rest of the document remains intact, the part that changes is said to be "invalidated" because it must be redrawn by the rendering engine. All invalidation tests are asynchronous tests to give us complete control over when the snapshots are taken of the canvas. To test invalidation, we capture a signal from the rendering engine to know when we may modify the page to invalidate the prior rendering. Once we invalidate the prior rendering, we remove the "reftest-wait" value and allow the snapshot to be taken.

A simple invalidation test would be to cover part of a document with an opaque shape, then remove that shape to cause the covered background to be redrawn. We would compare such a test to a static rendering of the page without the covering shape. This is what we'll do in Figure 19-1.

This time, let's start with the reference file. The reference for this test is merely a sentence with a green border around it (Example 19-3).

EXAMPLE 19-3. Reference file for invalidation test

```
<!DOCTYPE html PUBLIC "-//W3C//DTD HTML 4.01//EN">
<html>
  <head>
    <style>
      html, body {margin: 0px;}
      #textdiv {height: 100px; width: 100px; border: solid green;}
    </style>
  </head>
  <body>
    <div id="textdiv">The quick brown fox jumped over the lazy dog and it bit
him</div>
  </body>
</html>
```

Now for the test, we will partially cover the sentence with a red block. When the test runs, we capture the MozReftestInvalidate event and remove the red block at that moment. Once we remove the block, we will also clear the reftest-wait value to allow the framework to take the test's snapshot. In this example, we remove the big red block by adding the "disappear" class attribute to make it invisible (Example 19-4).

EXAMPLE 19-4. Test file for invalidation test

```
<!DOCTYPE html PUBLIC "-//W3C//DTD HTML 4.01//EN">
<html class="reftest-wait">
  <head>
    <style>
      html, body {margin: 0px;}
      #textdiv {height: 100px; width: 100px; border: solid green;}
      #block {position: fixed; top: 40px; left: 40px; width: 100px;
              height: 100px; background: red;}
      #textdiv + div.disappear {display: none;}
    </style>
    <script>
      function doTest(){
        document.getElementById("block").setAttribute("class", "disappear");
        document.documentElement.removeAttribute("class");
      }
      document.addEventListener("MozReftestInvalidate", doTest, false);
    </script>
  </head>
  <body>
    <div id="textdiv-id001">The quick brown fox jumped over the lazy dog and it bit
him</div>
    <div id="block"></div>
  </body>
</html>
```

Once the block is removed, we have our sentence, surrounded by a simple green border, which matches our reference.

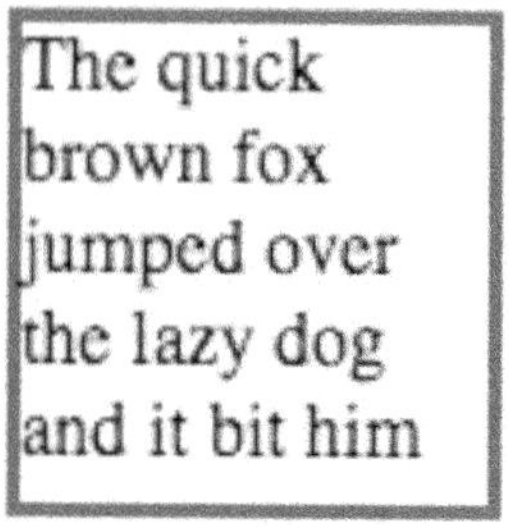

FIGURE 19-1. Final rendering of the invalidation test

Building Community

Everything we do on the Mozilla Project is done in ways that encourage participation and involvement from the worldwide community of people interested in making the open Web a reality. This has practical implications for all our test frameworks. We strive to make every test framework as simple as possible to run, understand, and create tests for.

This has concrete benefits for the immediate Mozilla testing community. When our bug triage corps finds an issue with a web page, they can narrow down the problem to a minimal test case. These minimal test cases can then be easily added to the reference test framework. Developers can also easily write tests to determine whether their fixes or new features are working as designed. However, to move outside of the reactive nature of regression testing, we are taking this one step further.

We are beginning a project that will do live comparisons of real-time websites. One of the chief motivations here is to understand the ramifications that our new, next-generation HTML 5 parser will have on websites at large. This real-time comparison engine is being built atop the reference test framework.

As part of the real-time site compare tool, we also plan to invite web developers to submit their own tests for parts of their websites that they would like to include in a special site-comparison test suite. For example, if you were working on a complex navigation system for a site, you might want to submit test markup or a link to a page that contains the navigation code. If the test markup and its previous renderings change between two Firefox milestone releases, we will send you a notice.

We are also submitting our reference tests to various W3C groups that are working on interoperable test suites for technologies such as CSS and SVG. By contributing our tests to these bodies, we will help move the Web forward by helping to ensure interoperability among all implementers of these specifications. We also have an initiative to run our own reference tests on other web browsers. By continuing to push the envelope of what is possible with a regression framework, we can extend our testing framework to make it useful to web developers and also as a mechanism for testing future web technologies.

The lessons here about keeping the testing framework simple and extensible are key for anyone wishing to move their regression testing from a reactive to a proactive orientation. Although those two items alone are almost enough, it is also important to create a test framework that can be repurposed by other developers for new projects. By ensuring that your test framework is simple, powerful, and extensible, you can create a resource for developers to extend it in ways you never imagined, creating an automated regression framework that helps test the latest technologies and behaviors. The Mozilla reference test framework is doing all of these things, aiming to benefit everyone, from the millions of people who depend on Mozilla products for their daily conduit to the Web, to the traveler printing a boarding pass, to the web developer implementing the latest HTML 5 specification on his site. Now, that is one beautiful framework.

## CHAPTER TWENTY

Clam Anti-Virus: Testing Open Source with Open Tools

Tomasz Kojm

SOFTWARE TESTING IS ALWAYS CHALLENGING, and no matter how hard you try, you can never be sure that your program is safe and bug-free. Even if you can prove your algorithms are perfect, the real world will quickly verify your beliefs. Bugs in compilers, operating systems, or third-party libraries are not uncommon and introduce additional layers of complexity. In order to make your testing procedures effective, you have to be flexible, think widely, and use proper tools for proper things.

Anti-virus scanners are really strong opponents when it comes to testing. Everyone expects them to be very stable, reliable, accurate, fast, etc. The developers need to perform dozens of tests to ensure that both software and signature databases meet the desired quality requirements. Everything needs to be tested and tuned up very carefully, to avoid unexpected surprises when the software reaches the end users.

During the last few years, the Clam Anti-Virus project has deployed a wide variety of testing techniques to keep the product ready for mission-critical applications. I'll try to explore these solutions as well as some common difficulties the developers still need to deal with. Testing methods may vary between different platforms, and this case study focuses on Unix, whose most famous design principle is KISS: Keep it Simple, Stupid! This harsh but very accurate rule also perfectly applies to testing. Simplicity is beautiful, and Unix is just a great example of this.

The Clam Anti-Virus Project

Clam Anti-Virus (ClamAV) is an open source antivirus toolkit for Unix, written in C and licensed under GNU GPLv2. Started in 2002 and acquired by Sourcefire five years later, the project has become one of the key players in the open source security world. ClamAV is being maintained by its international team of developers and provides an antivirus engine library (*libclamav*) together with a set of tools based around it, including a command-line scanner (*clamscan*) and a multithreaded scanning daemon (*clamd*). The scanner is coupled with a virus signature database that consists of more than 580,000 entries.

The main goal of the project is the integration with mail servers for the purpose of email scanning. This makes ClamAV a mission-critical application; the scanning must be both stable and reliable so that it does not affect delivery of legitimate messages. The scanner can be also used for many other purposes. Currently there exist more than 100 third-party applications, which extend ClamAV to provide various forms of on-access scanning, HTTP traffic inspection, or integration with FTP and other services.

Like all antivirus products, ClamAV is not just software but also a service. To provide accurate detection, the signature database needs to be kept up-to-date, cover all current threats, and be free from false positives. Extensive testing is required to keep the detection accuracy on an acceptable level.

Testing Methods

The Clam Anti-Virus project uses several black and white box testing methods to eliminate as many errors as possible and make the user experience both more efficient and enjoyable.

Black Box Versus White Box Testing

The *black box* and *white box* methods are the most common design methods for software testing. In the black box approach, the software is treated as a mysterious object, of which internal structure and design are unknown. It takes some input data, processes it, and spits out the results. A single test is considered successful when a program can both handle the data and give expected results. Whereas black box testing is based on the software specification, the white box approach requires knowledge about the internal implementation and focuses on testing specific paths in the program. The test cases need to be carefully selected by the programmers and cover all of the important units of code.

Black box and white box testing methods are complementary, but both share similar limitations, the major one being the fact that in practice, it's impossible to test the program completely. You need to be creative, design effectively, and, even better, develop beautiful tests that cover various use cases and detect problems before the software reaches your users.

Static Analysis

A static analysis of source code is a white box testing method, which doesn't require the code to be executed. The point of this method is to look for common programming errors and ensure that the source code meets all important requirements and standards. The analysis can be performed manually and automatically. Since a strictly manual code inspection would be a very laborious task, the developers take advantage of professional tools for automated code analysis, which perform checks based on techniques such as syntax, semantic, and data-flow analysis.

GCC

One of the most useful and commonly used kinds of static analysis tools are compilers. In the ClamAV project, we mostly use the famous GCC compiler, which performs both syntax and semantic checking during the compilation stage. Syntax errors, which break the C coding rules, are always fatal. The programmer needs to fix all of them in order to compile the application. Much more interesting is the semantic analysis. It's performed after syntax checking and focuses on the correctness of the program's internal design. The semantic analysis includes methods such as scoping (checking whether names of identifiers are handled properly) and type checking (making sure that operators are applied to proper operands), among others. In many cases the semantic bugs are treated as critical and GCC will refuse to compile code that, for example, defines the same identifier names twice in the same block of code. Somewhere else it will only issue a warning that some variable is being initialized from an incorrect type. After semantic analysis, GCC also performs other checks, such as data-flow analysis, that are mostly used to optimize the code. But some useful warnings can be issued during these phases as well. The GCC compiler is very flexible and provides dozens of options for fine-tuning the error detection. In all cases, it's important to carefully analyze the warnings and preferably fix all of them. A code free of warnings is easier to maintain and less error-prone. With the good habit of keeping the code clean, you will never get critical issues camouflaged by existing warnings.

Clang Static Analyzer

Clang Static Analyzer, also known as the Clang Checker, is a relatively young part of the Low Level Virtual Machine (LLVM) project. Despite the fact that it's still in heavy development, it already provides very good results and successfully detects nasty problems such as null and undefined pointer dereferences, divide by zero, invalid function calls, uninitialized arguments, and others. One of the major advantages of this tool is its output format; in contrast to other analyzers, Clang Checker creates an HTML report for each bug detected in the source code, with line numbers, colored syntax, and a complete problem description. By following the description, developers can easily see the origin of the bug (Example 20-1).

EXAMPLE 20-1. This snippet presents only the last four steps before the invalid dereference (complete report available at https: //wwws.clamav.net/bugzilla/show_bug.cgi?id=1292)

```
[...]
          [8] Taking false branch.

757       if(!i) {
758             cli_errmsg("lsigattribs: Empty TDB\n");
759             return -1;
760       }
761
          [9] Loop condition is true. Entering loop body.

762       for(i = 0; tokens[i]; i++) {

          [10] Loop condition is false. Execution continues on line 769.

763       for(j = 0; attrtab[j].name; j++) {
764             if(!strcmp(attrtab[j].name, tokens[i])) {
765                 apt = &attrtab[j];
766                 break;
767             }
768       }

          [11] Dereference of null pointer.

769       switch(apt->type) {
[...]
```

Splint

Before the compilers were equipped with advanced code analyzers, the programmers had to rely solely on external tools. The most common solution was Lint, which was bundled with the Version 7 Unix released in 1979. Since then, many equivalent tools were developed, all sharing similar concepts and even similar names. A tool that can be recommended nowadays is Splint. It's name stands for Secure Programming Lint, because in addition to the traditional semantic checks, it can also detect security-related issues such as null pointer dereferences, memory management errors, buffer overflows, dangerous aliasing, possible infinite loops, and other suspicious statements. Splint is a very sensitive tool. It will not only report dozens of possible problems for a piece of good-looking code, but it also may sometimes have problems with parsing more complex files; therefore, it often makes sense to isolate and separately check the parts of code you want to review.

Be patient

Like all static analyzers, GCC, Clang Static Analyzer, and especially Splint are not perfect and may generate spurious reports or not detect some problems. The ratio of false positives and negatives usually depends on the runtime options used for fine-tuning the tools. Don't go mad when a static analyzer reports problems for a perfectly valid piece of code! In almost all cases the false warnings can be suppressed with special options or by annotating the affected lines in the source code.

Memory Checkers

Memory management errors are one of the most common software bugs, and in large projects it's almost impossible to avoid them. The most popular faults are memory leaks, using undeclared or already released memory, writing out of bounds, or double frees. Memory-related issues might have very different symptoms. In the basic cases, they will result in a crash (caused by a segmentation fault) and will be repeatable. However, it's not unusual that the problems are hard to reproduce and sometimes not even deterministic. In such cases, looking for the reasons may be very time consuming, and just like searching for a needle in a haystack, you know it's there but good luck finding it! Fortunately enough, there exist advanced memory-debugging tools that can save a lot of time, significantly improving the developer's life. A dynamic code analysis with these tools is often more optimal and easier than the static approach, especially when the problem is reproducible. The ClamAV project most often makes use of Valgrind, Electric Fence and DUMA, and Mudflap.

Valgrind

Valgrind is both powerful and easy to use. Its major advantage is that the application you want to test doesn't need to be modified at all, and Valgrind works directly with binaries, meaning that your program can be written in any language (also interpreted ones!). It's not only a memory debugger; in fact, it's a complete suite that also provides tools for cache and heap profiling or detection of synchronization problems. The original version only supports Linux on some specific hardware platforms (x86, amd64, ppc32/64), but there exist unofficial ports to other systems. Valgrind emulates an environment similar to the one the program is supposed to run in. Since it also emulates a CPU, the execution is significantly slower (in the worst case, even up to 50 times slower). That's why it's very helpful to have some fast box at hand. See Example 20-2.

EXAMPLE 20-2. Valgrind reporting memory corruption in one of the unpackers for compressed executable files in ClamAV 0.92

```
==18030== Invalid write of size 1
==18030==    at 0x4E6D92A: unmew (packlibs.c:300)
==18030==    by 0x4E6F5DA: unmew11 (mew.c:799)
==18030==    by 0x4E61FE0: cli_scanpe (pe.c:1155)
==18030==    by 0x4E47F6A: cli_magic_scandesc (scanners.c:2234)
==18030==    by 0x4E498F0: cl_scandesc (scanners.c:2264)
==18030==    by 0x405737: checkfile (manager.c:651)
==18030==    by 0x40675A: scanfile (manager.c:1093)
==18030==    by 0x40733D: scanmanager (manager.c:371)
==18030==    by 0x404EA5: main (clamscan.c:213)
==18030==  Address 0x67594f0 is 0 bytes after a block of size 12,288 alloc'd
==18030==    at 0x4C216F4: calloc (vg_replace_malloc.c:397)
==18030==    by 0x4E42CD9: cli_calloc (others.c:330)
==18030==    by 0x4E61DF5: cli_scanpe (pe.c:1123)
```

```
==18030==    by 0x4E47F6A: cli_magic_scandesc (scanners.c:2234)
==18030==    by 0x4E498F0: cl_scandesc (scanners.c:2264)
==18030==    by 0x405737: checkfile (manager.c:651)
==18030==    by 0x40675A: scanfile (manager.c:1093)
==18030==    by 0x40733D: scanmanager (manager.c:371)
==18030==    by 0x404EA5: main (clamscan.c:213)
```

Electric Fence and DUMA

Besides Valgrind, we make use of Electric Fence and its fork, DUMA. They both are `malloc()`
debuggers and use the virtual memory hardware of the system to detect overruns of boundaries
for heap-allocated buffers and invalid memory access. This is accomplished by following each
memory allocation with an inaccessible memory page; as soon as the tested program attempts
to access such a page, it gets terminated and the invalid access reported. Similarly, all memory
released by `free()` is marked inaccessible and treated the same way. DUMA can also detect
memory leaks and has support for C++ memory management functions. The big advantage of
these tools is their portability; they can run on most operating systems and architectures. In
order to use them, the target application must be linked against libefence or libduma, which
replace the default memory management functions of the C library. On many systems it's
possible to avoid recompilation/relinking by preloading the libraries. These tools usually don't
cause as much of a runtime slowdown as Valgrind (although significant slowdowns may occur
when the code does lots of small allocations) but primarily make the applications much more
memory-hungry; therefore, their use should be limited to testing purposes.

Mudflap

Mudflap is a pointer-debugging tool and part of the GCC suite since version 4.0. It's an
advanced tool that detects memory reference violations by modifying the original GCC
constructs and instrumenting all possibly problematic pointer-dereferencing operations as well
as some other risky functions. Since Mudflap modifies the internal structures, the target
application needs to be recompiled with the `-fmudflap` switch of the gcc compiler and linked to
libmudflap. When it's done, Mudflap can be controlled via the environment variable
`MUDFLAP_OPTIONS`. The tool provides many runtime options for fine-tuning of the detection. The
big advantage of Mudflap is that it's part of GCC and no additional third-party components are
required. However, it's harder to use than other solutions and is also very sensitive. In the
default configuration it may throw out many warnings, which need to be carefully classified
by the tester. One of the greatest advantages of Mudflap is the ability to detect out-of-object
accesses, which can be perfectly legal from the memory point of view. Such a situation may
occur when a program reads or writes to some object out of boundary without violating the
memory itself but breaking the internal structure of another object. This kind of problem, often
caused by off-by-one errors, can be very nasty and hard to debug, and the tools described earlier
won't detect them. Mudflap has already saved us a lot of time debugging these errors.

Limitations

Although there are very good memory debuggers, the common problem is that memory leaks may occur at very rare execution paths, which highly complicates their detection. When looking for memory leaks, we usually run our scanner under Valgrind and test large collections of files. We have also developed our own tool that wraps calls to memory and file functions and checks for memory and descriptor leaks. Since its overhead is very low, it's more practical than Valgrind when we're just looking for leaks and need to scan huge amounts of data.

Since memory management errors may occur in any code unit, it's important to test as many modules as possible. For us this means we need to scan lots of files in as many different formats as possible. Of course, this still doesn't guarantee that we discover all the problems! Therefore, when performing general code testing, it's recommended to do both dynamic and static analysis to improve detection of bugs in less-visible code places, such as error paths, which are often overlooked.

Unit Testing

As part of white box testing, ClamAV makes use of unit tests. This solution allows us to check that individual units of code (such as single functions or modules) are working correctly: they properly handle input data, process it, and return expected values. Unit tests allow us to quickly check the code before committing any changes to our SVN repository and find out which particular units are not behaving properly. They're also priceless when it comes to testing on different platforms and architectures. The unit tests should be consistently implemented during the development stage and applied to all critical sections of code. They're another beautiful example of the KISS concept realized in practice. Integration of unit tests enforces good coding practices and leads to better code design and modularization.

We use the popular open source unit-testing framework for C called *Check*, which can be found at *http://check.sf.net*. It was originally inspired by the famous JUnit for Java as well as some other frameworks, and features a clear and simple interface. Due to the nature of C, all tests need to be separated from the framework to avoid situations when a crash in a single test affects the entire framework. Check runs its tests in separate processes and uses message queues to communicate with the framework what makes the solution stable and reliable. The framework was designed for easy integration with Autotools (Autoconf/Automake) and common Unix development environments for C. See Example 20-3.

EXAMPLE 20-3. Example test for one of the pattern matchers in ClamAV

```
START_TEST (test_bm_scanbuff) {
        struct cli_matcher *root;
        const char *virname = NULL;
        int ret;

    root = (struct cli_matcher *) cli_calloc(1, sizeof(struct cli_matcher));
    fail_unless(root != NULL, "root == NULL");
```

```
#ifdef USE_MPOOL
    root->mempool = mpool_create();
#endif
    ret = cli_bm_init(root);
    fail_unless(ret == CL_SUCCESS, "cli_bm_init() failed");

    ret = cli_parse_add(root, "Sig1", "deadbabe", 0, 0, NULL, 0, NULL, 0);
    fail_unless(ret == CL_SUCCESS, "cli_parse_add(Sig1) failed");
    ret = cli_parse_add(root, "Sig2", "deadbeef", 0, 0, NULL, 0, NULL, 0);
    fail_unless(ret == CL_SUCCESS, "cli_parse_add(Sig2) failed");
    ret = cli_parse_add(root, "Sig3", "babedead", 0, 0, NULL, 0, NULL, 0);
    fail_unless(ret == CL_SUCCESS, "cli_parse_add(Sig3) failed");

    ret = cli_bm_scanbuff("blah\xde\xad\xbe\xef", 12, &virname, root, 0, 0, -1);
    fail_unless(ret == CL_VIRUS, "cli_bm_scanbuff() failed");
    fail_unless(!strncmp(virname, "Sig2", 4), "Incorrect signature matched in
cli_bm_scanbuff()\n");
    cli_bm_free(root);
#ifdef USE_MPOOL
    mpool_destroy(root->mempool);
#endif
    free(root);
}
END_TEST
```

Test Scripts

Test scripts are sets of step-by-step instructions that reproduce various conditions and check that the program is functioning properly. We use a number of automated scripts that mimic the usual usage of our applications and expect correct results for given sets of the configuration and input data. This is a black box testing method that focuses only on the specification, not the internal details. Thanks to the fact that all the applications in the ClamAV package are console-based, it's relatively easy to create test cases that can be automatically reproduced in the console. Similar to unit tests, the big advantage of test scripts is that once created, they are executed automatically, making the testing procedure less painful and much faster. However, they also have to be designed very carefully and as extended as possible; otherwise, their benefits will be highly limited.

Fuzz Testing

In fuzzing, it's all about making a mess—very useful, often artistic messes that can help render possible failures in your algorithms. One of the main rules of fuzzing is there are no rules! And this is what makes this concept really simple and beautiful. One of the best ways to test a program is to do it in a very nonstandard way that may help discover various shortcomings that don't show up during regular usage.

The virus scanners need to handle hundreds of file formats, usually pretty complex ones. Let's take compressed archives of files, such as *.zip* or *.rar*, for example. In order to unpack and scan their contents, the scanner first needs to parse some special headers that store lists of compressed files together with all their characteristics (such as names, original sizes, file offsets in the compressed stream, checksums, etc.). If such headers include some bogus values and the code that handles them is missing proper checks, the code may attempt to perform an action that may result in abnormal termination of the program, e.g., due to a miscalculation of a buffer size and its later overflow. Although these problems can be avoided by performing a proper sanitization of the input data, real life shows that sometimes programmers cannot handle each and every case in the original implementation, even if they try hard. And this is where the fuzz tests enter the game!

We use file fuzzers, which create a specified amount of mutations of the original file. Each new copy should be different and should have some part randomly modified. The quality of the file fuzzer is crucial to the testing process. The best fuzzers are those dedicated to specific tasks that can handle file formats or protocols used by the target application. When the fuzzer understands the input format it's supposed to modify, it can create good quality modifications by affecting the most important parts of the original data. However, implementation of dedicated fuzzers is time-consuming, and since they're focused on single formats, their future use is highly limited.

In most cases, it's more optimal to use a general-purpose fuzzer. A good example of such a solution is *Fusil*, which is in fact a complete fuzzer framework and can be downloaded from *http://freshmeat.net/projects/fusil*. It's written in Python and comes with a set of so-called fuzzing projects that cover some popular applications such as ClamAV, Firefox, and MPlayer. It's also relatively easy to create other fuzzers or adapt Fusil to your own needs. The framework provides many ways to detect program crashes, deadlocks, and other problems by watching exit codes, log and standard output messages, CPU usage, or time taken to process the data. Additionally, Fusil makes efforts to keep the operating system stable by monitoring the load and memory usage, and making sure that the process being tested gets terminated at the end of the session. When started, it creates mutations of the original file and tests the application against them in separate sessions. For each session, it computes a score and reports possibly detected errors.

How many fuzzed files are needed to test a single file-format handler? Well, the more the better. Since fuzz testing is a brute-force method, it's impossible to say in advance how long it will take to give some interesting results or whether it will be able to detect anything at all. The fuzzer may discover some problems in five minutes, but they're not necessarily the most important bugs. On the other hand, if nothing is found for a few hours, it doesn't mean you should stop fuzzing and consider the code safe. Patience is the key to success. Still, if the program is able to handle a few million fuzzed files without any problems, this means the coder did his job pretty well!

Collection of Problematic Files

We collect all files that make our scanner crash. These come from our users or our own findings (e.g., from fuzzing, as described earlier), and we use them for further sanity testing. The experience has taught us that some problems have a tendency to reactivate under various conditions. For example, it may happen that some complex code gets cleaned up or rewritten from scratch for some reason, such as performance improvement, and due to design or implementation faults some important safety checks get missed. By keeping the problematic files and testing our software against them on a regular basis, we ensure that we don't reintroduce the old bugs. Such files are quite often a valuable source for further fuzzing!

Testing the Environment

Autoconf is a very popular tool that produces special configuration scripts for automatic configuration of source code packages. Like almost every open source project, ClamAV makes use of this solution. The configure script created by Autoconf performs a large number of tests, checking whether some features are available on the target system and making portable programming much easier. Besides checking for availability of various, often platform-dependent features, we use the configure script to test the system libraries and even the compilers for possible bugs that could render ClamAV vulnerable to security threats. For example, in 2007 we found out that GCC versions affected by bug PR27603 (versions 4.0.x, 4.1.0, and some versions of 4.1.1) incorrectly compile our bounds-checking routines, generating security-vulnerable binaries from completely safe source code! We added a configure check to detect this particular compiler bug and also a more generic test for a valid code generation of the important bounds-checking routine in libclamav. Some time later, thanks to our configure script, it turned out that another C compiler from Sun Studio is suffering from the same problem and can also create broken binaries while optimizing the code.

Buildbot

Buildbot (http://buildbot.net/) automates the rebuilding and testing of the source tree, making it very easy to validate new code changes. The tool is integrated with version control systems such as CVS or SVN and gets triggered when a developer commits a new code. It then runs the usual compilation procedure and performs unit tests. If some errors occur, the developer is informed immediately and provided with a complete report of failure. Buildbot uses a client-server architecture. The heart of Buildbot is *BuildMaster*, which manages one or more *BuildSlaves*. The slaves execute commands and send the results back to the master. The architecture makes it easy to add more BuildSlaves and simplifies multiplatform testing (we run it on a several flavors of Unix and different architectures). Once set up, Buildbot provides a fully automated testing system and significantly helps keep the code base free from obvious errors. Beautiful!

Compatibility Testing

The compatibility testing of ClamAV is multilayer and needs to cover both the software and the virus signature databases. Since ClamAV is an open source project, it's expected to compile and run correctly on a large variety of system platforms and architectures. We perform compatibility testing manually from time to time, and automatically on a per-change basis using Buildbot, which checks the current code on some of the major platforms. Beside this, we've developed a semi-automatic compile farm system, which performs daily and on-demand tests on many different systems (including Linux, Solaris, OpenBSD, Mac OS X, FreeBSD, and others) and presents us with detailed results of compilations and unit and test scripts (see Figure 20-1).

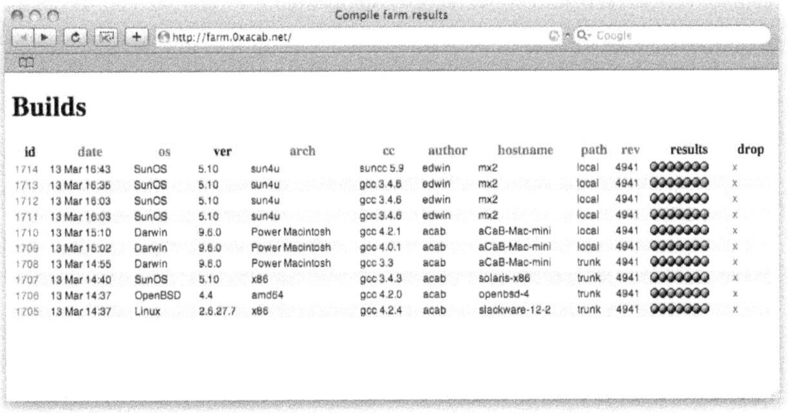
Compile farm results

http://farm.0xacab.net/

Builds

id	date	os	ver	arch	cc	author	hostname	path	rev	results	drop
1714	13 Mar 16:43	SunOS	5.10	sun4u	suncc 5.9	edwin	mx2	local	4941		x
1713	13 Mar 16:35	SunOS	5.10	sun4u	gcc 3.4.6	edwin	mx2	local	4941		x
1712	13 Mar 16:03	SunOS	5.10	sun4u	gcc 3.4.6	edwin	mx2	local	4941		x
1711	13 Mar 16:03	SunOS	5.10	sun4u	gcc 3.4.6	edwin	mx2	local	4941		x
1710	13 Mar 15:10	Darwin	9.6.0	Power Macintosh	gcc 4.2.1	acab	aCaB-Mac-mini	local	4941		x
1709	13 Mar 15:02	Darwin	9.6.0	Power Macintosh	gcc 4.0.1	acab	aCaB-Mac-mini	local	4941		x
1708	13 Mar 14:55	Darwin	9.6.0	Power Macintosh	gcc 3.3	acab	aCaB-Mac-mini	trunk	4941		x
1707	13 Mar 14:40	SunOS	5.10	x86	gcc 3.4.3	acab	solaris-x86	trunk	4941		x
1706	13 Mar 14:37	OpenBSD	4.4	amd64	gcc 4.2.0	acab	openbsd-4	trunk	4941		x
1705	13 Mar 14:37	Linux	2.6.27.7	x86	gcc 4.2.4	acab	slackware-12-2	trunk	4941		x

FIGURE 20-1. ClamAV's compile farm results at http://farm.0xacab.net

The antivirus technology needs constant improvements, which is why the releases of ClamAV have rather short life cycles and we regularly publish new versions with improved detection mechanisms. In many cases our users cannot follow these updates instantly, as they need to wait for their OS distributions to prepare the update or a policy manager to approve the software update. We put much effort into ensuring that our signature updates are backward compatible. By testing each and every database update against the current and previous ClamAV engines, we make sure that the updates don't break older installations.

Performance Testing

The antivirus software needs to handle hundreds of thousands of virus signatures and hundreds of file formats, and still must perform all the tasks fast enough to not bring the computer system to its knees. Sometimes performance problems can even lead to *denial-of-service* attacks when the scanner is spending too much time processing some special data. The attacker can make use of this fact to paralyze some important service, such as email delivery, by flooding it with data that cannot be handled in a timely way. That's why performance testing and elimination of various bottlenecks is another important issue the ClamAV developers need to face.

In the antivirus software there are many places where such bottlenecks may occur. It may be the pattern matching or other specialized detection engine, as well as one of the special file handlers. There exist special tools designed for code execution performance analysis, called *profilers*, which help to localize bottlenecks. A profiler produces an execution profile of a program with a statistical summary for each called function. It shows how many times a function was called and how much time was spent in it. Most profilers can also provide a detailed call graph showing how the functions are getting called and how much time was spent in specific subroutines of functions, thus allowing for better identification of places where bottlenecks may occur. However, even with profilers, it's usually not an easy task to identify portions of code that can result in slowdowns. One of the reasons is the fact that a problematic code can be hidden in routines that don't get called frequently. Therefore, when profiling ClamAV, we not only test it against regular data but also feed the scanner with thousands of files in different formats to raise the probability of a bottleneck occurring. As part of the performance testing we also perform stress testing. By creating heavy load with regular input data, we're trying to simulate the behavior of the scanner in busy environments, which need to handle hundreds of thousands or even millions of files or electronic messages daily. The stress testing helps discover possible problems with stability, robustness, and general efficiency of the software (see Example 20-4).

EXAMPLE 20-4. Example flat profile from gprof, showing that in this particular case libclamav is spending most time in the Boyer-Moore and Aho-Corasick pattern matchers

```
Each sample counts as 0.01 seconds.
  %   cumulative   self              self     total
 time   seconds   seconds    calls  s/call   s/call  name
48.74     4.65      4.65     5755     0.00     0.00  cli_bm_scanbuff
41.82     8.64      3.99     8068     0.00     0.00  cli_ac_scanbuff
 1.57     9.19      0.15   504155     0.00     0.00  cli_bm_addpatt
 0.52     9.24      0.05        7     0.01     0.01  cli_bm_free
 0.42     9.28      0.04  1664706     0.00     0.00  mpool_malloc
 0.42     9.32      0.04    90151     0.00     0.00  cli_parse_add
 0.31     9.35      0.03   411228     0.00     0.00  hashset_addkey_internal
 0.21     9.37      0.02   511472     0.00     0.00  cli_hex2str_to
 0.21     9.39      0.02    21345     0.00     0.00  cli_ac_addsig
 0.21     9.41      0.02     1248     0.00     0.00  text_normalize_buffer
 0.10     9.42      0.01  1664161     0.00     0.00  mpool_free
 0.10     9.43      0.01   525577     0.00     0.00  cli_mpool_virname
 0.10     9.44      0.01   514394     0.00     0.00  cli_chkign
 0.10     9.45      0.01   514394     0.00     0.00  hashset_contains
 0.10     9.46      0.01    33772     0.00     0.00  bfs_enqueue
 0.10     9.47      0.01    21652     0.00     0.00  cli_ac_addpatt
[...]
```

Testing for False Positive and False Negative Alerts

The antivirus scanners can sometimes produce false alerts. A false positive alert happens when a legitimate file gets incorrectly marked as infected. Similarly, we say a false negative alert happens when an infected file is wrongly confirmed as clean. Both of them are the common nightmare to all antivirus vendors. A high ratio of false positive alerts may render the scanner unusable. Desktop users will not accept virus notifications popping up here and there many times a day; similarly, the system administrators will quickly drop a product that marks a large volume of legitimate emails passing their mail servers as infected. The false negative alerts are a bit different and may occur due to at least two reasons. The obvious one is the lack of virus definitions in the scanner's database. The situation is complicated when the antivirus scanner includes proper virus signatures or other detection mechanisms for a particular virus, but then fails to identify it. This is usually related to bugs in the scanner's detection engine, such as invalid file processing (unpacking, extracting) or even problems with the pattern matcher, and should be treated with the utmost caution. A quick detection and elimination of false alerts, optimally before the product or its updates reaches the end users, is a must for all antivirus vendors.

False positives

Although the virus analysts of ClamAV put much effort into ensuring the best quality signatures, a positive result from a special, fully automated signature testing mechanism is required to publish them to the world. The core component of this system is a large collection of clean files. The size, quality, and especially the diversity of this collection is the key factor in eliminating false positive matches. It consists of hundreds of gigabytes of various executables, libraries, and other components of popular operating systems and software, which are all confirmed to be safe. When the author is ready to publish new signatures, he uploads them into a special interface and simply clicks one button. The system automatically scans the collection with these signatures and makes sure they don't generate any detection; if they do, the author gets notified and the publishing process is immediately stopped. It's very important that the testing phase is as fast as possible and there are no significant delays; otherwise, we could be too late in reacting to new threats. Since we need to scan large amounts of data, to do it effectively we distribute the process among multiple machines, which all store parts of the collection. The test is considered successful when all the nodes report no detections.

False negatives

How does this process look for false negatives? Well, usually when the scanner doesn't detect some malware, it means there's no signature for it. Then the only way to fix the problem is to update the database to cover the particular threat. However, it may happen that the scanner stops detecting some threats without a valid reason. In almost all cases, such situations are related to problems with the detection engine and may have very nasty consequences. Therefore, they should always be addressed as soon as possible. To avoid such problems in

ClamAV, we perform regular regression tests against our collection of malware. The aim of these tests is to compare the detection results generated by the new code to the old version and see how it's performing. We run two different versions of the scanner using the same set of signature databases to scan the same collection of files. Any differences in the results need special attention, especially when some malware is undetected by the new code.

Usability and User Acceptance Testing

The major strength of open source projects is their great user communities. The ClamAV users don't only supply us with the latest samples of malware, they also provide many useful suggestions, verify our development ideas, and help as the best black box testers. The usability and user acceptance testing is the last step before rolling out the final product. In our case, it's strictly connected to opinion polling and testing of release candidates. This testing phase is very important for at least two reasons. First, the software authors are never objective and critical enough when it comes to their own creations. Second, they never have a way to empirically test the application in all possible ways in which the users expect it to run. Testing performed by the users can show whether the new functions and changes work as intended and without problems in various environments and applications. It's primarily focused on the usability, stability, user interfaces, and visible behavior of programs.

Opinion polling

From time to time, each project needs to make changes that sound controversial or even unacceptable to part of its user base. Since ClamAV is mostly used for integration with other solutions and third-party software, any changes to user interfaces, APIs, report formats, and other user-visible mechanisms usually are not very welcome, because they may affect the cooperation between components. During the last few years, we quickly learned that we would never fully satisfy all our users but that we could reduce complaints by publicly discussing all major changes. We usually use the mailing lists for discussions and opinion polls about the upcoming changes. By discussing them with the community, we can verify our ideas and make sure the majority of interested people accept them; if they don't, we can see what should be improved or modified. Usually the users are quite responsive and provide useful suggestions or criticism, but sometimes the response is lower than expected. However, it's always worth doing the opinion polls because they not only make further user acceptance testing easier, but also give the authors a good argument for later discussions when the changes make it into a final release. Hey, you were warned! :-)

Release candidates

Since ClamAV is usually being used for mission-critical applications and users expect high stability, we generally don't publish any alpha or beta versions of the upcoming releases, as they wouldn't have a big audience. People interested in the latest code can always check out our SVN repository, but we don't recommend using it for production purposes. The only exceptions are release candidate versions of ClamAV, which we always publish before new major releases. We only publish a release candidate when the code passes all the important tests already described in this text and when it's free from fatal bugs. Such releases are usually of production quality; however, we still find that our users are rather uncomfortable installing them. Therefore, we make appeals to all users who don't have dedicated test environments and cannot run the prerelease versions in production to help by downloading them, compiling them, and running make check. This way we can find out on which platforms or setups the new versions don't compile or pass the internal tests. And this is just another beautiful example of the usefulness of unit tests and test scripts. The release candidates are part of the user acceptance testing. The focus of this test is to see how the code is performing in real-world scenarios, and also to make sure that the new version meets the requirements of our users.

Summary

The presented overview of the ClamAV testing procedures covers most techniques we use in day-to-day project maintenance. Although ClamAV testing is challenging and often time-consuming, the last seven years have showed us it can also be very exciting. In our efforts we almost solely depend on free, open source applications, which mature and get better each year, just like our project does. Better tools = better testing = better code quality provided back to the open source community. Isn't this beautiful?

Credits

The Clam Anti-Virus project would never be what it is now without the great ClamAV Team. I'd like to especially thank Török Edwin and Alberto Wu for proofreading this text and for taking ClamAV testing to the next level, and to Luca Gibelli for keeping our infrastructure running perfectly. They're some of the most brilliant nerds I've ever met! Finally, I'd like to thank my beautiful wife for her patience with my duties and hobbies.

## CHAPTER TWENTY-ONE

Web Application Testing with Windmill

Adam Christian

Introduction

THE UNSTOPPABLE FORCE OF DYNAMIC WEB APPLICATIONS has changed the technology industry forever, and as rapidly as they are built, they need to be tested. Testing applications rich with dynamic JavaScript and interactive AJAX (Asynchronous JavaScript and XML) require a much more advanced set of tools producing tests that can easily be considered beautiful. In many ways it takes a well-versed web developer to understand and appreciate the complexities of automated testing on the Web, but essentially anyone can see the vast array of benefits.

Windmill originated at the Open Source Applications Foundation (OSAF) in an effort to minimize the manual testing that was required to release new versions of the Cosmo Web User Interface. Initially, Selenium Core was explored, but it was still in the early stages of development and didn't provide the required tools for continuous integration or a responsive community. Thus, Windmill was born. The language of choice at OSAF was Python, and it lent itself as the obvious choice for Windmill.

Two years after its initial public announcement at O'Reilly's Open Source Convention (OSCON) 2007 in Portland, Windmill has gained a rapidly growing community and a set of very polished tools, allowing you to quickly create automated test cases for your web application.

Overview

The general purpose of the Windmill project is to provide an open source tool that allows you to create test cases as a series of actions, organized into collections called suites. These suites can then be executed in your browser of choice, either manually on your desktop or in an automated way using one of the readily available continuous integration tools.

Windmill is built in Python, and relies on a collection of open source Python libraries. This installation process is streamlined using PyPi or PIP, and you can choose to install the release version or the development trunk. It's important to understand that the other piece of Windmill is the JavaScript controller, which runs completely in the browser so that it can simulate your user session (Figure 21-1). This is why each Windmill test run requires that you specify the browser in which you would like to run your test.

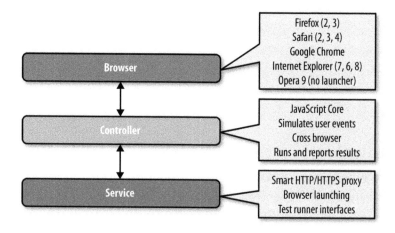

FIGURE 21-1. Overview of the Windmill architecture

Writing Tests

The Windmill integrated development environment (IDE), shown in Figure 21-2, provides a cross-browser solution for recording, editing, and testing your suites of test actions. This part of the tool isn't exactly beautiful, but after using it you will see the extensive utility that it brings to the project.

Of all the pieces covered in this section, the recorder comes the closest to something that could be described as beautiful in its ability to reliably guess what you as a user are trying to simulate. Even if the recorder doesn't make the cut as a beautiful feature, it can still save you a lot of time.

FIGURE 21-2. Snapshot of the Windmill IDE

At OSAF the quality assurance team working on Cosmo was pretty small: one and a half QA engineers for eight developers who were building features at a rapid pace. Like any other project, quality assurance is absolutely necessary, manual testing happens, and automation is one of those things you want but don't have the time or resources to implement. We managed to dedicate a small amount of time and some very concise requirements: fast and efficient test writing and editing, coverage of all the major features in our application, and features and compatibility for existing continuous integration software.

Accomplishing the speed aspect of test writing was tightly coupled to the recorder, which started out generating JavaScript Object Notation (JSON) strings that were then dumped into a file. As the test actions became more complex and we moved to Python and JavaScript, utilities were built around translating from the recorded actions and suites into Python and JavaScript, with the ability to add transformers for other languages. Both Python and JavaScript provide utilities for setup and teardown as well as their own set of unique strengths, which are outlined in the documentation on the project website.

The Windmill recorder encourages a different kind of workflow than most recording tools. Actions are added to the current suite you are working on, but in a way that encourages manipulation. The action is represented by a simple editable form (Figure 21-3), where each of the different options has a drop-down box or a text input that are populated by the recorder but allow you to easily change and run them as you go.

FIGURE 21-3. An assert action

The first step in building a recording tool is recognizing that half of the time it's not going to record what the user wants, but still needs to provide some value to the user that encourages them to correct it.

This same concept of constant editing was also used in the playback feature. It doesn't matter if you are building your test or running it for the 50th time, you can change values and replay actions, suites, or the whole test to see what happens. More often than expected, a user will find himself halfway through a test run to validate his product and discover there is a missing workflow, or something in the application has changed but isn't a bug. You can simply stop the playback, record that new workflow, and save it out to the filesystem. This reduces barriers for debugging, editing, and growing your tests repository.

As mentioned, another piece of the puzzle is saving out those created or edited tests in a way that you can store and run them later. The format you save them is configurable in the Windmill settings (Figure 21-4).

FIGURE 21-4. Save settings

Saving tests can be accomplished by clicking the save button for a suite: save . See Examples 21-1 and 21-2 for example Python and JavaScript tests.

Building and saving tests is really important, but editing and debugging is where you can waste a lot of time. Windmill allows you to load tests back into the Windmill IDE with the loadtest command-line parameter (Example 21-3). This will build each action but not execute it, so that you can walk through them one at a time to see which actions are failing and why.

The last major piece we tackled was the ability to run in continuous integration, which like most engineering challenges turned out to be more complicated than we had expected. The requirements included starting and stopping browsers reliably, returning the correct error codes from the test runs, and providing features to stop test runs in their tracks when there was a problem.

Knowing that a test is failing is significantly less useful than knowing why, and over time the reporting features have become more complete, and so has the stability of the code used for browser launching. Currently Windmill is being run with Buildbot and Hudson, and has thorough documentation on how to get this set up.

The Cosmo Web User Interface is rich with drag-and-drop functionality, allowing a user to manipulate her schedule, which made for one of the most beautiful web demos I have ever seen. Fortunately this beauty was enough to earn more time dedicated to working on Windmill, which gave our QA effort many more hands touching the application and resulted in many logged and fixed bugs. Part of that dedicated time allowed for some cycles spent fixing many of the community bugs found in Windmill and writing documentation.

EXAMPLE 21-1. Example of the Python test syntax

```
# Generated by the windmill services transformer
from windmill.authoring import WindmillTestClient

def test_googletest():
        client = WindmillTestClient(__name__)

        client.click(name=u'q')
        client.type(text=u'test', name=u'q')
        client.click(name=u'btnG')
        client.waits.forPageLoad(timeout=u'20000')
        client.waits.forElement(link=u'Test.com Web Based Testing', timeout=u'8000')
        client.click(link=u'Test.com Web Based Testing')
        client.waits.forPageLoad(timeout=u'20000')
```

EXAMPLE 21-2. Example of the JavaScript test syntax

```
// Generated by the windmill services transformer
var test_googletest = new function() {
    this.test_actions = [
        {"params": {"name": "q"}, "method": "click"},
        {"params": {"text": "test", "name": "q"}, "method": "type"},
        {"params": {"name": "btnG"}, "method": "click"},
        {"params": {"timeout": "20000"}, "method": "waits.forPageLoad"},
        {"params": {"link": "Test.com Web Based Testing", "timeout": "8000"},
        "method": "waits.forElement"},
        {"params": {"link": "Test.com Web Based Testing"}, "method": "click"},
        {"params": {"timeout": "20000"}, "method": "waits.forPageLoad"}
    ];
}
```

Running Tests

Windmill provides a command-line interface (CLI) that is used to load, run, and debug your tests. It also has a shell that can be used for debugging and allows for more interaction between Python and JavaScript (Figure 21-5). Windmill also provides the ability to debug from PDB (Python Debugger), if you're looking to go more in-depth.

FIGURE 21-5. Windmill shell snapshot

Python and JavaScript tests can be run two ways from the command line. The first is directly via command-line arguments, and the second is from the Windmill shell. The command line (Examples 21-3 and 21-5) is great for quickly firing off a test run, and is used more commonly for day-to-day test running and continuous integration (CI). The shell mode (Examples 21-4 and 21-6) is very useful for debugging, allowing you to directly access the functions inside of Windmill that run and load tests.

As the tests became more complex, we realized the dire need for a setup and teardown hierarchy. When you have an application that requires you to authenticate and then log out when you are finished, manually repeating this becomes difficult to maintain.

EXAMPLE 21-3. Example of running and loading Python tests from the CLI

```
Running: windmill 'browser' 'url' test=test_file.py (or a directory)
Loading: windmill 'browser' 'url' loadtest=test_file.py (or a directory)

Ex. windmill firefox http://www.google.com test=test_googlesearch.py
```

EXAMPLE 21-4. Example of running and loading Python tests from the shell

```
windmill shell 'browser' 'url'

Running: At the prompt, In [1]: run_test('path/to/test_file.py')
Loading: At the prompt, In [1]: load_test('path/to/test_file.py')
```

JavaScript tests are run as a directory hierarchy, so you are going to want to create a directory and put all of your saved JavaScript tests in it. These can both be run either from the CLI (Example 21-5) or from the Windmill shell (Example 21-6). Additionally, there are optional CLI arguments for JavaScript tests, which include jsfilter and jsphase. These can be used to specify subsets of test functions in the directory files to run.

EXAMPLE 21-5. Example of running JavaScript tests from the CLI

```
windmill 'browser' 'url' jsdir=js_tests_dir
ex. windmill firefox http://www.google.com jsdir=js_tests_dir
```

EXAMPLE 21-6. Example of running JavaScript tests from the shell

```
windmill shell 'browser' 'url'
Running: At prompt, In [1]: run_js_tests('/path/to/js_tests_dir')
```

Debugging Test

Windmill's most prominent debugging feature is the ability to execute Windmill actions directly from the shell; this allows you to control your browser without even touching it (Example 21-7).

EXAMPLE 21-7. Example shell session interacting with the browser

```
zsh% windmill shell firefox http://www.google.com
(Start the Windmill server in shell mode)
Started ['/Applications/Firefox.app/Contents/MacOS/firefox-bin', '-profile',
'/var/folders/YO/YOAvf2hSGtO+VnBIAKuImE+++TM/-Tmp-/tmpyOxq6y.mozrunner',
'http://www.google.com/windmill-serv/start.html']
(Windmill output telling you what was launched and from where)
In [1]: from windmill.authoring import WindmillTestClient
(Import the Windmill Test Client)
In [2]: client = WindmillTestClient(__name__)
(Access the Windmill client)
In [3]: client.click(name=u"q")
(Click on a DOM node in the browser with a name attribute of "q")
Out[3]: {u'endtime': u'2009-3-9T18:1:3.813Z',
 u'method': u'click',
 u'output': None,
 u'params': {u'name': u'q', u'uuid': u'101d4630-256b-11de-b49f-002332da2796'},
 u'result': True,
 u'starttime': u'2009-3-9T18:1:3.811Z',
 u'suite_name': u'windmill.bin.shell_objects',
 u'version': u'0.1'}
(All of the output associated with the click action)
```

In addition to the debugging features, Windmill also has some client-side features built in for debugging the Document Object Model (DOM) and JavaScript.

Firebug Lite

Firebug Lite is integrated into the Windmill IDE. It provides much of the same functionality found in the Firebug Firefox plug-in and is available on all of the browsers, in both your testing window and the Windmill IDE. The main goal of Firebug is to allow you to interact with any part of the web application at any time. This includes a DOM inspector, a JavaScript console, and the following views: HTML, CSS, Script, DOM, XML HTTP Request (XHR). See Figure 21-6.

FIGURE 21-6. Firebug Lite user interface

LookupNode

Using the Firebug Lite console, you can use built-in Windmill functionality for searching through the DOM for nodes. One of the most useful methods is lookupNode, because it will do a cross-window, frame, and iframe lookup of a locator to find a node (Example 21-8). LookupNode works by taking many different "locators" or ways of matching DOM node properties in order to help you find the one you are looking for. The simplest use case is ID, but it also searches by attributes, XPath, jQuery selector, and more.

EXAMPLE 21-8. Example session locating nodes with lookupNode

```
>>> lookupNode({name:'q'})
<input value="" title="Google Search" size="55" name="q" maxlength="2048" autocomplete="off">
>>> lookupNode({name:'q'}).name
"q"
>>> lookupNode({name:'q'}).parentNode
<td nowrap="" align="center">
//testing xpath lookup
>>> lookupNode({xpath:"/html/body/center/form/table[1]/tbody/tr/td[2]/input[2]"})
<input value="" title="Google Search" size="55" name="q" maxlength="2048" autocomplete="off">
```

The Project

Windmill is open source and freely available at *http://www.getwindmill.com*. The mailing list is used heavily for decision making, answering questions, and keeping the community up-to-date. Although the mailing list is very effective, the IRC channel is a constant flow of project chatter, and is a great way to get your questions answered quickly.

As the need for the ability to test web applications grows, the community and these tools will only get stronger. Windmill has made its bet on the JavaScript platform to continue running the Web, and the principals of open source to influence the direction of new features. The documentation has proven to be very comprehensive, and the community responsive.

Comparison

There are many solutions out there for testing web applications in the browser: Watir, Selenium, Twill, and WebDriver, to name a few. Although they all have strengths and weaknesses, Windmill clearly has some very useful features, and appears to have the least barriers to entry for new test writers, regardless of the platform or browser they need to test on.

Windmill boasts a recorder, integrated Firebug Lite, integrated inspector, and support for cross-domain and SSL testing. However, unlike Watir, Windmill operates within the content security model, which means that it can't access some parts of the browser, such as the confirmation dialog or file uploads. But Windmill has come up with a solution or workaround for many of these challenges.

Selenium boasts the GRID project, which allows for distributed tests running across many machines. Windmill has yet to come up with a comparable solution, but with test runtimes being such an important factor with large sets of tests, it's being factored into the roadmap.

Other projects such Twill can provide much faster test runtimes, and in many ways more humanly readable test syntax. However, these frameworks lack the ability to test applications that heavily use JavaScript, limiting the scope of their utility. If you find yourself testing an application that doesn't use any JavaScript and you don't worry about cross-browser bugs, you will probably find the test running experience much more enjoyable in a tool such as Twill.

Conclusions

Now that you have been introduced to the vast utility of Windmill, as well as its strengths, weaknesses, and competition, it's time for you to start testing! As web applications become exceedingly more commonplace, the need for testing grows, and so does the importance of the testing community.

It's hard to describe exactly why test automation is beautiful, because there are so many layers of technology involved in making it work. From the Python code talking to the browsers, to the JavaScript firing and capturing events against the DOM, each piece has its own complexity and elegance. Alone, each of these pieces isn't that impressive, but as soon as they are combined into a fluid system, they create an amazing amount of utility. In the ability to make a computer simulate a person, I see an unmistakable amount of beauty.

As soon as your automated test cases start finding bugs for you, it will be hard for you not to see the beauty in automated testing of the Web.

References

Gift, N. 2009. "Functional testing for Web applications: Using Selenium, Windmill, and twill to test Google App Engine applications." *http://www.ibm.com/developerworks/library/wa-aj -testing/.*

Jaffamonkey blog. "Windmill Testing Framework." *http://www.jaffamonkey.co.uk/2009/03/12/ windmill-testing-framework/.*

Selenium Core, *http://seleniumhq.org/projects/core/.*

Windmill Developers Google group, *http://groups.google.com/group/windmill-dev.*

Windmill Testing Framework, *http://www.getwindmill.com/* and *http://trac.getwindmill.com/.*

## CHAPTER TWENTY-TWO

Testing One Million Web Pages

Tim Riley

BEAUTY IS SEEING DISPARATE AND ROUGH TEST TOOLS come together at the right time to create a special testing capability. In this chapter's case, the test tools were originally developed six years ago when the Mozilla Project (where I am director of quality assurance) was a very different organization. These tools morphed from simple web *spidering*[1] tools to assertion and crash testers for a hundred web pages to an automated framework for testing one million web pages!

The resultant combined framework was needed to test a huge number of web pages in a very flexible way. This included testing on different operating systems, on different build types (e.g., standard and debug), across hangs and crashes, with highly selectable page sets.

It took the work of multiple people to innovate and collaborate to create interesting new tools along the way. These people built up tools, one upon another. The result was an amazing framework that can collect the top websites into sets. These can be 100 pages, 10,000 pages, or a million-plus pages. They can be the top pages across the world or the top shopping sites in Albania. And they can be tested using standard, debug, or optimized builds. The framework can test any combination of these that your mind can imagine or your test farm can handle.

What follows is the story of how the tools were refactored and morphed to test one million web pages.

---

1. Spidering refers to finding links on a web page and following those links to their respective web pages. This can be done recursively to any desired "depth" of follow-on links. The analogy is traversing a spider web of links.

In the Beginning...

...our small Mozilla Project team needed to verify if, and how often, web page elements such as HTML tags or DOM elements were used. To meet this need, we created the Spider tool[2] to walk through web pages and check for certain tags or elements. It did this checking in a modular way that allowed for quick addition or swapping of "user hooks" to add various test and analysis capabilities. We've made slight enhancements and added new user hooks over time, but the spidering part has generally remained the same.

The core of the Spider tool is this:

```
while (this.mCurrentUrl != null && !isGoodUrl)
{
    var href = this.mCurrentUrl.mUrl;
    var lhref = href.toLowerCase();

    if (this.mCurrentUrl.mDepth > this.mDepth)
    {
        dlog('CSpider.loadPage ignoring ' + this.mCurrentUrl.mUrl +
            ' mCurrentUrl.mDepth > ' + this.mCurrentUrl.mDepth+
            ' CSpider.mDepth ' + this.mDepth);
        this.mCurrentUrl = this.mPagesPending.pop();
    }
    elseif (        lhref.search(/\.aac$/) != -1 ||
        lhref.search(/\.ads$/) != -1 ||
        lhref.search(/\.adp$/) != -1 ||
        lhref.search(/\.app$/) != -1 ||
        ...
        lhref.search(/\.xls$/) != -1 ||
        lhref.search(/\.xpi$/) != -1 ||
        lhref.search(/\.zip$/) != -1
    )
    {
        dlog('CSpider.loadPage Bad Extension blocked ' + href);
        this.mCurrentUrl = this.mPagesPending.pop();
    }
    else if (this.mRespectRobotRules && isRobotBlocked(href, this.mUserAgent))
    {
        msg('CSpider.loadPage Robot Rules blocked ' + href);
        this.mCurrentUrl = this.mPagesPending.pop();
    }
    else
    {
        isGoodUrl= true;
    }
```

You can find the Spider tool extension at *http://bclary.com/projects/spider/spider/spider.xpi*.

Jump ahead three years. Our team was frustrated having to run JavaScript tests over and over again. Whenever we hoped to start focusing on new projects and new test development, we

2. Info about the Spider tool can be found here: *http://bclary.com/projects/spider/*.

would be called on to rerun the JavaScript tests that were semi-automated. So we decided to use the Spider tool to automate the JavaScript tests. We made a new JavaScript-based framework, which we called Sisyphus. (The name seemed appropriate because it refers to a Greek myth about a king cursed to roll a boulder up a hill over and over again.[3]) Spider was (and is) an essential part of the Sisyphus test framework for browser-based tests. It allowed the JavaScript tests to be run recursively across a large number of real-life web pages. Thanks to Sisyphus, we no longer needed to be on call to run JavaScript tests when significant changes were made or release regression testing was done. Life was good!

At that point, we had a diamond of a test tool that no one knew about. We ran Sisyphus by ourselves. The tests ran on a "magical box" that was specially configured for this testing. No one else knew how to run it or took the initiative to learn it. The next step for it would require someone else looking to solve other problems, finding a broader use for this tool, and bringing it out into the light.

Fast-forward six months to December 2008. We were using a tool that would load a predefined list of URLs to test. This tool was able to test about 500 web pages, but it didn't scale up from there, because the list had to be predefined. The purpose of this tool was to load the pages in Firefox and check for crashes and assertions. Memory leaks, assertions, and crashes were all recorded into a big logfile. Crashes were indicated via the exit status that was output into the log for each crashing top site. The following is a logfile example:

```
2009-04-25-14-41-02+0200,firefox,1.9.1,debug,darwin,tomcat2.local,
tests_mozilla.org_top-sites.log.
```

With text editor tools or commands such as grep, we could search the logs for crashes (shown in the exit status), etc.

This tool was a very simple command-line tool. We had used it for only one release test cycle, and we knew it had the potential to do more. We needed a way to generate and manage larger lists of URLs—several orders of magnitude larger!

Another nagging issue was that we had problems with interaction between Firefox rendering web pages and Firefox extensions. How could we load extensions so that they were in the mix?

The Tools Merge and Evolve

So we were looking for a mash-up with characteristics that would:

- Generate custom sets of URLs to test up to one million URLs using a URL list from *alexa.com*

---

3. Sisyphus was a king in Greek mythology punished in Tartarus with the curse of rolling a huge boulder up a hill, only to watch it roll back down, and then repeating this throughout eternity (see *http://wikipedia.org/wiki/Sisyphus*). Note how this curse relates to running semi-manual test cases over and over again. Sisyphus tool installation, usage, and script reference information can be found at *https://wiki.mozilla.org/Sisyphus*.

- Manage those large sets of URLs in the context of the test framework (Spider)
- Launch a selected version of Firefox, open a page, collect memory leak and assertion information, and then quit Firefox (Sisyphus)
- Load extensions (Sisyphus)
- Continue across crashes (Sisyphus)
- In addition to launching web pages, spider through their links for more rigorous testing (Spider)

We could pull the URLs from a site such as *alexa.com*. At first we only knew about Alexa's top-100 or top-500 URL lists. During a meeting we played with this idea and looked around the Alexa site (must have been a boring meeting). We discovered it had a *top-million* link.[4] Why stop at 50,000 or 100,000 websites? Now we were able to download large lists of top URLs, and we could scale our tests to 1,000, 50,000, or 1,000,000 sites! We could also create custom sets of sites.

We downloaded the Top 1,000,000 Sites list from Alexa (*http://s3.amazonaws.com/alexa-static/top-1m.csv.zip*) and converted the list into a format that the test script would understand (just a simple *.txt* file with a URL in the form of *http://example.com* on each line). This was very flexible, and we could add as many URLs as we liked.

We had a database as part of the Spider tool. This database could track URLs and related information more effectively and in a more flexible way. It could easily expand to 50,000 or more predefined URLs. We linked it with the Spider tool and the top-500 sites framework, and tried it out. It worked great!

When we first tried to scale the tests, we simply wanted to find a better way of running the leak tests. We needed something that would start Firefox, load a website, and then quit Firefox. Running a debug build provided the functionally to collect memory leak and assertion information, and to continue testing even if Firefox crashed. We wondered how to save a logfile. It turned out there was a preference to have leak data piped into a logfile. The next challenge was to be able to run this with different versions of Firefox. We had a special TraceMonkey build (TraceMonkey adds native-code compilation to Mozilla's JavaScript engine) along with trunk, 3.0, and 3.5 builds. We were able to easily bolt this onto Sisyphus.

We started running the automated JavaScript tests with Sisyphus. While browsing though the harness code, we discovered by accident that Sisyphus could load extensions. We thought this capability could be used more actively. If it could load the Spider extension automatically, then it could load any extension automatically. Initially we thought of Firebug, but it could be any extension. This got us thinking about extension testing. We had had some problems with people thinking that Firefox was leaking badly, and frequently the problem turned out to be extensions leaking. Firefox wasn't innocent of leaks, but we had come a long way in Firefox

4. See the "Free Download Top 1,000,000 Sites (Updated Daily)" link at *http://alexa.com/topsites*.

3.0 and 3.5 in cleaning this up. Consequently, the most likely source of leaks had dramatically shifted from Firefox itself to extensions.

At that point in time, Sisyphus just ran a list of URLs and could spider them to any depth desired. We added onto this the ability to automatically grab top sites from the Alexa list and collect leak-testing data.

For memory leaks,[5] we get an output in the logfile combined with the site URL, like this:

```
nsTraceRefcntImpl::DumpStatistics: 701 entries
nsStringStats
 => mAllocCount:         14412
 => mReallocCount:        1458
 => mFreeCount:          14256  -- LEAKED 156 !!!
 => mShareCount:          9327
 => mAdoptCount:          1150
 => mAdoptFreeCount:      1147  -- LEAKED 3 !!!
```

For assertions, we get something like the following:

```
###!!! ASSERTION: nsWyciwygChannel::GetOriginalURI - mOriginalURI not set! :
'mOriginalURI != mURI', file c:/work/mozilla/builds/1.9.1-trace-malloc/mozilla/
content/html/document/src/nsWyciwygChannel.cpp, line 182
```

Also, after every tested URL, an exit status is printed into the logfile. With this exit status we can see whether the test run crashed on a specific URL or passed (no crash).

For example, this:

```
http://www.cnn.com: EXIT STATUS: NORMAL (9.594268 seconds)
```

indicates with a NORMAL exit status that everything was fine (no crash), whereas this:

```
Assertion failure: !rt->gcRunning, at /work/mozilla/builds/1.9.1/mozilla/js/
src/jsgc.cpp:1873 http://www.download.com: EXIT STATUS: CRASHED signal 5 SIGTRAP
(100.560452 seconds)
```

shows a CRASHED exit status (this would be ABNORMAL on Windows), which indicates an assertion failure or crash. For the debug code that generates the various error and warning messages, see *http://mxr.mozilla.org/mozilla-central/source/xpcom/base/nsDebugImpl.cpp#254*.

The Nitty-Gritty

OK, so enough about the history. How does it work? Sisyphus doesn't install Firefox, but instead can launch any specific previously installed version of Firefox. This is good, in a way, as it allows you to easily substitute custom builds, such as special patched builds or debug builds. Still, it would be cool to just point at an installable binary and say, "Go!"—just pick your build, install it, and start throwing websites at it. Currently, the sequence is: pick an installed Firefox

---

5. See "Testing Extensions and Firefox for Memory Leaks with a Debug Build" at *https://wiki.mozilla.org/ MozillaQualityAssurance:Home_Page:Firefox_3.0_TestPlan:Leaks:LeakTesting-How-To* and "Debugging memory leaks" at *https://developer.mozilla.org/En/Debugging_memory_leaks*.

build, launch Firefox, install extensions, run the tests, exit Firefox, and repeat, a million times if you like.

The command line looks like this:

```
./tester.sh -t "$TEST_DIR/tests/mozilla.org/top-sites/test.sh \
-s $TEST_DIR/tests/mozilla.org/top-sites/global1000.txt -D 0 -r" \
firefox 1.9.1-tracemonkey debug

-t = which tests to run
-s = file containing URLs to test with
-D is how deep to spider (0 = just load the current URL)
-r = which revision of Firefox to test
```

The following are some key environment variables:

- `XPCOM_DEBUG_BREAK`=stack (capture the stack with assertions)
- `XPCOM_MEM_LOG`=1 (log leak data)

This is very flexible. We can focus on assertion testing, memory-leak testing, or whatever is most important to investigate at the time. Also, these are platform variables, so they also apply to Thunderbird, SeaMonkey, etc.

This tool allows us to load thousands of websites without having to enter them manually into the URL bar. (We actually used to do that quite a bit!) It also allows us to test websites for different locales without having to know anything about the language or culture. Keep in mind that this is not a functional test; we are not trying to QA the page for the site's developers. Testing that a web page is functionally correct is a different issue and has entire books dedicated to its treatment. We are just looking for the basic ability of Firefox to deal with all the crazy JavaScript, HTML, and CSS out there and load these pages. Does JavaScript throw any exceptions? Is the page causing memory leaks? Does it cause the browser to crash?

Some of these test sets take a long time to run. The million-URL list takes months. We call these the "long haul" tests. It may seem crazy to have a test take months, but we are still developing these tools and will consider optimizing the duration and the frequency of these tests soon. We have some issues with testing live websites too frequently and looking like a malicious bot. But that is another story.

One challenge we have encountered is that major breakages on active branches are naturally found and fixed quickly. So we don't want to take a month to find bugs only to discover that they were already found and fixed by our community. The TraceMonkey branch is an example of how we have addressed this, so the long-haul tests are saved for the maintenance branch (Firefox 3.0 as of this writing). We also have a 150,000-URL set that takes three to four weeks to run. We use the 1,000-URL set for the active branches; it takes about four hours, and we can get results daily. This is part of our automated constant-integration testing.

So, what happens when we find a crash?

The first thing we do is capture the page and save it locally. Web pages change frequently, so depending on a live page is too risky. Once it is captured, we have to reproduce the test, which can get a little labor-intensive. If it is reproducible, we have won most of the battle.

The next step is to reduce it down to its simplest form. A lot happens in a complete web page. The offending code needs to be isolated or a developer will have to spend an inordinate amount of time poring over code. The good news is that we have a tool for this, too, called Lithium.[6] It automatically reduces a failing web page down to a simpler test case. This tool was originally developed to take web pages found to crash by various fuzzers, including the jsfunfuzz[7] tool. Yet another example of repurposing in a beautiful way! With this tool, we can often reduce a web page from 3,000 lines to maybe 5–10 lines.

Summary

One thing to note about the original Spider tool: I consider it beautiful, but not because it was well-designed and elegant. It was not pretty, and the developer was hesitant to show it to others. But it was a workhorse. It was designed to solve a very specific problem in a very practical, reusable, and flexible way. It was *built to be used*. Like a beautiful Clydesdale or a well-worn tool, it has a natural beauty.

It is intriguing to see how these tools evolved, were discovered, and then were combined from the first simple Spider tool to a tool that can test a million websites, survive crashes, and keep testing to various depths on the Web. I find it fascinating how a tool used by one person for one reason can explode into a handy tool for many people to use for many purposes.

As tools become more visible, people use them in new ways and the tools evolve. Testing becomes more automated and flexible. A person's private "magical box" is less exclusive as the tools get more exposure.

It is a beautiful thing when this happens.

Acknowledgments

I'd like to express special thanks to Carsten Book (aka Tomcat) and Bob Clary for their technical assistance providing details for this chapter.

6. See *http://www.squarefree.com/2007/09/15/introducing-lithium-a-testcase-reduction-tool/* for more information about reducing troublesome web pages to reduced test cases. Also see *http://www .squarefree.com/2009/01/11/reducing-real-world-scripts/*.

7. *http://www.squarefree.com/2007/08/02/introducing-jsfunfuzz/*

## CHAPTER TWENTY-THREE

Testing Network Services in Multimachine Scenarios

Isaac Clerencia

The Need for an Advanced Testing Tool in eBox

WE HAD BEEN DEVELOPING eBox (*http://ebox-platform.com/*) for a bit over a year when we started to struggle to get new releases out. The main problem we faced every time we had to release a new version was the testing and quality assurance (QA) process, which had quickly become the lengthiest and most dreaded task among eBox developers, although it did face tight competition from documentation writing in that honor.

The eBox platform is a complex open source web tool to manage corporate networks. It integrates some homegrown services, such as network configuration, a firewall, or traffic shaping, and well-known existing services such as Squid, Samba, or OpenLDAP. It is released as a set of independent modules that have to be thoroughly tested to prevent regressions and to verify that every new feature works as expected.

Even though eBox just offers a simplified interface to these services, the number of test cases still grew overwhelmingly fast as new modules were added and existing ones got more features that required new tests.

Another problem we faced was the complexity of the scenarios required to perform the tests. In the beginning, most modules needed quite simple scenarios, such as the proxy one, which only required two machines, one client to try to browse from, and the proxy server managed by eBox that we wanted to test.

Later in the development process, new modules requiring far more complex scenarios, such as the OpenVPN module, started to appear. This module can be used to connect different offices or to allow road warriors to connect to a central office. To test the functionality of the module in certain setups, up to six machines may be needed. The tester not only had to install all these machines, but also had to configure each one of them for its particular role.

This configuration process was not only lengthy but also error-prone, as it required a lot of human intervention, including writing configuration files and setting up eBox through the web interface. Once the scenario is set up, determining whether the test has been successful is not a trivial task either. Appropriate tools have to be used for some modules, such as the traffic shaping one, to determine the outcome of the test.

To add to all these problems, eBox needs to be tested in several Ubuntu Linux and Debian GNU/Linux releases. Even if eBox is mainly targeted at the latest Ubuntu LTS (long-term support) release, we also release packages for the latest Ubuntu regular release and the latest Debian release to try to grow our user base. In addition, while making sure that all these releases work correctly, we have to start testing packages for the upcoming releases, to make sure our packages are ready as soon as the new releases are out. All of this adds up to a total of five different operating systems that we have to run tests for at a certain point.

The last problem is due to the fact that even if most members of the eBox team are in Spain, a few of them live in other countries. This makes it very difficult to have the required testing infrastructure in each of the different locations. Because of this, the ability to remotely schedule tests was an important requirement.

It can be argued that it is relatively easy to address some of these problems partially, for example, using virtual machines with predefined images to ease machine installation or writing scripts to automate configuration tasks. But even with these improvements, testing eBox would still have been a tiresome task. We wanted to aim for a beautiful solution that saved humans from having to do any daunting, repetitive task.

Development of ANSTE to Improve the eBox QA Process

We had decided to try to achieve full automatization for our tests. After a disappointing search for an existing solution for this problem, we set out to develop our own open source (*http://opensource.org*) testing suite. The new product had to be strongly focused on our requirements, but we also wanted to keep it flexible enough so that it could be used to enhance the testing process of other software projects.

The set of requirements was very well defined, as we had been manually testing eBox for a long time by then and were fully aware of all the pitfalls in our testing process. Based on the extensive list of requirements, we were expecting a long development process. Fortunately, building it on top of other open source software allowed us to speed up the process considerably, and after just three months of frenzied development by only one person, we had a tool that we could already use in our testing efforts. We named it Advanced Network Service Testing Environment, or ANSTE (*http://public.warp.es/anste/*).

The first feature developed in ANSTE was the ability to easily define complex network scenarios. Scenarios have the information about all the machines that will have to be created for a given test suite. The information for each machine includes basic details such as the amount of memory and hard disk space the machine will have and its hostname, but also more complex information, such as the number of network interfaces and their configuration, as well as the routing rules to reach other networks.

Defining the details for every machine in every scenario would be a daunting task, and in addition, building operating system images is a long process that takes a lot of memory and disk space. Thus, in order to avoid having to build images more often than strictly needed, the scenario framework supports inheritance for machine definitions, allowing the user to define as many base images as needed and that hosts can later inherit from.

A base image definition includes a name to refer to the image and an installation method. A program called *debootstrap* is used to install Debian-based distributions. This program is able to install a basic system on an empty disk, pulling the required packages from Internet mirrors and installing them in the new system. This installation method requires only one parameter: the name of the distribution to be installed.

Base images can be reused in different scenarios with just minor changes. Every machine in a scenario declares which base image to use, and then, if changes are required in the image, it specifies the values of the parameters that need to be different. Besides the network configuration, one of the most important parameters for customizing a machine is the one containing the software packages desired for that machine. As many as needed can be specified, and they will be installed on it using the system package manager once the machine has been set up.

ANSTE cannot provide a parameter for every minor detail that could be potentially configured in the installed operating system, so in order to allow further customization of the machines, scripts can be declared and will be run before and after performing the package installation.

These network scenarios will be automatically deployed when a test suite needs them. Scenarios are transformed into a number of configuration files for libvirt and a set of scripts that will be run at the right time. libvirt is a library developed by Red Hat that can interface easily with the different emerging virtualization systems. By using libvirt in ANSTE, different backends, such as KVM or Xen, can be used.

For every machine declared, a virtual machine is created and started using the preferred virtualization system, trying to replicate as closely as possible a real scenario, including the network links between machines. ANSTE is smart enough to put virtual machines in different virtual bridges to simulate the physical separation between the machines. This actually allows

ANSTE to work correctly with daemons that rely on broadcasting packets over the network, such as DHCP or Samba.

Once a scenario is correctly designed, it is possible to start running tests on it. In order to do that, test suites are defined. Test suites are simply files containing a set of tests that will be run sequentially on the same instance of a scenario. Running a few test suites at once is a common task, so a suite file can be used to aggregate several of them.

It is worth noticing that not all the tests in a suite are tests as such; some of them rather have a utility nature. The reason for this is that some individual tests may require certain preconfiguration before they are actually run. This configuration is usually performed using other tests, which could be seen as simple scripts. It could be argued that a test that requires the preconfiguration could do it by itself, but it is quite usual that the same configuration steps are required by different tests, so insulating them in a different script allows further reusability.

The tests in a test suite define several parameters. These include the machine where they will be executed and a directory containing the actual test. These directories can contain two types of tests, command-based and Selenium-based, which can and often will be mixed freely in a suite.

The first kind of tests, command-based ones, merely execute a command named `test`, which should be in the provided directory. If the command returns zero, the test is considered successfully passed; otherwise, it is considered to have failed. The use cases for these tests are really varied. For example, they can be used to modify configuration text files, restart involved daemons, or run any other command to make a functionality check.

Selenium-based tests use a web application testing framework called Selenium (*http:// seleniumhq.org/*). This framework is used to perform configuration steps using the web interface and to check the results of these actions. The main advantage of using Selenium is that it makes the tests not only cover the program logic but also the web interface.

Selenium tests are written in Selenese, a language that makes use of HTML tables to define a sequence of actions to run. A file named *suite.html* in the test directory is read first, and it declares in Selenese the rest of the files that are part of the test. These other files contain actions such as opening a given URL, clicking on a link, filling and sending a form, or checking whether a particular string exists in the response.

Network testing frameworks always have to deal with the problem of synchronization between the different machines. For example, most scenarios will involve at least one machine having to wait until another one is ready. Other frameworks opt for complex solutions, usually sending the jobs to every machine in parallel and then relying on synchronization primitives to coordinate the execution in the different machines. eBox goes for the simplest option: running the tests sequentially, with a master (the host machine) explicitly telling each machine when it should run each test.

When machines are deployed in a scenario, they notify their availability to the master, which will not start running tests until all of them have been successfully started. If it is important to make sure that a certain action has taken place in a machine before the master is notified, a post-install script can be defined that should wait and check whether such an action has already occurred.

As tests are run in a serialized manner, if we want two actions to be run in parallel, we have to write tests to launch processes asynchronously and leave them running in the background. Then it is the responsibility of the test writer to stop these processes when they are no longer needed, writing another test for that task.

Once the tests are ready, they can be scheduled to be run and ANSTE will notify the tester when they have finished. A full report is made available through a web interface. The report includes all the information that the developer may need to check the outcome of the tests. First of all, the result of every test is provided. In addition, it also has the output logs for all the scripts that were run during the test and a video recording of the browser for the tests that failed.

How eBox Uses ANSTE

Once ANSTE was ready, the next step was to introduce it into our testing process. A machine powerful enough to deploy even the largest scenarios was purchased, and ANSTE was installed on it.

Module developers started to write ANSTE tests for every feature that needed to be checked. Initially the tests were run only when new beta releases of a module came out, but soon developers wanted to take advantage of ANSTE to do preliminary tests as soon as they developed new features.

In the beginning, a first-come, first-served approach was taken, but it was soon obvious that it was not an optimal solution. Developers had to coordinate manually to share the access to the machine and check whether someone else was running tests at the moment.

To address this problem, a scheduling daemon was developed. Testing jobs can be submitted to this daemon by ANSTE users. Each job has a priority, which allows the scheduler to run them in the appropriate order. Users have different maximum priorities, so the release manager can schedule jobs with a higher priority than regular developers, as well as change the priority of any scheduled test. The scheduler might run some jobs out of order to try to optimize the use of resources. For example, if a test is being run and there is only one job in the queue that has a memory footprint small enough to allow it to be run at the same time, such a job will be processed immediately, regardless of its position in the queue.

When a job is scheduled, the user receives the URL of an RSS feed that can be used to keep track of the test results. In addition, the user can provide an email address and, once all the tests are finished, a notification will be sent to that address.

At the moment, there are 455 tests covering almost every feature in most modules. The whole suite of tests takes around three hours to be run with our current equipment.

ANSTE has been specially useful when merging large framework changes that affected every module. These kinds of merges are very likely to cause unexpected regressions that were very difficult to find in the past. Now almost every regression is immediately detected by the testing framework without any human effort.

Sample ANSTE Tests for eBox

The first example is a test from the proxy module.

The eBox machine acts as a router between the client and the gateway. The test is supposed to check whether the proxy service is configured properly, allowing the client to browse the Internet through the proxy.

The scenario is defined in a file called *proxy.xml*, which includes the machines required for the test. First of all, the router connecting the rest of the machines to the Internet is declared:

```
<host type="router">
    <name>router</name>
    <desc>Internet Router</desc>
    <baseimage>hardy-mini</baseimage>
    <network>
        <interface type="static">
            <name>eth1</name>
            <address>192.168.3.254</address>
            <netmask>255.255.255.0</netmask>
        </interface>
    </network>
</host>
```

A host of type router provides the rest of the machines with a connection to the Internet, setting up a network interface and the necessary parameters to provide the connection. A scenario without a host of type router will not have access to the Internet. The router uses a base image called hardy-mini, which contains a minimal Linux system using Ubuntu Hardy. Another network interface is added so that other machines in the scenario can connect to the router. In this case, just the eBox machine, which is described as follows, will be connected:

```
<host>
    <name>ebox-server</name>
    <desc>eBox server</desc>
    <baseimage>{$dist}-ebox-base</baseimage>
    <network>
        <interface type="static">
            <name>eth1</name>
            <address>192.168.2.1</address>
            <netmask>255.255.255.0</netmask>
        </interface>
        <interface type="static">
            <name>eth2</name>
```

```
                <address>192.168.3.1</address>
                <netmask>255.255.255.0</netmask>
                <gateway>192.168.3.254</gateway>
            </interface>
        </network>

        <post-install>
            <script>ebox-import-network.sh</script>
            <script>ebox-wait-start.sh</script>
        </post-install>
    </host>
```

Variables can be used in the XML scenario definition, as can be observed in the baseimage declaration. It uses the variable dist so the test can be used without any modifications for every supported distribution.

The eBox base image contains a complete and fresh installation of eBox. These base images are generated once and then copied as many times as needed. The images are always stored in a RAM disk to speed up the process.

Two static network interfaces are set up, and then the post-installation scripts are used to import the network configuration into eBox and to ensure that the testing process does not continue until eBox has been successfully started and is running correctly.

The only machine left to be defined in our scenario is the client that will try to browse through the eBox proxy, declared as follows:

```
    <host>
        <name>test-client</name>
        <desc>simple client host</desc>
        <baseimage>hardy-mini</baseimage>

        <network>
         <interface type="static">
            <name>eth1</name>
            <address>192.168.2.2</address>
            <netmask>255.255.255.0</netmask>
            <!-- ebox is the gateway -->
            <gateway>192.168.2.1</gateway>
         </interface>
        </network>

        <packages>
            <package>wget</package>
            <package>netcat</package>
        </packages>
    </host>
```

The hardy-mini image is used again for the browsing client. The machine is configured to use the eBox previously set up as gateway. This way, the HTTP requests made by the browser will go through the proxy.

Two extra packages are required to perform the tests in this scenario, wget and netcat. They are marked for installation in the packages section. This way, they will be available for the test scripts later.

The scenario file is ready now, and it can finally be used in the proxy test suite. This suite is declared in another XML file, which defines the name of the suite, a description, and the scenario to be used:

```
<suite>
    <name>eBox Proxy tests</name>
    <desc>
    Contains a set of tests to check
    that the eBox HTTP Proxy module works properly.
    </desc>

    <scenario>ebox/proxy.xml</scenario>

    ...
```

After these fields, the tests follow. The first ones are not functionality tests, but instead Selenium scripts to set up eBox through the web interface, although they also serve the purpose of testing the correctness of the web interface. For example:

```
<test type="selenium">
    <name>EnableModules</name>
    <desc>
    Enable network and firewall modules.
    </desc>

    <host>ebox-server</host>
    <dir>enable-modules</dir>
</test>
```

The *EnableModules* script enables the required modules in the eBox server. Enabling modules is a very common task, so there are scripts to enable each of the different modules that are shared along all the tests and then included as needed. These scripts programatically click on the appropriate interface links and buttons and wait until the actions are finished. The file *enable-proxy.html* contains a Selenium script to activate the proxy module:

```
<tr>
    <td>open</td>
    <td>/ebox/Summary/Index</td>
    <td></td>
</tr>
<tr>
    <td>click</td>
    <td>link=Module status</td>
    <td></td>
</tr>
<tr>
    <td>waitForElementPresent</td>
    <td>squid</td>
    <td></td>
```

```
    </tr>
    <tr>
        <td>click</td>
        <td>squid</td>
        <td></td>
    </tr>
    <tr>
        <td>waitForElementPresent</td>
        <td>accept</td>
        <td></td>
    </tr>
    <tr>
        <td>clickAndWait</td>
        <td>accept</td>
        <td></td>
    </tr>
```

The open function tells the browser to load the specified location. Once the page is loaded, we use the click function to make Selenium simulate a click on the link with the text "Module status." Then we wait until the squid element is loaded using waitForElementPresent. We continue using these functions to click on the required links to finally enable the Squid eBox module.

Selenium scripts are verbose and boring to write, but fortunately they can be written automatically using Selenium IDE (*http://seleniumhq.org/projects/ide/*), an integrated development environment for Selenium tests. This IDE allows the tester to perform the actions in a browser and have them automatically recorded as a Selenium test.

Selenium can perform a lot of actions besides opening locations and clicking on links. The functions most frequently used in eBox tests include typing into text fields, choosing an element in a selection combo, and checking whether a page contains a given text.

eBox uses AJAX pervasively, and a lot of user actions cause asynchronous requests. These alter parts of the page structure without actually loading it again completely, and it is not always easy for Selenium to detect when one of these requests has finished. To fix this, eBox provides a flag inside the HTML code of AJAX-enabled pages that gets changed when asynchronous requests are completed. This way, Selenium can just monitor this flag and know exactly when the request has finished, allowing the safe execution of the next steps.

Originally the flag had to be reset manually, by running a JavaScript function provided by eBox from Selenium. A click on a link that will cause an AJAX request would have looked like this:

```
    <tr>
        <td>runScript</td>
        <td>startAjaxRequest()</td>
        <td></td>
    </tr>
    <tr>
        <td>waitForValue</td>
        <td>ajax_request_cookie</td>
        <td>1</td>
```

```
    </tr>
    <tr>
        <td>click</td>
        <td>filter</td>
        <td></td>
    </tr>
    <tr>
        <td>waitForValue</td>
        <td>ajax_request_cookie</td>
        <td>0</td>
    </tr>
```

The function `startAjaxRequest` is called, which sets the flag, named `ajax_request_cookie`, to 1. Then, we have to wait until the variable value actually changes to 1. Once this has happened, we can safely click on an AJAX-enabled link and just wait until the value of the flag is 0 again.

All these steps are still happening now, but a Selenium extension has been developed that allows us to replace all that code with just:

```
<tr>
    <td>clickAjax</td>
    <td>filter</td>
    <td></td>
</tr>
```

Another common task across eBox tests is configuring an interface as external in the eBox interface. An external interface is one that provides access to other networks that can be potentially dangerous, such as the Internet. eBox services will usually listen only on internal interfaces, and the firewall for external interfaces is quite strict.

This script should be usable from most scenarios that might need to configure different interfaces as external. Selenium does not support passing variables to scripts, but ANSTE provides a simple templating system to do it. Variables can be used to make scripts more flexible and thus more easily usable from different scenarios, as it is done in the next one:

```
<test type="selenium">
    <name>ConfigNetworkSetExternal</name>
    <desc>
    Sets the interface as external.
    </desc>

    <host>ebox-server</host>
    <dir>set-external</dir>
    <var name="IFACE" value="eth2"/>
</test>
```

We set the variable `IFACE` to the name of the desired interface, and ANSTE will replace the variable in the script before invoking it so that it will have the appropriate value when it is actually run.

After these generic configuration scripts, the actual scripts to test the proxy follow. They usually come in pairs, with one setting some configuration through the web application, and thus testing the correctness of the user interface, and another one testing whether eBox works as expected after saving changes. The next set of scripts are:

```
<test type="selenium">
    <name>ConfigProxyFilter</name>
    <desc>
    Config the proxy with filter mode and forbid a host.
    </desc>

    <host>ebox-server</host>
    <dir>config-proxy-filter</dir>
    <var name="HOST" value="www.filterme.com"/>
</test>

<test>
    <name>FilterAllowDownload</name>
    <desc>Try to download a file from an allowed host</desc>

    <host>test-client</host>
    <dir>test-allow</dir>
    <var name="HOST" value="www.google.com"/>
</test>

<test type="selenium">
    <name>TestLogFilterAllowDownload</name>
    <desc>Tests if proxy logs works ok</desc>

    <host>ebox-server</host>
    <dir>test-logs</dir>
    <var name="URL" value="www.google.com"/>
    <var name="EVENT" value="Accepted"/>
</test>
```

The first script performs two actions. The first one is setting the proxy general policy to filter, meaning that every request will be filtered. The second one is adding a new domain, passed as a parameter to the script, and setting an "always deny" policy for it.

The second script is command-based and is run in the machine named test-client. It sets the proxy to be the eBox machine and then tries to download the specified URL using wget. Then the script tests whether it was able to download the file specified by the given URL. As it did not belong to the forbidden domain, the script will return a successful status if it did and one indicating failure otherwise.

The last script is again run against the web interface in the ebox-server machine. Its purpose is to verify that the access to the given URL was registered correctly in the logs for the proxy module and has an Accepted state. As this script is used often to check logs, it is properly parameterized to make it more reusable.

The proxy test suite includes many more scripts to continue checking other features of the proxy module, such as denying requests for forbidden domains or content filtering.

Checking the correct functionality of the Squid module is relatively easy, but other modules require far more elaborate tests. For example, to check whether the Jabber module is working correctly, a small script had to be written using the Net::Jabber Perl module. This script creates a pair of Jabber connections, verifies that the authentication is successful, and makes sure communication between the two connections is possible through the Jabber server.

Most eBox tests would have been really difficult to develop from scratch, but fortunately a whole set of libraries and commands is available on Linux systems. Besides the already mentioned Net::Jabber, other Perl libraries are used in the tests, for example Mail::IMAPClient or Net::SMTP. A plethora of small but handy Unix commands, such as netcat, wget, or traceroute, are used as well.

Another module with a difficult functionality verification process is the OpenVPN one. In this case, the complexity comes from the large number of machines involved in the scenario. As tests can affect only one machine, different tests have to interact with each other and leave running processes in the machines. Of course, tests are also required to stop these processes eventually.

First of all, the networking between the machines has to be set up. We have a machine running eBox, which will act as an OpenVPN server; two clients that will establish VPNs to the eBox machine; and a couple of routers connecting the clients with the server.

Once the machines are set up, the first test enables an OpenVPN server using the web interface in the eBox machine. The next step would be to have the OpenVPN clients connecting to eBox, but some things need to be configured before this can happen.

The first problem is that the clients cannot actually connect directly to the eBox machine. A redirection rule needs to be established in the routers in order to have connections to the router in the OpenVPN port automatically redirect to the eBox machine. This is achieved by running a utility test that adds the rule to the firewall in each of the hosts.

The next problem we have to deal with is the configuration of the clients. The eBox OpenVPN module provides configuration bundles that include all the necessary files for a given client. Unfortunately, Selenium does not allow downloading files, so we have to look for another way. In the end, this is done by a utility test that uses the eBox API to create the bundles in the server and then moves them into a place from which they can be downloaded through HTTP. These generated bundles are then downloaded to the client machines.

At this point, the clients are ready to connect. First of all, we want to check whether a client can connect successfully to the VPN server, so we start the OpenVPN connection from the first client and check whether it has been established successfully.

One of the options that needs to be tested is the one that enables client-to-client communication. This option determines whether clients connected to the eBox OpenVPN server should be able to communicate with each other. The option is set to false by default, so we have to check that clients indeed cannot communicate with each other. To accomplish this, we run a test that starts the OpenVPN client in the second machine and tries to connect to the other client. The test checks for a successful connection and returns successfully in that case. As we want just the opposite, we have to add a configuration option in the test to invert the result.

The next step is making sure that changing the configuration option actually changes the behavior. To do that, we modify the option using Selenium and then proceed to stop the VPN connections and restart the OpenVPN server. Now we can use the same test we used before, just not inverting the result this time, and thus verifying that the two clients can actually communicate between each other.

How Other Projects Can Benefit from ANSTE

ANSTE was developed explicitly to help in the testing process of software that involves several machines connected to a network. Any project that matches this description can easily improve its quality assurance process by using ANSTE to automate it.

One of the projects that can easily take advantage of ANSTE is MySQL. MySQL is a widely used open source database management system. It already has a great testing framework, but it is heavily oriented toward SQL testing on a single host. However, there are some parts of MySQL, such as replication and clustering, that require several MySQL servers.

The testing framework can run multiple servers in the same machine to perform these tests, but although these tests might cover the most usual behavior, they do not faithfully reflect the real scenarios with several machines, as they fail to take into account possible failures in the connections between the machines, which actually is a very important test case for database clusters.

ANSTE has already been successfully used to test MySQL clusters. As ANSTE is designed to deal with several machines, it can replicate more closely a real cluster scenario. For example, a network failure can be easily simulated by bringing down the network interface from a script, making testing this issue a straightforward and completely automated task.

It is quite easy to find further examples of projects that can benefit from ANSTE. There is no need to even look away from eBox, as most of its tests actually check functionality provided by the underlying daemons. Software such as jabberd, the Jabber server behind the eBox instant messaging module, or Squid, the web proxy, are perfect candidates for ANSTE testing. eBox uses and tests only a small subset of the features of these projects, but they have a complete feature set that could be covered by ANSTE tests, providing a thorough and automatic way to enhance the current QA process.

Contributors

JENNITTA ANDREA has been a multifaceted, hands-on practitioner (analyst, tester, developer, manager), and coach on over a dozen different types of agile projects since 2000. Naturally a keen observer of teams and processes, Jennitta has published many experience-based papers for conferences and software journals, and delivers practical, simulation-based tutorials and in-house training covering agile requirements, process adaptation, automated examples, and project retrospectives. Jennitta's ongoing work has culminated in international recognition as a thought leader in the area of agile requirements and automated examples. She is very active in the agile community, serving a third term on the Agile Alliance Board of Directors, director of the Agile Alliance Functional Test Tool Program to advance the state of the art of automated functional test tools, member of the Advisory Board of IEEE Software, and member of many conference committees. Jennitta founded The Andrea Group in 2007 where she remains actively engaged on agile projects as a hands-on practitioner and coach, and continues to bridge theory and practice in her writing and teaching.

SCOTT BARBER is the chief technologist of PerfTestPlus, executive director of the Association for Software Testing, cofounder of the Workshop on Performance and Reliability, and coauthor of *Performance Testing Guidance for Web Applications* (Microsoft Press). He is widely recognized as a thought leader in software performance testing and is an international keynote speaker. A trainer of software testers, Mr. Barber is an AST-certified On-Line Lead Instructor who has authored over 100 educational articles on software testing. He is a member of ACM, IEEE, American Mensa, and the Context-Driven School of Software Testing, and is a signatory to the Manifesto for Agile Software Development. See *http://www.perftestplus.com/ScottBarber* for more information.

Rex Black, who has a quarter-century of software and systems engineering experience, is president of RBCS (*http://www.rbcs-us.com*), a leader in software, hardware, and systems testing. For over 15 years, RBCS has delivered services in consulting, outsourcing, and training for software and hardware testing. Employing the industry's most experienced and recognized consultants, RBCS conducts product testing, builds and improves testing groups, and hires testing staff for hundreds of clients worldwide. Ranging from Fortune 20 companies to startups, RBCS clients save time and money through improved product development, decreased tech support calls, improved corporate reputation, and more. As the leader of RBCS, Rex is the most prolific author practicing in the field of software testing today. His popular first book, *Managing the Testing Process* (Wiley), has sold over 35,000 copies around the world, including Japanese, Chinese, and Indian releases, and is now in its third edition. His five other books on testing, *Advanced Software Testing: Volume I*, *Advanced Software Testing: Volume II* (Rocky Nook), *Critical Testing Processes* (Addison-Wesley Professional), *Foundations of Software Testing* (Cengage), and *Pragmatic Software Testing* (Wiley), have also sold tens of thousands of copies, including Hebrew, Indian, Chinese, Japanese, and Russian editions. He has written over 30 articles, presented hundreds of papers, workshops, and seminars, and given about 50 keynotes and other speeches at conferences and events around the world. Rex has also served as the president of the International Software Testing Qualifications Board and of the American Software Testing Qualifications Board.

Emily Chen is a software engineer working on OpenSolaris desktop. Now she is responsible for the quality of Mozilla products such as Firefox and Thunderbird on OpenSolaris. She is passionate about open source. She is a core contributor of the OpenSolaris community, and she worked on the Google Summer of Code program as a mentor in 2006 and 2007. She organized the first-ever GNOME.Asia Summit 2008 in Beijing and founded the Beijing GNOME Users Group. She graduated from the Beijing Institute of Technology with a master's degree in computer science. In her spare time, she likes snowboarding, hiking, and swimming.

Adam Christian is a JavaScript developer doing test automation and AJAX UI development. He is the cocreator of the Windmill Testing Framework, Mozmill, and various other open source projects. He grew up in the northwest as an avid hiker, skier, and sailer and attended Washington State University studying computer science and business. His personal blog is at *http://www.adamchristian.com*. He is currently employed by Slide, Inc.

Isaac Clerencia is a software developer at eBox Technologies. Since 2001 he has been involved in several free software projects, including Debian and Battle for Wesnoth. He, along with other partners, founded Warp Networks in 2004. Warp Networks is the open source–oriented software company from which eBox Technologies was later spun off. Other interests of his are artificial intelligence and natural language processing.

John D. Cook is a very applied mathematician. After receiving a Ph.D. in from the University of Texas, he taught mathematics at Vanderbilt University. He then left academia to work as a software developer and consultant. He currently works as a research statistician at M. D. Anderson Cancer Center. His career has been a blend of research, software development, consulting, and management. His areas of application have ranged from the search for oil deposits to the search for a cure for cancer. He lives in Houston with his wife and four daughters. He writes a blog at *http://www.johndcook.com/blog*.

LISA CRISPIN is an agile testing coach and practitioner. She is the coauthor, with Janet Gregory, of *Agile Testing: A Practical Guide for Testers and Agile Teams* (Addison-Wesley). She works as the director of agile software development at Ultimate Software. Lisa specializes in showing testers and agile teams how testers can add value and how to guide development with business-facing tests. Her mission is to bring agile joy to the software testing world and testing joy to the agile development world. Lisa joined her first agile team in 2000, having enjoyed many years working as a programmer, analyst, tester, and QA director. From 2003 until 2009, she was a tester on a Scrum/XP team at ePlan Services, Inc. She frequently leads tutorials and workshops on agile testing at conferences in North America and Europe. Lisa regularly contributes articles about agile testing to publications such as *Better Software* magazine, *IEEE Software*, and *Methods and Tools*. Lisa also coauthored *Testing Extreme Programming* (Addison-Wesley) with Tip House. For more about Lisa's work, visit *http://www.lisacrispin.com*.

ADAM GOUCHER has been testing software professionally for over 10 years. In that time he has worked with startups, large multinationals, and those in between, in both traditional and agile testing environments. A believer in the communication of ideas big and small, he writes frequently at *http://adam.goucher.ca* and teaches testing skills at a Toronto-area technical college. In his off hours he can be found either playing or coaching box lacrosse—and then promptly applying lessons learned to testing. He is also an active member of the Association for Software Testing.

MATTHEW HEUSSER is a member of the technical staff ("QA lead") at Socialtext and has spent his adult life developing, testing, and managing software projects. In addition to Socialtext, Matthew is a contributing editor for *Software Test and Performance Magazine* and an adjunct instructor in the computer science department at Calvin College. He is the lead organizer of both the Great Lakes Software Excellence Conference and the peer workshop on Technical Debt. Matthew's blog, Creative Chaos (*http://xndev.blogspot.com*), is consistently ranked in the top-100 blogs for developers and dev managers, and the top-10 for software test automation. Equally important, Matthew is a whole person with a lifetime of experience. As a cadet, and later officer, in the Civil Air Patrol, Matthew soloed in a Cessna 172 light aircraft before he had a driver's license. He currently resides in Allegan, Michigan with his family, and has even been known to coach soccer.

KAREN N. JOHNSON is an independent software test consultant based in Chicago, Illinois. She views software testing as an intellectual challenge and believes in context-driven testing (*http://www.context-driven-testing.com/*). She teaches and consults on a variety of topics in software testing and frequently speaks at software testing conferences. She's been published in *Better Software* and *Software Test and Performance* magazines and on InformIT.com and StickyMinds.com. She is the cofounder of WREST, the Workshop on Regulated Software Testing (*http://www.wrestworkshop.com/Home.html*). Karen is also a hosted software testing expert on Tech Target's website (*http://searchsoftwarequality.techtarget.com/expert/ KnowledgebaseBio/0,289623,sid92_cid1093127,00.html*). For more information about Karen, visit *http://www.karennjohnson.com*.

KAMRAN KHAN contributes to a number of open source office projects, including AbiWord (a word processor), Gnumeric (a spreadsheet program), libwpd and libwpg (WordPerfect libraries), and libgoffice and libgsf (general office libraries). He has been testing office software for more than five years, focusing particularly on bugs that affect reliability and stability.

TOMASZ KOJM is the original author of Clam AntiVirus, an open source antivirus solution. ClamAV is freely available under the GNU General Public License, and as of 2009, has been installed on more than two million computer systems, primarily email gateways. Together with his team, Tomasz has been researching and deploying antivirus testing techniques since 2002 to make the software meet mission-critical requirements for reliability and availability.

MICHELLE LEVESQUE is the tech lead of Ads UI at Google, where she works to make useful, beautiful ads on the search results page. She also writes and directs internal educational videos, teaches Python classes, leads the readability team, helps coordinate the massive postering of Google restroom stalls with weekly flyers that promote testing, and interviews potential chefs and masseuses.

CHRIS MCMAHON is a dedicated agile tester and a dedicated telecommuter. He has amassed a remarkable amount of professional experience in more than a decade of testing, from telecom networks to social networking, from COBOL to Ruby. A three-time college dropout and former professional musician, librarian, and waiter, Chris got his start as a software tester a little later than most, but his unique and varied background gives his work a sense of maturity that few others have. He lives in rural southwest Colorado, but contributes to a couple of magazines, several mailing lists, and is even a character in a book about software testing.

MURALI NANDIGAMA is a quality consultant and has more than 15 years of experience in various organizations, including TCS, Sun, Oracle, and Mozilla. Murali is a Certified Software Quality Analyst, Six Sigma lead, and senior member of IEEE. He has been awarded with multiple software patents in advanced software testing methodologies and has published in international journals and presented at many conferences. Murali holds a doctorate from the University of Hyderabad, India.

BRIAN NITZ has been a software engineer since 1988. He has spent time working on all aspects of the software life cycle, from design and development to QA and support. His accomplishments include development of a dataflow-based visual compiler, support of radiology workstations, QA, performance, and service productivity tools, and the successful deployment of over 7,000 Linux desktops at a large bank. He lives in Ireland with his wife and two kids where he enjoys travel, sailing, and photography.

NEAL NORWITZ is a software developer at Google and a Python committer. He has been involved with most aspects of testing within Google and Python, including leading the Testing

Grouplet at Google and setting up and maintaining much of the Python testing infrastructure. He got deeply involved with testing when he learned how much his code sucked.

ALAN PAGE began his career as a tester in 1993. He joined Microsoft in 1995, and is currently the director of test excellence, where he oversees the technical training program for testers and various other activities focused on improving testers, testing, and test tools. Alan writes about testing on his blog (*http://blogs.msdn.com/alanpa*), and is the lead author on *How We Test Software at Microsoft* (Microsoft Press). You can contact him at *alan.page@microsoft.com*.

TIM RILEY is the director of quality assurance at Mozilla. He has tested software for 18 years, including everything from spacecraft simulators, ground control systems, high-security operating systems, language platforms, application servers, hosted services, and open source web applications. He has managed software testing teams in companies from startups to large corporations, consisting of 3 to 120 people, in six countries. He has a software patent for a testing execution framework that matches test suites to available test systems. He enjoys being a breeder caretaker for Canine Companions for Independence (*http://cci.org*), as well as live and studio sound engineering.

MARTIN SCHRÖDER studied computer science at the University of Würzburg, Germany, from which he also received his master's degree in 2009. While studying, he started to volunteer in the community-driven Mozilla Calendar Project in 2006. Since mid-2007, he has been coordinating the QA volunteer team. His interests center on working in open source software projects involving development, quality assurance, and community building.

DAVID SCHULER is a research assistant at the software engineering chair at Saarland University, Germany. His research interests include mutation testing and dynamic program analysis, focusing on techniques that characterize program runs to detect equivalent mutants. For that purpose, he has developed the Javalanche mutation-testing framework, which allows efficient mutation testing and assessing the impact of mutations.

CLINT TALBERT has been working as a software engineer for over 10 years, bouncing between development and testing at established companies and startups. His accomplishments include working on a peer-to-peer database replication engine, designing a rational way for applications to get time zone data, and bringing people from all over the world to work on testing projects. These days, he leads the Mozilla Test Development team concentrating on QA for the Gecko platform, which is the substrate layer for Firefox and many other applications. He is also an aspiring fiction writer. When not testing or writing, he loves to rock climb and surf everywhere from Austin, Texas to Ocean Beach, California.

REMKO TRONÇON is a member of the XMPP Standards Foundation's council, coauthor of several XMPP protocol extensions, former lead developer of Psi, developer of the Swift Jabber/XMPP project, and a coauthor of the book *XMPP: The Definitive Guide* (O'Reilly). He holds a Ph.D. in engineering (computer science) from the Katholieke Universiteit Leuven. His blog can be found at *http://el-tramo.be*.

LINDA WILKINSON is a QA manager with more than 25 years of software testing experience. She has worked in the nonprofit, banking, insurance, telecom, retail, state and federal government, travel, and aviation fields. Linda's blog is available at *http://practicalqa.com*, and she has been known to drop in at the forums on *http://softwaretestingclub.com* to talk to her Cohorts in Crime (i.e., other testing professionals).

JEFFREY YASSKIN is a software developer at Google and a Python committer. He works on the Unladen Swallow project, which is trying to dramatically improve Python's performance by compiling hot functions to machine code and taking advantage of the last 30 years of virtual machine research. He got into testing when he noticed how much it reduced the knowledge needed to make safe changes.

ANDREAS ZELLER is a professor of software engineering at Saarland University, Germany. His research centers on programmer productivity—in particular, on finding and fixing problems in code and development processes. He is best known for GNU DDD (Data Display Debugger), a visual debugger for Linux and Unix; for Delta Debugging, a technique that automatically isolates failure causes for computer programs; and for his work on mining the software repositories of companies such as Microsoft, IBM, and SAP. His recent work focuses on assessing and improving test suite quality, in particular mutation testing.

We'd like to hear your suggestions for improving our indexes. Send email to *index@oreilly.com*.

COLOPHON

The cover image is from Getty Images. The cover fonts are Akzidenz Grotesk and Orator. The text font is Adobe's Meridien; the heading font is ITC Bailey.

Get even more
for your money.

Join the O'Reilly Community, and register the O'Reilly books you own. It's free, and you'll get:

- $4.99 ebook upgrade offer
- 40% upgrade offer on O'Reilly print books
- Membership discounts on books and events
- Free lifetime updates to ebooks and videos
- Multiple ebook formats, DRM FREE
- Participation in the O'Reilly community
- Newsletters
- Account management
- 100% Satisfaction Guarantee

Signing up is easy:

1. **Go to: oreilly.com/go/register**
2. **Create an O'Reilly login.**
3. **Provide your address.**
4. **Register your books.**

Note: English-language books only

To order books online:
oreilly.com/store

For questions about products or an order:
orders@oreilly.com

To sign up to get topic-specific email announcements and/or news about upcoming books, conferences, special offers, and new technologies:
elists@oreilly.com

For technical questions about book content:
booktech@oreilly.com

To submit new book proposals to our editors:
proposals@oreilly.com

O'Reilly books are available in multiple DRM-free ebook formats. For more information:
oreilly.com/ebooks

O'REILLY®

Spreading the knowledge of innovators   oreilly.com

Have it your way.